Communications
in Computer and Information Science 1456

More information about this series at http://www.springer.com/series/7899

Juan Pablo Salgado Guerrero ·
Janneth Chicaiza Espinosa ·
Mariela Cerrada Lozada ·
Santiago Berrezueta-Guzman (Eds.)

Information and Communication Technologies

9th Conference of Ecuador, TICEC 2021
Guayaquil, Ecuador, November 24–26, 2021
Proceedings

 Springer

Editors
Juan Pablo Salgado Guerrero (iD)
Politecnica Salesiana University
Cuenca, Ecuador

Mariela Cerrada Lozada (iD)
Politecnica Salesiana University
Cuenca, Ecuador

Janneth Chicaiza Espinosa (iD)
Universidad Técnica Particular de Loja
Loja, Ecuador

Santiago Berrezueta-Guzman (iD)
CEDIA
Cuenca, Ecuador

ISSN 1865-0929   ISSN 1865-0937 (electronic)
Communications in Computer and Information Science
ISBN 978-3-030-89940-0   ISBN 978-3-030-89941-7 (eBook)
https://doi.org/10.1007/978-3-030-89941-7

This Springer imprint is published by the registered company Springer Nature Switzerland AG
The registered company address is: Gewerbestrasse 11, 6330 Cham, Switzerland

Preface

The nineth edition of the Information and Communication Technologies Conference of Ecuador (TICEC 2021) took place in Guayaquil during November 24–26, 2021, in hybrid mode, at the Universidad Politécnica Salesiana (UPS) campus. TICEC is one of the most important conferences in Ecuador on information and communications technologies (ICTs). This event brings together researchers, educators, professionals, and students from different parts of the world for the dissemination of results and research activities regarding the development, problems, and forecasts of the use of ICTs in multiple fields of application. This important academic and scientific event is organized by UPS and the Corporación Ecuatoriana para el Desarrollo de la Investigación y la Academia (CEDIA).

According to the research area, the conference included more than 24 presentations distributed across the event's sessions. The content of this volume has been divided into the following areas:

- Data Science
- ICTs Applications
- Industry 4.0
- Technology and Environment
- Biomedical Sensors and Wearables Systems

The nineth edition of TICEC received 126 manuscripts from 309 authors in thirteen countries. All articles passed the control of the maximum percentage of similarity with previous works, and were reviewed by peers by the TICEC 2021 Program Committee, consisting of 150 highly experienced researchers from 40 countries. To ensure a high-quality and careful review process, we assigned at least three reviewers to each article. Based on the peer review results, 24 full articles were accepted, representing an acceptance rate of 19%.

November 2021

Juan Pablo Salgado Guerrero
Janneth Chicaiza Espinosa
Mariela Cerrada Lozada
Santiago Berrezueta-Guzman

Organization

Honorary Committee

Cecilia Paredes	CEDIA, Ecuador
Juan Cárdenas Tapia	Universidad Politécnica Salesiana, Ecuador
Juan Pablo Carvallo Vega	CEDIA, Ecuador

General Chair

Juan Pablo Salgado Guerrero	Universidad Politécnica Salesiana, Ecuador

Steering Committee

Germania Rodriguez Morales	Universidad Técnica Particular de Loja, Ecuador
Efrain R. Fonseca C.	Universidad de las Fuerzas Armadas, Ecuador
Pablo Pérez-Gosende	Universidad Politécnica Salesiana, Ecuador
Marcos Orellana	Universidad del Azuay, Ecuador

Program Committee Chairs

Janneth Chicaiza Espinosa	Universidad Técnica Particular de Loja, Ecuador
Mariela Cerrada Lozada	Universidad Politécnica Salesiana, Ecuador

Organizing Committee

María Isabel Carpio	Universidad Politécnica Salesiana, Ecuador
César Andrade Martínez	Universidad Politécnica Salesiana, Ecuador
David Mora Bocca	Universidad Politécnica Salesiana, Ecuador
Wendy Luna Ramos	Universidad Politécnica Salesiana, Ecuador
Pablo Pérez-Gosende	Universidad Politécnica Salesiana, Ecuador
María José Llanos	Universidad Politécnica Salesiana, Ecuador
Galia Rivas Toral	CEDIA, Ecuador
Ana Isabel Ordoñez	CEDIA, Ecuador
Santiago Ruilova	CEDIA, Ecuador
Francisco Toral	CEDIA, Ecuador
Santiago Morales	CEDIA, Ecuador
Santiago Berrezueta	CEDIA, Ecuador

Program Committee

Adam Wojciechowski	Lodz University of Technology, Poland
Agustin L. Herrera-May	Universidad Veracruzana, Mexico
Agustín Yagüe	Universidad Politécnica de Madrid, Spain
Alex F. Buitrago Hurtado	Universidad Externado de Colombia, Colombia
Alexandros Liapis	ESDA Lab, Greece
Alexandros Spournias	ESDA Lab, Greece
Alvaro Llaria	University of Bordeaux, France
Alvaro Suarez	Universidad de Las Palmas de Gran Canaria, Spain
Ángel Alberto Magreñán	Universidad de La Rioja, Spain
Angel Hernandez-Martinez	Universidad Nacional Autónoma de México, Mexico
Ankit Maurya	Indian Institute of Technology Roorkee, India
Antonio Mogro	Tecnológico de Monterrey, Mexico
Arash Arami	University of Waterloo, Canada
Arcangelo Castiglione	University of Salerno, Italy
Artur Rydosz	AGH University of Science and Technology, Poland
Belen Bermejo	University of the Balearic Islands, Spain
Belen Curto	Universidad of Salamanca, Spain
Benoît Parrein	École Polytechnique de l'Université de Nantes, France
Bugra Alkan	London South Bank University, UK
Carlos Abreu	Instituto Politécnico de Viana do Castelo, Portugal
Carme Quer	Universitat Politècnica de Catalunya, Spain
Cecilio Angulo	Universitat Politècnica de Catalunya, Spain
Chao Min	Nanjing University, China
Che-Wei Lin	National Cheng Kung University, Taiwan
Christos Antonopoulos	University of the Peloponnese, Greece
Christos Mourtzios	Aristotle University of Thessaloniki, Greece
Christos Panagiotou	ESDA Lab, Greece
Claudia Ayala	Universitat Politècnica de Catalunya, Spain
Claudia Marzi	Italian National Research Council, Italy
Coral Calero	Universidad de Castilla-La Mancha, Spain
Corina Namaj	University of Istanbul, Turkey
Cristian Vasar	Politehnica University of Timisoara, Romania
Dan Pescaru	Politehnica University of Timisoara, Romania
Darius Andriukaitis	Kaunas University of Technology, Lituania
David Valiente	Miguel Hernandez University, Spain
Dhruba Panthi	Kent State University Tuscarawas, USA
Diego Brandao	CEFET/RJ, Brazil
Dionisis Kandris	University of West Attica, Greece
Eduardo Almentero	UFRRJ, Brazil
Eduardo Juarez	Universidad Politécnica de Madrid, Spain
Eike Petersen	Universität zu Lübeck, Germany
Engin Zeydan	Tecnològic de Telecomunicacions de Catalunya, Spain
Emil Pricop	Pro-Innovation, Romania
Fabio Arena	University of Enna "Kore", Italy

Firas Raheem	University of Technology, Iraq
Francisco Prieto-Castrillo	Universidad Politécnica de Madrid, Spain
Gabor Sziebig	The Arctic University of Norway, Norway
George Adam	University of Thessaly, Greece
Gerasimos Vonitsanos	University of Patras, Greece
Giuseppe Ciaburro	Università degli Studi della Campania Luigi Vanvitelli, Italy
Gyanendra Prasad Joshi	Sejong University, South Korea
Ho-Lung Hung	Chienkuo Technology University, Taiwan
Hugo Almeida-Ferreira	Polytechnic Institute of Oporto, Portugal
Ibraheem Kasim-Ibraheem	Baghdad University, Iraq
Ioan Viorel-Banu	Gheorghe Asachi Technical University of Iasi, Romania
Iosif Szeidert	Politehnica University of Timisoara, Romania
Irina Georgiana Mocanu	Politehnica University of Bucharest, Romania
Isabel-Sofia Sousa-Brito	Instituto Politécnico de Beja, Portugal
Iván Pau	Universidad Politécnica de Madrid, Spain
Ivan Virgala	Technical University of Košice, Slovakia
Jai Singh	Charles Darwin University, Australia
Janusz Dudczyk	WB Electronics S.A., Poland
Jari Hannu	University of Oulu, Finland
Jason Wu	Texas A&M Transportation Institute, USA
Javier Gomez	Universidad Autónoma de México, Mexico
Jean-Fu Kiang	National Taiwan University, Taiwan
Jerwin Prabu-A.	Bharati Robotic Systems India Pvt Ltd, India
Jessica Maradey	Universidad Autonoma de Bucaramanga, Colombia
Jianbin Qiu	Harbin Institute of Technology, China
John Castro	Universidad de Atacama, Chile
José Martinez-Carranza	Instituto Nacional de Astrofísica, Óptica y Electrónica, Mexico
Jose Huertas	Tecnologico de Monterrey, Mexico
José Olivas-Varela	Universidad Castilla la Mancha, Spain
José Joaquim de Moura Ramos	University of A Coruña, Spain
José J. Pazos Arias	Universidad de Vigo, Spain
José Fernán Martínez	Universidad Politécnica de Madrid, Spain
José Tenreiro Machado	ISEP University, France
Josip Music	University of Split, Croatia
Kester Quist-Aphetsi	Ghana Technology University College, Ghana
Khalid Saeed	Bialystok University of Technology, Poland
Kiril Alexiev	IICT-BAS, Bulgaria
Konstantinos Antonopoulos	ESDA Lab, Greece
Krzysztof Bernacki	Silesian University of Technology, Poland
Kwan-Ho You	Sungkyunkwan University, South Korea
Lidia Lopez	Barcelona Supercomputing Center, Spain
Liyanage Kithsiri Perera	USQ, Australia

Loredana Stanciu	Politehnica University of Timisoara, Romania
Lucian Pislaru-Danescu	INCDIE ICPE-CA, Romania
Luis Martin-Pomares	Qatar Environment and Energy Research Institute, Qatar
Luise Wolfshagen	Universität Heidenheim, Germany
Lukasz Sobaszek	Lublin University of Technology, Poland
Lydia Schawe	Hochschule Bremerhaven, Germany
Mahendra Babu G. R.	Karpagam Academy of Higher Education, India
Marcin Ciecholewski	University of Gdansk, Poland
Marcin Górski	Silesian University of Technology, Poland
Marco Zappatore	University of Salento, Italy
Marco Antônio P. Araújo	UFJF, Brazil
Maria Francesca Bruno	Politecnico di Bari, Italy
María Cristina Rodriguez	Rey Juan Carlos University, Spain
María-Luisa Martín-Ruíz	Universidad Politécnica de Madrid, Spain
Marian Wysocki	Rzeszow University of Technology, Poland
Marija Seder	University of Zagreb, Croatia
Mario Miličević	University of Dubrovnik, Croatia
Mariusz Kostrzewski	Warsaw University of Technology, Poland
Marta Gabaldón	Universidad Politécnica de Madrid, Spain
Martín López-Nores	Universidad de Vigo, Spain
Massimo Donelli	University of Trento, Italy
Massimo Merenda	Università Mediterranea di Reggio Calabria, Italy
Michał Tomczak	Gdańsk University of Technology, Poland
Modestos Stavrakis	University of the Aegean, Greece
Mohiuddin Ahmed	Edith Cowan University, Australia
Natasa Zivic	Institute for Data Communications Systems, UK
Noman Naseer	Pusan University, South Korea
Noor Zaman	Taylor's University, Malaysia
Omar Abdul Wahab	Université du Québec en Outaouais, Canada
Panagiota Yota-Katsikouli	Technical University of Denmark, Denmark
Patricio Galdames	Universidad del Bio-Bio, Chile
Paul Nicolae Borza	Transilvania University of Brasov, Romania
Piotr Borkowski	Maritime University of Szczecin, Poland
Prasanta Ghosh	ICEEM, India
Przemysław Mazurek	West Pomeranian University of Technology, Poland
Raúl Antonio Aguilar Vera	Universidad Autónoma de Yucatán, Mexico
Robert-Alexandru Dobre	Politehnica University of Bucharest, Romania
Roberto Murphy	INAOE, Mexico
Roemi Fernandez	Universidad Politecnica de Madrid, Spain
Rosaria Rucco	University of Naples Parthenope, Italy
Rostom Mabrouk	Bishop's University, Canada
Rui Zhao	University of Nebraska Omaha, USA
Ruoyu Su	Memorial University of Newfoundland, Canada
Saleh Mobayen	University of Zanjan, Iran
Samanta Kolsch	Steinbeis Hochschule Berlin, Germany

Samuel Ortega-Sarmiento	University of Las Palmas de Gran Canaria, Spain
Sara Paiva	Oviedo University, Spain
Shaibal Barua	Mälardalen University, Sweden
Shernon Osepa	Internet Society, The Netherlands
Silvia Grassi	Università degli Studi di Milano, Italy
Stavros Souravlas	University of Macedonia, North Macedonia
Stefano Mariani	Università degli Studi Modena e Reggio Emilia, Italy
Sule Yildirim-Yayilgan	Norwegian University of Science and Technology, Norway
Sunday-Cookeyn Ekpo	Manchester Metropolitan University, UK
Thomas Usländer	Fraunhofer IOSB, Germany
Tomasz Bieniek	Institute of Electron Technology, Poland
Tuan Nguyen-Gia	University of Turku, Finland
Utkarsh Singh	Depsys SA, Switzerland
Valerio Baiocchi	Sapienza University of Rome, Italy
Vera Ferreira	Federal University of the Pampa, Brazil
Vinayak Elangovan	Penn State Abington, USA
Vladimir Sobeslav	University of Hradec Kralove, Czech Republic
Wojciech Zabierowski	Lodz University of Technology, Poland
Xavier Franch	Universitat Politècnica de Catalunya, Spain
Yanhua Luo	University of New South Wales, Australia
Yu Huang	Chinese Academy of Sciences, China
Zoltán Ádám Tamus	Budapest University of Technology, Hungary

Contents

xiv   Contents

Technology and Environment

Biomedical Sensors and Wearables Systems

Data Science

Estimation of Ordinary Differential Equations Solutions with Gaussian Processes and Polynomial Chaos Expansion

Naomi Cedeño[1]([⊠])(iD) and Saba Infante[1,2](iD)

[1] School of Mathematical and Computational Sciences, Yachay Tech,
San Miguel de Urcuqui 100115, Ecuador
{helen.cedeno,sinfante}@yachaytech.edu.ec
[2] Departamento de Matematicas, FACyT, Universidad de Carabobo,
Naguanagua 2005, Venezuela

Abstract. Derivative modeling is a wide-used technique in the estimation of solutions of systems of differential equations whose numerical solution has an intractable computational complexity or in which the presence of error or infinitesimal perturbations could result in their divergence. The quantification of the uncertainty that is produced when estimating the solution in a finite mesh is an open problem and has been addressed from various probabilistic approaches. In this work, uncertainty estimation of solutions of ordinary differential equations by means of a GP process in a space of smoothed functions is addressed by implementing an algorithm that allows estimating the solution states $x(t)$ and their derivatives in a sequential way. Besides, the addition of polynomial chaos expansions (PCE) using the resulting distributions of the algorithm is proposed to improve the prediction of the algorithm. To illustrate the methodology, the algorithms were tested on three known systems of ordinary differential equations and their effectiveness was quantified by three performance measures, resulting in an overall improvement in prediction by adding the polynomial chaos expansion.

Keywords: Ordinary differential equation models · Gaussian processes · Polynomial chaos expansion

1 Introduction

Mathematical models used to infer and predict real-life phenomena usually have a non-linear structure, partially observed functions and complex dynamics are part of the problems that occur frequently in many fields of science. The estimation of the parameters in these models is carried out with observations measured with errors and in some cases with missing data. A way to quantify the experimental information is to measure the observations of the trajectories generated

© Springer Nature Switzerland AG 2021
J. P. Salgado Guerrero et al. (Eds.): TICEC 2021, CCIS 1456, pp. 3–17, 2021.
https://doi.org/10.1007/978-3-030-89941-7_1

by dynamical systems, and then use it to perform estimation. Thus, the solution states and parameters of ordinary differential equation models that describe the natural dependence between the system states and their rates of change in an open space-time domain are estimated. In practice, solving these problems is complicated since the observed state variables are not exact representations of the solutions, or they can not be found analytically.

Ramsay et al. [11] and Huang et al. [6] developed a Bayesian method to estimate the parameters in ODE systems from noisy data using a nonparametric procedure based on a hybrid Monte Carlo algorithm. On the other hand, Tronarp et al. [18] proposed a probabilistic numerical approximation to solutions of ODE systems as a Gaussian process (GP) regression problem with nonlinear measurement functions. Also, Heinonen et al. [5] developed a novel paradigm of nonparametric modeling of ODEs, where functions learn from observations of the unknown states using a Gaussian process. Schober et al. [13] studied the connections between ODE solvers and probabilistic regression methods, introducing a new approach for inference in stochastic differential equations models. Finally, Chkrebtii et al.[2] developed a framework for making inference and quantifying uncertainty in models defined by general systems of analytically intractable differential equations. This approach provides a statistical alternative to deterministic numerical integration for the estimation of complex dynamical systems, and characterizes the solution uncertainty introduced when models are chaotic considering estimation of solutions as an inference problem that allows quantifying numerical uncertainty by means of functional estimation tools that can propagate through uncertainty in model parameters and posterior predictions. Other alternative methods of approximation, such as Gaussian mixtures [7] and polynomial chaos based in Kalman filters [16], were also studied in the literature.

In this work, we introduce a Bayesian estimation methodology based on functional data obtained as realizations of smooth random variable functions and collected over a discrete time set, taking into account measurement errors. Specifically, we propose the implementation of a time sequential sampling and updating algorithm that estimates functions as Gaussian process, its derivative and the solution states of an ODE. The probabilistic solutions are based on a Gaussian process (GP) prior regression proposed by Chkrebtii [2] and the addition of polynomial chaos expansions (PCE) to the result is proposed to achieve more accurate estimated values. The rest of the article is written as follows: In Sect. 2, the methodology will be established and fundamental concepts about Gaussian Processes, Probabilistic solver model, and Polynomial Chaos Expansion will be defined. In Sect. 3, the results obtained are shown and discussed, and in Sect. 4 the conclusions and possible future works are determined.

2   Methodology

2.1   Gaussian Process Priors

Gaussian processes (GP) define a distribution over functions f where f is a function that maps some space of $\mathcal{X}$ entries to $\mathbb{R}$; i.e., $f : \mathcal{X} \to \mathbb{R}$. Formally, for some finite set of elements taken from $\mathcal{X}$, f is a Gaussian process defined by:

$$f(x) \sim GP\left(m(x), k\left(x, x'\right)\right)$$

Functions supported for $m : \mathcal{X} \to \mathbb{R}$ y $k(.,.) : \mathcal{X} \times \mathcal{X} \to \mathbb{R}$ satisfy the condition that the marginals are Gaussian distributed, with $m(.)$ as a parametric function and $k(.,.)$ as a function that admits a positive semi-definite matrix when evaluated at the points $x \in \mathcal{X}$. The function $k\left(x, x'\right)$ models the dependence between the functional values at different input points x and x'. The choice of $k\left(x, x'\right)$ that will use in this article is the radial basis function, which is defined as:

$$k\left(x, x'\right) = \sigma_f^2 \exp\left(-\frac{\|x - x'\|}{2\lambda^2}\right) \tag{1}$$

where (1) provides a transition kernel that serves to model smooth and stationary functions, λ is a scaling parameter, and σ_f^2 is the variance of the signal. If we consider $m(x) = 0$, we sample values of f at input x_{new} as follows:

$$f_{new}(x_{new}) \sim N\left(0, K\left(x_{new}, x_{new}\right)\right) \tag{2}$$

where $f_{new} = f_{new}(x_{new})$. Let $\mathcal{D}_t = \{x_t, y_t\}$ be a collection of observations, predictions can be made using new data x_{new} if we sample $f_{new}(x_{new})$ from the posterior distribution $p\left(f_{new}(x_{new})|\mathcal{D}_t\right)$. The observations $y_t = f(x_t)$ and the function $f_{new}(x_{new})$ would follow a joint multivariate normal distribution:

$$\begin{pmatrix} f \\ f_{new} \end{pmatrix} \sim N\left(\begin{pmatrix} m(x) \\ m(x_{new}) \end{pmatrix}; \begin{pmatrix} K(x, x) & K(x, x_{new}) \\ K(x_{new}, x) & K(x_{new}, x_{new}) \end{pmatrix}\right) \tag{3}$$

with $K\left(x, x\right)$, the kernel evaluated at x. The marginal distribution $f_{new}|f, x, y$ is given by:

$$f_{new}|f, x, y \sim N\left(m\left(x_{new},\right)^{post}, K^{post}\left(f(x_{new}), f(x_{new})\right)\right) \tag{4}$$

where:

$$m^{post}\left(x_{new}\right) = m\left(x_{new}\right) + K\left(x_{new}, x\right) K^{-1}\left(x, x\right) \left[f - m\left(x\right)\right]$$

$$K^{post}\left(f(x_{new}), f(x_{new})\right) = K\left(x_{new}, x_{new}\right) - K\left(x_{new}, x\right) K^{-1}\left(x, x\right) K\left(x, x_{new}\right)$$

Generalizing, if we look at the real values of f by adding noise, we have that:

$$y_i = f(x_i) + \epsilon_i \quad , \quad \epsilon_i \sim N\left(0, \sigma_\epsilon^2\right) \quad , \quad y|f \sim N\left(f(x_i), \sigma_\epsilon^2 I\right) \tag{5}$$

where I is the identity matrix. The noise can be included in the covariance function, so that:

$$k\left(f(x_i), f(x_j)\right) = k\left(x_i, x_j\right) + \delta_{ij}\sigma_\epsilon^2 \tag{6}$$

where δ_{ij} is the Kronecker delta function. The uncertainty is now present in the observations, and the joint distribution over the unknown data and the known data is augmented in the covariance equation by:

$$\begin{pmatrix} f \\ f_{new} \end{pmatrix} \sim N\left(\begin{pmatrix} m(x) \\ m(x_{new}) \end{pmatrix}; \begin{pmatrix} K(x, x) + \sigma_\epsilon^2 I & K(x, x_{new}) \\ K(x_{new}, x) & K(x_{new}, x_{new}) + \sigma_\epsilon^2 \end{pmatrix}\right) \tag{7}$$

$$f_{new}|f,x,y \sim N\left(m\left(x_{new},\right)^{post}, K^{post}\left(f(x_{new}), f(x_{new})\right)\right)$$

with:

$$m^{post}\left(x_{new}\right) = m\left(x_{new}\right) + K\left(x_{new}, x\right)\left(K\left(x,x\right) + \sigma_\epsilon^2 I\right)^{-1}\left[f - m\left(x\right)\right]$$

$$K^{post}\left(f(x_{new}), f(x_{new})\right) = K\left(x_{new}, x_{new}\right) - K\left(x_{new}, x\right)\left(K\left(x,x\right) + \sigma_\epsilon^2 I\right)^{-1} K\left(x, x_{new}\right) + \sigma_\epsilon^2$$

2.2 Probabilistic Solver Model

In this section, a probabilistic model that allows to characterize the error of the solution of an initial-valued ODE is introduced, where the solution states are not defined in closed form. In the considered model, the exact solution $x(t)$ is replaced with a finite dimensional representation $x^n(t, \theta)$ such that:

$$\dot{x}(t) = f\left(x(t), t\right), \quad x(t_0) = x_0 \tag{8}$$

$$y(t) = h\left(x^n(t, \theta)\right) + \epsilon(t), \quad \epsilon(t) \sim N\left(0, \sigma_\epsilon^2\right) \tag{9}$$

Equation (8) represents an unobserved theoretical model, while (9) represents an observational model. We formulate the approximation of (8) at discrete points $\{t_i\}_{i=1}^n$ as a Bayesian inference problem. If $y_{1:t} := (y_1, y_2 \ldots, y_n)$ are the observed data and $x_{1:t} := (x_1, x_2 \ldots, x_n)$ the unknown states, $p\left(y_{1:t}|x_{1:t}\right)$ is the likelihood, and $p_y\left(\theta\right)$ is the prior distribution over the solution space, the posterior distribution is obtained by:

$$p\left(y_{1:t}|x_{1:t}\right) = \frac{p\left(y_{1:t}|x_{1:t}p_y\left(\theta\right)\right)}{\int p\left(y_{1:t}|x_{1:t}p_y\left(\theta\right)\right)d\theta} \tag{10}$$

Following the theory developed in Skilling [15] and Chkrebtii's [2] works, it is proposed to model the uncertainty of the solution by a GP process in a smoothed function space in an interval $[0, T]$, by estimating $x(t)$ and the derivative of the solution sequentially. The existence of the solutions is well founded as long as they satisfy the Lipschitz conditions [1]. Let (x_i, y_i), $i = 1, 2, \ldots, n$ be the observations where x_i is the input variable and $y_i = f(x_i) + \epsilon_i$ is the response variable, where the error $\epsilon_i \sim N\left(0, \sigma_\epsilon^2\right)$. To estimate the derivative of the curve of observations $\dot{f}(x)$, it is assumed that:

$$f(x) \sim GP\left(m(.), k\left(., .\right)\right) \tag{11}$$

If $k\left(., .\right)$ is twice differentiable at the origin, $f(x)$ is differentiable in root mean square [19]. Then:

$$\dot{f}(x) \sim GP\left(0, \frac{dk\left(x, x'\right)}{dxdx'}\right) \tag{12}$$

Therefore, given the parametric form of $k\left(., .\right)$, we can use the data (x_i, y_i) to estimate the parameters of $k\left(., .\right)$ and use:

$$k''(., .) = \frac{dk\left(x, x'\right)}{dxdx'} \tag{13}$$

to make inference about $\dot{f}(x)$. An alternative method is to assume that the derived process $\dot{f}(x)$ is a GP. The integrated process with noisy observations is:

$$f(x) = \int_0^x \dot{f}(s)ds \tag{14}$$

The covariance function of $f(x)$ can be obtained using a double integration over the covariance function of $\dot{f}(x)$. If $\dot{y} =\sim GP\left(0, k\left(x, x'\right)\right)$, then:

$$y = f(x) \sim GP\left(0, \int_0^x \int_0^{x'} k\left(s, s'\right) ds ds'\right) \tag{15}$$

In the context of this paper, the solutions of the ODE are approximated at n points $\{t_1, t_2, \ldots, t_n\}$, and are denoted by:

$$\hat{x}(t) = \left(\hat{x}(t_1), \hat{x}(t_2), \ldots, \hat{x}(t_n)\right)^T \tag{16}$$

and evaluating in the vector field $y = f\left(\hat{x}(t)\right)$:

$$f(x) = \left(f\left(\hat{x}(t_1)\right), f\left(\hat{x}(t_2)\right) \ldots, f\left(\hat{x}(t_n)\right)\right)^T \tag{17}$$

The likelihood of the model depends on (15), so that for each pair of locations $(x(t_i), x(t_j))$a double integral is required to be computed, so a large n implies high computational costs. Consider a set of points $\{\tau_1, \tau_2, \ldots, \tau_n\}$, obtaining:

$$\hat{x}^*(t) = \left(\hat{x}^*(\tau_1), \hat{x}^*(\tau_2), \ldots, \hat{x}^*(\tau_n)\right)^T \tag{18}$$

To estimate the probabilistic model that quantifies the estimation error produced when approximating the solution in a finite lattice, we set the parameters θ of the continuous model, the hyperparameters $\Sigma = \left(\sigma_f^2, \lambda, \sigma_\epsilon^2, x_0\right)$ associated with the estimation errors and write the likelihood of the model, which represents the probabilistic solution of the system:

$$p\left(x\left(t, \theta\right), y, \dot{y}, \theta, \Sigma\right) \propto p\left(x\left(t, \theta\right) | y, \dot{y}, \theta, \Sigma\right) p\left(y | \dot{y}, \theta, \Sigma\right) p\left(\dot{y} | \Sigma\right) \tag{19}$$

The posterior distribution is estimated by:

$$p\left(x\left(t, \theta\right), \theta, \Sigma | y(t), \dot{y}(t)\right) \propto p\left(x\left(t, \theta\right) | y, \dot{y}, \theta, \Sigma\right) p\left(y | \dot{y}, \theta, \Sigma\right) p\left(\dot{y} | \Sigma\right) p\left(\theta, \Sigma\right) \tag{20}$$

In this study we propose to estimate the solution of an ODE defined in the structure of the space-state models (8) and (9). A prior distribution is considered to model the solution function of the ODE considering a GP and $d-1$ derivatives:

$$\left(x(t), \dot{x}(t), x^{(2)}(t), \ldots, x^{(q-1)}(t)\right) : [0, T] \rightarrow \mathbb{R}^d \tag{21}$$

which are obtained from a Wiener process integrated $d-$times. We consider prior distributions given by a GP, of the form:

$$x(t) \sim GP\left(m(.), k(t, t')\right) \tag{22}$$

where $x^{(1)}(t)$ y $x^{(2)}(t)$ model $x(t)$ and $\dot{x}(t)$, respectively. The remaining $q - 1$ sub-vectors in $x(t)$ can be used to model the higher order derivatives in $x(t)$ [8,13].

A joint initial prior distribution of uncertainty is proposed via the solution and its derivative $(\dot{x}(t), x(t))^T$ using a GP prior [2,18], with mean vectors given by $\dot{m}_0$ and m_0, covariance matrices $\dot{k}_0(t,t')$ and $k_0(t,t')$, cross-covariance matrices $\tilde{k}_0(t,t')$, and $\tilde{k}_0(t',t)$, with the following constraints on the marginal mean:

$$m_0(t) = \int_0^t \dot{m}_0(z)dz + x_0$$

The initial joint GP prior distribution for the solution at a vector of evaluation times t_i and its time derivative at a possibly different vector of evaluation times t_j, is given by:

$$(\dot{x}(t_i), x(t_j))^T \,|f_0 \sim GP\left(\begin{pmatrix} \dot{m}_0(t_i) \\ m_0(t_j) \end{pmatrix}; \begin{pmatrix} \dot{k}_0(t_i, t_i) & \tilde{k}_0(t_i, t_j) \\ \tilde{k}_0(t_j, t_i) & k_0(t_j, t_j) \end{pmatrix}\right) \tag{23}$$

The matrix $\dot{k}_0(t_i, t_j)$ has entries given by:

$$\dot{k}_0(t_i, t_j) = \int_0^{t_i} \int_0^{t_j} \dot{k}_0(z, w)dzdw$$

and the covariance-cross matrices have entries given by:

$$\tilde{k}_0(t_i, t_j) = \int_0^{t_j} \dot{k}_0(t_i, z)\,dz, \quad and \quad \tilde{k}_0(t_j, t_i) = \int_0^{t_j} \dot{k}_0(z, t_i)\,dz$$

The solution $x(t)$ and its derivative $\dot{x}(t)$ in (23) can be updated by conditioning on its partition information $\tau = (\tau_1, \ldots, \tau_n)$. The model is evaluated in:

$$f_n = f(\tau_n, x(\tau_n), \theta) = \dot{x}(\tau_n)$$

from the predictive distribution to marginal posterior $x(\tau_n)|\dot{x}(\tau_{n-1})$. The marginal distributions follow the distribution of a GP [2,10,17]. The solution vector is:

$$x(t_j)|\dot{x}(t_i) \sim GP\left(\dot{m}_0, \dot{k}(.,.)\right)$$

The marginal distribution of the derivatives is obtained in a similar way:

$$\dot{x}(t_i)|x(t_j) \sim GP\left(m_0, k_0(.,.)\right) \tag{24}$$

The update of the Eq. (23) is performed sequentially, the derivative of the exact solution in the initial condition $\dot{x}_0^*(\tau_1)$ at $\tau_1 = 0$ is obtained by evaluating:

$$f_1 = f(\tau_1, x_0^*(\tau_1), \theta) = \dot{x}^*(\tau_1) \tag{25}$$

the next iteration will be:

$$(\dot{x}(t_i), x(t_j))^T \,|f_1 \sim N\left(\begin{pmatrix} \dot{m}_1(t_i) \\ m_1(t_j) \end{pmatrix}; \begin{pmatrix} \dot{k}_1(t_i, t_i) & \tilde{k}_1(t_i, t_j) \\ \dot{k}_1(t_j, t_i) & k_1(t_j, t_j) \end{pmatrix}\right) \tag{26}$$

Means and covariances are updated in the time vectors t_i and t_j:

$$\dot{m}_1(t_i) = \dot{m}_0(t_i) + \dot{k}_0(t_i, \tau_1)\,\dot{k}_0(\tau_1, \tau_1)^{-1}\,[f_1 - \dot{m}_0(\tau_1)]$$
$$m_1(t_j) = m_0(t_j) + \dot{k}_0(\tau_1, \tau_1)^{-1}\,\tilde{k}_0(t_j, \tau_1)\,[f_1 - \dot{m}_0(\tau_1)],$$
$$\dot{k}_1(t_i, t_i) = \dot{k}_0(t_i, t_i) - \dot{k}_0(t_i, \tau_1)\,\dot{k}_0(\tau_1, \tau_1)^{-1}\,\dot{k}_0(\tau_1, t_i)$$
$$k_1(t_j, t_j) = k_0(t_j, t_j) - \tilde{k}_0(t_j, \tau_1)\,\dot{k}_0(\tau_1, \tau_1)^{-1}\,\left(\tilde{k}_0(t_j, \tau_1)\right)^T$$

For the n-th iteration, we generate the data $x(\tau_n)$ at time τ_n from the predicted marginal posterior distribution:

$$x(\tau_n)\,|f_{n-1}, \ldots, f_1 \sim GP\left(\dot{m}(\tau_n), \Lambda_{n-1}(\tau_n)\right) \tag{27}$$

where $\Lambda_{n-1}(\tau_n) = \dot{k}_{n-1}(\tau_n, \tau_n)$. Updates of the predictive model (26) are carried out by evaluating at times t_i and t_j as follows:

$$(\dot{x}(t), x(t))^T \,|f_n, \ldots, f_1 \sim N\left(\begin{pmatrix} \dot{m}_n(t_i) \\ m_n(t_j) \end{pmatrix}; \begin{pmatrix} \dot{k}_n(t_i, t_i) & \tilde{k}_n(t_i, t_j) \\ \tilde{k}_n(t_j, t_i) & k_n(t_j, t_j) \end{pmatrix}\right) \tag{28}$$

The marginal means and covariances evaluated on the time vectors t_i and t_j are updated by:

$$\dot{m}_n(t_i) = \dot{m}_{n-1}(t_i) + \dot{k}_{n-1}(t_i, \tau_n)\left(\dot{k}_{n-1}(\tau_n, \tau_n) + \Lambda_{n-1}(\tau_n)\right)^{-1}[f_n - \dot{m}_{n-1}(\tau_n)]$$
$$m_n(t_j) = m_{n-1}(t_j) + \left(\dot{k}_{n-1}(\tau_n, \tau_n) + \Lambda_{n-1}(\tau_n)\right)^{-1}\tilde{k}_n(t_j, t_i)\,[f_n - \dot{m}_{n-1}(\tau_n)]$$
$$\dot{k}_n(t_i, t_j) = \dot{k}_{n-1}(t_i, t_j) - \dot{k}_{n-1}(t_i, \tau_n)\left(\dot{k}_{n-1}(\tau_n, \tau_n) + \Lambda_{n-1}(\tau_n)\right)^{-1}\left(\tilde{k}_{n-1}(\tau_n, t_j)\right)^T$$
$$\dot{k}_n(t_i, t_j) = \dot{k}_{n-1}(t_i, t_j) - \left(\dot{k}_{n-1}(\tau_n, \tau_n) + \Lambda_{n-1}(\tau_n)\right)^{-1}\tilde{k}_{n-1}(t_i, \tau_n)\left(\tilde{k}_{n-1}(t_j, \tau_n)\right)^T$$

Chkrebtii [2], and Overstall [10] proposed a sequential algorithm to update and sample on $\mathbf{t} = (t_1, \ldots, t_n)^T$ a GP between $x(t)$ and $\dot{x}(t)$, and a mesh $\boldsymbol{\tau} = (\tau_1, \ldots, \tau_n)^T$ to evaluate the derivatives $\dot{x}(t) = (\dot{x}(\tau_1), \ldots, \dot{x}(\tau_n))^T$, respectively.

2.3 Polynomial Chaos Expansion and Gaussian Processes

Consider a dynamic system whose behavior is represented by a mathematical model:

$$Y = f(X), \quad X \in \mathcal{D}_X \subset \mathbb{R}^M$$

where $X = (X_1, \ldots, X_M)^T$ are the input parameters of the system, and Y is the response. When the data are assumed to be independent, the joint distribution can be defined by a set of marginal distributions:

$$f_X(x_1, \ldots, x_M) = \prod_{i=1}^{M} f_{X_i}(x_i) \qquad (29)$$

Then, $Y = f(X)$ becomes a random variable with properties implicitly defined by the propagation of uncertainty. Assuming that Y is a second-order stochastic process having finite variance, it belongs to a Hilbert space and is given by:

$$f_{PCE}(X) = \sum_{i=0}^{\infty} \beta_i Z_i \qquad (30)$$

where Y is an infinite series, $\{Z_i\}_{i=0}^{\infty}$ is a numberable set of random variables forming a basis in Hilbert space, and $\{\beta_i\}$ are the coefficients of the series. Hilbert spaces guarantee the existence of such bases and their representation. In the case of polynomial chaos expansions, in which the terms of the bases $\{Z_i\}_{i=0}^{\infty}$ are multivariate orthonormal polynomials with input vector X, i.e., $Z_i = \Psi_i(X)$, and the approximation (30) can be rewritten by truncating the series, so that:

$$f_{PCE}(X) = \sum_{i=0}^{M} \beta_i \Psi_i(X) \qquad (31)$$

In practice, the experimental data are obtained considering an error rate, i.e.:

$$Y_i = \hat{f}_{PCE}(X_i) + \epsilon_i, \quad \epsilon_i \sim N\left(0, \sigma^2\right), \quad i = 1, \ldots, N$$

then $\hat{f}_{PCE}(X_i)$ remains unknown. The above allows us to connect the polynomial chaos expansion with Gaussian processes. For an input data $X = \{X_i\}$ and an output response $Y = \{Y_i\}$ with $i = 1, \ldots, n$, where:

$$Y = f(X) + \epsilon, \quad \epsilon \sim N\left(0, \sigma_\epsilon^2 I\right), \quad f(X) \sim GP\left(m_{prior}(X), k_{prior}(X, X)\right)$$

Using Bayes' theorem, new data with its respective error can be predicted using the posterior distribution:

$$f(x)|Y, X, x, \theta \sim N\left(m_{post}(x), k_{post}(x, x)\right)$$

where:

$$m_{post}(x) = \mathbb{E}\left(f(x)|Y, X, x, \theta\right) = K_x^T\left(K + \sigma_\epsilon^2 I\right)^{-1} Y \qquad (32)$$

$$k_{post}(x, x) = K_{xx} - K_x^T\left(K + \sigma_\epsilon^2 I\right)^{-1} K_x \qquad (33)$$

Here, $K = k(X, X) \in \mathbb{R}^{N \times N}$, $K_{ij} = k(X_i, X_j)$, $K_x = k(X, x) \in \mathbb{R}^{N \times 1}$ and $K_{xx} = k(x, x) \in \mathbb{R}$. Note that (33) can be represented as a combination of N kernels of functions:

$$m_{post}(x) = \hat{f}_{GP}(x) = \sum_{i=1}^{N} \beta_i k(X_i, x), \quad \beta = \left(K + \sigma_\epsilon^2 I\right)^{-1} Y$$

PCEs and GPs are linked through the reproduction of kernels of covariance functions in Hilbert spaces.

3   Results and Discussion

To exemplify the methodology proposed above, three coupled differential equation models which are widely used in physics, epidemiology and biology have been proposed. In these systems, uncertainty is evaluated by comparing the estimated solutions with the numerical solution provided by the Python dependency scipy.integrate, and the effectiveness of the proposed solvers is quantified by performance measures such as root mean squared error (RMSE), standardized mean squared error (SMSE) and mean standardized log loss (MSLL).

3.1   Lorenz Attractor Model

The Lorenz attractor model simulates the fluid motion induced by the temperature difference between surfaces. It is expressed as:

$$\dot{x}(t) = \frac{dx}{dt} = \sigma(y(t) - x(t))$$

$$\dot{y}(t) = \frac{dy}{dt} = \rho x(t) - y(t) - x(t)z(t) \tag{34}$$

$$\dot{z}(t) = \frac{dz}{dt} = -\beta z(t) + x(t)y(t)$$

where $\sigma, \rho, \beta \in \mathbb{R}^+$ are known parameters. In this work we will use $(\sigma, \beta, \rho) = (10, 8/3, 28)$ since at these points the attractor exhibits chaotic behavior [9]. A vector of initial conditions $(x_0, y_0, z_0) = (-12, 15, 38)$ in an interval of $T = [0, 20]$ was considered. After running 2000 realizations of Chkrebtii's algorithm, the three-dimensional model was constructed (Fig. 1).

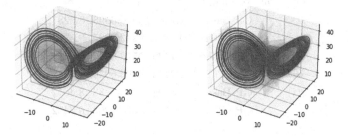

Fig. 1. 3D reconstructed solutions for the Lorenz model. Left, GP-Based vs. Numerical solutions. Right, GP+PCE vs. Numerical solutions.

Here, the blue trajectory is numerical solution and the light blue spectrum are the model realizations with uncertainty, noting that the perturbed trajectories represent a modification of the attractor orientation but do not change radically its overall behavior. On the other hand, a generalized polynomial chaos sampling was performed, with Legendre polynomials of order 4 that generated 50 basis functions fitted by Gaussian quadrature. Due to the geometry of the attractor, approximate it by this method can be complicated in initial conditions in which the dynamics of the attractor results in chaos. In fact, note that the calculated realizations become spare and depart from the expected trajectory as time goes by, presenting an increase in the standard deviation and therefore in the variance of the realizations (Fig. 2).

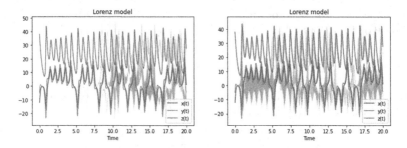

Fig. 2. Individual solutions.

Comparing the numerical solution with the sampling of the solutions with the GP-based method and with addition of the polynomial chaos expansion, we observe that the polynomial chaos simulation has a rather more unstable behavior with a clear variability in the functions $x(t)$ and $y(t)$, which is noticeable from the beginning of the time interval (Table 1).

Table 1. Performance measures for Lorenz model

Function	Technique	RMSE	SMSE	MSLL
$x(t)$	GP-Based	11.7409	5566.6898	8.5237
	GP+PCE	10.0168	9242.2935	9.5369
$y(t)$	GP-Based	13.1429	5578.0299	8.7529
	GP+PCE	11.2242	9166.5040	9.7348
$z(t)$	GP-Based	11.3804	5566.4833	8.4612
	GP+PCE	6.9450	2570.9264	6.7482

Taking the mean of the realizations to compute the performance measures, we can observe that a considerably higher error rate is present in the functions $x(t)$ and $y(t)$, according with what was observed in the plot of the trajectories. In general, polynomial chaos expansions did not help to estimate the model adequately, perhaps due to its complex structure [12].

3.2   Kermack-McKendrick SIR Model

The SIR epidemiological model aims to predict the evolution of infectious diseases that are transmitted between people. Under the assumption of dynamic suppression, this system is detailed as:

$$\dot{S}(t) = \frac{dS}{dt} = -\beta S(t)I(t) \tag{35}$$

$$\dot{I}(t) = \frac{dI}{dt} = \beta S(t)I(t) - \gamma I(t)$$

$$\dot{R}(t) = \frac{dR}{dt} = \gamma I(t)$$

where a population of $N(t) = S(t) + I(t) + R(t) \in \mathbb{R}^+$ individuals are classified according to various disease status at a point in time t. Within the population, $S(t)$ represents the susceptible individuals, $I(t)$ the infectious population, and $R(t)$ the recovered inhabitants [3]. On the other hand, $\beta, \gamma \in \mathbb{R}^+$ is considered as fixed parameters, representing the infection rate and the recovery rate. In this work, we will use the set of parameters $(\beta, \gamma) = (0.22, 0.1)$ and initial conditions $(S(0), I(0), R(0)) = (1, 0, 0)$ in an interval $T = [0, 200]$ (Fig. 3).

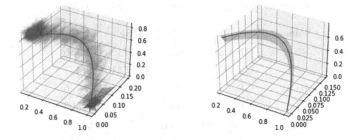

Fig. 3. 3D reconstructed solutions for SIR model. Left, GP-Based vs. Numerical solutions. Right, GP+PCE vs. Numerical solutions.

A wide range of disturbances can be observed in the estimation of the GP technique, with unstable and periodic trajectories, which are concentrated at the beginning of the time interval. On the other hand, the trajectories returned by increasing the polynomial chaos fit are smoother and have a mean closer to the numerical estimated paths of the solution. The method was applied with Legendre polynomials of order 3 resulting in 50 basis functions. The effect of the variability of the trajectories has a better understanding in the three-dimensional projection of the model (Fig. 4).

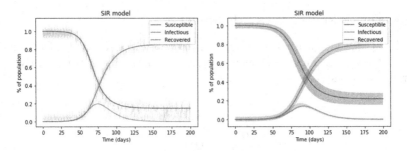

Fig. 4. Individual solutions.

On the other hand, the mean squared error rates do not differ considerably between methods, but the standardized error shows a lower error in the method based on GPs. This may occur because the mean of the realizations is closer to the original solution; however, the high variability of data must be considered. Although as the polynomial chaos increases the error is higher, the sampled functions are smoother which allows a more adequate prediction of the function at all its points (Table 2).

Table 2. Performance measures for SIR model.

Function	Technique	RMSE	SMSE	MSLL
S(t)	GP-Based	0.0325	8.1571	0.1750
	GP+PCE	0.1480	193.7416	0.1471
I(t)	GP-Based	0.0355	420.2386	1.7746
	GP+PCE	0.0403	736.1283	0.2806
R(t)	GP-Based	0.0337	8.8735	0.1035
	GP+PCE	0.1404	176.2106	0.1750

3.3 FitzHugh-Nagumo Model

The FitzHugh-Nagumo equations describe the excitation and propagation properties of neurons under electrochemical reactions. These are given by:

$$\dot{v}(t) = \frac{dv}{dt} = v(t) - \frac{v^3(t)}{3} - w(t) + I \tag{36}$$
$$\dot{w}(t) = \frac{dw}{dt} = \frac{v(t) + a - bw(t)}{\tau}$$

where $v(t)$ describes the voltage evolution in the neuronal membrane, while $w(t)$ simulates the recuperative action between the sodium channel deactivation currents and the potassium channel deactivation [14]. In (36), $a, b, \tau \in \mathbb{R}^+$ are constant parameters, and $I \in \mathbb{R}^+$ represents the applied external current. For the simulations, the values of the parameters used in [4] will be used, which are $(a, b, \tau) = (0.5, 0.7, 0.8)$ and a current amount $I = 12.5$. In this study, we have considered the initial conditions $(v(0), w(0) = (0,0)$ to run simulations in a interval time $T = [0, 200]$. For the implementation of polynomial chaos, 56 basis functions were generated from Legendre polynomials of degree 3, using the Gaussian quadrature rule (Fig. 5).

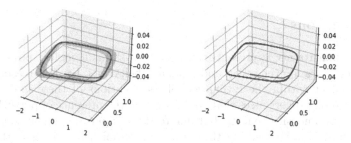

Fig. 5. 3D reconstructed solutions for FitzHugh-Nagumo model. Left, GP-Based vs. Numerical solutions. Right, GP+PCE vs. Numerical solutions.

A good overall estimation can be observed using the GP-based algorithm, where the distance between the simulated trajectories and the numerical solution is small. Moreover, the simulations follow very closely the shape of the numerical trajectory so we can affirm that its variability is low. On the other hand, the addition of the chaos component considerably improves the prediction, resulting in trajectories that overlap the numerical solution (Fig. 6).

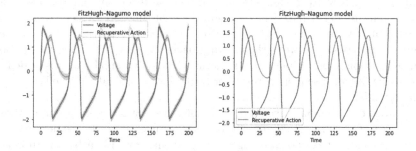

Fig. 6. Individual solutions.

The above-mentioned observations are confirmed by the performance measures, which show a much lower error than in the rest of the models. Both methods yielded very small error rates, indicating that in this model there is no substantial modification of the solutions when simulations are generated (Table 3).

Table 3. Performance measures for FitzHugh-Nagumo model

Function	Technique	RMSE	SMSE	MSLL
v(t)	GP-Based	$3.5874e^{-17}$	$1.4399e^{-30}$	2.4187
	GP+PCE	0.1153	1.4772	2.4335
w(t)	GP-Based	$1.0268e^{-17}$	$6.3392e^{-31}$	0.7372
	GP+PCE	0.0310	0.5823	0.7359

4   Conclusions

In real life, uncertainty is present in almost all systems modeling physical, biological, chemical and even social and economic behaviors. For this reason, quantifying its effect within the estimation of the solutions of these models helps experts to predict divergences that could occur in the presence of perturbations. This can cause undesired effects, but due to the computational complexity that it usually has, it is ignored. In this work, this problem is addressed by using a GP-based algorithm and its combination with recently studied components, such as polynomial chaos expansions.

To check the outcome of both techniques, they were tested on models which can be challenging case studies due to their dynamics. The algorithm proposed by Chkrebtii showed a mean relatively close to the numerical solution in all the cases, but the randomness of the samplings resulted in the existence of several sparse trajectories. This shows that the uncertainty rate in the estimation of the solutions is significant, especially in the SIR model where constant perturbations are shown.

On the other hand, the polynomial chaos addition yielded good results in terms of similarity to the mean of the GP-based simulations, as it was expected, and approached toward the numerical solutions. However, simulated trajectories of the Lorenz model depart from the solutions as time progressed, which may suggest that this technique is sensitive to the chaotic structure of the model. Finally, a comparison between the two approaches versus the numerical solution given by Python shows a better estimation when polynomial chaos is added in two systems. As a consequence, the error rate is lower, specially in the FitzHugh-Nagumo model.

However, the tests on these models do not represent a decisive opinion about the contrast of both methods in terms of performance, so future studies on other systems of chaotic behavior are suggested that may provide a better approach to the interpretation of the results of the techniques. On the other hand, it is recommended to make modifications in the basis functions of the polynomial chaos, such as changing the type of polynomial, their order or their quadrature fitting, in order to have a broaden perspective of the results obtained.

References

1. Butcher, J.: Numerical methods for ordinary differential equations, pp. i–xxiv, August 2016
2. Chkrebtii, O., Campbell, D., Girolami, M., Calderhead, B.: Bayesian solution uncertainty quantification for differential equations. Bayesian Anal. **11**, 1239–1267 (2013)
3. Doungmo Goufo, E.F., Maritz, R., Munganga, J.: Some properties of the Kermack-McKendrick epidemic model with fractional derivative and nonlinear incidence. Adv. Differ. Equ. **2014**(1), 1–9 (2014)
4. FitzHugh, R.: Impulses and physiological states in theoretical models of nerve membrane. Biophys. J . **1**(6), 445–466 (1961)
5. Heinonen, M., Yildiz, C., Mannerstrm, H., Intosalmi, J., Lhdesmki, H.: Learning unknown ode models with Gaussian processes, March 2018
6. Huang, H., Handel, A., Song, X.: A Bayesian approach to estimate parameters of ordinary differential equation. Comput. Stat. **35** (2020)
7. Infante, S., Luna, C., Snchez, L., Hernndez, A.: Approximations of the solutions of a stochastic differential equation using Dirichlet process mixtures and Gaussian mixtures. Stat. Optim. Inf. Comput. **4**, 289–307 (2016)
8. Kersting, H., Hennig, P.: Active uncertainty calibration in Bayesian ODE solvers, May 2016
9. Lorenz, E.: Deterministic nonperiodic flow. J. Atmos. Sci. **20**, 130–141 (1963)
10. Overstall, A., Woods, D., Parker, B.: Bayesian optimal design for ordinary differential equation models with application in biological science. J. Am. Stat. Assoc. **115** (2019)
11. Ramsay, J., Dalzell, C.: Some tools for functional data analysis. J. R. Stat. Soc. Ser. B (Methodol.) **53**, 539–561 (1991)
12. Sandu, C., Sandu, A., Ahmadian, M.: Modeling multibody systems with uncertainties. Part II: Numerical applications. Multibody Syst. Dyn. **15**, 241–262 (2006)
13. Schober, M., Srkk, S., Hennig, P.: A probabilistic model for the numerical solution of initial value problems. Stat. Comput. **29** (2019)
14. Sherwood, W.E.: FitzHugh-Nagumo Model, pp. 1–11. Springer, New York (2013)
15. Skilling, J.: Bayesian Solution of Ordinary Differential Equations, pp. 23–37. Springer, Dordrecht (1992)
16. Sánchez, L., Infante, S., Marcano, J., Griffin, V.: Polynomial chaos based on the parallelized Ensamble Kalman filter to estimate precipitation states. Stat. Optim. Inf. Comput. **3**, 79–95 (2015)
17. Solak, E., Murray-Smith, R., Leithead, W., Leith, D., Rasmussen, C.: Derivative observations in gaussian process models of dynamic systems. In: Appear Advance Neural Information Processing Systems, vol. 16 (2003)
18. Tronarp, F., Kersting, H., Srkk, S., Hennig, P.: Probabilistic solutions to ordinary differential equations as nonlinear Bayesian filtering: a new perspective. Stat. Comput. **29** (2019)
19. Yaglom, A., Newell, G.: An introduction to the theory of stationary random functions. J. Appl. Mech. **30**, 479 (1963)

Forecasting Energy Consumption in Residential Department Using Convolutional Neural Networks

Julio Barzola-Monteses[1,2]($\boxtimes$) ⓘ, Marcos Guerrero[3] ⓘ, Franklin Parrales-Bravo[3] ⓘ, and Mayken Espinoza-Andaluz[4] ⓘ

[1] Artificial Intelligence and Information Technology Research Group, University of Guayaquil, Av. Delta y Av. Kennedy, 090514 Guayaquil, Ecuador
`julio.barzolam@ug.edu.ec`
[2] Department of Computer Science and Artificial Intelligence, Escuela Técnica Superior de Ingenierías Informática y de Telecomunicación, Universidad de Granada, 18071 Granada, Spain
[3] Faculty of Mathematics and Physical Sciences, University of Guayaquil, Av. Delta y Av. Kennedy, 090514 Guayaquil, Ecuador
[4] Facultad de Ingeniería Mecánica y Ciencias de la Producción, Centro de Energías Renovables y Alternativas, Escuela Superior Politécnica del Litoral, ESPOL, Campus Gustavo Galindo, Km. 30.5 Vía Perimetral, P.O. Box, 09-01-5863 Guayaquil, Ecuador

Abstract. During 2017, the construction and operation of buildings worldwide represented more than a third (36%) of the final energy used and 40% of the carbon dioxide emissions. Hence, in the last decade, there has been great interest in analyzing the energy efficiency in buildings from different approaches. In this paper, black-box approaches based on artificial neural networks to predict the energy consumption of a selected residential department building are proposed. The potential of convolutional neural networks (CNN) applied to images and videos is tested in time series as one-dimensional (1D) sequences. CNN models and other combinations with Long Short-Term Memory (LSTM) such as CNN-LSTM and ConvLSTM are proposed to make predictions in two scenarios, i.e., for predicting energy consumption in the next 24 h and 7 days. The results showed that the best model was CNN for the first scenario, and in the second scenario, CNN-LSTM performed better. These models can be very useful in predictive control systems considered in buildings to foresee with great precision the energy consumption behavior in the short, medium, and long term.

Keywords: Buildings · CNN · CNN-LSTM · ConvLSTM · Energy efficiency · Prediction models · Time series

1 Introduction

A report issued by the International Energy Agency shows that during 2017, the construction and building operations sector was one of the largest consumers of energy worldwide, consuming around 36% of primary energy and responsible for the emission of 40% of CO2 [1].

© Springer Nature Switzerland AG 2021
J. P. Salgado Guerrero et al. (Eds.): TICEC 2021, CCIS 1456, pp. 18–30, 2021.
https://doi.org/10.1007/978-3-030-89941-7_2

In the Ecuadorian case, as reported by the Geological and Energy Research Institute (IIGE) in 2018, the national consumption for residential, commercial, service, and public administration buildings was approximately 21% of total consumption. The primary energy source used by buildings was electricity, which represented 57.6%, i.e., 29.7% of the residential group and 27.9% of the commercial, services and public administration group. The total energy demand in 2018 was 3.8% higher than in 2017, which can be evidenced in the historical data of each year, i.e., presents an increasing trend annually until the current dates [2].

Due to the above described, in the last decade, interest has increased in the research line of optimizing the energy associated with the manufacture of construction materials, elaboration of new eco-friendly materials with the environment, efficient building designs, and predictive control systems of the energy consumption in residential homes, and buildings in general.

The predictive control systems considered in buildings require to foresee with great precision the energy consumption behavior in the short, medium, and long term [3]–[6]. There are some techniques to predict the demand for electrical energy, such as statistical models, thermal-mathematical models involving differential equations, or models considering machine learning, such as deep learning [7]. In this article, a deep learning approach based on artificial neural networks (ANN) will be applied to forecast the energy consumption of a residence. We will consider three of the less analyzed structures in previous studies for the energy field: a 1D CNN structure and two hybrid structures between CNN and LSTM networks.

The rest of the paper is organized as follows: Sect. 2 summarizes the ANN techniques used in this work, Sect. 3 shows the experiment setup. Experimental results and discussion are shown in Sect. 4. Finally, Sect. 5 presents the conclusions and future work.

2 Artificial Neural Network Techniques

An ANN is a structure that contains a simple processing unit mainly inspired by biologic neurons with the same components, i.e., dendrites, axons, and synapses [8]. Artificially understood, there are three specific characteristics that every ANN has, which are: a) the connections and the input values that will pass through each neuron in the network; b) the training process where a summation of the input values with their respective weights is made; c) an activation function is applied to the input and output values of each neuron [9].

For this work, a CNN and two additional combinations with an LSTM network were considered, i.e., CNN-LSTM and ConvLSTM structures. These supervised ANN structures will be applied to time series, and prediction scenarios will be analyzed.

2.1 Convolutional Neural Network

A CNN is a type of feed-forward neural network in which the computations proceed only in the forward direction. Specifically, in a CNN, there are two processes, convolution and pooling. Convolution allows the network to collect information on characteristics or visual features in two dimensions: images or videos, such as color, lines, edges, etc. Pooling simplifies the information that results in the convolution operation and creates a new version with different dimensions considering the fully condensed data [10].

CNNs are widely used for image and video processing. These neural networks work in the same way as normal neural networks. It only differs in that each neuron of each layer has a two-dimensional filter in which a convolution is made for the next layer, allowing a different characteristic to be extracted in each layer of the convolutional network [11].

CNNs have been applied to recognize or classify images that correspond to two dimensions, but this is not a limitation for analyzing sequential data of one dimension, such as time series. Figure 1 depicts a block diagram showing the structure of the model to be used in the experimentation stage.

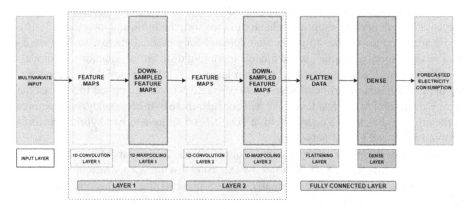

Fig. 1. Fully CNN architecture for time series prediction.

In this work, CNN will be applied to multivariate time series to forecast the energy consumption of a residential apartment.

2.2 CNN-LSTM Hybrid Structure

A recurrent neural network (RNN) consists of feedback with loops included in the entire neural network. This allows processing information sequentially, such as time series. The mentioned process is performed considering the previous process state [11].

LSTM is a type of RNN and is widely recognized as a universally applied ANN for analyzing and forecasting time series. These networks allow data to travel backward and forward, with a robust and powerful architecture. Since each neuron possesses internal memory, exchanging information between the cycles of the network is enhanced [7, 12].

CNN-LSTM hybrid structure complements the individual advantages of CNN and LSTM structures. The CNN structures perform well for spatial information extraction, but it is not that good for temporal information. On the other hand, LSTM structures are insufficient for spatial information and can learn temporal information [13, 14].

In this work context, the CNN-LSTM structure will be applied to extract spatio-temporal information to predict energy consumption time series effectively. Figure 2 shows a block diagram of the structure to be used in the experimentation stage.

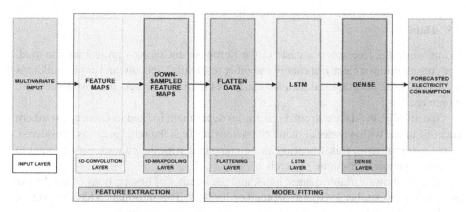

Fig. 2. Fully CNN-LSTM architecture for time series prediction.

2.3 Conv-LSTM Hybrid Structure

ConvLSTM and CNN-LSTM networks are a combination of CNN and LSTM structures, with the difference that ConvLSTM networks work in the same LSTM block, making the convolution and analysis process at the same layer [15].

Figure 3 depicts the block diagram of the structure to be used in the experimentation stage. The ConvLSTM layer has inside a convolution operator that reads the data and extracts the spatial characteristics of the time series. Then, its output will feed the inputs of the LSTM unit. The data passes into a pair of layers called fully connected layers that compile the data extracted by previous layers to generate the final output.

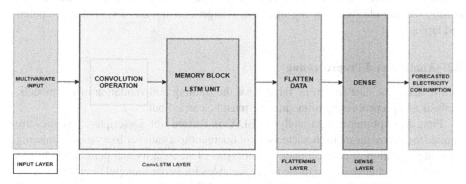

Fig. 3. Fully ConvLSTM architecture for time series prediction.

3 Experimental Setup

This section details the experimental design considered for the configurations of the CNN, CNN-LSTM, and ConvLSTM models.

3.1 Data

In this work, the free access dataset of the European enCompass project will be used. The consumption of electrical energy and other residential, schools, and public buildings located in three geographical locations such as Germany, Greece and Switzerland are monitored [16].

Specifically, the dataset from a residential department located in Greece, a southern area of Europe with warmer climatic characteristics than the other areas, is considered. In the medium term, this scenario can be compared with the characteristics found in Ecuador to implement future research.

Table 1 shows variable names, units, and the number of observations of the dataset collected from October 1, 2018 to September 30, 2019. This information has a resolution of 15 min.

Table 1. Variables of the dataset considered for the experimentation of the models.

Variable	Units	Number of records
Energy consumption	kWh	35040
Relative humidity	% RH	12944
Indoor temperature	°C	12868

In addition, the apartment has the following characteristics: Number of people: 4, number of rooms: 5, type of heating: radiators, heating source: gas. It is also equipped with a water heater, lighting: incandescent light bulb. The following items complete the consumer elements: air conditioning, electric oven, microwave, electric kettle, coffee maker, vacuum cleaner, washing machine, refrigerator, freezer, TV, HI-FI, computer, and laptop.

3.2 Analysis and Preprocessing

Before using the data shown in Table 1 for the training and validation of the models, analysis and preprocessing of the models must be carried out.

First, an exploratory data analysis (EDA) is carried out. Descriptive statistics are applied to analyze the main characteristics of fluctuation of values, observation of missing data, identification of atypical data, and analysis of stationarity and periodicity. In this phase, a name change is also made to the variables for better manipulation. Thus, E for energy consumption, H for relative humidity, and T for indoor temperature are defined.

After performing the EDA, the preprocessing data is carried out. Initially, for each variable, there was a dataset. All datasets were merged into a single dataset in which each column identified the respective variables E, H, and T. The rows represent the measurements of each variable collected by the sensors at time t. In addition, during the data collection, readings problems can occur, which have an impact on missing or lost data. Therefore, statistical imputation techniques such as mean substitution are applied. Finally, treatment of outliers or atypical data is conducted [17, 18].

3.3 Definition of the Problem

A multivariate problem of time series will be approached by applying deep learning, i.e., regression models. There will be three input variables (regressor variables) E, H and T. As output variable (predictor variable) is selected E, the variable of interest in this research.

To analyze the performance of the CNN structures in the energy consumption forecasts, two scenarios are evaluated in the experimentation:

Given the recent energy consumption, relative humidity, and temperature measurements inside the apartment, What will the energy consumption be in the next 24 h, i.e., the next day?

Given the recent energy consumption, relative humidity, and temperature measurements inside the apartment, What will the energy consumption be in the next 7 days, i.e., next week?

In each scenario, a transformation of the data is considered by applying a normalization, whose new values will fluctuate between -1 and + 1. This is due to the hyperbolic tangent activation function present in the LSTM memories.

For experimentation with each scenario proposed, the dataset is resampled with resolutions of one hour and one day, respectively. For both scenarios, the proportion of the dataset is 80% and 20% for training and validation, respectively.

Therefore, in the first scenario, there are 2424 observations, of which 1939 and 485 are used for training and testing, respectively; while for the second scenario, the dataset has 107 observations, from which 85 and 22 are used for training and testing, respectively.

Model Evaluation: A continuous forecast scenario, also called walk-forward validation (WFV), is used. It consists of going through the data set only once concerning each step of time [19].

Performance Evaluation: The root mean squared error (RMSE) is used for the evaluation applied to time series, which corresponds to the most commonly employed in energy studies. Other supporting metrics are the mean absolute error (MAE) and mean absolute percentage error (MAPE).

$$RMSE = \sqrt{\frac{1}{N_{test}} \sum_{n=1}^{N_{test}} (y_n - \tilde{y}_n)^2} \tag{1}$$

$$MAE = \frac{1}{N_{test}} \sum_{n=1}^{N_{test}} |y_n - \tilde{y}_n| \tag{2}$$

$$MAPE = \frac{1}{N_{test}} \sum_{n=1}^{Ntest} \left| \frac{y_n - \tilde{y}_n}{y_n} \right|$$ (3)

where N_{test} in the number of tests set samples, y_n refers to the actual value of the *nth* forecasting point, and $\tilde{y}_n$ is the corresponding predicted value [19].

3.4 Experimental Models

CNN, CNN-LSTM, and ConvLSTM structures were configured for multi-step time series forecasting with multivariate inputs.

For the experimentation of CNN, CNN-LSTM, and ConvLSTM models in each scenario: 288, 288, and 72 model configurations were designed. Tables 2 and 3 show the hyperparameter values used in each scenario. According to the specified characteristics, almost 650 configurations were executed.

Table 2. Hyperparameters used for the experiments - scenario 1: Forecast for the next 24 h

CNN y CNN-LSTM		ConvLSTM	
Hyperparameters	Values	Hyperparameters	Values
n_input	24, 48, 72	n_input	24, 48, 72
n_nodes	8, 16, 32, 64	n_filters	8, 24
n_filters	8, 24	n_kernel	(1, 2), (1, 5)
n_kernel	2, 5	n_epochs	25, 50
n_epochs	25, 50	n_batch	8, 16, 48
n_batch	8, 16, 48	act_hid	Tanh
act_hid	tanh	act_out	Linear
act_out	linear		

As presented in Tables 2 and 3, the hyperparameters are described as follows: n_input is the number of prior inputs to use as input for the model, n_nodes is the number of nodes that are used in the hidden layer, n_filters are the number of filters of the convolutional layer, n_kernel is the kernel number to be used in the convolutional layer, n_epochs is the number of training epochs, n_batch is the number of samples to include in each mini-batch, act_hid is the activation function used in the hidden layer, and act_out corresponds to the activation function for the output layer.

Due to the stochastic nature of neural network models, each model is trained and validated ten times to obtain a mean of RMSE error values.

All experiments were run on Windows 10, Python 3.8, Anaconda 2020.11, Spyder 4.2.0, and Tensorflow library. Additionally, hardware with the following characteristics was used: Acer, Intel® Core (TM) i7–8550 U CPU @ 1.80 GHz 1.99 GHz, 16 GB of RAM.

Table 3. Hyperparameters used for the experiments - scenario 2: Forecast for the next 7 days

CNN y CNN-LSTM		ConvLSTM	
Hyperparameters	Values	Hyperparameters	Values
n_input	7, 14, 21	n_input	7, 14, 21
n_nodes	8, 16, 32, 64	n_filters	8, 24
n_filters	8, 24	n_kernel	(1, 1), (1, 2)
n_kernel	2, 2	n_epochs	25, 50
n_epochs	25, 50	n_batch	8, 16, 48
n_batch	8, 16, 48	act_hid	tanh
act_hid	tanh	act_out	linear
act_out	linear		

4 Experimental Results and Discussion

Once the experimentation has been carried out configuring the models with the hyper-parameters established for training and validation in the dataset, the best model configurations with their respective hyperparameters are determined.

4.1 Scenario 1: Forecast of the Next 24 h

Table 4 shows the top five of the best configurations of each ANN structure obtained after carried out the experimentation. It is noted that among the three analyzed convolutional neural network structures, CNN has the best metric. The best CNN configuration has the following hyperparameters: n_input = 24, n_nodes = 32, n_filters = 8, n_kernel = 5, n_epochs = 25, n_batch = 8, act_hid = tanh, act_out = linear.

The execution time of the experiments in this scenario with CNN, CNN-LSTM, and ConvLSTM was 636, 664, and 517 min, respectively; i.e., on average: 2.2 min/model, 2.3 min/model, and 7.18 min/model, respectively. Figure 4 shows a contrast between the average execution times of the models and the associated error. The CNN models have the shortest computational time compared to the other models studied. The worst error is with the ConvLSTM structure by a factor of 3.26 compared to the CNN model.

4.2 Scenario 2: Forecast for the Next 7 days

Table 5 shows the top five of the best configurations of each model obtained after carried out the experimentation. It is noted that among the three analyzed CNN structures, CNN-LSTM has the best metric with the following hyperparameters: n_input = 14, n_nodes = 8, n_filters = 8, n_kernel = 2, n_epochs = 25, n_batch = 8, act_hid = tanh, act_out = linear.

Table 4. Configurations of the best models obtained - scenario 1

Model	Hyperparameters	RMSE
CNN	**[24, 32, 8, 5, 25, 8, 'tanh', 'linear']**	**0.0645**
	[24, 8, 8, 5, 25, 8, 'tanh', 'linear']	0.0649
	[24, 16, 8, 5, 25, 8, 'tanh', 'linear']	0.0649
	[24, 64, 8, 5, 25, 8, 'tanh', 'linear']	0.0653
	[24, 64, 24, 5, 25, 8, 'tanh', 'linear']	0.0653
CNN-LSTM	**[72, 8, 24, 5, 25, 8, 'tanh', 'linear']**	**0.0661**
	[72, 8, 24, 2, 25, 8, 'tanh', 'linear']	0.0665
	[48, 8, 24, 5, 25, 8, 'tanh', 'linear']	0.0669
	[48, 8, 24, 2, 25, 8, 'tanh', 'linear']	0.0671
	[48, 8, 8, 5, 25, 8, 'tanh', 'linear']	0.0681
ConvLSTM	**[48, 8, (1, 5), 50, 48, 'tanh', 'linear']**	**0.0751**
	[48, 8, (1, 2), 50, 48, 'tanh', 'linear']	0.0770
	[48, 8, (1, 2), 25, 16, 'tanh', 'linear']	0.0774
	[48, 8, (1, 5), 25, 48, 'tanh', 'linear']	0.0779
	[24, 8, (1, 2), 50, 16, 'tanh', 'linear']	0.0780

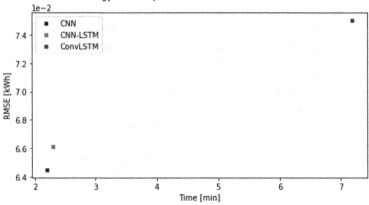

Fig. 4. Comparative error/time of the three observed models – scenario 1

The execution time of the experiments with CNN, CNN-LSTM, and ConvLSTM was 52, 152, and 60 min, respectively; that is, on average: 0.18 min/model, 0.53 min/model, and 0.83 min/model, respectively. Figure 5 shows a contrast between the average execution times of the models and the associated error. The CNN model achieves the best execution time. However, its error is high and occupies second place among the analyzed models. The worst execution time is the ConvLSTM model, which is higher than

Table 5. Configurations of the best models obtained - scenario 2

Model	Hyperparameters	RMSE
CNN	**[14, 8, 8, 1, 50, 48, 'tanh', 'linear']**	**0.9288**
	[21, 8, 8, 2, 25, 16, 'tanh', 'linear']	0.9324
	[14, 8, 8, 1, 25, 16, 'tanh', 'linear']	0.9400
	[21, 8, 8, 1, 25, 48, 'tanh', 'linear']	0.9488
	[14, 8, 8, 2, 25, 8, 'tanh', 'linear']	0.9500
CNN-LSTM	**[14, 8, 8, 2, 25, 8, 'tanh', 'linear']**	**0.8827**
	[21, 16, 8, 1, 25, 48, 'tanh', 'linear']	0.8833
	[14, 16, 8, 2, 50, 48, 'tanh', 'linear']	0.8841
	[14, 8, 24, 2, 50, 16, 'tanh', 'linear']	0.8865
	[14, 8, 24, 2, 50, 48, 'tanh', 'linear']	0.8870
ConvLSTM	**[14, 8, (1, 2), 25, 16, 'tanh', 'linear']**	**0.9427**
	[14, 8, (1, 2), 25, 48, 'tanh', 'linear']	0.9475
	[14, 8, (1, 1), 25, 48, 'tanh', 'linear']	0.9482
	[21, 8, (1, 2), 25, 16, 'tanh', 'linear']	0.9663
	[21, 8, (1, 1), 50, 48, 'tanh', 'linear']	0.9681

CNN by a factor of 4.61. This model also matches the worst RMSE error among all the structures analyzed in this scenario.

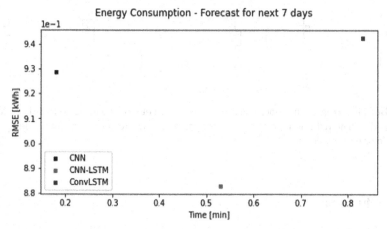

Fig. 5. Comparative error/time of the three observed models – scenario 2

4.3   General Comparison of Scenarios

According to the RMSE, it is evident that scenario 1 has surpassed scenario 2. In addition, the CNN model of scenario 1 exceeds the best model of scenario 2 (CNN-LSTM) by a factor of 13.69.

Regarding execution times, scenario 1 has higher execution times compared to scenario 2. This is mainly due to the amount of data used in training models, i.e., considering the two different resolutions and timesteps, there was a lower amount of data for scenario 2, which resulted in faster execution. However, scenario 2 presented worse learning and generalization for the predictions.

On the other hand, Figs. 6 and 7 show the distribution of errors using a box diagram of each scenario and structures analyzed. For this purpose, each structure was repeated 30 times. It is visually ratified that the CNN architecture of scenario 1 presents the best metrics, while in both scenarios, the ConvLSTM models present the worst values.

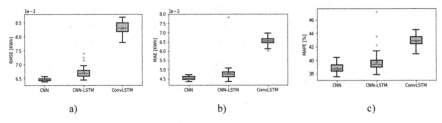

Fig. 6. Box plot errors of the experiment's models carried out in scenario 1. a) RMSE, b) MAE, and c) MAPE. The red line represents the median, while the green triangle corresponds to the mean. (Color figure online)

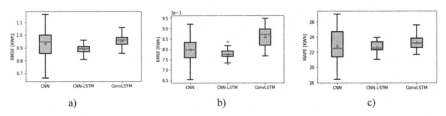

Fig. 7. Box plot errors of the experiment's models carried out in scenario 2. a) RMSE, b) MAE, and c) MAPE. The red line represents the median, while the green triangle corresponds to the mean. (Color figure online)

5   Conclusions

In this study, CNN models were applied to forecast the energy consumption of a residential apartment. Experiments using a dataset of variables such as energy consumption, relative humidity, and temperature inside the apartment were carried out.

According to the resolution of time (hours and days), two scenarios were considered: next day and next week. Almost 650 CNN, CNN-LSTM, and ConvLSTM models were configured, trained, and validated. RMSE, MAE, and MAPE were used to select the best model for each type of architecture. CNN and ConvLSTM obtained the best results in scenario 1 and scenario 2, respectively. However, the CNN model of scenario 1 obtained the best results of this work.

On the other hand, the average execution times of the models in scenario 1 and scenario 2 are 3.89 and 0.51 min per model, respectively. It is noted that data resolution affects computational times. Higher resolution (timestep) of the dataset implies less computational time to run a model in our case study.

This research provides a different approach to ANN deep learning applied to multivariate time series using CNN one-dimension (1D). These models can be taken into account as a reference for use in predictive control systems considered in buildings to foresee with great precision the energy consumption.

In further studies, it is expected that the analysis of CNN considers univariate series and a more extensive range of values with hyperparameters. In addition, make forecast comparisons with other neural network techniques such as MLP, LSTM, GRU, seq2seq, among others is expected.

References

1. GLOBALABC: Global Alliance for Buildings and Construction. 2018 Global Status Report. United Nations Environ. Int. Energy Agency, p. 325 (2018)
2. IIGE: Balance Energético Nacional 2018. Quito (2018)
3. Huang, H., Chen, L., Hu, E.: A neural network-based multi-zone modelling approach for predictive control system design in commercial buildings. Energy Build. 97, 86–97 (2015)
4. Reynolds, J., Rezgui, Y., Kwan, A., Piriou, S.: A zone-level, building energy optimisation combining an artificial neural network, a genetic algorithm, and model predictive control. Energy 151, 729–739 (2018). https://doi.org/10.1016/j.energy.2018.03.113
5. Gomez-Romero, J., et al.: A probabilistic algorithm for predictive control with full-complexity models in non-residential buildings. IEEE Access 7, 1 (2019)
6. Finck, C., Li, R., Zeiler, W.: Economic model predictive control for demand flexibility of a residential building. Energy 176, 365–379 (2019)
7. Barzola-Monteses, J., Espinoza-andaluz, M., Mite-León, M., Flores-Morán, M.: Energy consumption of a building by using long short-term memory network : a forecasting study. In: 39th International Conference of the Chilean Computer Science Society SCCC 2020, pp. 1–6 (2020)
8. Shanmuganathan, S.: Artificial neural network modelling: an introduction. Stud. Comput. Intell. 628, 1–14 (2016)
9. Savoy, J.: Machine Learning Methods for Stylometry: Authorship Attribution and Author Profiling. Springer International Publishing, Cham (2020). https://doi.org/10.1007/978-3-030-53360-1
10. Torres, J.: Deep Learning, 2nd edn. Watch this Space, Barcelona (2018)
11. Khan, S., Rahmani, H., Shah, S.A.A., Bennamoun, M.: A Guide to Convolutional Neural Networks for Computer Vision. Morgan & Claypoo, Crawley (2018)
12. Somu, N., Gauthama Raman, M.R., Ramamritham, K.: A hybrid model for building energy consumption forecasting using long short term memory networks. Appl. Energy 261, 114131 (2020). https://doi.org/10.1016/j.apenergy.2019.114131
13. Khan, Z.A., Ullah, A., Ullah, W., Rho, S., Lee, M., Baik, S.W.: Electrical energy prediction in residential buildings for short-term horizons using hybrid deep learning strategy. Appl. Sci. 10(23), 1–12 (2020)

14. Segura, G., Guamán, J., Mite-León, M., Macas-Espinosa, V., Barzola-Monteses, J.: Applied LSTM neural network time series to forecast household energy consumption. In: 19th LAC-CEI International Multi-Conference for Engineering, Education, and Technology: "Prospective and Trends in Technology and Skills for Sustainable Social Development" "Leveraging Emerging Technologies to Construct the Future", pp. 1–6 (2021)

15. Shi, X., Chen, Z., Wang, H., Yeung, D.Y., Wong, W.K., Woo, W.C.: Convolutional LSTM network: a machine learning approach for precipitation nowcasting. Adv. Neural Inf. Process. Syst. **2015**(Janua), 802–810 (2015)

16. Fraternali, P., et al.: enCOMPASS - an integrative approach to behavioural change for energy saving. In: Global Internet of Things Summit (GIoTS), pp. 1–6 (2017)

17. García, S., Ramírez-Gallego, S., Luengo, J., Benítez, J.M., Herrera, F.: Big data preprocessing: methods and prospects. Big Data Anal. **1**(1), 1–22 (2016)

18. Tomar, D., Agarwal, S.: a survey on pre-processing and post-processing techniques in data mining. Int. J. Database Theory Appl. **7**(4), 99–128 (2014)

19. Bergmeir, C., Benítez, J.M.: On the use of cross-validation for time series predictor evaluation. Inf. Sci. (Ny) **191**, 192–213 (2012)

Estimation of the State Space Models: An Application in Macroeconomic Series of Ecuador

Henry Bautista Vega[1]([✉])[iD], Saba Infante[1,2][iD], and Isidro R. Amaro[1][iD]

[1] Universidad Yachay Tech, Urcuquí, Ecuador
{henry.bautista,sinfante,iamaro}@yachaytech.edu.ec
[2] Universidad de Carabobo, Valencia, Venezuela

Abstract. This paper develops a framework for the analysis of state-space models combined with Kalman and smoothed Kalman filters for the estimation of unknown states, and parameters, determining the accuracy of the algorithms, with the purpose of analyzing some time series of the macroeconomy of Ecuador. This methodology plays an important role in the area of economics and finance and has many advantages because it allows describing how observed macroeconomic variables can be related to potentially unobserved state variables, determining the evolution in real time, estimating unobserved trends, changes of structures and make forecasts in future times. To achieve the objectives, three models are proposed: the first model is used to estimate the Ecuador's gross domestic product. The second model combines a state space model with the classic ARIMA (p, q, r) model to adjust the GDP rate and finally it is considered a model for the simultaneous stress time series analysis related to: consumer price index, industrial production index and active interest rate. In all the cases studied, the estimates obtained reflect the real behavior of the Ecuadorian economy. The square root of the mean square error was used as a measure of goodness of fit to measure the quality of estimation of the algorithms, obtaining small errors.

Keywords: Dynamic system · Kalman filter · State space model · ARIMA model · Gross domestic product

1 Introduction

In this work, a methodology based on filtering algorithms is applied to estimate states and parameters in time series models that are used to model dynamic phenomena that evolve over time. It is interesting to study the behavior of stochastic processes with partially observed dynamics measured with errors; It is particularly interesting to study financial time series of macroeconomic variables such as gross domestic product, unemployment rate, prices of shares in the stock market, volatility of interest rates in the short and medium term, commodity prices of primary products, and the neutral density of active risk among other financial series.

© Springer Nature Switzerland AG 2021
J. P. Salgado Guerrero et al. (Eds.): TICEC 2021, CCIS 1456, pp. 31–45, 2021.
https://doi.org/10.1007/978-3-030-89941-7_3

There is an extensive literature on state space models beginning with the works of [1–6] classical time series models such as those studied in [7], model of Markov hidden discrete [8–11]; stochastic volatility model used to model the time variance of logarithmic returns on assets [12]; and the point change models used to model stock prices [13]. The methodology allows estimating smoothed states with linear and non-linear structures by implementing efficient computational algorithms.

Related works to this research highlight: In [14] was implemented the algorithms: Gibbs, Kalman filter, extended Kalman filter and particles filters, they analyze series of oil gross domestic product (GDP), and not oil; and the dollar to bolivar exchange rate of the Venezuelan economy; They also conducted a simulation study, demonstrating that the algorithms estimate adequately.

In [15] describes a general procedure to make Bayesian inference based on the evaluation of the plausibility of stochastic general equilibrium models through the Markov Chain Monte Carlo methods, they implemented the Kalman filter to evaluate the likelihood function and finally apply the Metropolis Hastings algorithm to estimate the parameters of the posterior distribution. They illustrate the methodology by using the basic stochastic growth model, considering quarterly data for the Venezuelan economy from the first quarter of (1984) to the third quarter of (2004). The empirical analysis carried out allows us to conclude that the algorithms used works efficiently and at a low computational cost, the estimates obtained are consistent, and the estimates of the predictions adequately reflect the behavior of the product, employment, consumption and investment per capital of the country. In [16] propose a methodology based on the state-space structure applying filtering techniques such as the auxiliary particle filter to estimate the underlying volatility of the system.

Additionally, they used a Markov chain Monte Carlo algorithm to estimate the parameters. The methodology was illustrated using a series of returns from simulated data, and the series of returns corresponding to the Standard and Poor's 500 price index for the period 1999–2003. The results show that the proposed methodology allows to adequately explain the dynamics of volatility when there is an asymmetric response to a shock of a different sign. In [17] a methodology was applied based on state space models inspired by the Monte Carlo Markov Chain sampling schemes, which simplifies the estimation and prediction process of the Markov switching model. The general objective of this study was to simultaneously determine: non-linearity, structural changes, asymmetries and outliers that are characteristics present in many financial series. The methodology was empirically illustrated using series that measure the annual growth rate of industrial production in the MERCOSUR countries. The study concludes that there is no reduction in economic volatility, there is no reduction in the depth of economic cycles. At breakpoints, outliers and non-linearity are observed in the data. It is evident that there are no common economic cycles for the countries analyzed. In [18], two recursive filtering algorithms were implemented, the optimized particle filter, and the Viterbi algorithm, which allow the joint estimation of states and parameters of stochastic volatility models in continuous time, such as the Cox Ingersoll Ross and Heston model, using daily empirical data from the time series of the S & P500 stock index returns. Furthermore, these parameters prove that the Viterbi algorithm has less execution time than the optimized particle filter. In [19] several algorithms related to the Kalman filter are used to carry out linear and non-linear approximations. In [20] an estimation methodology based on the Monte Carlo sequential algorithm is proposed, which jointly estimates the states and parameters, the relationship between the prices of futures contracts and the spot prices of primary products, they determined the evolution of prices and volatility of the historical data of the primary market (Gold and Soybeans), using three algorithms: the sampling algorithm of sequential importance with resampling (SISR), the Storvik algorithm, and the particle learning and smoothing algorithm (PLS). The results conclude that the prices of products for future delivery at different expiration dates with the spot price are highly correlated.

The contribution of this work presents an adjustment of a state space model to estimate macroeconomic indicators of Ecuador. To achieve the objectives, three models are proposed: the first model analyzes the gross domestic product of Ecuador corresponding to the period 2000–2020. The second model is a combination of a state space model with the ARIMA (p, q, r) models which will be used to adjust the GDP rate and finally it is considered a model for the simultaneous analysis of several time series related to: consumer price index, industrial production index and active interest rate. Each of these models are estimated using the Kalman filter and Smoothed Kalman filter.

The rest of the article is as follows: in Sect. 2, the state space models and the Kalman filter are described; Sect. 3 specifies the variables, models, and parameters to be used; In Sect. 4 the results and discussion of the studies carried out are presented; Sect. 5 ends with the conclusions.

2   State Space Models

State space models (SSM) are mathematical structures customized to the study of stochastic processes, especially when data are contaminated with error. A generalized SSM is the form:

$$State\ equation: \qquad x_t = h(\mathbf{x}_{t-1}, \epsilon_t) \ \ or \ \ x_t \sim q_t(\cdot \mid \mathbf{x}_{t-1}). \qquad (1)$$

$$Observation\ equation: \qquad y_t = g(\mathbf{x}_t, e_t) \ \ or \ \ y_t \sim f_t(\cdot \mid \mathbf{x}_t) \qquad (2)$$

where y_t is the observation, x_t is the (unobservable) state variable. Let $\mathbf{y_t} = (y_1, \ldots, y_t)'$ denote the entire past sequence of the observations at time t and $\mathbf{x_t} = (x_1, \ldots, x_t)'$ denotes the entire history of the state before and at time t. Let's recall that y_t can be multi-dimensional, moreover x_t evolves through the conditional distribution $q_t(\cdot)$ and underlying states evolve with the function $h_t(\cdot)$. Conditional distribution $q_t(\cdot)$ and state innovation ϵ_t (or equivalent the function $h_t(\cdot)$) are assumed to be known.

Using statistical inference that at any time t the states $x_1, \ldots, x_t$ can be found given the observation $y_1, \ldots, y_t$, up to time t we can obtain the posteriors distribution

$$p(x_1, ..., x_t | \mathbf{y}_t) \propto p(x_1, ..., x_t, y_1, ..., y_t)$$

$$\propto \prod_{i=1}^{t} p(y_i | x_1, ..., x_i, y_1, ..., y_{i-1}) p(x_i | x_1, ... x_{i-1}, y_1, ..., y_{i-1}) \tag{3}$$

$$\propto \prod_{i=1}^{t} f_i(y_i | x_i) q_i(x_i | x_{i-1})$$

We can see that state variable, x_t, gives information to obtain y_t through $g(\cdot)$. x_{t+1} is obtained using x_t and provides information to obtain y_{t+1}.

2.1 Statistical Inference and Kalman Filter

Principal objective of statistical inference is first obtain the marginal posterior distribution $p(x_t | \mathbf{y}_t)$ and $E[\phi(x_t | \mathbf{y}_t)]$. Second, compute the marginal posterior distribution $p(x_{t+1} | y_1, ..., y_t)$ (prediction) and $E[\phi(x_{t+1} | \mathbf{y}_t)]$. Finally, found the posterior distribution $p(x_1, ..., x_{t-1} | y_1, ..., y_t)$ and estimate a value that maximize $p(x_1, ..., x_t | y_1, ..., y_t)$.

Let θ be a collection unknown parameter's associated whit to with the distributions of ϵ_t. Given all observation $\mathbf{y}_t = \{y_t, t = 1, ..., T\}$ likelihood function is

$$L(\theta) = p(\mathbf{y}_T | \theta) = \int p(y_1, ..., y_T, x_1, ..., x_T | \theta) dx_1 ... dx_T \tag{4}$$

Another formulation is

$$L(\theta) = p(\mathbf{y}_T | \theta) = \prod_{t=1}^{T} p(y_t | \mathbf{y}_{t-1}, \theta) \tag{5}$$

where

$$p(y_t | \mathbf{y}_{t-1}, \theta) = \int p(y_t | x_t, \mathbf{y}_{t-1}, \theta) p(x_t | \mathbf{y}_{t-1}, \theta) dx_t \tag{6}$$

Kalman filter needs a specific model to work and all theory developed is supported by the following model.

2.2 Linear Gaussian State Space Models

If the function are linear and the noise is Gaussian, we can rewrite (1) and (2) as

$$x_t = \mathbf{H}_t x_{t-1} + \mathbf{B}_t b_t + \mathbf{W}_t w_t$$
$$y_t = \mathbf{G}_t x_t + \mathbf{C}_t c_t + \mathbf{V}_t v_t, \tag{7}$$

where $\mathbf{H}_t$, $\mathbf{G}_t$, $\mathbf{B}_t$, $\mathbf{C}_t$, $\mathbf{W}_t$ and $\mathbf{V}_t$ are matrices, the input series (c_t and b_t) are known and $w_t \sim N(0, \mathbf{I})$ and $v_t \sim N(0, \mathbf{I})$. In literature model (7) is known as dynamic linear model see [5].

Kalman Filter. Before to continue is indispensable the use of lemma 1 and lemma 2:

Lemma 1. *If* $X \sim N(\mu_x, \Sigma_x)'$ *and* $\mathbf{Y} = c + \mathbf{G}X + \mathbf{V}v$, *where* $v \sim N(0, \mathbf{I})$ *and is independent with* X, *then the join distribution of* (X, Y) *is*

$$\binom{X}{Y} \sim N\left(\binom{\mu_X}{\mu_Y}, \begin{bmatrix} \Sigma_{xx} & \Sigma_{xy} \\ \Sigma_{yx} & \Sigma_{yy} \end{bmatrix}\right) \tag{8}$$

where

$$\begin{aligned}
\Sigma_{xx} &= \Sigma_x \\
\mu_y &= E[Y] = E[c + \mathbf{G}x + \mathbf{V}v] = c + \mathbf{G}E[X] = c + \mathbf{G}\mu_x \\
\Sigma_{xy} &= \Sigma_x \mathbf{G}', \\
\Sigma_{yx} &= \mathbf{G}\Sigma_x, \\
\Sigma_{yy} &= \mathbf{G}\Sigma_x \mathbf{G}' + \mathbf{V}\mathbf{V}'.
\end{aligned} \tag{9}$$

Lemma 2. *If*

$$\binom{X}{Y} \sim N\left(\binom{\mu_X}{\mu_Y}, \begin{bmatrix} \Sigma_{xx} & \Sigma_{xy} \\ \Sigma_{yx} & \Sigma_{yy} \end{bmatrix}\right) \tag{10}$$

and we assume that Σ_{yy}^{-1} *exist, then*

$$\begin{aligned}
E(X|Y = y) &= \mu_x - \Sigma_{xy}\Sigma_{yy}^{-1}(y - \mu_y) \\
Var(X|Y = y) &= \Sigma_{xx} - \Sigma_{xy}\Sigma_{yy}^{-1}\Sigma_{yx}
\end{aligned} \tag{11}$$

Initial step: Suppose at time $t - 1$ we have obtained μ_{t-1} and Σ_{t-1},

$$p(x_{t-1}|\mathbf{y}_{t-1}) \sim N(\mu_{t-1}, \Sigma_{t-1}) \tag{12}$$

The one-step-ahead predictive density for the states is

$$p(x_t|\mathbf{y}_{t-1}) \sim N(\mu_{t|t-1}, \Sigma_{t|t-1}) \tag{13}$$

where

$$\begin{aligned}
\mu_{t|t-1} &= E[\mathbf{H}_t x_{t-1} + \mathbf{B}_t b_t + \mathbf{W}_t w_t|\mathbf{y}_{t-1}] \\
&= \mathbf{H}_t E[x_{t-1}|\mathbf{y}_{t-1}] + \mathbf{B}_t b_t \\
&= \mathbf{H}_t \mu_{t-1}|\mathbf{y}_{t-1}] + \mathbf{B}_t b_t
\end{aligned} \tag{14}$$

$$\begin{aligned}
\Sigma_{t|t-1} &= Var[\mathbf{H}_t x_{t-1} + \mathbf{B}_t b_t + \mathbf{W}_t w_t|\mathbf{y}_{t-1}] \\
&= Var[\mathbf{H}_t x_{t-1}|\mathbf{y}_{t-1}] + \mathbf{W}_t \mathbf{W}_t \\
&= \mathbf{H}_t \Sigma_{t-1} \mathbf{H}_t' + \mathbf{W}_t \mathbf{W}_t'
\end{aligned} \tag{15}$$

joint distribution $p(x_t, y_t|y_1, \ldots, y_{t-1})$ can be obtained with the use of (14), (15), (7) and Lemma 1. Finally, using the new observation y_t and from Lemma 2, we get

$$p(x_t|y_1, \ldots, y_t) \sim N(\mu_t, \Sigma_t) \tag{16}$$

$$\mu_t = \mu_{t|t-1} + \mathbf{K}_t(y_t - \mathbf{C}_t c_t - \mathbf{G}_t \mu_{t|t-1})$$
$$\mathbf{\Sigma}_t = \mathbf{\Sigma}_{t|t-1} - \mathbf{K}_t \mathbf{G}_t \mathbf{\Sigma}_{t|t-1}, \tag{17}$$

where

$$\mathbf{K}_t = \mathbf{\Sigma}_{t|t-1}\mathbf{G}'_t[\mathbf{G}_t\mathbf{\Sigma}_{t|t-1}\mathbf{G}'_t + \mathbf{V}'_t\mathbf{V}_t]^{-1} \tag{18}$$

In the literature the matrix $\mathbf{K}_t$ is called the Kalman gain matrix [21].

Kalman Smoothing. Kalman Smoothing aims to find $p(x_1, ..., x_T | \mathbf{y}_T)$ given the entire observed sequence $\mathbf{y}_T = (y_1, ..., y_T)$ and recursively obtains $\mu_{t|T}$ and $\mathbf{\Sigma}_{t|T}$ in a forward and backward two-pass algorithm.

Algorithm 1

$$\mu_{t|t-1} = \mathbf{H}_t \mu_{t-1} + \mathbf{B}_t b_t$$
$$\mathbf{\Sigma}_{t|t-1} = \mathbf{H}_t \mathbf{\Sigma}_{t-1} \mathbf{H}'_t + \mathbf{W}_t \mathbf{W}'_t$$
$$\mu_t = \mu_{t|t-1} + \mathbf{K}_t(y_t - \mathbf{C}_t c_t - \mathbf{G}_t \mu_{t|t-1})$$
$$\mathbf{\Sigma}_t = \mathbf{\Sigma}_{t|t-1} - \mathbf{K}_t \mathbf{G}_t \mathbf{\Sigma}_{t|t-1}, \tag{19}$$

where

$$\mathbf{K}_t = \mathbf{\Sigma}_{t|t-1}\mathbf{G}'_t[\mathbf{G}_t\mathbf{\Sigma}_{t|t-1}\mathbf{G}'_t + \mathbf{V}'_t\mathbf{V}_t]^{-1} \tag{20}$$

Prediction and Missing Data. The main idea of prediction is obtain $p(\mu_{t+d}|y_1, ..., y_t)$, we can do it of recursive way

$$\begin{aligned}\mu_{t+d|t} &= E(x_{t+d}|\mathbf{y}_t) \\ &= E[E(x_{t+d}|x_{t+d-1}, \mathbf{y}_y)|\mathbf{y}_t] \\ &= \mathbf{H}_{t+d}\mu_{t+d-1|d} + \mathbf{B}_{t+d}b_{t+d}, \end{aligned} \tag{21}$$

and

$$\begin{aligned}\mathbf{\Sigma}_{t+d|t} &= Var(x_{t+d}|\mathbf{y}_t) \\ &= Var[E(x_{t+d}|x_{t+d-1}, \mathbf{y}_t)|\mathbf{y}_t] \\ &+ E[Var(x_{t+d}|x_{t+d-1}, \mathbf{y}_t)|\mathbf{y}_t] \\ &= \mathbf{H}'_{t+d}\mathbf{\Sigma}_{t+d-1}\mathbf{H}_{t+d} + \mathbf{W}'_{t+d}W_{t+d} \end{aligned} \tag{22}$$

For missing data, y_t, just do a substitution $\mu_{t|t} = \mu_{t|t-1}$ and $\mathbf{\Sigma}_{t|t} = \mathbf{\Sigma}_{t|t-1}$.

3   Analysis of Ecuadorian Macroeconomic Time Series

3.1   Data Information

In the first part of this work, a model for the gross domestic product and another model for the GDP rate are presented. The quarterly time series that involves a total of 84 observations can be obtained from https://contenido. bce.fin.ec/home1/estadisticas/bolmensual/IEMensual.jsp and correspond to the period 2000–2020. The 80% of data was used for filtering models, corresponding to the period 2000–2017. In the forecast Sect. 4.4, this 80% of the data was used as training and the rest as testing [22] corresponding to the period 2017–2020. In the second part of the work, a model for multivariate analysis is proposed in which we will include three monthly time series: consumer price index (CPI), industrial production index (IPI) and active interest rate (ACI). Due to the limited accessibility of the data, the study covers the period 2016–2019, the observations corresponding to CPI, IPI and ACI can be downloaded from https://www.ecuadorencifras.gob.ec/estadisticas/.

3.2   Model for Gross Domestic Product of Ecuador

Using the time series corresponding to GDP, the model given in (23) was fitted. To initialize the Kalman filters, prior values ($\mu_{1|0}$ and $\Sigma_{1|0}$) were taken as (24).

$$
\begin{aligned}
y_t &= \mathbf{G}_g x_t + \mathbf{V}_g v_t, & v_t &\sim N(0,1), \\
x_t &= \mathbf{F}_g x_{t-1} + \mathbf{W}_g w_t, & w_t &\sim N(0,1),
\end{aligned}
\tag{23}
$$

where

$$
\mu_{1|0} = (2,2), \qquad \mathbf{G}_g = \begin{bmatrix} 1 & 1 \\ 0 & 1 \end{bmatrix}, \qquad \mathbf{F}_g = \begin{bmatrix} 1 & 0 \end{bmatrix}
$$

$$
\Sigma_{1|0} = \begin{bmatrix} 1 & 0 \\ 0 & 1 \end{bmatrix}, \qquad \mathbf{V}_g = \begin{bmatrix} 0.05771 \end{bmatrix}, \quad \mathbf{W}_g = \begin{bmatrix} 0.02610 & 0.000 \\ 0.000 & 0.000249 \end{bmatrix}.
\tag{24}
$$

For estimation of V and W the maximum likelihood (MLE) estimation method is used, provides by [23].

3.3   Model for Gross Domestic Product of Ecuador Rate

ARIMA models need the data to be stationary but the Kalman filter is an adequate methodology since allows us to work regardless of the stationarity of the data. After carrying out the respective study of the autocorrelation function (ACF) and (PACF) partial autocorrelation, the GDP rate data show stationarity and an AR (1) model with joined intersection is proposed. To be able to work with the ARIMA models, it is necessary to perform a representation in the state space models (26).

$$
y_t - \mu = \phi(y_{t-1} - \mu) + \epsilon_t, \qquad \epsilon \sim N(0, \sigma^2).
\tag{25}
$$

In this model the observation and state equation are:

$$
\begin{aligned}
y_t &= [1,1]x_t, \\
x_t &= \begin{bmatrix} \mu \\ y_t - \mu \end{bmatrix} = \begin{bmatrix} 1 & 0 \\ 0 & \phi \end{bmatrix} \begin{bmatrix} \mu \\ y_{t-1} - \mu \end{bmatrix} + \begin{bmatrix} 0 \\ \epsilon_t \end{bmatrix}.
\end{aligned}
\tag{26}
$$

The missing parameters were estimated by MLE with the help of [23] and the results are shown below

$$\mu_{1|0} = (2,2); \quad \mathbf{G}_p = \begin{bmatrix} 1 & 0 \\ 0 & 0.5254 \end{bmatrix}, \quad \mathbf{F}_p = \begin{bmatrix} 1 & 1 \end{bmatrix},$$

$$\Sigma_{1|0} = \begin{bmatrix} 1 & 0 \\ 0 & 1 \end{bmatrix}; \quad \mathbf{V}_p = \begin{bmatrix} 0 \end{bmatrix}, \quad \mathbf{W}_p = \begin{bmatrix} 0 & 0 \\ 0 & 1.35 \times 10^{-8} \end{bmatrix}. \quad (27)$$

3.4 Multiple Variables

State space models allow us the possibility of working with several time series, together with the ARIMA(p,q,r) models there is a great variety of analyzes. In model (28) presented below, the matrix V[1,1] and V[2,2] obtained by MLE were altered in order to give the reader a demonstration on the accuracy of the filtering [24].

$$y_t = \begin{bmatrix} y_{t1} \\ y_{t2} \\ y_{t3} \end{bmatrix} = \begin{bmatrix} 1 & 0 & 0 \\ 0 & 1 & 0 \\ 0 & 0 & 1 \end{bmatrix} x_t + \begin{bmatrix} 20 & 0 & 0 \\ 0 & 0.5 & 0 \\ 0 & 0 & 2.93 \end{bmatrix} \begin{bmatrix} v_{t1} \\ v_{t2} \\ v_{t3} \end{bmatrix} \quad v_{ti} \sim N(0,1)$$

$$x_t = \begin{bmatrix} x_{t1} \\ x_{t2} \\ x_{t3} \end{bmatrix} = \begin{bmatrix} 1 & 0 & 0 \\ 0 & 1 & 0 \\ 0 & 0 & 1 \end{bmatrix} x_{t-1} + \begin{bmatrix} 8.88 & 0 & 0 \\ 0 & 7.81 & 0 \\ 0 & 0 & 3.31 \end{bmatrix} \begin{bmatrix} w_{t1} \\ w_{t2} \\ w_{t3} \end{bmatrix} \quad w_t \sim N(0,1).$$

$$(28)$$

4 Results and Discussions

Macroeconomic processes are usually described by mathematical models with linear and non-linear structures with Gaussian and non-Gaussian distributions that involve multiple parameters and partially observed dynamic processes measured with errors that must be estimated from data using classical statistics techniques such as the maximum likelihood estimator or methods of Bayesian statistics. State space models provide a general structure to study these stochastic processes. The filtering algorithms in the stage of the State space models involve the sequential calculation of the subsequent distribution of the unknown states x_t given the observations $y_1, \ldots, y_n$. For this, powerful computational algorithms such as Kalman filter and its variants are required when models are linear with Gaussian distributions, and when models are non-linear with non-Gaussian distribution, it is recommended to use particle filters and other approach techniques. In this work we focus on Gaussian linear models and are analyzed series of macroeconomics of Ecuador and the Kalman filter and Kalman smoothed are implemented to estimate and predict unknown states.

The development of technologies and calculation capacity in recent years has made it possible to have massive sets of economic data and techniques to analyze these economic indices. Finance ministries and central banks need easy-to-interpret macroeconomic information to enable them to design policies to strengthen economic growth and preserve society's quality of life. Key economic indicators on which decision making is based are usually published late, information is incomplete and economists can only gauge economic conditions at the moment, information at a future time is scarce, which makes forecasting and predicting the economy difficult to understand. There are also other interconnected factors in global economies, in which small disturbances that originate in one country spill over into other economies, resulting in low productivity levels, loss of employment and imbalance in the different economies.

This paper analyzes some economic indices in Ecuador to observe the behavior of these variables in the last decades. The variables analyzed are: GPD, GPD rate, CPI, IPI, and ACI, and to achieve this objective a dynamic Bayesian model and two learning algorithms were considered, this combination includes missing data information and allows evaluating the economic reaction to possible shocks and provides real time information and allows forecasting to market policy makers.

4.1   Gross Domestic Product of Ecuador

In Fig. 1 shows the evolution of the average mean of the Gross Domestic Product series during the period between the years $2000 - 2017$, estimated by the Kalman filter and Kalman smoothed together with true data. In the graph you can observe continuous growth over time, and a very similar adjustment between estimated states and true observations. It can also be appreciated that the algorithms mimic well the behavior of real data, these algorithms have the property of reducing noise and softening the series. The Kalman Smoothed filter captures the fluctuations of the economy and detects the peaks caused by the sudden jumps in the GDP and are characterized by being less pronounced.

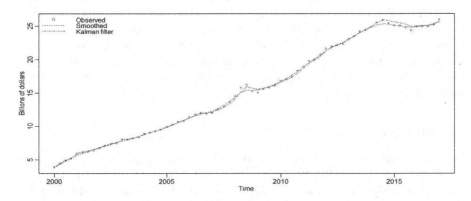

Fig. 1. Evolution of the posterior mean of the proposed model for the gross domestic product of Ecuador.

4.2 Gross Domestic Product Rate of Ecuador

Using the model proposed in (26) together with the values presented in (27), you can be show in Fig. 2 the evolution of the posterior mean of the series of the GDP rate of Ecuador during the period between the years 2000 − 2017. Time series of this style with constant mean and bounded variance as they are known in the literature [24] are usually very complex to filter. The results obtained see Table 1 shows that the ARIMA models together with the Kalman filter are a good option in time series analysis.

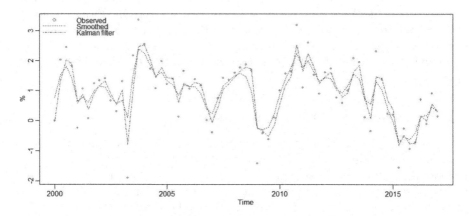

Fig. 2. Evolution of the posterior mean of the proposed model for the gross domestic product of Ecuador rate.

In the Fig. 3, we can see the residual of the proposed system to GDP and in Fig. 4 to GDP rate. Kalman filter and the Kalman smoothed show good behavior in the simulation of observations, however smoothed filter shows a greater error in the estimation of the data. The dynamics of the state space models allow us an independent adjustment of the W and V matrices. In the present work we use algorithms that allowed us to obtain the values for mentioned matrices, but the researcher could change these parameters and thus obtain a smaller or larger error in filtering the data.

4.3 Multiple Variables

The use of matrices in state space models allows us to work with several time series, in Fig. 5 the results obtained by the model (16) are presented. As mentioned previously, the values of matrix V were modified, these would allow us to control the accuracy of the filtering. It can be seen in Fig. 5 that the filtering and smoothing values fit almost perfectly to the true observations while the CPI observations show a large error, finally the ACI value was the one obtained by MLE.

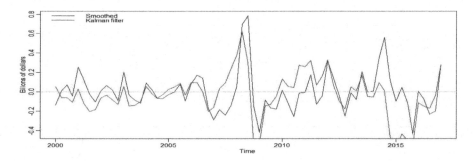

Fig. 3. Estimation errors for the Kalman filter and Kalman smoothed, models (24) and (23).

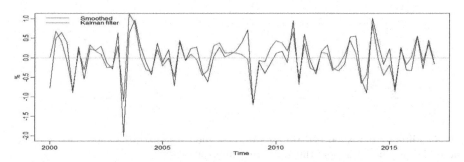

Fig. 4. Estimation errors for the Kalman filter and Kalman smoothed, models (26) and (27).

Table 1 shows a measure of goodness of fit calculated in order to measure the quality of estimation of the algorithms for all the series considered in the study, the mean square error metric was evaluated for each filter used, obtaining small estimation errors.

4.4   Forecast and New Observations

The dynamics of the state space models also allow us to make predictions, build confidence intervals and extract the new observations from (2). Using the equation proposed in (21) together with the model (23) the prediction of the posterior mean of GDP together with the new observations are presented in Fig. 6. Similarly, using the proposed adjustments for the GDP rate, the posterior mean prediction is shown in Fig. 7. The values with the MSE metric (see Table 1) suggest an acceptable prediction of the data.

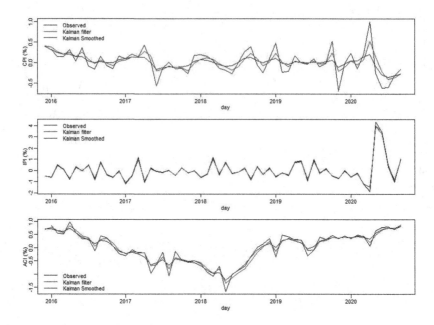

Fig. 5. Filtered and smoothed time series, first the consumer price index; second, the industrial production index; third, activate interest rate.

Table 1. Mean squared error for Kalman and smoothing filter

MSE	GDP	GDP rate	CPI	IPI	ACI	GDP forecast	GDP rate forecast
Kalman filter	0.0508	0.1803	0.0299	0.0057	0.0154	4.2840	10.2366
Kalman smoothed	0.0443	0.2861	0.0437	0.014	0.0245	–	–

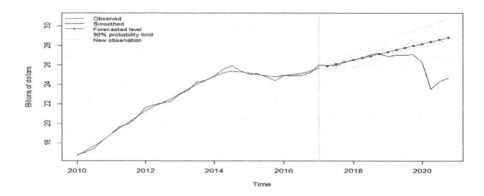

Fig. 6. Forescast, model GDP.

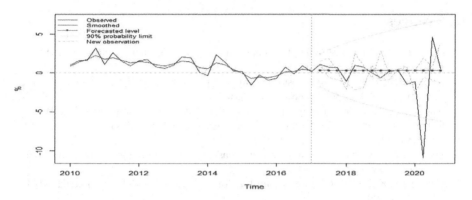

Fig. 7. Forescast, model GDP rate.

5   Conclusions

This article shows some applications of the space-state model in macroeconomics time series of Ecuador, considering filtering algorithm techniques under a Bayesian statistical approach. The objectives of the research are addressed as follows: the implementation of statistical tools in macroeconomic problems that have a lot of variability in time, non-linearity, non-stationary, structural changes, asymmetries and outliers that are characteristics present in many financial series. The estimation capacity of the algorithms to characterize and predict the nature of the stochastic phenomenon studied is compared, and the influence of external factors that may be causing fluctuations in the economic system in Ecuador is analyzed in real time. To illustrate the methodology, the macroeconomic series are analyzed: Gross domestic product, GPD rate, consumer price index (CPI), industrial production index (IPI) and active interest rate (ACI). An estimation of a linear Gaussian state space model and an ARIMA model with state space structure is performed using the Kalman and Kalman smoothed filters and forecasts are obtained outside the range of the analyzed data with the purpose of validating the model. In the results, a linear growth in the GPD variable can be observed with a fall in the last period of the series studied, which agrees with the reality of the economies in the world, the existence of an economic pattern or atypical values is not detected, nor changes of structures. The variable GPD rate shows fluctuations with a downward trend at the end of the analyzed period, the same behavior shows the series CPI, IPI, and ACI. When the simultaneous analysis of the CPI, IPI, and ACI series is carried out, fluctuations can be observed in time, with a slight rebound around the year 2020. In reference to the predicted values, it can be observed that the filters maintain a linear estimation trend. Both filters offer relatively good predictive performance. It was used as a measure of goodness of fit to calibrate the estimation quality of the algorithms, the mean square error metric, obtaining small estimation errors.

References

1. Kalman, R.: New approach to linear filtering and prediction problems. Trans. ASME-J. Basic Eng. **82**(Series D), 35–45 (2016)
2. Kalman, R., Bucy, R.: New results in linear filtering and prediction theory. J. Basic Eng. Trans. ASME Ser. D **83**, 95–108 (2016)
3. Anderson, B., Moore, J.: Optimal Filtering. Prentice Hall, New Jersy (1979)
4. Harvey, A.: Forecasting, Stuctural Time Series and the Kalman Filter, 1st edn. Cambridge University Press, UK (1989)
5. West, M., Harrison, J.: Bayesian Forecasting and Dynamic Model, 2nd edn. Springer, New York (1989)
6. Carter, C., Kohn, R.: On Gibbs sampling for state space models. Biometrika **81**(3), 541–553 (1994)
7. Box, G., Jenkins, G.: Time Series Analysis Forecasting and Control. San Francisco (1970)
8. Ball, F., Rice, J.: Stochastic models for ion channels: introduction and bibliography. Biometrika **112**, 189 (1992)
9. Hodgson, M.: A Bayesian restoration of an ion channel signal. J. Roy. Stat. Soc. Ser. B **61**, 95–114 (1999)
10. Boys, R., Henderson, D., Wilkinson, D.: Detecting homogeneous segments in DNA sequences by using hidden Markov models. J. Roy. Stat. Soc. Ser. C **49**, 269–285 (2000)
11. Juang, B., Rabiner, L.: Hidden Markov models for speech recognition. Technometrics **33**, 251–272 (1991)
12. Hull, J., White, A.: The pricing of options on assets with stochastic volatilities. J. Financ. **42**, 281–300 (1987)
13. Chen, J., Gupta, A.: Testing and locating changepoints with application to stock prices. J. Am. Stat. Assoc. **92**, 739–747 (1997)
14. Infante, S., Rojas, J., Hernández, A., Cartaya, V.: AModelos de espacio estado basados en la distribución normal inversa gaussiana: una aplicación al análisis de series de tiempo de la economía venezolana estadística. Rev. Inst. Interamericano Estadística **61**(178), 5–36 (2010)
15. Estévez, G., Infante, S., Sáez, F.: Estimation of general equilibium model in dynamic economies using Markov chain monte carlo methods. Rev. Mat. Teoría Aplicaciones **19**(1), 7–36 (2012)
16. Trosel, Y., Hernandez, A., F., Infante, S.: Estimación de modelos de volatilidad estocástica vía filtro auxiliar de partículas. Rev. Mat. Teoría Aplicaciones **26**(1), 45–81 (2019). https://doi.org/10.15517/rmta.v26i1.35518
17. Infante, S., Gomez, E., Sánchez, L., Hernández, A.: An estimation of the industrial production dynamic in the mercosur countries using the markov switching model. Rev. Electrón. Comun. Trabajos ASEPUMA Rect@ **20**, 21–42 (2019a)
18. Infante, S., Luna, C., Sánchez, L., Hernández, A.: Estimation of stochastic volatility models using optimized filtering algorithms. Aust. J. Stat. **48**, 73–96 (2019b)
19. Roth, M.: Advanced Kalman filtering approaches to Bayesian state estimation. LiU-Tryck, Sweden (2017)
20. Infante, S., Sánchez, L., Hernández, A., Marcano, J.: Sequential Monte Carlo filters with parameters learning for commodity pricing models. Stat. Optim. Inf. Comput. **9**(3), 694–716 (2021). https://doi.org/10.19139/soic-2310-5070-814
21. Ruey, S., Rong, C.: Nonlinear Time Series Analysis, 1st edn. Wiley, Hoboken (2019)

22. Petropoulos, F., Spiliotis, E.: The wisdom of the data: getting the most out of univariate time series forecasting. Forecasting **3**, 478–497 (2021). https://doi.org/10.3390/forecast3030029
23. Petris, G.: An R package for dynamic linear models. J. Stat. Softw. **2**(5), 99–110 (2010)
24. Shumway, R., Stoffer, D.: Time Series Analysis and Its Applications, 4th edn. Springer, New York (2016). https://doi.org/10.1007/978-3-319-52452-8

Financial Time Series Forecasting Applying Deep Learning Algorithms

Erik Solís[(⊠)][iD], Sherald Noboa[(⊠)][iD], and Erick Cuenca[(⊠)][iD]

Yachay Tech University, Urcuquí, Ecuador
{erik.solis,sherald.noboa,ecuenca}@yachaytech.edu.ec

Abstract. Deep learning methods can identify and analyze complex patterns and interactions within the data to optimize the trading process. This work presents a deep learning algorithm for intraday stock prices forecasting of Amazon, Inc. We focus on deep architectures such as convolutional neural networks (CNN), long short-term memory (LSTM), and densely-connected neural networks (NN). Results have shown that the combination of these architectures increases the accuracy when forecasting non-stationary time series. Furthermore, the evaluation of the proposed method has resulted in a mean absolute error (MAE) of 6.7 for one-step-ahead forecasting and 9.94 for four-step ahead forecasting.

Keywords: Forecasting · Financial time series · Deep learning · State-of-the-art

1 Introduction

A time series is an ordered sequence of values that are usually equally spaced over time [9]. Time series are encounter in stock prices, weather forecasts, or historical trends. For instance, Moore's law is empirical historical forecasting about the development of microchips [28]. This law describes the regularity in which the number of transistors on integrated circuits doubles approximately every two years. In this case, there is a single value describing each time step, so these types of series are called *univariate*. There are also multivariate time series, where the sequence is composed of multiple values at each time step. An example of multivariate time series is the register of births versus deaths in a period of time. Multivariate time series are useful for understanding the correlation between variables allowing to analyze the impact of the related data. For example, if the number of deaths passes to the number of births, it leads to a population decline [22].

Univariate temporal data could contains patterns describing different behaviors. One of these patterns is the trend, where time series have a specific direction that they are moving in. Another is seasonality, which occurs when patterns repeat at predictable intervals [19]. Also, there are time series with a completely random behavior producing what is typically called white noise. Another type is auto-correlated time series, where the value at each time step is dependent

J. P. Salgado Guerrero et al. (Eds.): TICEC 2021, CCIS 1456, pp. 46–60, 2021.
https://doi.org/10.1007/978-3-030-89941-7_4

on previous ones. Commonly, time series such as weather forecast, stock prices, or population statistics are described as a combination of trend, seasonality, auto-correlation, and noise [37].

Algorithms focused on forecasting time series are known as *sequential models* [39]. These models are designed to spot patterns within the data. Once the model spot these patterns, it is possible to make predictions. Traditional sequential models are based on the assumption that patterns that existed in the past will continue in the future. However, this assumption can not be translated to stock price prediction since the stock market behavior is influence by different external interrelated factors such as economic, industry, company, psychological, and political variables [14]. These variables interact in a very complex manner leading to the assumption that stock markets can not be predicted. Therefore, analyzing stock market movements has become an extremely challenging task for both investors and researchers. The complexity related to this task is based on the behavior of the stock market characterized by being non-stationary, i.e., unpredictable. In this sense, the efficient market hypothesis states that those asset prices reflect all available information at the moment. This hypothesis implies that it is impossible to predict the market behavior consistently since market prices should only react to new information [20]. Nevertheless, some researchers state that markets are inefficient, in part due to the psychological variables of market participants and the inability of the markets to immediately respond to newly released information [15]. Based on this hypothesis, financial variables such as stock prices are thought to be predictable. Thus, due to potential market inefficiencies, market participants have focused on the development of accurate forecasting strategies of financial variables.

To analyze the stock markets, statistical and machine learning methods have been explored. On the one hand, statistical approaches often employ Autoregressive Moving Average (ARMA) [33], Autoregressive Integrated Moving Average (ARIMA) [30] or Linear Discriminant Analysis (LDA) [1]. On the other hand, machine learning techniques used to forecast financial variables has been Artificial Neural Networks (ANNs). Conventional ANNs were mostly used in stock market prediction in the latter part of the last century [36]. The following trend of machine learning application on financial markets focused on applying Multilayer Perceptron (MLP) [31]. Nevertheless, ANNs are not the most accurate method for dealing with time series containing noise and complex dimensionality that extends for long periods [4]. However, deep architectures can overcome these problems. In this sense, sequential models such as Recurrent Neural Networks (RNNs) and specially Long Short Term Memory (LSTM) have transformed speech recognition, natural language processing, and other areas focused on the analysis of time series [18]. Other approaches focused on combining deep architectures such as LSTM for dealing with sequential data and Convolutional Neural Networks (CNNs) for identifying features within the data such as interdependencies among the companies to understand the market dynamics [29].

This paper presents the capability of deep architectures for forecasting non-stationary time series composed of stock prices. A deep learning model composed of deep architecture such as CNNs, LSTMs, and densely-connected neural networks is evaluated to forecast intraday stock prices of Amazon Inc. (AMZN). The proposed model uses as input a batch dataset composed of sequences with a period of time long enough to capture a high diversity in price movements; the sequence construction is based on a sliding window approach. The evaluation of this model consists of one-step and multi-step ahead forecasting. The obtained results suggest that deep learning techniques can optimize the development of trading strategies allowing to speed up the trading process.

This paper is organized as follows. Section 2 describes a brief literature review. The proposed methodology is presented in Sect. 3. The experiments are performed in Sect. 4, while the results are discussed in Sect. 5. Finally, Sect. 6 concludes this study and presents future work.

2   Background

Stock market prediction is generally regarded as one of the most challenging problems among time series predictions because this market is dynamic, non-linear, non-stationary, non-parametric, noisy, and chaotic [8,35]. Accurate prediction of stock price movement remains an open question due to a broad set of factors interacting in complex ways and affecting equity markets. These variables are financial (interest, exchange, or monetary growth rates), related to the company (changes in company policies, income statements), psychological (investor expectations or institutional investment options), and political (occurrence of an important event) [21]. Despite these challenges, several empirical studies have shown that financial markets are, to some extent, predictable [5,10,17].

Most of the standard methods for price prediction are based on fundamental and technical analysis. The first one is the traditional approach using company parameters, while the second is based on Dow Theory and uses price history for prediction [23]. In this sense, different approaches for stock prediction have been proposed, such as statistical or artificial neural network approaches.

2.1   Statistical Techniques

In the case of statistical approaches, techniques such as autoregressive integrated moving average (ARIMA) [2], the generalized autoregressive conditional heteroskedastic volatility (GARCH) [11] or the smooth transition autoregressive model (STAR) [27] have been applied, mostly for univariate time series analysis (the time series itself is used as input). Considering multivariate time series analysis, where multiple variables can be used as input, statistical approaches have been proposed, such as linear regression (LR) [6], support vector machines (SVMs) [26] or quadratic discriminant analysis (QDA) [24]. A drawback of methods mentioned above is that the data must meet requirements such as linearity, stationarity, and normality. In other cases the input data must be treated before been used.

Different methods including statistical approaches and data mining classification algorithms [13,32] have been compared to artificial neural networks (ANN) [3]. These studies suggest that ANN algorithms produce better performance, although it has some drawbacks, such as handling sequential data. ANN approaches cannot deal with sequential information since, in these techniques, all the units of the input vectors are independent of each other, which makes it impossible to capture the relationship between the before and after values of a sequence. In this sense, the introduction of deep architectures can overcome this problem and they have already yielded good results in tasks using sequential data such as speech recognition or machine translation. The success of deep architectures on the tasks mentioned above leads to the idea that sequential data (e.g., financial time series) can also be predicted by using deep architectures.

2.2   Deep Learning Techniques

Deep learning algorithms are capable of identifying hidden patterns and underlying dynamics in the data through a self-learning process based on supervised learning. Unlike other approaches, deep learning architectures can effectively model large, non-linear data that returns good prediction. One of the most used deep architectures for forecasting sequential data is Recurrent Neural Networks (RNN). In this sense, researchers have applied RNNs with different approaches. Certain works consider using data from a single time series as input [16] and others focused on multivariate financial time series with the inclusion of heterogeneous market information and macroeconomic variables [25]. With the introduction of Long Short-Term Memory network (LSTM), the analysis of time-dependent data become more efficient. The capability of LSTMs for holding information in extended periods of time improved the performance of stock price predictions [12,16].

RNNs are not the only type of neural network used in sequential data, recently convolutional neural networks (CNN) have take part in this field of research. CNNs are dedicated especially for images because of the feature extraction nature by using kernels [34]; however, they can also be applied to model sequential data [38]. CNNs can be implemented more efficiently than RNNs, and forecasting performance can even be improved when it comes to multivariate time series [7]. Nonetheless, state-of-the-art studies suggest hybrid models using different deep learning architectures to get each model's best features. Hybrid models utilize CNNs to extract features within the data, LSTMs to handle the long-term dependencies of time series, and deep neural networks for increasing the inferring capabilities of the model.

3   Methodology

This section describes the methodology followed in the proposed work. First, we obtain a suitable dataset of time series; after that, the dataset is split, obtaining training and test data. Then, the architecture of the model is proposed to carry out experiments and finally discuss the results.

3.1   Dataset

The data used in this work involves the intraday stock prices of Amazon (ticker: AMZN). The stock prices are collected with intervals of two and five minutes during the trading hours from the last sixty days, from January 25 to March 25 of 2021. The time series used for building the dataset consists of the intraday opening prices for two and five minutes intervals composed of 6425, and 3274 data points respectively. This data was obtained through yfinance[1], a library that collects historical market data from Yahoo! finance.

3.2   Obtaining Training and Testing Data

The data is divided into two time series, one for training and one for testing. For the data with two and five-minute intervals, 3500 and 2000 observations are selected respectively for training, and the leftover observations are used for the testing. In order to capture a high diversity in price movements, a window slice mechanism is used. A window of 60 data points corresponding to 2 h of stock prices is selected for the two-minute intervals dataset, and 108 data points related to 9 h of stock prices for the five-minute intervals dataset. This process of choosing an optimal window size focuses on overcoming the characteristic of non-stationary time series and thus increasing the model's accuracy.

3.3   Model Architecture

Figure 1 shows the architecture of a 7 layers model. A batch dataset composed of the sequences generated by a sliding window approach is presented as the input. Each batch is 1D-convolved with 60 filters, each of size 5, using a stride of 1 in the x-axis, causal padding, and ReLU activation function. The resulting feature maps are then passed through a LSTM layer where each cell is composed of 60 units and returns its output sequence. The resulting sequences serve as inputs for another LSTM layer with the same characteristics which also outputs the sequence generated by each cell.

The following layers are three regular densely-connected neural networks. The first dense layer composed of 30 units processes the outputs from the second LSTM layer. Similar operations are performed by the second layer composed of 10 units. The final dense layer is composed of 1 unit which output dimension is batch size by sequence length by dense layer units. To conclude a Lambda layer is applied to scale up the output values of the last dense layer in order to help the learning.

3.4   Training the Model

The process of training the model consists of fine-tuning parameters such as the learning rate, optimizer, loss function, and the number of epochs for training.

---

[1] https://github.com/ranaroussi/yfinance, Last access: June, 2021.

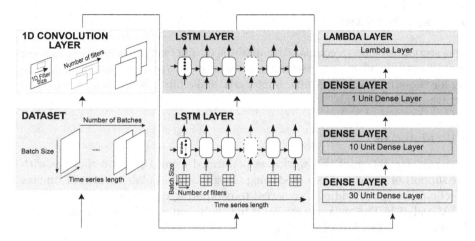

Fig. 1. Model Architecture composed of CNN, LSTMs, dense, and lambda layers.

The loss function used in this work is the Huber function, this function tends to be less sensitive to outliers. Therefore, the Huber loss function is able to perform well for intraday stocks characterized by having a high variance and noisy behavior. For this model, the optimizer used is Stochastic Gradient Descent (SGD). This gradient is an iterative method for optimizing an objective function with suitable smoothness properties. It can be regarded as a stochastic approximation of gradient descent optimization since it replaces the actual gradient by an estimation of itself.

A learning rate scheduler (LR) is used to define the optimum value for the stochastic gradient descent. This rate is used to modulate the learning rate over time of SGD. In this regard, the model is trained for a short number of epochs where the LR is modified to analyze the returning loss values. Defining a high LR will make the learning jump over minima, and a low LR will either take too long to converge or get stuck in an undesirable local minimum.

3.5 Testing the Model

The metric for measuring the error between the values predicted by the model and the observed values in this study is the mean absolute error (MAE). A characteristic of this metric is not penalizing significant errors as much as the MSE or RMSE does. The mean absolute error is a common measure of forecast error in time series analysis since the loss values tend to be proportional to the size of the error. Two types of prediction were performed over the test dataset to evaluate the performance of the model. The first evaluation consists of one-step forecasting over the whole test data with a stride of one. The second evaluation consists of four-step forecasting given an input sequence. Additionally, in order to test the performance of the model when forecasting extended periods of time, a fifteen-step ahead forecasting was performed for five-minute stock price intervals.

4 Experiments

This section provides a comparative analysis of different experiments consisting of varying the window size, learning rate selection, one-set and four-step forecasting for two-minute and five-minute intervals, and a fifteen-step ahead forecasting for five-minute intervals.

4.1 Materials

The implementation of this work was performed using Python 3 routines with the support of Keras and executed using Google Colab. Colab is a hosted Jupyter notebook service providing free access to computing resources including GPUs, RAM and disk. The resources available in Colab used for this project was a GPU Nvidia K80s, 12.69 GB of RAM, and 68.35 GB of disk.

4.2 Experimental Setup

Different window sizes were tested for both datasets (two and five minutes intervals dataset). For the two-minute dataset, window sizes of 40, 60, and 80 were tested. And for the five-minute dataset, window sizes of 46, 72, and 108. Testing different window sizes allow the selection of an optimum period of time capturing a high diversity in price movements. The result of this process is a set of sequences with a length equal to the window size. Then, the dataset is built by creating batches of 100 sequences. Figure 2 shows the experiments performed by varying the window size.

The parameters used for training the model were Huber loss function, SGD for optimizing the loss function with a momentum of 0.9, and mean absolute error for the metrics. In order to define an optimum learning rate, the model is trained for 100 epochs where at each epoch the learning rate is modified. Starting with a learning rate of $1e^{-8}$, at each epoch, the learning rate is modified as following $1e^{-8} * 10^{epoch/20}$. This process provides an approximation for selecting an optimum learning rate.

The model was trained on the two datasets by varying the number of data points used for training and testing. The used library to obtain data (see Sect. 3.1) returns sequences containing around 6000 and 6500 data points in the case of stock prices with two-minute intervals and around 3000 and 3500 data points for five-minute intervals. The number of data points returned by the library varies depending on the day and hour that the query is performed. In this sense, the number of data points for consolidating the training set were 2500, 3500, and 4500 for two-minute intervals, and in the case of four-minute intervals, the number of data points for training was 1500, 2000, and 2500.

4.3 Varying Window Sizes

Experiment varying the widow size were performed, the purpose of this experiment is to define an optimum window size in order to face the characteristic of

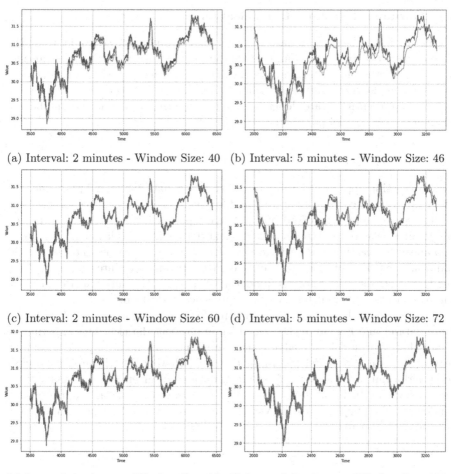

(a) Interval: 2 minutes - Window Size: 40   (b) Interval: 5 minutes - Window Size: 46

(c) Interval: 2 minutes - Window Size: 60   (d) Interval: 5 minutes - Window Size: 72

(e) Interval: 2 minutes - Window Size: 80   (f) Interval: 5 minutes - Window Size: 108

Fig. 2. One-step ahead forecasting (Orange) vs. Test Dataset (Blue). A window size of 40 provides the best results in the case of two-minute intervals and a window size of 108 for five-minute intervals. (Color figure online)

non-stationary time series. The experiments show that for timer series with two-minute intervals, the optimum window size consists of 60 data points. Figure 2a shows the one-step-ahead prediction over the test dataset with a window size of 40, this plot shows how the forecasted values tend to be below the actual values. Figure 2e shows the prediction of using a window size of 80, in this case, the forecasted values tend to be above the actual ones. Figure 2c shows how the forecasted values are quite close to the actual values. In the case of five-minute intervals, Fig. 2f shows the one-step-ahead predictions using a window size of 108 correspondings to a period of time of 9 trading hours. This window size provides the best forecastings over the test dataset.

4.4 Optimum Learning Rate Selection

In order to define the learning rate for training. A learning rate scheduler provides
an approximation of the optimum learning rate. This process consists on varying
the learning rate for 100 training epochs. The performed experiments show that
the optimum learning rate for both datasets varies between $5e^{-7}$ and $5e^{-6}$.
The optimum learning rate depends on multiple factors such as the number of
training epochs, model parameters, or dataset.

4.5 Forecasting

Two forecasting approaches were performed to evaluate the model performance.
These approaches consist of one-step and four-step ahead stock price forecasting.
In this sense, sequences of 60 and 108 data points for two-minute and five-
minute intervals are used to forecast the next data points. Additionally, a fifteen-
step ahead forecasting was performed for five-minute stock price intervals. This
additional experiment was only considered for two-minute interval forecasting
due to the characteristics of the model developed for this interval. Figures 3, 4
and 5 shows the different forecasting approaches performed.

Figure 3 shows how the model performs for one-step forecasting, Fig. 3a for
2 min dataset and Fig. 3b in the case of 5 min intervals dataset. This experiment
shows that the model trained for the 2-min intervals dataset performs more
accurately than the model for 5-min intervals. However, both models provide
good performance for forecasting the next data point given non-stationary time
series as input. In both cases, the selected number of training examples and
window sizes corresponds to the values which provide the best performance on
previous experiments.

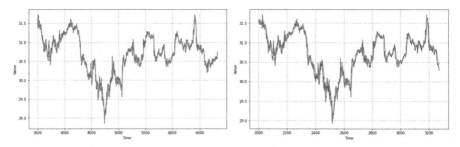

(a) One-step ahead forecasting for 2-minute
intervals dataset.

(b) One-step ahead forecasting for 5-minute
intervals dataset.

Fig. 3. One-step ahead forecasting (Blue) vs. Test Dataset (Orange). (Color figure
online)

For the two-minute intervals dataset, window sizes of 60 and 3500 training
examples. For the five-minute intervals dataset, window sizes of 108 and 2000

training examples. Figure 4 shows the model behavior for four-step ahead forecasting. The first row corresponds to the forecasted values for 2-min and 5-min intervals datasets. The second row corresponds to the input sequence followed by the four predicted values.

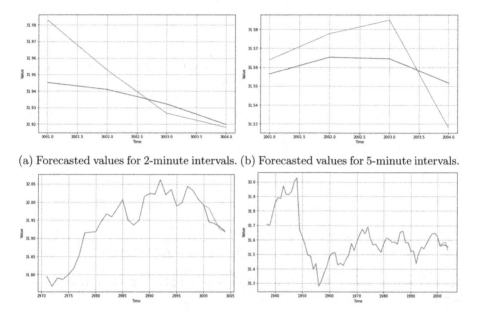

(a) Forecasted values for 2-minute intervals. (b) Forecasted values for 5-minute intervals.

(c) Input sequence followed by forecasted values for 2-minute intervals dataset. (d) Input sequence followed by forecasted values for 5-minute intervals dataset.

Fig. 4. Four-step ahead forecasting (Blue) vs. Actual values (Orange). (Color figure online)

In order to test the performance of the model for predicting longer periods of time, an additional experiment for fifteen-step ahead forecasting was performed. The results showed that the model trained for forecasting 5 min intervals time series provides much more accurate results than the model for 2-min intervals. Figure 5 only corresponds to the results provided by the model trained for forecasting 5-min intervals. In this experiment the same forecasting approach is performed for two different time series, the first corresponds to the stock prices from the last sixty days ending at March 24 and the second corresponds to the last sixty days ending at March 25, 2021. Figure 5a and 5b shows the model performance for fifteen-step ahead forecasting, this experiment shows that the model trained for 5-min intervals can forecast the trend in which the non-stationary time series behaves for at least 15 data points ahead.

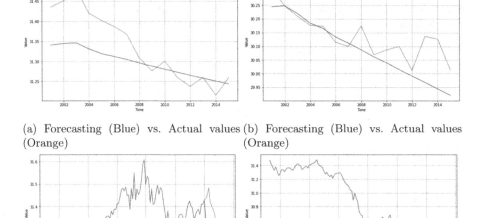

(a) Forecasting (Blue) vs. Actual values (Orange)

(b) Forecasting (Blue) vs. Actual values (Orange)

(c) Forecasting (Blue) vs. Actual values and input sequence (Orange).

(d) Forecasting (Blue) vs. Actual values and input sequence (Orange).

Fig. 5. Fifteen-step ahead forecasting for March 24 and March 25, 2021. (Color figure online)

5   Results

The results of the model for one-step, four-step, and fifteen-step ahead prediction are shown in Table 1. This table describes the most important parameters used to achieve these results and the average error rate returned by the models that performed these experiments. Table 2 shows the experimental results for varying the window size in order to face the drawbacks of treating with non-stationary time series and define an optimum period of time long enough to capture a high diversity in price movements.

The experimental results show that the proposed architecture provides the best performance for a short period of time, the best performance was achieved training the model with two-minute intervals time series, in this case, the error rate of the model is equal to 6.7. By using five minute intervals time series for training, the model provides an error rate of 9.94, which is higher than the model trained for two-minute intervals but also provides good performance for a longer period of time. Figure 3a and 3b shows the forecasted values compared to the actual values for two and five minute intervals. In the case of four-step ahead forecasting, the model trained with two-minute intervals time series also provides a better error rate, 3.49 for two-minute intervals time series and 8.07 in the case of five-minute intervals time series.

Table 1. Performance results in terms of mean absolute error (MAE) for one-step and multi-step forecasting.

Approach	Interval	Window size	Training examples	MAE
One-step ahead forecasting	2 min	60	3500	6.7
One-step ahead forecasting	5 min	108	2000	9.94
Four-step ahead forecasting	2 min	60	3500	3.49
Four-step ahead forecasting	5 min	108	2000	8.07
Fifteen-step ahead forecasting	5 min	108	2000	9.84

Table 2. Experimental results for experiments varying the window size.

Approach	Interval	Window size	MAE
One-step ahead forecasting	2 min	40	11.53
One-step ahead forecasting	2 min	60	5.7
One-step ahead forecasting	2 min	80	9.49
One-step ahead forecasting	5 min	46	11.57
One-step ahead forecasting	5 min	72	10.32
One-step ahead forecasting	5 min	108	9.11

Although the models trained for two-minute intervals time series provides better performance, the results show that models trained with five-minute intervals time series forecast more precisely the longer period of time than the two-minute intervals approach. The results show that for fifteen-step ahead forecasting, the model is able to maintain the error rate closer to 9 while the error rate for models trained with two-minute intervals time series is affected drastically. These results suggest that models trained with longer intervals time series are able to forecast the trend in which the market data behaves for at least fifteen steps ahead.

Regarding the analysis of non-stationary time series, the experimental results show that defining an optimum window size is fundamental for increasing the model accuracy. The selection of an optimum window size depends on the intervals of the time series. It was found that for two-minute intervals time series, the optimal window size is equal to 60 data points. In the case of five minute interval time series, the optimal window size is 108 data points.

The results show that deep architecture performs accurately when forecasting stock market prices. In this sense, one-step and four-step ahead forecasting can be applied to high-frequency trading strategies. Since high-frequency trading strategies focused on short-term positions, the forecasted values by the model can be used as an indicator for determining a position. An advantage of using deep learning models in high-frequency trading is the speed at which the model provides accurate forecasting, this approach enables the possibility to exploit trading opportunities that may open up for milliseconds or seconds.

Since the financial market is a highly dynamic system, the patterns and dynamics existing within the model will not always correspond to the current dynamics of the financial market. Therefore, in order to maintain the performance of the model, a limitation of this approach is that the model must be trained constantly to allow the model to learn the current behavior of the financial market. In this sense, further researches could focus on extending the variables provided to the model to identify more complex features and increase the model accuracy.

6   Conclusion

This work has presented a deep learning model that combines a CNN layer with two LSTM layers and three regular densely-connected NN layers for intraday stock price forecasting. The model uses as input a batch dataset built from non-stationary time series. Results presented in Table 1 show that the model can perform one-step and multi-step ahead forecasting with a low error rate.

The proposed model uses a sliding window approach that shows the importance of selecting shorter sequences of data points to train the model and thus helps to overcome the drawbacks when dealing with non-stationary time series. In addition, the experimental results show that choosing an optimal window size can improve the model's accuracy.

Regarding the model architecture, it can be concluded that the combination of different deep architectures improves the capability of the model for identifying interrelations within the time series to allow to forecast changes in trends of the stock market. Furthermore, the results show that deep architectures can be applied successfully to trading strategies due to the speed at which the model performs accurate forecasting of stock prices.

Although the proposed model has a satisfactory forecasting performance, it still has some improvements for future studies. For example, a multivariate dataset could identify more complex features within the data to improve the model accuracy. Moreover, since the model must be constantly trained to learn the current behavior of the stock prices, this process becomes a time-consuming problem that high-performance computing (HPC) techniques can address.

References

1. Altman, E.I., Marco, G., Varetto, F.: Corporate distress diagnosis: comparisons using linear discriminant analysis and neural networks (the Italian experience). J. Bank. Financ. **18**(3), 505–529 (1994)
2. Ariyo, A.A., Adewumi, A.O., Ayo, C.K.: Stock price prediction using the ARIMA model. In: 16th International Conference on Computer Modelling and Simulation, pp. 106–112. IEEE (2014)
3. Atsalakis, G.S., Valavanis, K.P.: Surveying stock market forecasting techniques-part II: soft computing methods. Expert Syst. Appl. **36**(3), 5932–5941 (2009)
4. Bengio, Y., Lamblin, P., Popovici, D., Larochelle, H., et al.: Greedy layer-wise training of deep networks. Adv. Neural Inf. Process. Syst. **19**, 153 (2007)

5. Bollerslev, T., Marrone, J., Xu, L., Zhou, H.: Stock return predictability and variance risk premia: statistical inference and international evidence. J. Financ. Quantit. Anal. **49**, 633–661 (2014)
6. Cakra, Y.E., Trisedya, B.D.: Stock price prediction using linear regression based on sentiment analysis. In: International Conference on Advanced Computer Science and Information Systems, pp. 147–154. IEEE (2015)
7. Chen, Y., Kang, Y., Chen, Y., Wang, Z.: Probabilistic forecasting with temporal convolutional neural network. ArXiv preprint arXiv: 1906.04397 (2020)
8. Deboeck, G.J.: Trading on the Edge: Neural, Genetic, and Fuzzy Systems for Chaotic Financial Markets, vol. 39. Wiley, Hoboken (1994)
9. Durbin, J., Koopman, S.J.: Time Series Analysis by State Space Methods. Oxford University Press, Oxford (2012)
10. Ferreira, M.A., Santa-Clara, P.: Forecasting stock market returns: the sum of the parts is more than the whole. J. Financ. Econ. **100**(3), 514–537 (2011)
11. Franses, P.H., Ghijsels, H.: Additive outliers, GARCH and forecasting volatility. Int. J. Forecast. **15**(1), 1–9 (1999)
12. Heaton, J., Polson, N.G., Witte, J.H.: Deep learning in finance. ArXiv preprint arXiv:1602.06561 (2016)
13. Huang, C.J., Yang, D.X., Chuang, Y.T.: Application of wrapper approach and composite classifier to the stock trend prediction. Expert Syst. Appl. **34**(4), 2870–2878 (2008)
14. Huang, N.E., Wu, M.L., Qu, W., Long, S.R., Shen, S.S.: Applications of Hilbert-Huang transform to non-stationary financial time series analysis. Appl. Stochast. Models Bus. Ind. **19**(3), 245–268 (2003)
15. Jensen, M.C.: Some anomalous evidence regarding market efficiency. J. Financ. Econ. **6**(2/3), 95–101 (1978)
16. Jia, H.: Investigation into the effectiveness of long short term memory networks for stock price prediction. ArXiv preprint arXiv:1603.07893 (2016)
17. Kim, J.H., Shamsuddin, A., Lim, K.P.: Stock return predictability and the adaptive markets hypothesis: evidence from century-long us data. J. Empir. Financ. **18**(5), 868–879 (2011)
18. LeCun, Y., Bengio, Y., Hinton, G.: Deep learning. Nature **521**, 436–44 (2015)
19. MacDonald, J.M.: Demand, information, and competition: why do food prices fall at seasonal demand peaks? J. Ind. Econ. **48**(1), 27–45 (2000)
20. Malkiel, B.G.: The efficient market hypothesis and its critics. J. Econ. Perspect. **17**(1), 59–82 (2003)
21. Malkiel, B.G.: A Random Walk Down Wall Street the Time-Tested Strategy for Successful Investing (2021)
22. Mizuno, R.: The male/female ratio of fetal deaths and births in Japan. Lancet **356**(9231), 738–739 (2000)
23. Murphy, J.J.: Technical Analysis of the Financial Markets: A Comprehensive Guide to Trading Methods and Applications. Penguin, New York (1999)
24. Ou, P., Wang, H.: Prediction of stock market index movement by ten data mining techniques. Mod. Appl. Sci. **3**(12), 28–42 (2009)
25. Roman, J., Jameel, A.: Backpropagation and recurrent neural networks in financial analysis of multiple stock market returns. In: International Conference on System Sciences, vol. 2, pp. 454–460. IEEE (1996)
26. Sapankevych, N.I., Sankar, R.: Time series prediction using support vector machines: a survey. IEEE Comput. Intell. Mag. **4**(2), 24–38 (2009)
27. Sarantis, N.: Nonlinearities, cyclical behaviour and predictability in stock markets: international evidence. Int. J. Forecast. **17**(3), 459–482 (2001)

28. Schaller, R.R.: Moore's law: past, present and future. IEEE Spectr. **34**(6), 52–59 (1997)
29. Selvin, S., Vinayakumar, R., Gopalakrishnan, E., Menon, V.K., Soman, K.: Stock price prediction using LSTM, RNN and CNN-sliding window model. In: International Conference on Advances in Computing, Communications and Informatics, pp. 1643–1647. IEEE (2017)
30. Siami-Namini, S., Namin, A.S.: Forecasting economics and financial time series: ARIMA vs. LSTM. ArXiv preprint arXiv:1803.06386 (2018)
31. Situngkir, H., Surya, Y.: Neural network revisited: perception on modified Poincare map of financial time-series data. Phys. A: Stat. Mech. Appl. **344**(1–2), 100–103 (2004)
32. Teixeira, L.A., De Oliveira, A.L.I.: A method for automatic stock trading combining technical analysis and nearest neighbor classification. Expert Syst. Appl. **37**(10), 6885–6890 (2010)
33. Tsay, R.S.: Analysis of Financial Time Series, vol. 543. Wiley, Hoboken (2005)
34. Valueva, M., Nagornov, N., Lyakhov, P., Valuev, G., Chervyakov, N.: Application of the residue number system to reduce hardware costs of the convolutional neural network implementation. Math. Comput. Simul. **177**, 232–243 (2020)
35. Wang, B., Huang, H., Wang, X.: A novel text mining approach to financial time series forecasting. Neurocomputing **83**, 136–145 (2012)
36. White, H.: Economic prediction using neural networks: the case of IBM daily stock returns. In: ICNN, vol. 2, pp. 451–458 (1988)
37. Wu, J., Wei, S.: Time series analysis. Hum. Sci. Technol. Press **20**, 2018 (1989)
38. Yosinski, J., Clune, J., Nguyen, A.M., Fuchs, T.J., Lipson, H.: Understanding neural networks through deep visualization. ArXiv preprint arXiv:1506.06579 (2015)
39. Zhang, Q., Luo, R., Yang, Y., Liu, Y.: Benchmarking deep sequential models on volatility predictions for financial time series. ArXiv preprint arXiv:1811.03711 (2018)

Detection of Space and Time Patterns in the ECU 911 Integrated Security System Using Data Mining Techniques

Gustavo Chacón-Encalada[1](✉), Lorena Jaramillo-Mediavilla[1] ⓘ,
Wilson Rivera-Montesdeoca[2], Luis Suárez-Zambrano[1] ⓘ,
and Iván García-Santillán[1] ⓘ

[1] Universidad Técnica del Norte, Ibarra, Ecuador
{cgchacone,ljaramillo,lesuarez,idgarcia}@utn.edu.ec
[2] Servicio Integrado de Seguridad ECU 911, Ibarra, Ecuador
wilson.rivera@ecu911.gob.ec

Abstract. The integrated security SIS ECU 911 will oversee monitoring emergency situations, video surveillance, and alarm monitoring reported through 911 services throughout the Ecuadorian territory. This research addresses space and time pattern detection at SIS ECU 911 (Imbabura-Ecuador) using mining data techniques to support decision-making processes in addition to operating costs. In 2018–2019, 47.4% of placed calls were ill-intentioned generating significant unnecessary operating costs. The study was conducted in four phases (i) caller location and call data gathering (ii) Creation of a Geo-database and hotspots (iii) Making of data clocks (iv) Prediction model applying a Geo-graphical Weighted Regression (GWR). Hotspots determined that the largest number of ill-intentioned came from Ibarra and Otavalo cities. Data clocks showed a temporary pattern in the months of July and August as they are the most critical months. The GWR model identified that the rate for this type of phone call partially corresponds to a spatial predominant pattern that originated in the rural areas of Ibarra and Pimampiro. Therefore, all ill-intentioned calls respond to certain temporary spatial patterns that help us understand this problem aiming to pose mitigating alternatives.

Keywords: Mining data · Space-time patterns · Hotspots · Data clock · GWR · ECU 911

1 Introduction

The integrated security system (SIS) ECU 911 will be in charge of monitoring emergency situations, video surveillance and alarm monitoring reported through 911 services throughout the Ecuadorian territory. The service is performed through specialized immediate response dispatching systems linked to ECU 911 including the fire and police departments and ambulance services aiming to efficiently contribute to the population's comprehensive safety of [1].

© Springer Nature Switzerland AG 2021
J. P. Salgado Guerrero et al. (Eds.): TICEC 2021, CCIS 1456, pp. 61–74, 2021.
https://doi.org/10.1007/978-3-030-89941-7_5

In 2018 the SIS ECU 911 reported at a national level 12,6 million of emergency calls from which 6 million (47.4%) were false alarms [2]. Compared to 5′300,000 emergency calls placed during the first quarter in 2019 and 2′056.000 (40%) were also considered false alarms causing a mayor economic and social issues in this province. Some of the difficulties encountered are response time spent by the dispatcher registering false information and the unnecessary use of emergency resources like ambulances, national police task force and fire department crew hindering real emergency response procedures. As far as the economic impact in 2018 caused by unnecessary false emergency calls there is an estimate of around $12 455 169 USD in contrast to the first 2019 quarter reporting a $616.800 loss [2].

Specifically at the Imbabura province in Ecuador, where this study took place, in 2017 statistics show that 439.614 calls are equivalent to 3.52% from the national total emergency calls whereas in 2018 434.576 calls represented 3.46% from the national total. Finally in 2019 402.698 amounted to 3.19%. While 196,898 emergency ill-intentioned 9-1-1 calls in this province during 2019 equate to 48,89%, in 2020 a total of 92.207 amounts to 46,94% of total calls placed [3]. With that in mind, the public entity ECU 911 has implemented a campaign called "Make proper use of 911" with the purpose of raising awareness about the use of this emergency service to lower the number of those subject to punishment by law. Current legal regulations indicate that every individual that makes improper use of 911 emergency services which results in the unnecessary activation emergency service resources will be arrested and penalized from 15 to 30-day period [4].

ECU 911 manages a great deal of information from public safety activities such as call records, user data and network communication. Each record must have call time and date, call origin and duration. Such enormous source of information could be impossible to manage manually so the use of data mining techniques comes into play to enhance this process.

Data mining is the technique used for the extraction of useful and comprehensive information capable of managing massive amounts of data whose fundamental task is determining intelligible models starting at data entered. Technically speaking, it is the process of finding a correlation or patterns between stored information in relational data bases [5] following the process in Fig. 1. Data mining used properly becomes a strategic tool. For instance, effective decision-making processes rely on the speed in which crucial information is identified and analyzed so that competitive advantage is reached. [6]. Such techniques automatically extract and analyze data characteristics from different application contexts [7–10] compared to Expert Systems [11] based on extracted knowledge from human experts resulting in a more difficult and expensive extraction process.

A relevant project for this study [12] where the issue of perturbing calls made either accidentally or voluntary to the only emergency 911 service line was addressed, focusing on calls under the "system error" category, with no caller and ill-intentioned calls known as missiles. A software application supporting SIG—Geographical Information Systems—was created to find calls real-time location, missile calls processing, in addition to report a temporary and territorial analysis identifying tendency patterns regarding calls temporal-space at the Imbabura province.

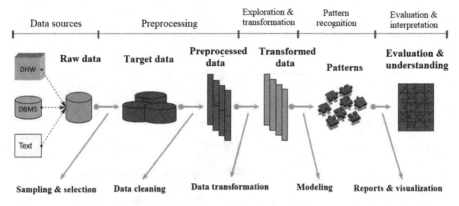

Fig. 1. Data mining process [13]

Based on previous projects the aim of this study is the application of certain data mining techniques to the SIS ECU 911 system for time-space pattern detection and to better identify the most sensitive areas in this province to mitigate the repetition of ill-intentioned calls.

This study was performed in 4 phases: (i) Data gathering (incoming call points and geographical positioning) (ii) Geo-database creation and hotspots, (iii) Data clocks development (iv) Prediction model applying Geographically Weighted Regression. (GWR) ArcGIS software version 10.2.2 was available and used throughout the process [14] at ECU 911.

The rest of the manuscript is as follows: Sect. 2 describes how the 4 phases in the studio were performed in detail. In Sect. 3 the most relevant results are revealed together with the discussion of current relative projects. Finally, Sect. 4 introduces conclusions and future projects.

2   Materials and Methods

This project was performed at the SIS ECU 911 agency in Imbabura-Ecuador in charge of the management of emergency entry calls from the province's six main cities and towns: Ibarra, Otavalo, Cotacachi, Antonio Ante, Pimampiro y Urcuquí. As previously mentioned, the ill-intentioned use of the emergency lines causes significant socio-economic issues.

Study developed and detailed in 4 phases as indicated in Fig. 2 above:

Phase One: First, data gathering required was performed. Such data is found in alphanumeric format archived in the Oracle 11g database [15] at the SIS ECU 911 data servers. Next, the way in which calls are entered in the system was identified along with data storage and the way in which call entry points are located.

In Ecuador mobile communication is possible by Global System for Mobile Communication—GSM technology, which allows for the location of mobile phones just by being turned on. Phone operators need to do signal measurements in several network

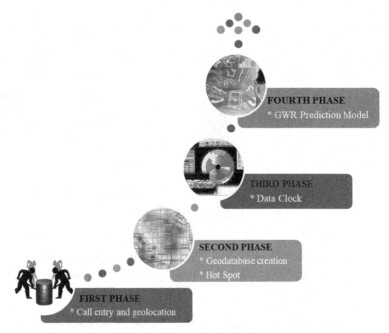

Fig. 2. Proposed project phases

reference points to locate calls. Then data is sent to a processing center and so the Mobil station position is determined. This process is known as Data Triangulation, as seen in Fig. 3. Once the mobile phone's global position is identified it is sent to SIS ECU 911 Ibarra.

Data Triangulation process for calls global positioning is summarized in three features: the closest antenna captures the call signal from the user's mobile phone, transmits positioning data to its phone service provider and in turn, the provider sends data to SIS ECU 911. The global positioning accuracy depends on factors like the number of radiobase stations or antennas in the geographical area where the mobile phone is located. The more antennas available, the more accurate will be the phone's information location [17].

Mobile phone positioning is performed by a phone's built-in Global Positioning System (GPS) whose function is activated in most smart phones. By using this method there is a higher level of accuracy regarding location information. Once the operator sends the location information to the SIS ECU 911emergency services technological platform, it can be instantly visualized on the Geographical Information System ArcGIS [14] available at the agency.

SIS ECU 911 has a server called *MobileLocator* which receives incoming call's geographical location through an application as many Mobil operators agreed to. To do this, an internal procedure that interacts with SMA web services providers. Then calls' latitudes and longitudes positioning coordinates are obtained to be stored in an alphanumeric data base in the server from the Oracle 11g database.

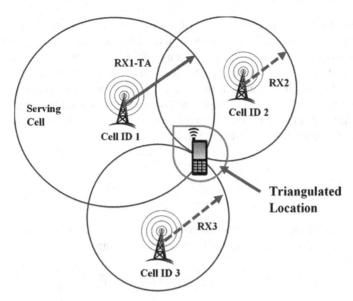

Fig. 3. Triangulation of a phone call [16]

After the information has been saved in the data base, personalized scripts (queries) are entered in the Oracle data base with the purpose of obtaining information such as calls per day, per month, as well as calls latitude and longitude Such information is extracted in a separate format by commas csv. Similarly, this information is imperative for the creation of a geo-database with the ability to store geographical information which will be the basis for the spatial and temporal analysis in this research.

Phase two: This phase dealt with the transformation of data previously obtained into spatial information resulting in the creation of a spatial-data base (geodatabase).

After that, the correlation technique was applied so that the relation between data obtained is analyzed, particularly the main connection between attributes. In this technique there is no assumption of dependent or independent variables, nor there is a previous model for data. Additionally, models are automatically created from spatial pattern recognition. For this technique, the ArcGIS Crime Analyst technique was used with the aim of creating hotspots and detect existing hotspots so a geographical pattern is determined considering high, mid-high, mean, mean-low, and low visualizing the color of each hotspot category in the map [18].

Based on KDD –Knowledge Discovery in Databases—data selection took place, in other words, filtering from January 2018 to December 2019. In this stage, data cleaning and filtering was performed aiming to have valid data for the objective of this study. With results from the script ran in the previous step, a separate file by csv commas is obtained. The scrip is owned by SIS ECU 911 and it is also run by the data base operated in this agency. In this study, the first step is to eliminate fields from calls containing incomplete information such as latitude and longitude, namely when a call was not located by the system at SIS ECU911 strictly owing to operators' technical problems. Once the final file is created in cvs format, ArcGIS tools were used for the creation of a geo-database.

HotSpot are processes used to visualize geographical data with the purpose of showing highest activity concentration [19]. Such processes imply a statistical calculation Gi* of Getis-Ord [20] and for each agency a dataset is assigned. A dataset is a collection of related agencies that share a common coordinates system used to integrate spatial or thematically types of interrelated agencies that generate a topology. Mathematically speaking, Gi* statistic is represented in Eq. 1:

$$G_i^* = \frac{\sum_{j=1}^{n} w_{i,j} x_j - \bar{x} \sum_{j=1}^{n} w_{i,j}}{S \sqrt{\frac{\left[n \sum_{j=1}^{n} w_{i,j}^2 - \left(\sum_{j=1}^{n} w_{i,j} \right)^2 \right]}{n-1}}} \tag{1}$$

χj is the attribute's value for characteristic j, $\omega_{i,j}$ is spatial weight between characteristics i and j, n is equal to the total number of characteristics.

$$\bar{x} = \frac{\sum_{j=1}^{n} x_j}{n} \quad S = \sqrt{\frac{\sum_{j=1}^{n} x_j^2}{n} - (\bar{x})^2} \tag{2}$$

Statistic Gi* is score z, are standard variations and P-values represent probability. For pattern analysis tool, when the P-value is small, it means that the likeliness for the spatial pattern is the result of random processes. As results are obtained, they show spatially where entities with high or low values are grouped thus, groups and associations are formed between entities showing high and low values. This tool works through the search of each entity within the scope of nearby entities [21].

It must be pointed out that a high-value entity is important, however it is possible that it is not a statistically significant hotspot which would require a high-valued P and to be surrounded by other high-value entities. The local sum for and entity and its neighbors are proportionally compared to the sum of all entities. Alternatively, when the local sum is quite different from the expected, the discrepancy is critical if in fact, the result originates from a random option and consequently, a z score is statistically significant. Table 1 show P values and the z critical score without correction for varied confidence levels.

Table 1. Information to measure the level of confidence between de P and z values [20]

Score z (Standard Deviations)	P value (Probability)	Confidence level
< -1,65 o > + 1,65	<0,10	90%
< -1,96 o > + 1,96	<0,05	95%
< -2,58 o > + 2,58	<0,01	99%

Statistic Gi* returned for each entity in the dataset means a z score. Scores z positive is significant statistically speaking, the higher the z score, the more intense the clustering of high values is –hotspot. While z negative scores being statistically significant the smaller the z score is, the more intense is the low clustering value –cold spot.

Phase 3: This phase allowed the creation of data clocks which show a temporal distribution able to analyze data patterns that might not be easily identifiable. A Crime Analyst for ArcGIS tool was used since it is widely used by agencies dedicated to crime pattern analysis, managing special operations and patrolling. Maps at the Geographical Information System (SIG) assist in the processing of information so it can be visualized and analyzed as well as sharing data using interactive maps. Besides, with this information, personnel may be trained about real-time location and positioning for decision-making processes. Each decision taken should start with the analysis of information generated by data clocks since they provide more accurate results compared to hotspots. Therefore, such information helps to react in time to make sensible decisions thus reducing risks and improving operations performance based on real data.

In this phase, this tool functions 24/7 so to create data clocks, they are divided into cells through concentric circles where they days of the week can be visualized and in the radial lines representing hours of the day. Each color in a cell indicates the number of events in that time. Data clocks enabled us to look in detail ill-intentioned calls from each city and town in 2018 and 2019 determining tendencies per area. In the same way, a rectangular data clock capable of registering days and months was created, so in this case the use of colors will define and highlight higher values of ill-intentioned calls made during months and days which is the objective of this study.

Phase 4: In this phase the software ArcGIS—GWR Geographically Weighted Regression Model tool was used to achieve time and space future predictions based on the relations between the number of calls and area population. In the GWR Model a dependent variable is represented by ILL-INTENTIONED calls rate while the population functions as an independent variable. This model delineates ill-intentioned calls geographical area. Additionally, it serves as a local statistic able to produce a set of local parameter estimations that show how relations vary in space linked to call origin, cell phone number, motive, and the like to have a better understanding what lies behind the motives for this pattern as local parameter-estimation [22].

Values interpretation is based on the R^2 local determination coefficient [0, 1] one being the most suitable value. In this study, credibility ranges described in Table 2 were used for the analysis of Geographically Weighted Regression.

Table 2. R^2 determination coefficient acceptability criteria for regression analysis GWR [23]

R^2 Range	Acceptability
0–0.25	Very Low
0.25–0.50	Low
0.50–0.75	High
0.75–1.00	Very high

With the aim of validating this behavior, the 20-year-old time variable was considered. Such data was accessed from population referential projections by areas from 2010 to 2030 [24] where future population size is estimated.

3   Results and Discussion

As previously mentioned, the duration of this research was from January 1st, 2018, to December 31st, 2019. The SIS ECU 911 started operating in 2014 but starting 2018 the location of ill-intentioned call process started. Table 3 shows a percentage of mobile pones incoming calls to the only emergency number –911 in the Imbabura province. Included are both complete georeferencing information valid records and those considered incomplete or non-valid because of the lack of location confirmation by operators.

Table 3. Summary of ill-intentioned calls 2018–2019 in Imbabura

Call type	Number	Percentage (%)
Recorded ill-intentioned calls	34036	100%
Non-valid records	3728	10.95%
Valid records	30308	89.05%

Once the ill-intentioned calls information has been processed in the Imbabura province, the identification of Hot Spots is crucial to focus on the concentration of these types of calls in the territory. Next, the map displays ill-intended calls hotspots obtained in the second phase in cities and towns—Fig. 4.

It is observed that in red zones there are statistically important high-value groups – hotspots—ill-intended calls. In this case the highest number of calls come from Ibarra and Otavalo cities therefore, a higher concentration calls from the medium-high and high categories is evident, while in towns like Atuntaqui, Cotacachi, Urcuquí and Pimampiro fall into the medium-low, and medium categories, so these types of calls do not have significant values.

Furthermore, as evidenced in the phase 3 temporal patters in certain periods related to information cross-over between 2018 and 2019. From Monday to Friday the hours in which the greatest number of ill-intentioned calls placed was from 1pm until 9pm, highlighting the highest concentration of calls from 2pm to 6pm as seen in Fig. 5. Additionally, between the months of July and August a critical ill-intentioned calls pattern took place, in consequence the detection of critical patterns on the following days Monday, Tuesday, Friday and Saturday was also identified during the same months.

Comparative charts 5 and 6 between 2018 and 2019 show the data circular clock displaying days and hours, while the rectangular clock displays days and months. As far as days, critical patterns are detected in days 2, 5, 6, 12, 13, and 30 in the most disconcerting months (Fig. 6).

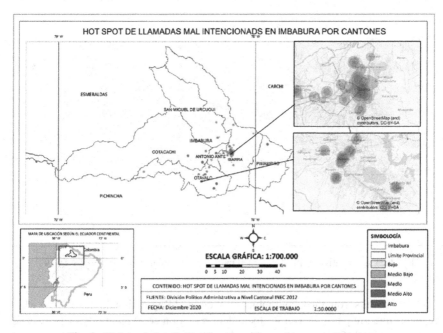

Fig. 4. Ill-intended calls Hot Spot by cities and towns in Imbabura

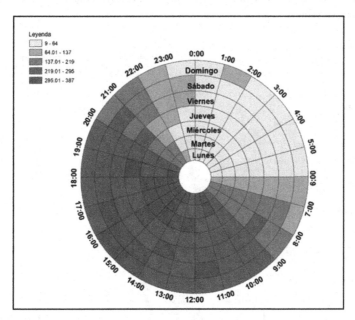

Fig. 5. Ill-intentioned calls comparative chart -circular data clock 2018–2019

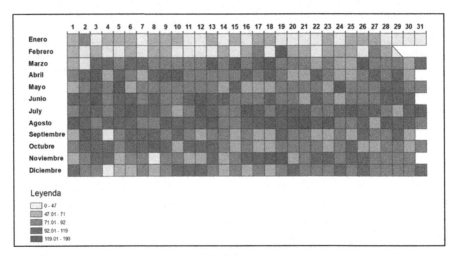

Fig. 6. Comparative of ill-intentioned calls—rectangular data clock 2018–2019

In Fig. 7 results from the Geographically Weighted Regression model (GWR) which were determined in phase 4. The R2 local determination coefficient fluctuated between 0.43248 -- 0.43404. Cities and towns like Pimampiro, Ambuquí, Ibarra, Salinas, Pablo Arenas and Lita stand out in this model. Besides, the model justified up to 43% variance of ill-intentioned calls in connection with the population in the Imbabura province. Despite minimum variability from the R2 local coefficient, spatial dependency is not as high between variables.

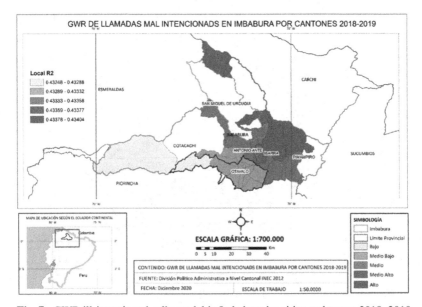

Fig. 7. GWR ill-intentioned calls model in Imbabura by cities and towns 2018–2019

In Fig. 8 the GWR model went through a change related to the independent variable –population. According to the 2030's population projection from the National Information System [24] the urban area from the towns of Pimampiro and rural areas from de Ambuquí, Salinas y Lita have 43% variance in connection with ill-intentioned calls and the population of this area which does not happened in the rural areas of González Suárez, Pablo Arenas, and Selva Alegre since the model has not geographically focused on a spatial dependency that determines a significant predictable pattern. In this respect the ill-intentioned call rate partially responds to a spatial pattern, mainly from Ibarra and Pimampiro rural areas.

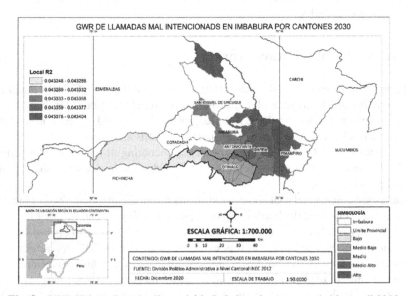

Fig. 8. GWR ill-intentioned calls model in Imbabura by towns and cities until 2030

3.1 Discussion

The contribution of this study is primarily the implementation of certain mining data techniques to explore and discover relationships between spatial and non-spatial data from a geographical data base –geodatabase. The collection of patterns/relations between stored information in relational data bases are not only an index result, a percentage, value, or number from a simple statistical process, but also a result that implies the visualization of spatial components through maps which helps in the development of analysis and interpretation in addition to providing support to the decision-taking process [25].

In [12] a conclusive spatial pattern was not found, according to weighted regression between missiles calls and socio-demographic variables unless there is a possible way to identify a high level of spatial dependency that generate plausible hypothesis for the reasons behind such calls. In our study, the Geographically Weighted Regression model—GWR partially responds to a spatial pattern, mostly in the rural areas of the Ibarra city and Pimampiro. Both projects used a similar methodology with the help of SIG, hotspots, data clocks and GWR with the aim to finding and revealing - spatial patterns and stational tendencies in the long run, trying to focus the limited resources of the SIS ECU911 on real emergencies.

Thus, the application of Data Mining at SIS ECU 911 becomes a strategic tool that enhances competitiveness and effectiveness in decision-making processes based on real data having an inevitable socio-economic impact which will have to be quantified in future projects. At the same time, the implementation of a data warehouse for the automation of results-processing with the objective of attaining considerable technical cost-reduction is desirable.

4   Conclusions and Future Work

This project addresses time and space pattern detection at the SIS ECU 911 integrated system in Imbabura, Ecuador applying certain data mining techniques for the decision-making processes. Reviewing the GWR Geographical Weighted Regression model in Fig. 7, there is 43% variance between ill-intentioned calls and population -related variables, in other words it is partially confirmed that incoming ill-intentioned calls made to ECU 911 emergency services reflects a spatial distribution pattern, since spatial dependence is low.

Data clock determined that there were ill-intentioned calls made 24/7. However, time behavior focuses on the hours between 2 pm–6 pm, Fig. 5. On the other hand, the greatest number of ill-intentioned calls were made between 2018 and 2019 during the critical months of July and August. It is evident that ill-intentioned calls respond to a time pattern. As far as territorial levels are concerned, there is a high concentration of this type of calls in the towns of González Suarez and Selva Alegre along with their points of interest. For instance, in street markets and bus stations there is an evident spatial relation shown by hotspots.

To sum up, - hotspots determine that the highest number of ill-intentioned calls come from Ibarra and Otavalo cities. In like manner, Data clocks show a time pattern between the months of July and August, while the Geographically Weighted Regression model GWR partly reflects a spatial pattern, for the most part in Ibarra and Pimampiro rural areas. The socio-economic impact of the Mining data application at SIS ECU 911 will be quantified in future projects.

References

1. ECU 911: Misión y visión del ECU 911 (2019). [En línea]. https://www.ecu911.gob.ec/mision-y-vision/
2. ECU 911: «INFORME RENDICIÓN DE CUENTAS PLANTA CENTRAL –ECU 911,» (2018) [En línea]. https://www.ecu911.gob.ec/wp-content/uploads/2019/02/Informe-Preliminar-Rendici%C3%B3n-de-Cuentas_-Planta-Central.pdf
3. ECU 911: «¿Como reportar al 9–1–1?,» (2021). [En línea] https://www.ecu911.gob.ec/como-reportar-al-9-1-1/

4. COIP: Código Orgánico Integral Penal. Quito-Ecuador (2018)
5. Witten, I.H., Frank, E., Hall, M., Pal, C.: Data Mining: Practical Machine Learning Tools and Techniques, 4th edn. Morgan Kaufmann, USA (2016)
6. Marcano Aular, Y.J., Talavera Pereira, R.: Minería de Datos como soporte a la toma de decisiones empresariales. Opción. **23**(52), 104–118 (2007)
7. Vila, D., Cisneros, S., Granda, P., Ortega, C., Posso-Yépez, M., García-Santillán, I.: Detection of desertion patterns in university students using data mining techniques: a case study. In: Botto-Tobar, M., Pizarro, G., Zúñiga-Prieto, M., D'Armas, M., Sánchez, M.Z. (eds.) CITT 2018. CCIS, vol. 895, pp. 420–429. Springer, Cham (2019). https://doi.org/10.1007/978-3-030-05532-5_31
8. Herrera-Granda, I.D., et al.: Artificial neural networks for bottled water demand forecasting: a small business case study. In: Rojas, I., Joya, G., Catala, A. (eds.) IWANN 2019. LNCS, vol. 11507, pp. 362–373. Springer, Cham (2019). https://doi.org/10.1007/978-3-030-20518-8_31
9. Roldán, P., Umaquinga, A., García, J., Herrera, I., García-Santillán, I.: A conceptual architecture for content analysis about abortion using the Twitter platform. Risti N°. E22, pp. 363–374 (2019). ISSN: 1646–9895. http://risti.xyz/issues/ristie22.pdf
10. Chacua, B., et al.: People identificarion through facial recognition using deep learning. In: IEEE Latin American Conference on Computational Intelligence (LA-CCI), Guayaquil, Ecuador, pp. 1–6 (2019). https://doi.org/10.1109/LA-CCI47412.2019.9037043
11. Sandoval, L., Tarupi, A., Basantes, A., Granda, P., García-Santillán, I.: Expert system for diagnosis of motor failures in electronic injection vehicles. In: International Conference on Information System and Computer Science (INCISCOS), Quito -Ecuador, pp. 259–266 (2019). https://doi.org/10.1109/INCISCOS49368.2019.00048
12. Rivera, W.: Geolocalización de llamadas perturbadoras al sistema de emergencias 911 en Imbabura (Ecuador). Universidad de Salzburg, Tesis de Maestría (2020)
13. de Núñez Cárdenas, F.J.: El proceso de minería de datos (2018). [En línea]. https://www.uaeh.edu.mx/scige/boletin/huejutla/n1/m2.html
14. ARCGIS: «Qué es una geodatabase» (2019). [En línea]. https://desktop.arcgis.com/es/arcmap/10.3/manage-data/geodatabases/what-is-a-geodatabase.htm
15. Oracle: «¿Quées, exactamente, big data?» (2020). [En línea]. https://www.oracle.com/es/bigdata/what-is-big-data.html
16. El Informador: «Triangulación de una llamada telefónica» 21 Junio 2020 [En línea]. https://www.elinformadorchile.cl/2020/06/21/noticias-chile-gobierno-rastreara-antenas-de-celular-para-poder-ver-la-movilidad-de-los-chilenos-en-cuarentena/
17. SIS ECU 911: «Servicio Integrado de Seguridad ECU 911: Localizador Móvil - La geolocalización» (2021). [En línea] https://www.ecu911.gob.ec/localizador-mobil/
18. Álvarez-Menéndez, J.: «Minería de Datos: Aplicaciones en el sector de las telecomunicaciones» (2008)
19. LISA Institute: «Análisis criminal de los hotspots o puntos calientes» (2020). [En línea] https://www.lisainstitute.com/blogs/blog/analisis-criminal-hot-spots-puntos-calientes-1
20. ARCGIS: «Cómo funciona el Análisis de puntos calientes» (2017). [En línea] https://desktop.arcgis.com/es/arcmap/10.3/tools/spatial-statistics-toolbox/h-how-hotspot-analysis-getis-ord-gi-spatial-stati.htm
21. Anselin, L., Rey, S.: Perspectives on Spatial Data Analysis. Springer-Verlag, Berlin, Heidelberg (2010)
22. Fotheringham, A., Brunsdon, M., Charlton, M.: Geographically Weighted Regression: The Analysis of Spatially Varying Relationships, p. 284. Wiley, USA (2002)
23. Novales, A.: «Análisis de regresión» 20 septiembre 2010. [En línea]. https://www.ucm.es/data/cont/docs/518-2013-11-13-Analisis%20de%20Regresion.pdf

24. SIN: «Sistema Nacional de Información: Proyecciónes y estudios demográficos» enero 2021. [En línea]. https://sni.gob.ec/proyecciones-y-estudios-demograficos
25. Peña Suárez, A.: Modelo para la Caracterización del Delito en la Ciudad de Bogotá Aplicando Técnicas de Minería de Datos Espaciales. Universidad Distrital Francisco José de Caldas, Bogotá (2018)

VitaApp: Augmentative and Alternative Communication System Aimed at Older Adults

Priscila Cedillo(⊠) ⓘ, Christian Collaguazo-Malla ⓘ, William Sánchez ⓘ,
Paúl Cárdenas-Delgado ⓘ, and Daniela Prado-Cabrera ⓘ

Universidad de Cuenca, Cuenca - Azuay Av. 12 de abril s/n, Cuenca, Ecuador
{priscila.cedillo,christian.collaguazo,william.sanchez,
paul.cardenasd,daniela.pradoc}@ucuenca.edu.ec

Abstract. Augmentative and Alternative Communication Systems (AACs) is an important study area for people who need alternative ways to communicate their ideas. An AAC web system based on pictograms for the elderly VitaApp is presented in this paper. The system results from the implementation of the last phase of the UIAAC method, which guides the design and implementation of AAC systems aimed at older adults. VitaApp is based on a client-server architecture, divided into three roles: a) administrator, carer: these oversee customizing the interface and have dedicated web applications; b) elderly: they use the AAC application that their caregiver personalizes for them. The graphical interface of the AAC application is evaluated through a case study that was applied to an older adult, his caregiver, and a clinical psychologist; in this, the ease of use, usefulness, and future use of the web application were evaluated. The results show that its users perceive VitaApp as an alternative communication support tool, useful, easy to use, and considered to be used in the future.

Keywords: AAC · Web application · Elderlies · Software engineering · User interfaces

1 Introduction

At present, the population of older adults has increased and differs from one country to another. For example, around 16.5% United States population was 65 years or older in 2019; in 2014, 21% of the elderly in Germany and Italy and 20.5% in Greece [1–3]. In Ecuador, according to the institute of statistics and censuses (INEC), by the end of 2020, Ecuador had a population of 1.3 million older adults; this would mean 33% more than in 2010 [4]. Due to their vulnerability situation, older adults face various problems linked to their age. Among the most common are physical, hearing, and visual impairment, appropriate to their age, and significantly affect how they communicate and interact with other people [5].

Communication is an essential element throughout human life; it allows the transmission of ideas, feelings, and needs. The primary forms of communication are spoken and written language [6]. Alternative communication modalities to spoken language

© Springer Nature Switzerland AG 2021
J. P. Salgado Guerrero et al. (Eds.): TICEC 2021, CCIS 1456, pp. 75–86, 2021.
https://doi.org/10.1007/978-3-030-89941-7_6

should be sought and geared towards older adults. Augmentative and Alternative Communication (AAC) is defined by the American Speech-Language-Hearing Association [7] as "the development of alternative technology or methods to help people to develop or regain communication skills". AAC systems use a series of techniques, technological means, voice generators, eye tracking, signs, gestures, tangible objects, computerized communication systems, voice generating devices, image communication boards, pictographic symbols [6, 7].

Generally, technological solutions are built considering users' needs in general, without considering the specific requirements of some groups, such as adults over 65 years of age [8]. In this context, interfaces focused on this type of user require considering accessibility and usability aspects based on their needs [9]. Thus, creating methods and solutions for this vulnerable population segment has become a priority [10]. The problems that affect technology design can be reduced to [11]:

– A poorly designed interface can confuse how to use the application and, consequently, make it challenging to adopt the technology.
– Tasks that are simple for a specific age group, such as adolescents, are not immediately understandable for older adults.

There are several types of AAC systems designed to support people with communication problems. These include both assisted and unassisted options. Unaided AAC systems do not need any external equipment or technology, while assisted AAC systems to require technological means to interact with the user [12].

Several AAC systems available on the market support a wide range of users with severe communication problems. Some years ago, one of the main problems to implement an AAC solution was its high cost, and this made it not available to many potential users [13], but in recent years with the advancement of mobile technology, the costs of implementing an AAC system have decreased [14]. In addition, the widespread use of mobile technologies has made more people more aware and accepting of AAC [14, 15]. This advance is reflected in many applications and new forms of interaction, such as eye-tracking aimed at people with severe motor disabilities [14, 16, 17]. However, the fact of having several applications is that many have incomplete systems or that they are oriented to specific users.

On the other hand, it is important to consider quality aspects in terms of the design of an AAC graphical interface. For this, quality models are used that measure the degree to which a software satisfies user requirements. According to Abad et al. [18], a quality model for AAC systems focused on usability is presented; this paper highlights the importance of measuring metrics based on i) the capacity for recocibility; (ii) learning capacity; (iii) operability; (iv) protection against user error; v) Aesthetics of the interface. Usability is an ergonomic approach and a set of techniques for product creation, based on a user-centred approach [19, 20].

User interfaces should be adapted to this age group, considering their limitations and providing tools to their caregivers that help them communicate efficiently and effectively with the elderly [21]. In this sense, this work presents the architecture of the web system called VitaApp that implements the graphic interface design method for alternative and augmentative communication (UIAAC) [21], and that is oriented towards creating AAC interfaces for older adults. VitaApp differs from other AAC alternatives available as it is a system created following a method that considers software development processes and development focused on older adults with communication problems; the result of the work is a system that allows an elderly adult to use an AAC system and their caregiver to configure the AAC system.

The rest of the article is organized as follows. It begins with a review of the current work and explains the method used to build the web application. Next is introduced the architecture of the VitaApp web system. In addition, the results obtained by conducting a case study in an older adult, their caregiver, and a clinical psychologist are shown. Finally, there is a discussion of the results and suggestions for future work.

2 Related Works

This section presents studies that implement and design augmentative and alternative communication systems (AAC) aimed at different age groups or people with some disability [13, 17, 22, 23]. The objective is to verify these AAC systems, their architecture, and results when implemented with the end-user. In work [13], SymbolChat is presented, an AAC instant messaging system with assisted technology, based on a grid of pictograms and aimed at people with intellectual disabilities. SymbolChat is a customizable system for the end-user and their support staff. Interaction is done through a method of touch input and voice output. This research shows that people with intellectual disabilities can improve their communication by creating customizable messaging systems.

On the other hand, in the study [17], a prototype provides alphabetic and pictographic options to allow end-user communication. This system is aimed at people with severe motor disabilities who cannot move their bodies. The means of interaction with the graphic interface is based on eye-tracking. The system was evaluated through previous training, and it was shown that an expert user requires less than two seconds to select a pictogram, allowing a 30-character phrase to be formed in less than a minute. Another example of eye-tracking as a form of interaction can be observed at work [22]. This work shows both the design and implementation of the AAC system and that it is aimed at people who have suffered a stroke, cerebral palsy (CP), amyotrophic lateral sclerosis (ALS). The system tests were carried out with healthy patients in order to analyze the performance of the system.

Finally, in [23], an AAC tool aimed at people with cognitive disabilities is presented; this system has a method of mechanical interaction through the use of a special keyboard or remotely using infrared signals that are activated with the movement of the head. Tests show that this system is easy to use and transport, with short response times.

The review of different technological implementations for augmentative and alternative communication shows various forms of interaction with their graphical interfaces and technological systems. In addition, all focus on a design focused on the target user looking for ease of use, customization by the user or its caregiver. The research shows the lack of AAC solutions oriented towards older adults in particular and who have communication problems.

3 Interface Design for Older Adults

The design of AAC interfaces for older adults is a multi-phase process. It is possible to start with the three principles of user-centered design [24]: i) The early focus on users; ii) empirical measurement using prototypes; iii) iterative design. In this sense, it is necessary to know the possible users' needs and carry out tests to know if the people's capacities coincide with the system to be developed [25]. Before any design, the objectives and needs of the user must be clear [21, 24]. At the time of design, prototypes or simulations must be available, and their results must be observed, recorded, and analyzed [24]. Any problems in the tests should be fixed or redesigned if necessary [24, 25].

Another necessary approach is universal design, a process where systems are built and designed flexible enough to be used by users regardless of their physical or intellectual limitations [25, 26]. Older adults may suffer certain physical limitations that affect their sight, hearing, mobility, or cognitive problems, which must be considered when designing a system [26].

3.1 UIAAC Method

The UIAAC method [21] proposes a series of phases to create AAC user interfaces aimed at older adults. This method integrates the principles of user-centered design, usability and accessibility criteria, and other ones. The method consists of six phases:

1. Scope phase: obtaining artifacts (user needs, problems, user definition, user profile, project structure).
2. Analysis phase: obtaining requirements, choosing the pictograms and ideal vocabulary.
3. Prototyping phase: this phase consists of the conceptual design and the prototype of the AAC interface to be used by the elderly.
4. Evaluation of the prototype phase: the prototype is evaluated and iterated until a final version is obtained.
5. Implementation phase: A functional AAC interface and the systems that support it are implemented.

4 VitaApp

VitaApp is a web system that implements the UIAAC method. The design process began with the first phase, the scoping phase, where the project's objectives, the client's needs, and the possible user profile were defined through a case study. The second phase consisted of obtaining requirements, choosing the vocabulary and pictograms to make the interface prototype for the elderly. In the third phase, a prototype was created in the Figma prototyping tool. In the fourth phase, the prototype was validated. The last phase uses traditional software engineering methods to design the architecture required for the functional implementation of VitaApp, which is detailed in subsequent subsections.

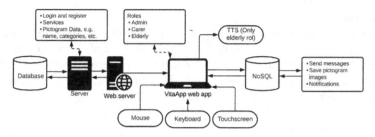

Fig. 1. VitaApp architecture

4.1 VitaApp Web System

VitaApp is made up of a client-server architecture Fig. 1 that communicates through microservices. VitaApp is divided into three user profiles (admin, carer, elderly); for each user profile, a web application was created in the Angular web development framework.

VitaApp Admin

The administrator application allows entering a classification of general pictograms (Fig. 2) divided into categories (e.g., Food), subcategories (e.g., meat, dairy, fruits), and pictograms within a subcategory (e.g., Apple, pear, grapes). This type of grouping seeks to enter the largest number of grouped pictograms, which allows the caregiver to choose and customize the interface of the elderly. However, the pictograms entered and the messages that complement them seek that the caregiver has to personalize them only if these are not adapted to the needs of the elderly.

Fig. 2. Example of hierarchical division within VitaApp

Another part is creating aids, pictograms, and messages that help give shape and meaning to the message created by an older adult; an example of this can be seen in Fig. 3. In the same way, these aids can be personalized by the caregiver if necessary, so that the adult can form messages correctly.

Fig. 3. Example of help pictograms within VitaApp

VitaApp Carer

The caregiver web application is used by prior registration. VitaApp Carer application allows registering the number of older adults under the care of a caregiver, nurse, and family member. The application allows customizing the categories, subcategories, pictograms, and aids entered by the administrator. In addition, the caregiver can create and customize the board that will be used by the elderly; it can:

– Select aids for a board.
– Select the general category to display on the board.
– Change the position of the pictograms.
– Assign a board to an older adult or several older adults.
    Finally, the caregiver can receive the messages in real-time, which the older adult forms in their application. This messaging is unidirectional; that is, the caregiver only receives the messages, and the older adult sends a message. This to make the application of the elderly as less complex as possible.

VitaApp Elderly

The application of the elderly adult is the implementation of the prototype created in phase 3 of the UIAAC method and allows an elderly adult, through a username created by their caregiver, to enter a personalized panel divided into categories Fig. 4 (area 1). When an older adult selects a category, a board will be displayed Fig. 5 in the form of a grid divided into aids (area 1), pictograms (area 2), and subcategories (area 3). The older adult can form a message by clicking on the pictograms displayed on the board (area 5). In addition, it is possible to switch between the subcategories contained in the general category (area 3). Furthermore, the older adult can erase one or all the pictograms (area 4) that make up a message if an error or a new message is to be entered. Finally, by clicking on send the message, which is sent to the caregiver application to determine what to do with the information.

    It is adapted to support mouse and keyboard input methods and a touch screen to interact with the user interface. The output of each interaction is visual and audible through TTS (Text-to-Speech) software. In addition, this application has features of a progressive web app (PWA), which works in a simulated way to a native application, but that runs within a web browser. The PWA is compatible with IOS, Android and desktop environments.

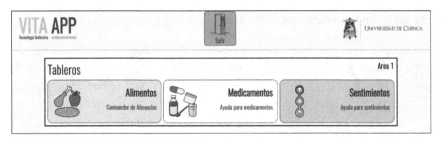

Fig. 4. Main panel of the elderly panel

The interface of this application has a usability evaluation carried out as part of phase 3 of the UIAAC method. This evaluation was carried out taking into account metrics of the quality model proposed by Abad *et al.* [18], and with the help of quality engineers; the details of the evaluation and its results are detailed in the thesis of Collaguazo & Sanchez [27].

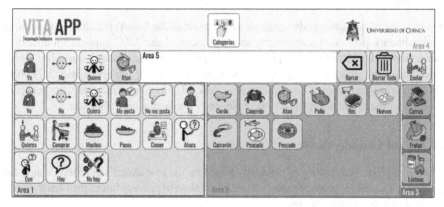

Fig. 5. AAC panel that is displayed when clicking on a category

VitaApp Server

The VitaApp server is responsible for providing the different services to be used in web applications by administrators, caregivers, and older adults. The communication between the client-server is carried out with HTTP methods through a REST API Fig. 1. The VitaApp client-server architecture was implemented using the Spring Framework. Among the primary services there are:

– User registration and authentication.
– CRUD operations (Create, Read, Update, Delete) categories, subcategories, pictograms, aids, general or personalized, created by administrators and caregivers.

The messaging and saving of images are managed by a NoSQL database that allows the creation and sending of data in real-time. In addition, this database is responsible for sending notifications to devices where a caregiver has logged in.

5 Case Study

This section shows the case study carried out on the application of the elderly that resulted from the implementation of the UIAAC method [21]. The application evaluated was VitaApp Elderly, and it is the result of the last implementation phase of the UIAAC method. The evaluation of the design of the graphical interface of the VitaApp application that is part of the third phase of the UIAAC method can be seen in its published article [21].

To carry out the case study, the activities of the methodology proposed by Runeson [28] are followed. 1) design; 2) ethical considerations; 3) preparation for data collection; 4) collection of evidence; 5) analysis of collected data and reporting; 6) threats of validity analysis.

5.1 Design

The objective of this case study is to evaluate the use of the VitaApp Elderly application with healthcare personnel, caregivers, and end-users of the AAC application aimed at older adults with communication problems. In this context, the research questions were: 1) How does the psychologist perceive the clinical utility of the application? 2) How does the caregiver perceive the application? Also, 3) How does the end-user perceive the utility of the application? Thus, the case study method is multi-holistic.

5.2 Ethical Considerations

As noted in [29], a case study is primarily based on the researcher's confidence and the case study. Therefore, some measures have been taken to prevent future problems, given the vulnerability of older adults.

In this case study, the ethical factors considered are 1) consent of both the elderly and their primary caregivers; 2) the approval of an ethics committee for this type of test; 3) confidentiality; 4) feedback. In addition, due to the global pandemic Covid-19, the necessary biosecurity protocols have been considered to safeguard the integrity of the elderly.

5.3 Preparation for Data Collection

A survey have been designed based on the technology assessment model (TAM) proposed in [30]. This model consists of evaluating the Perceived Ease Of Use (PEOU), the Perceived Usefulness (PU), and the Intention To Use (ITU) in the future [30]. The survey design focused on clinical psychologists, caregivers, and older adults. This questionnaire uses a 5-point Likert scale.

5.4 Collecting Evidence

As a first step, la PWA de la aplicacion VitaApp Elderly se instaló en una tableta Samsung S6 lite, con sistema operativo Android. Later, the clinical psychologist presented the VitaApp application to the elderly caregiver and taught him how to access and navigate it. Finally, the caregiver presents the application to the elderly to interact with it by forming messages.

5.5 Data Analysis and Results Reporting

By analyzing the data obtained, it can provide answers to the questions posed in the case study. In the open questions, caregivers and older adults conclude that the application is a useful tool to support communication. A future proposal proposed by caregivers is creating a mobile application; in this case, the app has a progressive web app PWA that simulates this requirement, but in the future, it is not ruled out to implement a native solution for mobile devices. In the same way as the case study of the UIAAC method [18] that evaluates the design of the interface of this application, the expert concludes that other ways should be sought to interact with the interface apart from the traditional methods of mouse and keyboard or touch screen. In Fig. 6 it can see the results of PEOU, PU and ITU. As a result, both the caregiver, the elderly, and the clinical psychologist indicate that the interface is easy to use and valuable as a CAA support tool. Finally, they conclude that the tool can be considered in the future for use as a form of communication or support.

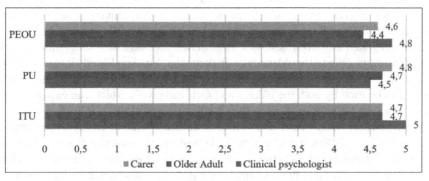

Fig. 6. Results of the case study: user perceptions.

5.6 Threats of Validity

Threats to validity are discussed to reveal possible interferences with this study.

Construct Validity
Construct validity refers to the relationship between the theory behind the case study and the empirical reality; it analyzes whether the operational measures studied represent what was planned to be investigated and what was investigated. For this, validated questionnaires were used, which have an ideal Cronbach's alpha. Finally, the constructs of the interview questions were interpreted in the same way by the researcher and the interviewees.

Internal and External Validity
Depending on how the group subjects are selected, the results may vary. In this study, age, degree of pathology, and previous experience on the part of the elderly may influence the ease of use when using the application.

For external validity, selecting the sample of individuals was carried out at convenience; given the COVID-19 pandemic, it is impossible for the elderly population with disabilities to access.

Reliability

The chain for data collection was carried out respecting their fidelity, from the interviews to the analysis. In addition, the qualitative responses were quantified using a Likert scale to avoid bias in interpretation.

6   Conclusions and Future Work

This document presents the Web VitaApp system, a set of applications divided into roles (admin, carer, elderly); This system helps older adults with communication problems to solve these problems, allowing them to increase their communication skills. The VitaApp creation integrated traditional software engineering methods, web programming, and aspects of design-oriented to older adults. In particular, VitaApp Elderly integrates ways of creating AAC graphical interfaces following the UIAAC method. The application is intended to be used by both the elderly and their caregivers, which can customize the interface in a way that helps increase their communication skills.

The application architecture allows it to be updated, given its ability to be scalable. Thanks to this, more content can be integrated into the application (for example, new categories, pictograms, or aids) and future functionalities such as i) new forms of interaction (for example, eye tracking, brain-computer interface); ii) machine learning techniques for text prediction; iii) evaluate other aspects related to the ergonomics and ergonomic convergence of the graphical interface of the VitaApp Elderly application, which differ from the usability of the interface; Finally, this allowed new studies to be carried out with other types of users so that the platform can be launched and used by any user with internet access.

Acknowledgements. This work is part of the research projects: "Design of architectures and interaction models for assisted living environments aimed at older adults. Case study: playful and social environments" and "Fog Computing applied to monitor devices used in assisted living environments; study case: a platform for the elderly", winners of the call for research projects DIUC XVIII and DIUC XVII. Therefore, the authors thank to the *Dirección de Investigación de la Universidad de Cuenca* (DIUC) of *Universidad de Cuenca* for its support.

References

1. Statista Research Department: U.S. - seniors as a percentage of the population 2050. In: Statistics Research Department (2021). https://www.statista.com/statistics/457822/share-of-old-age-population-in-the-total-us-population/. Accessed 3 Jun 2021
2. Cedillo, P., Beltran, P., Rodríguez, P.: Evaluación de la accesibilidad de MOOC orientados a la tercera edad. Undefined (2017)
3. Office Statistics: Eurostat Statistics Explained (2015). 2443-8219

4. Machado, J.: Ecuador tendrá 1,3 millones de adultos mayores a finales de 2020. Primicias (2019)
5. Wolrd Health Organitation: World Report on Disability (2011)
6. Carvalho, D.N., et al.: Augmentative and alternative communication with adults and elderly in the hospital environment: an integrative literature review. Rev CEFAC **22**, 1–11 (2020). https://doi.org/10.1590/1982-0216/202022516019
7. Hustad, K.C.: Augmentative and alternative communication. In: Weissbrod, P.A., Francis, D.O. (eds.) Neurologic and Neurodegenerative Diseases of the Larynx, pp. 407–413. Springer, Cham (2020). https://doi.org/10.1007/978-3-030-28852-5_34
8. Gregor, P., Newell, A.F., Zajicek, M.: Designing for dynamic diversity. In: Association for Computing Machinery (ACM), p. 151 (2002)
9. Dodd, C., Athauda, R., Adam, M.T.P.: Designing user interfaces for the elderly: a systematic literature review. In: Proceedings of 28th Australas Conference on Information Systems ACIS 2017 (2017)
10. Arnott, J.L., Alm, N.: Towards the improvement of augmentative and alternative communication through the modelling of conversation. Comput Speech Lang **27**, 1194–1211 (2013). https://doi.org/10.1016/j.csl.2012.10.008
11. Williams, D.M.: Designing Educational and Intelligent Human-Computer Interfaces for Older Adults (2009)
12. Beukelman, D., Light, J.: Augmentative & Alternative Communication: Supporting Children and Adults with Complex Communication Needs, 5th edn. Brookes Publishing, Baltimore (2020)
13. Keskinen, T., Heimonen, T., Turunen, M., Rajaniemi, J.P., Kauppinen, S.: SymbolChat: picture-based communication platform for users with intellectual disabilities. In: Miesenberger, K., Karshmer, A., Penaz, P., Zagler, W. (eds) Computers Helping People with Special Needs. ICCHP 2012. Lecture Notes in Computer Science, vol. 7383, pp. 279–286. Springer, Berlin, Heidelberg (2012). https://doi.org/10.1007/978-3-642-31534-3_43
14. Bircanin, F., et al.: Challenges and Opportunities in Using Augmentative and Alternative Communication (AAC) Technologies. In: Proceedings of the 31st Australian Conference on Human-Computer-Interaction. ACM, New York, NY, USA, pp 184–196 (2019)
15. Light, J., McNaughton, D.: Putting people first: Re-thinking the role of technology in augmentative and alternative communication intervention. AAC Augment. Altern. Commun. **29**, 299–309 (2013). https://doi.org/10.3109/07434618.2013.848935
16. Wołk, K.: Emergency, pictogram-based augmented reality medical communicator prototype using precise eye-tracking technology. Cyberpsychol. Behav. Soc. Netw. **22**, 151–157 (2019). https://doi.org/10.1089/cyber.2018.0035
17. Arias, E., López, G., Quesada, L., Guerrero, L.: Alternative and augmentative communication for people with disabilities and language problems: an eye gaze tracking approach. In: Di Bucchianico, G., Kercher, P. (eds.) Advances in Design for Inclusion, pp. 451–461. Springer International Publishing, Cham (2016). https://doi.org/10.1007/978-3-319-41962-6_40
18. Abad, F., Collaguazo, C., Sánchez, W.: Usability Model of Augmentative and Alternative Communication Systems and Pictographic Systems in People with Disabilities (2021)
19. Nunes, I.: Ergonomics and usability – key factors in knowledge society. Enterp. Work Innov. Stud. **2**, 88–94 (2006)
20. Dudczyk, J., Zielinska, M.: Ergonomic convergence of a modular integrator in aspect of soldier's situational awareness on the battlefield. J. Ergon. **06**, 1–6 (2016). https://doi.org/10.4172/2165-7556.1000155
21. Sanchez, W., Collaguazo, C., Prado, D., Cedillo, P.: UIAAC: a method for designing of graphical user interface for augmentative and alternative communication. In: Proceedings of the 7th International Conference on Information and Communication Technologies for Ageing Well and e-Health. SCITEPRESS - Science and Technology Publications, pp 256–264 (2021)

22. Pal, S., Mangal, N.K., Khosla, A.: Development of assistive application for patients with communication disability. In: 2017 International Conference on Innovations in Green Energy and Healthcare Technologies (IGEHT), pp. 1–4. IEEE, Coimbatore, India (2017)
23. Liegel, L.A., Nogueira, G.N., Nohama, P.: Portable system for alternative communication. In: 2019 Global Medical Engineering Physics Exchanges/ Pan American Health Care Exchanges (GMEPE/PAHCE), pp. 1–4. IEEE, Buenos Aires, Argentina (2019)
24. Gould, J.D., Lewis, C.: Designing for usability---key principles and what designers think. In: Proceedings of the SIGCHI Conference on Human Factors in Computing Systems - CHI 1983, pp 50–53. ACM Press, New York, New York, USA (1983)
25. Czaja, S.J., Boot, W.R., Charness, N., Rogers, W.A.: Designing for Older Adults, 3rd edn. CRC Press, Boca Raton (2019)
26. Nes, M., Ribu, K., Tollefsen, M.: Universal Design in Computer Science Education and Systems Development (2007)
27. Collaguazo, C., Sanchez, W.: Método para el diseño de interfaces de usuario orientadas al adulto mayor, que incluyen modalidades de comunicación aumentativa y alternativa simbólica soportadas por medios tecnológicos. Universidad de Cuenca (2021)
28. Runeson, P., Höst, M., Rainer, A., Regnell, B.: Case Study Research in Software Engineering. John Wiley & Sons Inc, Hoboken (2012)
29. Andrews, A.A., Pradhan, A.S.: Ethical issues in empirical software engineering: the limits of policy. Empir. Softw. Eng. **6**, 105–110 (2001). https://doi.org/10.1023/A:1011442319273
30. Davis, F.D.: A technology acceptance model for empirically testing new end-user information systems : theory and results (1985)

A Methodological Framework for Creating Large-Scale Corpus for Natural Language Processing Models

David Santos[1,4]([✉]) [iD], Andrés Auquilla[2,4] [iD], Lorena Siguenza-Guzman[2,3,4] [iD], and Mario Peña[3,4] [iD]

[1] Faculty of Engineering, University of Cuenca, 010107 Cuenca, Ecuador
david.santos@ucuenca.edu.ec
[2] Department of Computer Sciences, Faculty of Engineering, University of Cuenca, 010107 Cuenca, Ecuador
{andres.auquilla,lorena.siguenza}@ucuenca.edu.ec
[3] Research Centre Accountancy, Faculty of Economics and Business, KU Leuven, Leuven, Belgium
mario.penao@ucuenca.edu.ec
[4] Research Department (DIUC), University of Cuenca, 010107 Cuenca, Ecuador

Abstract. Currently, there is a boom in introducing Machine Learning models to various aspects of everyday life. A relevant field consists of Natural Language Processing (NLP) that seeks to model human language. A key and basic component for these models to learn properly consists of the data. This article proposes a methodological framework for constructing a large-scale corpus to feed NLP models. The development of this framework emerges from the problem of finding inputs in languages other than English to feed NLP models. With an approach focused on producing a high-quality resource, the construction phases were designed along with the considerations that must be taken. The stages implemented consist of the corpus characterization to be obtained, collecting documents, cleaning, translation, storage, and evaluation. The proposed approach implemented automatic translators to take advantage of the vast amount of English literature and implemented through non-cost libraries. Finally, a case study was developed, resulting in a corpus in Spanish with more than 170,000 documents within a specific domain, i.e., opinions on textile products. Through the evaluations carried out, it is established that the proposed framework can build a large-scale and high-quality corpus.

Keywords: Corpus construction · Corpus in Spanish · Large-scale corpus · Methodological framework · Supplies for NLP

1 Introduction

In 2020, the BBC media published: "Microsoft replaces journalists with robots" [1]. It details how Artificial Intelligence (AI) will take care of the article curation

© Springer Nature Switzerland AG 2021
J. P. Salgado Guerrero et al. (Eds.): TICEC 2021, CCIS 1456, pp. 87–100, 2021.
https://doi.org/10.1007/978-3-030-89941-7_7

work within the Microsoft News portal carried out by around 50 journalists. These types of tasks are within the field of Natural Language Processing (NLP), a discipline that faces one of the oldest and most difficult problems in AI [2], i.e., human language modeling.

Research carried out within NLP has achieved promising results in recent years. For instance, generation of complete descriptive articles [3], sentences within defined categories [4], sets of sentences resulting from interpolating between two sentences [5]; and even sentences for controlling feelings, tone, time, voice and humor [7]. Despite using different approaches and architectures, these investigations have two factors in common: 1) they use Deep Learning (DL) techniques, which is a subfield of AI where complex tasks can be addressed through neural networks organized in multiple layers [8], and 2) these algorithms are trained with a vast amount of documents in English. These factors are closely connected: DL algorithms require huge amounts of data [9], typically through text corpus; these are defined as large bodies of linguistic evidence composed of the use of attested language [10] that are mainly written in English [11]. The predominance of supplies in English results in an impediment to reproduce the results of cutting-edge research in other languages. [12] mention that the existence of large-scale corpus in other languages is extremely rare and, if they exist, contains deficiencies in terms of open access or data quality.

This work presents a framework to build a large-scale corpus to reduce the complexity of the adaptation of techniques making use of English corpus through three elements, 1) the retrieval of documents in social networks, 2) the adaptation of public corpora in the target language, and 3) the adaptation of public corpora with documents in English to be used in the target language through automatic translators. The rest of the paper is organized as follows. Section 2 reviews related works. Section 3 presents the new proposed methodological framework. Section 4 shows the application of the framework and the results obtained in a case study. Finally, Sect. 5 concludes the paper.

2   Related Works

For the English language, researchers have focused their efforts on creating supplies that feed DL models. In [6] created a large-scale balanced corpus in English called Stanford Natural Language Inference (SNLI). It has 570 thousand pairs of sentences written and labeled by people, around 2500 workers hired through Amazon Mechanical Turk (AMT). The authors in [13] identified limitations in the SNLI corpus. For instance, the lack of diversity in topics, styles, and degrees of formality. Therefore, they created a corpus that integrates these aspects to be used as benchmarks for Machine Learning (ML) models. The result, called the Multi-Genre NLI Corpus (MultiNLI), contains 433 thousand documents based on sentences. In [14] the researchers sought to generate automatic justifications for an opinion given as input. To do this, they built a corpus of more than 1 million documents by combining a subset of the Yelp dataset with the Amazon Clothing dataset.

Additionally, several investigations have been conducted to bridge the gap between supplies in English and other languages. In [15] recognized a lack in the development of supplies for languages other than English. They proposed a methodology to build a corpus from the translation of texts using automatic systems, such as Bing Translator, Google Translate, and Moses. In this manner, they generated three different corpora in German, Spanish, and French from a corpus in English with 12 thousand documents. To evaluate the results, they manually analyzed a set of translated documents, concluding that the translation systems at that time had a reasonable level of maturity to be used in specific languages. The work developed in [12] created a large-scale multilingual corpus from data provided by the private company Amazon. The researchers collected documents (with a publication between 2015 and 2019) and, through language detection algorithms, generated subsets for six languages, including Spanish, each containing 210 thousand documents.

3   Methodology

This section details the design of the framework, as well as the criteria for its implementation. The general scheme of the model developed for the construction and evaluation of an objective corpus is depicted in Fig. 1.

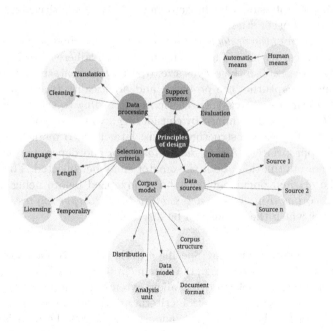

Fig. 1. Framework representation for building large-scale corpus.

3.1   Characterization of the Target Corpus

The main characteristics of the constructed corpus are presented below; thus, NLP models can generate comments on a specific domain.

Definition of the Corpus Domain. A domain was determined in which the contents of the documents were related, for example, politics, health, or industry. A corpus can be of a public domain, which includes documents related to different topics. However, according to [16], within the field of AI, the best language models are highly restricted to a specific domain.

Principles of Design. A good domain-specific corpus consists of much more than a series of randomly collected documents. It requires the documents to be related in some manner that they can be considered part of the same distribution. From this distribution, a model learns patterns that it can replicate in new contexts. Additionally, the corpus guide's objective includes data privacy and whether this input will be open to the general public or private. The proposed principles that constitute a transversal axis within the framework are the characteristics of the original documents, the number of documents, the diversity, the data anonymity, and the accessibility to the corpus. The *characteristics of the documents* to be collected should be detailed, for example, having been written by people with a professional language domain, having a positive sentiment, or being validated by other studies.

Regarding the *number of documents*, there is some ambiguity when referring to the size that a corpus should have. This framework adheres to [17], who point out two factors to establish the corpus size, that is, representativeness (the number of documents capturing the problem) and practicality (the collection time is under the research resources). Furthermore, according to the research objectives, *diversity* must be determined by considering a wide range of semantics and variations in their syntactic structures. Thus, later trained models will be able to generalize appropriately. About *data anonymity* and depending on the data source, personal information about the creators may be collected. This information from the original document must be anonymized before being integrated into the final corpus. Finally, the *accessibility to the corpus* expresses the type of license under which the corpus will be distributed.

Document Selection Criteria. Specific criteria are established to collect the texts from delimiting the scope, e.g., the infrequent texts are eliminated, and documents with licenses are selected that allow extending functionalities in future research. Thus, the document selection criteria are the idiom, license, temporality, and text length. The *language* or languages in which the data is collected must be specified. The *license* types to be taken into account in the data for the target corpus need to be identified. Authors in [18] mention that the use of language changes over time. In the experimental design phase, a uniform distribution must be preserved, in terms of *temporality*, due to the frequency of word usage. Therefore, a time interval must be defined to collect documents. Lastly, a document must exceed a minimum number of words to be considered suitable for inclusion in the corpus. If necessary, a maximum *length* is also set. Documents that exceed this value will be truncated.

Corpus Model. The structural design of the input and the format that the documents must have been defined as the unit of analysis, data model, document format, corpus structure, and means of distribution of the corpus. The *unit of analysis* is considered a document within the corpus. It can be a word, a sentence, a set of sentences, a paragraph, a group of paragraphs, or even a set of documents. The *data model* details the attributes and data types linked to the document text, such as a date, language, original annotations, and source. A differentiation must be made between required and non-mandatory attributes. Various types of *formats* are used to store documents and facilitate their later retrieval. These formats make up a particular abstract model [19], and in some cases, they are combined to take advantage of their strengths [20]. The formats to consider for the documents are the following: Comma Separated Values (CSV), Tab Separated Values (TSV), JavaScript Object Notation (JSON), JSON Lines, Extensible Markup Language (XML). The *corpus structure* consists of the convention for structuring the corpus to be built within the file system. And, there are two main trends to distribute a corpus: 1) through a private website and 2) through public repositories. In the former, the corpus is available under the domain and hosting of the party that provides it. In the latter, the corpus is hosted on third-party services. The *means of distribution* must be established for the final corpus.

Selection of Document Sources and Data Model Integration Design. Every year the number of corpus available to researchers increases. In [17] recommend that before building a corpus, researchers must carry out an exhaustive search and verify that a similar corpus does not already exist, in order to take advantage of existing inputs for its construction. Under this premise, a hybrid approach to construction is proposed through the collection of documents within social networks or digital platforms, together with the integration of subsets of existing corpus documents relevant to the objective of the study. In Annex A several data sources to consider are presented.

After selecting the relevant sources for the study, the attributes equivalent to the data model described must be selected for the corpus to be built and then define how these will be integrated into the proposed data model.

3.2 Document Processing

Cleaning. Document cleaning consists of executing a set of processes to improve the text quality, aiming to eliminate noise in the data, redundancies, and documents that do not comply with the design principles established for the corpus. A record is kept of each cleaning to verify the losses occurring during the corpus construction. Within the framework, a first cleaning stage, called pre-cleaning, is executed on the document immediately after its collection and before being added to the corpus under construction. This cleaning stage consists of completing a minimum length control to verify if the document length is within the established limit, eliminating Uniform Resource Locators (URLs) found within the messages through regular expressions, transforming user identifiers into unique tokens (e.g., account names), transforming platform's jargon into unique tokens (e.g., hashtags). Moreover, it includes cleaning up repeated words to preserve only one word, cleaning repeated special characters to preserve only one special character, truncating text if it has a length more significant than the established limit, and converting text to lowercase. It also comprises replacing numeric characters with a unique token, removing emoticons through their Unicode character, and refining rules. A set of rules is generated to increase the quality of the document. These rules seek to solve errors such as vowels written as *à* or punctuation as *word1.word2*. Finally, it covers encoding text according to UTF-8 encoding to facilitate cross-platform and multi-language handling.

Next, the document is stored within the corpus and the collection of documents continued once the previous tasks have been completed. At the end of the collection stage, a second cleaning stage is carried out, called post-cleaning, keeping a copy of the original corpus as a backup. This step consists of eliminating duplicate documents (i.e., all records with complete repeated texts are deleted), uncommon word auto-correction, and cleaning documents with unusual words. Words that do not exceed a defined frequency are replaced within a word dictionary built from the same corpus, in which each key is a word, and the value is the frequency of occurrence. In this manner, words like *corect* or *corrrect* are replaced by *correct*. Furthermore, after the previous, documents that have at least one word with a frequency lower than the limit established in the created dictionary are eliminated.

Translation. The translation phase is carried out after completing the collection of documents. Within the proposed data model, there has to be an attribute to indicate the original document language. Due to their extensive availability, the texts in English are selected for their posterior translation through Cloud Translation and Translator Text methods. Both APIs are implemented according to the available quota.

The implementation is carried out through external libraries to obtain the functionalities without providing payment information. For Cloud Translation, the googletrans and TextBlob libraries are proposed, and for Translator Text, the bing-tr library; all written in Python.

Unlike working directly with the official APIs, this methodology has to control the number of requests made in a time interval; otherwise, the translation platform would block the IP from which the requests are made. A virtual private network (VPN) is used to overcome this limitation.

3.3 Corpus Evaluation

After collecting and processing the documents, the corpus obtained is evaluated through automatic and human mechanisms. There is a dependency between the two; through human evaluations, some inputs are brought to serve the automatic evaluation. This workflow is shown in Fig. 2.

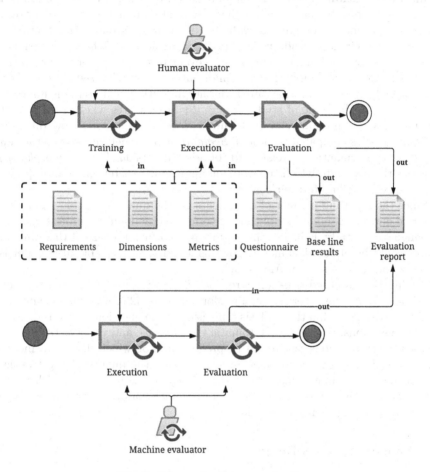

Fig. 2. Scheme for corpus evaluation.

Automatic Evaluation. The metrics to quantify the quality of a text generated by automatic means are Bilingual Evaluation Understudy (BLEU) and Distinct-N. The former, presented by [21], consists of a metric to measure the quality of a translation by automatic methods. Its central idea is to quantify how similar a translation performed by a model is compared to the same translation performed by a professional translator (person). The latter, proposed by [22], consists of a metric measuring the diversity of a sentence generated by a system. It analyzes the number of different degrees of n-grams and penalizes sentences with several repeated n-grams. In its typical form, an analysis is performed in unigrams and bigrams, Distinct-1 and Distinct-2, respectively.

Human Evaluation. There is no standard regarding the human evaluation of a constructed corpus. In general, researchers, in addition to automatic evaluations, generate experimental designs to evaluate the content through human criteria according to their needs and availability. A compendium of the characteristics to be assessed by the human component relevant to the framework is presented by [14] and [24]. It includes relevance, informativity, diversity, semantic fidelity, and morphology. *Relevance* measures whether an output text contains information relevant to the topic of study. *Informativity* measures whether an output text includes information relevant to users. *Diversity* measures how different an output text is compared to others. *Semantic fidelity* determines whether an output text is semantically related to its original version. Finally, *morphology* measures the degree to which the words in an output text retain an appropriate morphology according to their context.

Since the resulting number of documents can be quite large, this evaluation is carried out on a random sample and is performed by linguistic professionals in the language of study. Following [23] for a large corpus, the size of this random sample could be of 100 documents. For this activity, the suitable instrument is a questionnaire presented in Annex B.

Within the proposed questionnaire, each dimension was quantified through closed questions. The Likert scale, a conformity scale [25], was implemented to obtain an average within the analysis dimensions. The questionnaire was divided into three sections, translation, automatic translations, and variety. *Translation* received the translations carried out by professionals on which the BLEU metric was obtained. The *automatic translations* assessed the quality of the translations made by automated means and the quality of the original English documents. *Variety* quantified the perception of the evaluators regarding the type that existed among their analysis documents.

3.4   Support Systems Design

Except for the human evaluation component, the tasks were designed to be completely automated through software supporting distributed computing to parallelize the data collection, processing, and evaluation tasks.

4   Results and Discussion

Through the proposed framework, a case study was developed. It was possible to generate a large-scale corpus in Spanish whose domain corresponded to comments from people about textile products. The selected sources consisted of the social network Twitter, the Multilingual Amazon Reviews Corpus (MARC)

[12], and the Amazon Customer Reviews (ACR) corpus [26]. Table 1 shows the conformation of the corpus.

Table 1. Composition of the raw corpus built according to the data source.

Source	Documents quantity
Twitter	5312
MARC	8948
ACR	237977
Total	252237

After the collection step, more than 250 thousand documents were obtained, of which 96% were initially in English. The documents were translated, in parallel, through the libraries proposed in the framework and the development of a support system. The result was integrated into the corpus under construction. For the post-cleaning phase, an autocorrect was developed based on the editing distance metric: 1-edit. Subsequently, the comments that still had words considered as infrequent were removed. The final result consisted of a corpus with more than 170 thousand documents. The record of how the number of documents varied after each processing phase is detailed in Fig. 3. The initial corpus consists of the corpus before the post-cleaning step. The value registered in Processing 1 refers to the number of documents after the repeated documents have been removed from the initial corpus. They were then sent to the translation process. In Processing 2 are the documents that passed the translation phase resulting from the translation. The loss that existed at this point is because the automatic translator returned null values in some cases. In Processing 3 are the documents that passed the language detection phase, with a loss of 11% compared to the previous stage. In some cases, the translator returned the same document without translating, an uncontrollable factor by the system which was taken into account by languages detectors. Lastly, as indicated above, the final corpus corresponded to the documents that passed the self-correction phase. There was elimination of documents with infrequent words, corresponding to 68.7% of the initial corpus.

The final corpus went on to the phase of evaluation of the translations by automatic means. For this, the BLEU metric was used in a configuration of unigrams, bigrams, trigrams, quadgrams, and a weighted configuration where each n-gram component was assigned a weight of 0.25 as the default value. These results are summarized in Fig. 4.

Even though the score decreases as the order of the n-grams increases, it exceeds the value of 0.5 in all configurations. According to [27], a score higher than 0.5 reflects a good and fluent translation. Although BLEU is a widely used metric and scored high in the current research, additional evaluations were performed. In [28] stated that this metric has limitations since it is based solely

---

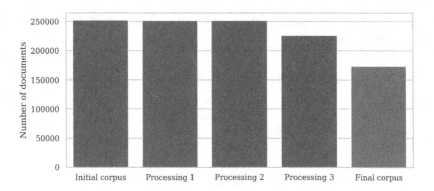

Fig. 3. Number of documents in the corpus through different stages.

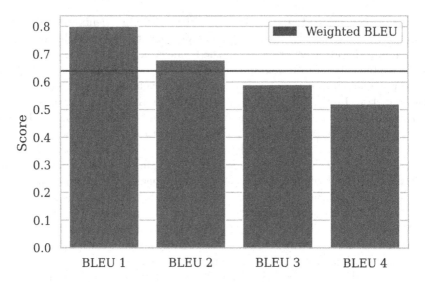

Fig. 4. BLEU scores.

on the precision of n-grams. Thus, to provide greater robustness to the evaluation, a human assessment was implemented. Figure 5 presents the evaluation of how adequate the translations were concerning the original text. Only 4% of evaluators consider that it does not have an adequate translation compared to the original text, 72% believe it has a satisfactory quality. In comparison, the remaining 24% maintain a neutral stance towards the translation. This last value is attributed to the fact that the input texts were confused even in their original language due to poor writing. Therefore, the evaluators did not have a clear position on whether the automatic translation was adequate or not.

In addition to the translation quality assessment, verification was performed on whether the collected texts correspond to the specified domain, which is depicted in Fig. 6. In this case, 63% of the documents were clearly within the

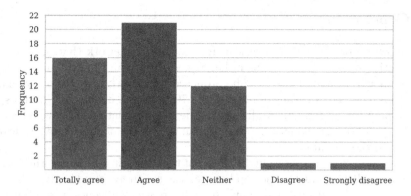

Fig. 5. Adequate translation quality.

established field. 12% of the documents did not correspond to the established domain. And, for the remaining 25%, they were valued in an intermediate position. Regarding these documents, it was identified that they consisted of texts with a generic nature and that their content could be considered from any domain, such as the text "I loved it, I would buy it again without thinking twice".

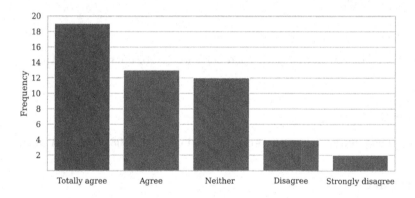

Fig. 6. Adequate domain of the collected documents.

The final corpus built through the described framework, has high-quality documents in Spanish and can be implemented to feed NLP Models. This result is highly relevant because it allows the generation of large-scale inputs in languages other than English, reducing the gap between research across different languages. All this at a lower cost than that implied by methodologies such as those of [12] and [5], and on a scale greater than that described by [15].

5   Conclusions

The objective of this research was to introduce a framework that allowed the construction of large-scale corpus in languages other than English and in which its documents have high quality. The proposed framework was tested through a case study in which a corpus of more than 170 thousand documents from a specific domain was generated. Additionally, the corpus mentioned above obtained a BLEU score higher than 0.5, and more than 60% of the documents were clearly relevant to the domain.

This framework becomes a highly relevant tool since, in addition to the results obtained, it allows reducing the gap between the resources found in English compared to other languages. Also, applied in different time frames, it can capture changes in how people use language. Furthermore, in different contexts, the same words would have various connotations, giving relevance to the domain-specific corpus.

Acknowledgments. This study is part of the research project "Incorporating Sustainability concepts to management models of textile Micro, Small and Medium Enterprises (SUMA)", supported by the Flemish Interuniversity Council (VLIR) and the Research Vice-rector of the University of Cuenca (DIUC).

A   Annexes

Annex A

https://imagineresearch.org/wp-content/uploads/2021/08/Corpus_AnnexA.pdf

Annex B

https://imagineresearch.org/wp-content/uploads/2021/08/Corpus_AnnexB.pdf

References

1. BBC. https://www.bbc.com/news/world-us-canada-52860247. Accessed 21 Jan 2021
2. Vieira, A., Ribeiro, B.: Introduction to Deep Learning Business Applications for Developers. Springer, Hiedelberg (2018). https://doi.org/10.1007/978-1-4842-3453-2
3. Brown, T., Mann, B., Ryder, N., Subbiah, M.: Language models are few-shot learners. arXiv (2020)
4. Li, Y., Pan, Q., Wang, S., Yang, T., Cambria, E.: A generative model for category text generation. Inf. Sci. **450**, 301–315 (2018)
5. Bowman, S.R., Angeli, G., Potts, C., Manning, C.: A large annotated corpus for learning natural language inference. In: Empirical Methods in Natural Language Processing, EMNLP 2015, pp. 632–642 (2015)

6. Bowman, S.R., Vilnis, L., Vinyals, O., Dai, A.M., Jozefowicz, R., Bengio, S.: Generating sentences from a continuous space. In: Computational Natural Language Learning, SIGNLL 2015, pp. 10–21 (2015)
7. Logeswaran, L., Honglak, L., Bengio, S.: Content preserving text generation with attribute controls. arXiv:1811.01135 (2018)
8. Chassagnon, G., Vakalopolou, M., Paragios, N., Revel, M.P.: Deep learning: definition and perspectives for thoracic imaging. Eur. Radiol. **30**, 2021–2030 (2020)
9. Ng, A., Katanforoosh, K., Bensouda, Y.: Deep Learning [MOOC]. COURSERA (2017)
10. McEnery, T.: Corpus Linguistics. Oxford University Press, Oxford (2012)
11. Ray, S.K., Ahmad, A., Kumar, C.A.: Review and implementation of topic modeling in Hindi. Appl. Artif. Intell. **33**(11), 979–1007 (2019)
12. Keung, P., Lu, Y., Szarvas, G., Smith, N.: The multilingual Amazon reviews corpus. arXiv:2010.02573 (2020)
13. Williams, A., Nangia, N., Bowman, S.: A broad-coverage challenge corpus for sentence understanding through inference. arXiv preprint arXiv:1704.05426 (2017)
14. Ni, J., Li, J., McAuley, J.: Justifying recommendations using distantly-labeled reviews and fine-grained aspects. In: Empirical Methods in Natural Language Processing 2020, EMNLP-IJCNLP, pp. 188–197 (2020)
15. Balahur, A., Turchi, M.: Comparative experiments using supervised learning and machine translation for multilingual sentiment analysis. Comput. Speech Lang. **28**(1), 56–75 (2014)
16. Bengfort, B., Bilbreo, R., Ojeda, T.: Applied Text Analysis with Python, 1st edn. O'Reilly, Sebastopol (2018)
17. O'Keeffe, A., McCarthy, M.: The Routledge Handbook of Corpus Linguistics. Routledge, Abingdon (2010)
18. Liu, C. J. Han, S.: Bilingual corpus research on Chinese English machine translation in computer centres of Chinese universities. In: Proceedings - 2012 International Conference on Computer Science and Service System, CSSS 2012, pp. 1720–1723 (2012)
19. Hogan, A.: Web of data. In: The Web of Data, pp. 15–57. Springer, Cham (2016). https://doi.org/10.1007/978-3-030-51580-5_2
20. Minard, A.L., et al.: MEANTIME, the NewsReader multilingual event and time corpus. In: Proceedings of the Tenth International Conference on Language Resources and Evaluation 2016, LREC, pp. 4417–4422 (2016)
21. Papineni, K., Roukos, S., Ward, T., Zhu, W.J.: BLEU: a method for automatic evaluation of machine translation. In: Proceedings of the 40th Annual Meeting of the Association for Computational Linguistics 2002, pp. 311–318 (2002)
22. Li, J., Galley, M., Brockett, C., Gao, J., Dolan, B.: A diversity-promoting objective function for neural conversation models. In: Conference of the North American Chapter of the Association for Computational Linguistics: Human Language Technologies 2016, LREC, pp. 110–119 (2016)
23. Conneau, A., et al.: XNLI: evaluating cross-lingual sentence representations. arXiv preprint arXiv:1809.05053 (2018)
24. Fan, A., Gardent, C.: Multilingual AMR-to-text generation. arXiv:2011.05443 (2020)
25. Albaum, G.: The Likert scale revisited. Mark. Res. Soc. **39**, 1–21 (1997)
26. He, R., McAuley, J.: Ups and downs: modeling the visual evolution of fashion trends with one-class collaborative filtering. In: Proceedings of the 25th International Conference on World Wide Web, pp. 507–517 (2016)

27. Lavie, A: Evaluating the output of machine translation systems (2011). https://www.cs.cmu.edu/~alavie/Presentations/MT-Evaluation-MT-Summit-Tutorial-19Sep11.pdf

28. Zhang, Y., Vogel, S., Waibel, A.: Interpreting BLEU/NIST scores: how much improvement do we need to have a better system? In: LREC (2004)

ICT's Applications

Tourism Analysis in Ecuador Through Airbnb

Ester Melo$^{(\boxtimes)}$ ⓘ, Daniel Arroyo$^{(\boxtimes)}$ ⓘ, Manuel Lecaroⓘ, and Alex Macas

Escuela Superior Politécnica del Litoral, Guayaquil, Ecuador
{emelo,darroyo,mnlecaro,admacas}@espol.edu.ec

Abstract. In this work, the tourism analysis of Ecuador is carried out based on data of the accommodations offered through Airbnb (Ecuador) from May to July 2019; Twitter comments on the terms: accommodation, hotel and Airbnb, which resulted in the creation of a data set for each term; and finally, data extracted from the National Institute of Statistics and Censuses of Ecuador (INEC) (INEC - Inicio, [1].), which refer to the population of the cantons of that country. From these records, data analysis techniques were applied such as: sentiment analysis, language analysis and clustering. The analysis of language and feelings is applied to data extracted from Twitter, to later unify the variable of feelings with data from Airbnb and the population. Subsequently, three quantitative variables (price, density, and revisions) of the data set were considered, which facilitated the execution of the clustering. All this to describe the interaction between users and Airbnb, as well as to understand the preferences of these users over accommodation and finally, locate the cities that contribute to tourism through this platform. Considering that the coronavirus pandemic affected tourism activities in 2020, this paper provides a basis on which the pre-pandemic context can be understood.

Keywords: Tourism · Twitter · Airbnb · Sentiment analysis

1 Introduction

The heyday of Airbnb in Ecuador, as well as in many countries of the world, has generated changes in the development of the country's real estate sector. It has opened new possibilities for home and apartment owners and allowed them to have an extra source of income. For many people, "this income has become a source of family support (...)" [2]. This way, in Ecuador, the expansion of the offer of accommodation has been given through this platform and that, without a doubt, has had an impact on tourism due to the visibility it grants to the national territory, making it more attractive. In this regard, it is worth mentioning that until 2018 "tourism contributed to the Ecuadorian economy with 2,392 million dollars, which maintains it as the third source of non-oil income, after bananas and shrimp" [3]. This indicates that the contribution that Airbnb gives to tourism transcends nationally and thus also benefits the country's economy.

While Airbnb has three clearly identified sections (accommodation, experiences, and adventures), this work will only focus on the accommodation section. However, it is necessary to emphasize that each of these sections have a relevant tourist and economic impact.

J. P. Salgado Guerrero et al. (Eds.): TICEC 2021, CCIS 1456, pp. 103–114, 2021.
https://doi.org/10.1007/978-3-030-89941-7_8

When reviewing the literature to guide the development of this research, it was discovered that "Airbnb currently competes with traditional hotels for the price" [4]. That is, what makes Airbnb competitive is not only the experience it offers and the diversity of hosts it has, but also the affordable prices for its users.

For all these changes that Airbnb generates within the economy of a particular place and because the applicant, user or tourist is one of the main actors in this context, it was necessary to know in detail how they influence ratings of the accommodations and the characteristics of their location (in Ecuador) in the degree of user satisfaction. This leads to some questions such as Q1: what is the affinity or relationship that users have about Airbnb and its competition (hotels)? Q2: how do users express themselves about Airbnb and its competition? Q3: Is it possible to discriminate city groups based on certain parameters?

The main interest in carrying out this study is that there is little information on the interaction of Airbnb in Ecuador and its users, which is important to determine because it is possible to explore the new needs of the consumer that other types of accommodation are not considering to be competitive. In addition, they also do not include an analysis from the user's point of view and then fully understand their preference for the use of this platform.

Finally, considering that the coronavirus pandemic caused an imbalance in the flow of tourist activities during 2020, this paper explores Airbnb information from the year 2019. Thus, providing a basis on which the pre-pandemic context can be understood.

2   Related Work

Studies recognize tourism as a key development factor in all countries and an important economic source. In addition, it promotes the image and international perception of a country, for this reason, analyzing tourism in a particular place facilitates the determination of important features of that place, being these of any type (social, economic, cultural and relaxation). Hence, the relevance of this work is also reinforced [5].

When referring to consumer aspects, it is simple to issue the idea of analyzing their profiles and their influx. However, a well-known method, which greatly optimizes this analysis, is based on the comments made by such users and on creating networks. Then, as a metric, a well-accepted measure of non-parametric range correlations is used, the Kendall range correlation [6], which is based on peer agreements between tourist locations.

Additionally, another significant measure regarding user comments is visitor satisfaction, which is an important qualitative indicator from the demand side. Customer demand is determined by a variety of factors that include the experience and recommendation of others, which in turn play an important role in the decision-making of many travelers [5]. The declared preferences of the visitors are also important to determine the probability of repeated visits and, therefore, the future competitiveness to generate economic benefits [7].

3   Methodology

This document has followed a series of steps to obtain some results. These are broadly described by:

- Data extraction
- Preprocessing of the data sets
- Geographical visualizations
- Sentiment analysis
- Language analysis
- Clustering

3.1   Data Extraction

For the purposes of this investigation, three sets of data extracted from three different sources were used: Airbnb, Twitter, and INEC (National Institute of Statistics and Census, Ecuador). From Airbnb (Ecuador) [8] 5000 records were obtained covering a period of two months, from May 17 to July 17 of 219. This first database had 25 variables, of which mainly these were used: location, only price, accuracy, and reviews. Comments were extracted from Twitter (located in Ecuador) about Airbnb's hosting service, as well as mentions of travel, accommodation, and hotels. Finally, from the INEC website, demographic data from Ecuador (regions, provinces, and cities) such as density, territory extension and the number of houses with internet access was obtained.

It is worth mentioning that the data extraction process was different for each data set. For the Airbnb data, a Python tracker called Selenium was used, because the Airbnb page requires an automatic human click interaction with the website. While the tweet data set was extracted using a library called GetOldTweets3 [9], as it allows users to query tweets within a range of specific dates. Finally, the population data from INEC was downloaded and analyzed within a .lxml file.

3.2   Data Preprocessing

As for the preprocessing stage, data encoded in utf-8 (Spanish chars) was removed, and NaN type values were replaced by zeros to maintain the consistency. In addition, new columns were added to some data sets, such as "sentiment" in the twitter comment data set, which would be used in subsequent analyzes. After these processes, the data sets were ready to be used with the panda library and later enrich the analysis by grouping records. Through that, the representation of the data was carried out in scatter diagrams, histograms, and choropleth maps (as for geographical representation).

All the different data sets (Airbnb, Airbnb sna, hotel sna, hosting sna and population data of Ecuador) were unified to have in the same set all the variables, especially the variables of interest and those resulting from the sentiment analysis (later explained). The problem of having all the variables in the same data set was that not all of them would contribute significantly to the study and, in turn, the high dimensionality of the data would require higher computational resources. For this reason, the principal components analysis was carried out.

3.3 Geographical Visualizations

Here, a new metric was created: the popularity metric, which determines the degree of acceptance and consumption of the leases of the accommodations by province (since the Airbnb data had been georeferenced by province). That is, to know the provinces that users prefer when renting temporary accommodation and analyze how they contribute to tourism given their popularity. For a better understanding, this visualization was shown in a choropleth map of Ecuador. The details associated with the popularity metric can be seen below:

$$p_i = \frac{reviews_i}{accommodations_i}$$

Where p is the popularity of a province, and i is the province (each one of the 24 provinces).

3.4 Sentiment Analysis

Once the preprocessed data was obtained, the sentiment analysis was carried out to study the comments of the users regarding three terms: Airbnb, hotel and lodging. For this process, the data set referring to Twitter comments was sectorized by towns and then divided into the previously mentioned terms, which ultimately resulted in the construction of three data sets.

To carry out the sentiment analysis [10], the indico.io library was used and was applied in each data set (Airbnb, hotel, lodging). When obtaining the sentiment for each tweet, this was added as a new column to the respective data set, then the results of the average sentiment analysis by city were grouped, thus obtaining a ranking of the cities with the best results.

3.5 Language Analysis

For the language analysis, the twitter comment data set was used for each term (Airbnb, hotel, and lodging). To begin, the stop words were removed using the "stopwords" [11] tool from the Natural Language Toolkit (nltk) library, as well as irrelevant terms such as numbers, URL, asterisks, among others. Then, by using this same library, the frequency of each term was calculated, which was then represented in the same graph. This to know what the most used terms at the time were when users referred to each type of temporary leasing service.

Once the frequency of all the terms of each data set was obtained, a top 10 common expressions between each set was made, to know the similarity of the comments. All this analysis finally allowed to answer the second question of this investigation, which refers to the expressions that users use about Airbnb and its competitors (in this case, hotel, and lodging).

3.6 Clustering

For the Kmeans [12] the variables that were standardized were considered: density, price, and review. Then, data on the results of the sentiment analysis was added in the tweets about the term Airbnb, in addition to the population density, area and Internet access, also by city, so it was sought to identify groups between the cities of the country. To determine the optimal number of classes, the elbow method was used through which it was identified that the optimum was three. From the groups obtained by this technique, the provinces and cities that maintained common characteristics were identified, mainly regarding density, price, and revision. And in this way, clarify the understanding of the contribution to tourism by said provinces and cities, in congruence with the information known about them.

4   Results

4.1   Hypothesis and Insights

As a result of the techniques implemented, insights were found regarding the terms that went together according to the corresponding theme (Airbnb, hotels, and lodgings). However, there is no relationship between the number of retweets within a city with respect to a topic and the number of retweets, also with the other variables taken from the interactions on Twitter: reactions and responses, this was discovered when applying the correlation Kendall's tau [6].

The second metric applied in this work is the possibility of locating the cities that contribute to tourism through Airbnb by applying K-Means based on three parameters: average price, density, and average popularity. These parameters are considered because the accommodation price is one of the factors that most influence the user's preference, the density corresponds to a measure of the city and finally, the popularity is a referential measure of the times that the users have stayed in rooms offered on Airbnb.

4.2   User Relationship Between Airbnb and Its Competition (Hotels)

The metric created called 'popularity', allowed to determine the provinces that users prefer when leasing a temporary accommodation, in this case, an accommodation offered on the Airbnb platform. It turned out that Guayas and Pichincha are the provinces with the highest demand or user preference. This is because these provinces, specifically, the cities of Guayaquil and Quito represent the main tourist points of Ecuador, followed by the city of Cuenca. However, the preference of the users measured through this metric, distributes this preference in some provinces of the Coast, Sierra, and Galapagos, and not precisely in the city of Cuenca. This indicates that it is not only Guayaquil and Quito that contribute to the tourism level of the province to which they belong, but also other sister towns. This was later showed using a geographic visualization, (Fig. 1).

Fig. 1. Popular provinces according to the preference of users when renting temporary accommodation on the Airbnb platform.

The sentiment analysis was also divided by cities which later helped to create rankings for cities with better "feelings" left on the tourist (Figs. 2 and 3).

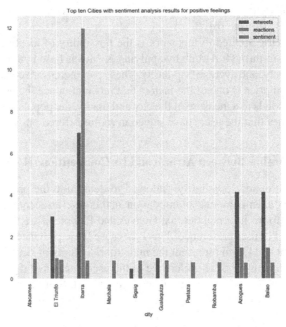

Fig. 2. Positive perception of tourists towards the cities of Ecuador

Popularity was passed through the Kendall's rank correlation on the tweets data sets after applying the sentiment analysis phase and obtained the following results:

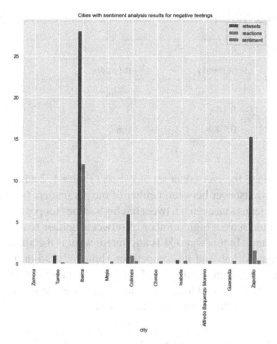

Fig. 3. Negative perception of tourists towards the cities of Ecuador

Table 1. Kendall correlation results for Hotel related tweets

Hotel			
	sentiments	retweets	reactions
Sentiments	1	– 0.33	– 0.30
Retweets	– 0.33	1	0.066
Reactions	– 0.30	0.066	1

Table 2. Kendall correlation results for Airbnb related tweets

Airbnb			
	sentiments	retweets	reactions
Sentiments	1	– 0.18	0.05
Retweets	– 0.18	1	– 0.29
Reactions	0.05	– 0.29	1

Table 3. Kendall correlation results for Lodging related tweets

Lodging			
	sentiments	retweets	reactions
Sentiments	1	– 0.14	– 0.14
Retweets	– 0.14	1	0.87
Reactions	– 0.14	0.87	1

The results obtained for every data set of tweets (Tables 1, 2 and 3) mean that there are no correlations whatsoever between neither of the parameters (sentiments, retweets and reactions), that means that even if a tweet has high values for positive feelings, it does not means that it could have a high number of retweets neither reactions and the same for the other parameters. In this way, Q1 is answered: what is the affinity or relationship that users have about Airbnb and its competition (hotels)? And in the same context it can be affirmed that, although the degree of affinity or relationship (feeling) of people with respect to Airbnb, hotel, and lodging, is positive, this is not reflected in the number of retweets or reactions of the tweets, but in its own content.

4.3   User Perception of Airbnb and Its Competition (Hotels)

On the other hand, regarding Language Analysis, it was obtained that among the comments regarding hotel and lodging there are several common terms that users use to refer to these and they are: hotel, better, Guayaquil, fun, enjoy, facilities, among others. While, when referring to lodging and Airbnb, they use expressions such as: travel, lodging, enjoy, direct, among others. Finally, to refer to hotel and Airbnb, the terms in common are enjoy, week, walk, lodging, better, among others. This indicates that the comments continue to be positive and reaffirms the use that users give to these types of temporary leases. These results can be found on Fig. 4.

However, the word frequency graph for each set of comments shows that, when referring to hotel, users use terms such as: Guayaquil, Mexico, Hilton, better, party,

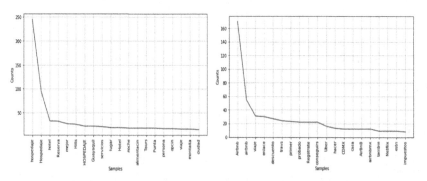

Fig. 4. Common user comments regarding Airbnb and hosting

among others (Fig. 5). On the other hand, to refer to lodging use: hotel, reservation, Guayaquil, services, place, night, food, tours, among others. Finally, to refer to Airbnb, they use expressions such as: travel, link, discount, register, Uber, and home. This study allows answering the Q2: how do users express themselves about Airbnb and its competition? whose response is much broader than expected, then, the comments denote that Guayaquil and Mexico are the city and country, respectively, of those most commented when referring to this type of services (temporary lease), even when these Tweets come from cities and/or provinces of Ecuador. When referring to hotels, the Hilton Colon hotel appears as the most mentioned, which could be said to represent a strong competition. And as for Airbnb, it can be said that this is conducive to travel given the discounts it offers for those who register and, in turn, maintains a relationship with another shared economy platform: Uber.

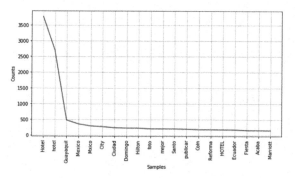

Fig. 5. Common user comments regarding hotel

4.4 Popular Cities According to Price, Review, and Density

After applying the clustering algorithm, four groups were obtained as a result. Cluster 0 (purple) represents the cities that are the most popular and have some of the lowest prices, including cities like Guayaquil, Cuenca, and Salinas, which are known for their touristic offers on holidays. Cluster 1 (blue) has the most cities and should represent average to low price-density-popularity cities. Cluster 3 (green) includes the most populated cities and low popularity, such as Muisne and Esmeraldas. Finally, cluster 4 (yellow) shows cities with high prices and thus, low popularity, were cities like Montecristi and Patate are grouped. In this way, it was possible to answer the Q3: Is it possible to discriminate city groups based on certain parameters? The results of this question can be seen on Table 4 and Fig. 6.

Table 4. Composition of the clusters obtained from clustering.

Cluster	Reviews	Mean price	Mean density
0	16.488	48.490	212.381
1	1.332	31.255	101.379
2	1.197	48.241	3124.578
3	0.690	106.036	119.567

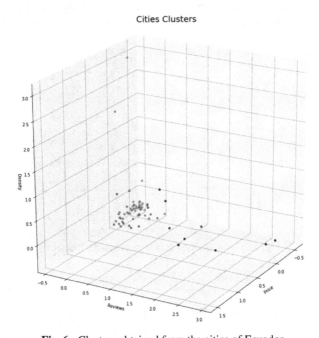

Fig. 6. Clusters obtained from the cities of Ecuador.

5 Discussion and Conclusion

In the first instance, the applied popularity metric allowed to locate those provinces whose contribution to tourism is significant; likewise, those that contribute in an average level and those that do not have visibility or that are scarcely visited.

The second part is the application of sentiment analysis techniques, which gave us the fact that in Ecuador the way of expressing about Airbnb has a better means of analyzing feelings than the tweets about accommodation and hotels.

Then, when applying the word analysis of tweets according to the terms Airbnb, accommodation, and a new term: hotel, many tweets were expected to be extracted due to the generality of those terms, but contrary to our prediction the number of tweets was quite low in contrast to other topics. The language analysis showed us the expressions most used by users regarding Airbnb, and these were "link" and "discount", this refers to Airbnb has a system to capture users through discount links, which confirms that cost is an important factor in user preference.

Finally, Kmeans was applied as a clustering algorithm applied in accommodation by cities considering three parameters (average price, density, and average popularity). Four clearly differentiated groups were obtained from this: economic-popular, average-popular-economic, non- popular-economic and non-popular-economic.

Despite the existing challenges, this approach gave us a significant way to describe the interaction between users and Airbnb, as well as internalize consumer preferences regarding the accommodation offered on this platform and all this located in cities in Ecuador.

In this sense, we suggest that the public sector or the hotel sector should consider this study to understand the new demands or preferences of users and thus be more competitive.

6 Recommendations

Among the general recommendations are to create a data set as robust and extensive as possible, preferably to carry out a data extraction planning that covers all the time that the project will take, when using platforms such as Airbnb that have a system to present offers where there are thirty results by search, it is best to create specific search criteria, such criteria can be the price range, the number of rooms available, the number of hosts, so you can also start categorizing the data by economic factors, characteristics of the hosting and by characteristics of the hosts.

Regarding tweets extraction, perform the extraction with the objective of having data with time and, if possible, geolocation so that it is easier to create geographical visualizations that can give rise to future insights.

Airbnb does not deliver specific latitude and longitude data to georeference the lodging places, it gives the city name and some descriptions such as the number of the streets and the position of the property with respect to the city (if it is in the center of the city, the south, north, east) in addition to the description added by the owner, so for jobs that require specific locations to be able to detect maps or relationships between nearby areas of populations regarding objects such as streets or buildings, Airbnb would not be a good source to get study data.

7 Future Works

In this work it was contemplated to have historical data to be able to define the impact that Airbnb brought to the national tourist movement, however this would require having records of the interactions between host and guests for longer, so a research that includes analysis is proposed of time and the movement that there is at the time of the year on Airbnb.

Within the techniques of exploratory data analysis, the movement of foreign tourists to Ecuador was reviewed. A future work is to determine the areas towards which for-eigners arrive and moves next to in Ecuador, so it could be possible to map the traveling patterns inside Ecuador of foreign tourists by country of origin and place of destination by season.

The analysis of tweets served to measure the degree of satisfaction on some issues by users in geographical regions of the country, but the maximum degree of precision counted in this work was the city of origin of the tweet, not only this entails problems because it is not completely certain that the location of the tweet is the one that the Twitter API gives us, yet the creation of a data set with geolocated Twitter data to relate them is considered with the areas of the Airbnb lodgings.

Each city has activities that attracts tourists and those have a different range of public interest which could be designated by the number of lodgings nearby, this could help in the detection of new points of interest for tourists, so a future work is to define a method to find the possible new areas of interest and the reason for an attractive touristic point to appear.

Airbnb shows recreational options available near the areas, these recommendations also have their own ratings and comments from other users by which in future work the impact of nearby recreational areas on lodgings and the tourist attraction's type that get more attention.

References

1. INEC – Inicio, https://www.ecuadorencifras.gob.ec/estadisticas
2. El Universo: Guillermo Lasso le pide al Gobierno que 'deje en paz las casas de los ecuatorianos' tras anuncio del Reglamento de alojamiento informal (2021). https://www.elcomercio.com/actualidad/politica/guillermo-lasso-reglamento-alojamiento-airbnb.html
3. Ministerio de Turismo: El turismo ecuatoriano creció un 11% en 2018. Quito (2021). https://www.turismo.gob.ec/el-turismo-ecuatoriano-crecio-un-11-en-2018/
4. Zervas, G., Proserpio, D., Byers, J.: The rise of the sharing economy: estimating the impact of Airbnb on the hotel industry. J. Mark. Res. **54**, 687–705 (2017)
5. Dhiratara, A., Yang, J., Bozzon, A., Houben, G.: Social media data analytics for tourism: a preliminary study. In: KDWEB 2016 (2016)
6. Dupeyras, A., MacCallum, N.: Indicators for measuring competitiveness in tourism. In: OECD Tourism Papers (2013)
7. Koh, V., Li, W., Livan, G., Capra, L.: Offline biases in online platforms: a study of diversity and homophily in Airbnb. EPJ Data Sci. **8**(1), 1–17 (2019). https://doi.org/10.1140/epjds/s13688-019-0189-5
8. Airbnb: Encuentra alojamientos para vacaciones, cabañas, casas en la playa, espacios únicos y experiencias en todo el mundo. Los anfitriones lo hacen posible en Airbnb., https://www.airbnb.com.ec/
9. Mottl, D.: GetOldTweets3. GitHub (2017)
10. Woldemariam, Y.: Sentiment analysis in a cross-media analysis framework. In: 2016 IEEE International Conference on Big Data Analysis (ICBDA) (2016)
11. Rakholia, R., Saini, J.: Lexical classes based stop words categorization for Gujarati language. In: 2016 2nd International Conference on Advances in Computing, Communication, & Automation (ICACCA) (Fall) (2016)
12. Lu, S., et al.: Clustering method of raw meal composition based on PCA and Kmeans. In: 2018 37th Chinese Control Conference (CCC) (2018)

Satisfaction with Information for Health Care and Prevention of Medical Fake News on Facebook During the COVID-19 Pandemic in Peru

Yuliana Mercedes De La Cruz-Ramirez[1]([⊠]) [iD], Augusto Felix Olaza-Maguiña[1] [iD], and Nadezhda Tarcila De La Cruz-Ramirez[2] [iD]

[1] Universidad Nacional Santiago Antúnez de Mayolo, Centenario 200, Huaraz 02002, Peru
{ydelacruzr,aolazam}@unasam.edu.pe
[2] Hospital Víctor Ramos Guardia, Luzuriaga 1248, Huaraz 02001, Peru

Abstract. The objective of the study was to determine the satisfaction with respect to the information received about health care and the prevention of medical fake news on Facebook during the COVID-19 pandemic in Peru, identifying differences with respect to gender and age. A cross-sectional investigation was carried out with 290 people who previously participated for 5 months on a voluntary basis in a Facebook group managed by health professionals. Data collection and analysis was performed using an online questionnaire and the SPSS program, respectively. The Chi square test was applied. A majority proportion of people satisfied with the information received was evidenced, with an average score of 4.14 on a scale of 1 to 5. Young people and women presented higher satisfaction values. It was concluded that there were high levels of satisfaction with the information received on health care and the prevention of medical fake news on Facebook during the COVID-19 pandemic in Peru. The promotion of netiquette or rules of cordiality on Facebook is an aspect that needs to be improved.

Keywords: COVID-19 · Health care · Medical fake news · Social network

1 Introduction

The massive use of social networks has meant worldwide the possibility of improving communication between people, thus overcoming the barriers that for so long limited access to important information sources for the development of human activities [1, 2].

In the medical area, the use of social networks has favored not only the work of health professionals in general, but also the care of patients themselves [3]. Various studies carried out in countries in Europe, the United States and Asia, have revealed the different activities that can be carried out for the benefit of the population through these social networks. Among the activities that stand out are telemedicine, telemonitoring and training in health issues [4, 5].

However, along with the benefits mentioned in the preceding paragraphs, there have also been problems of insecurity and danger to the health of patients [2, 6]. In this way,

© Springer Nature Switzerland AG 2021
J. P. Salgado Guerrero et al. (Eds.): TICEC 2021, CCIS 1456, pp. 115–126, 2021.
https://doi.org/10.1007/978-3-030-89941-7_9

the abundant information on social networks implies in many cases an overwhelming situation for people, for whom it is very difficult to identify the most appropriate sources of information for their needs [1, 7, 8]. This aspect is still very little addressed in existing research, not finding a consensus on how to face this situation [1, 9, 10].

The declaration of the global health emergency due to COVID-19 and the restrictive measures applied by the authorities have affected the face-to-face care of people in general, with the consequent reduction in medical appointments [11–13]. Faced with this reality, social networks have become an alternative to try to make up for this lack of attention, among which the use of Facebook has stood out [6, 14].

The situation described above has had a different context in developing countries such as Peru, especially in the cities furthest from the interior of that country, where the scarce access to modern technological means and the little training of the general population on the use of Facebook for educational purposes in the medical area, have brought different complications. An example of these complications is the disproportionate increase in fake news during the COVID-19 pandemic [7, 8], whose repercussions have been even more negative in the Peruvian population, not only due to the previously described context, but also due to the disinterest of the authorities and the lack of legislation that sanctions such practices [1, 15].

On the other hand, existing research in this regard has been primarily focused on the application of Facebook as a means of disseminating information, but with very little emphasis on the medical area [16, 17]. Thus, there is little knowledge about the particularities of the Facebook application during a health emergency situation such as the pandemic that currently affects the entire planet, especially in South American countries such as Peru. The aspects that have been studied so far have been basically focused on the repercussions that the inappropriate use of said social network may have, which is why its usefulness and the satisfaction of people are unknown when it is applied by properly trained health professionals, as well as the aspects in which some improvements can be made.

In this sense, the questions that have been sought to be resolved in this research have been the following:

What is the level of satisfaction of people regarding the information received on health care and the prevention of medical fake news on Facebook during the COVID-19 pandemic in Peru?

Are there differences in the level of satisfaction of people with the information received about health care and the prevention of medical fake news on Facebook according to gender?

Are there differences in the level of satisfaction of people with the information received about health care and the prevention of medical fake news on Facebook according to age?

In order to address the aforementioned questions, it was considered as a general objective to determine the satisfaction with respect to the information received about health care and the prevention of medical fake news on Facebook during the COVID-19 pandemic in Peru, identifying differences with respect to gender and age.

In this way, at the end of the research it has been possible to determine a majority proportion of people satisfied with the information received, with an average score of 4.14 on a scale of 1 to 5. Young people and women presented higher values of satisfaction. These results demonstrate the existence of high levels of satisfaction regarding the information received on health care and the prevention of medical fake news on Facebook during the COVID-19 pandemic in Peru. Likewise, the promotion of rules of cordiality on Facebook is an aspect that should be improved and whose analysis may be the subject of research in future studies.

2 Methodology

2.1 Research Design and Characteristics of the Population

A cross-sectional investigation was carried out with 336 people who previously participated for 5 months on a voluntary basis in a Facebook group managed by health professionals such as doctors, obstetricians and nurses. The population under study was made up of people of Peruvian nationality, over 18 years of age and whose participation or interaction in the Facebook group had to be at least 2 times a week.

Of the 336 people who are members of the Facebook group, 40 people agreed to participate in a pilot test in order to evaluate the suitability of the data collection instrument. Of the remaining 296 people, only 6 refused to answer the questionnaire, which resulted in a voluntary response from 290 people, who completed the final version of the online questionnaire.

2.2 Research Variables

First, the demographic variables of the population under study were considered, such as gender (male, female), age (18–39 years, ≥ 40 years) and occupation (student, housewife, salaried worker).

Next, the main variable of the research was addressed, which was related to satisfaction with the information received about health care and the prevention of medical fake news on Facebook during the COVID-19 pandemic in Peru. In this sense, as a result of the review and analysis of the theoretical bases and antecedents regarding the subject, the study of 6 dimensions was considered, such as the diversity of topics covered, thematic relevance, application of information in daily life, perception of veracity of information, quick response to inquiries and netiquette or rules of cordiality on Facebook.

A Likert-type scale was applied to the response alternatives to each of the aforementioned dimensions, with values from 1 to 5, where option 1 meant total dissatisfaction and option 5 total satisfaction. Within this scale, option 3 meant "indifference". All this information was properly recorded in the online questionnaire form.

2.3 Characteristics of the Data Collection Instrument

Based on the information described in the previous section, an online questionnaire was prepared, consisting of 9 questions, which were referred to the research variables.

The wording of the initial questions was modified as a consequence of the process of evaluating the validity and reliability of said questionnaire.

In this sense, for the validity of the questionnaire, the participation of 8 experts in telemedicine and telemonitoring in social networks was requested. In addition to the suggestions made regarding the content of the instrument, their responses were analyzed using Kendall's concordance test, with a result that demonstrated its validity ($p = 0.001$).

On the other hand, regarding the evaluation of the reliability of the questionnaire, as described above, the voluntary participation of 40 people was requested within the Facebook group, who participated in a pilot test. Suggestions made regarding the doubts raised about the wording of some questions were recorded. Likewise, after the use of the test-retest technique with an interval of 4 weeks, the analysis of the results of the pilot test was carried out using the intraclass correlation coefficient and the kappa index, through which the reliability of the instrument was demonstrated (0.843 and 0.894, respectively). The Cronbach's alpha index was also applied at the end of said process (0.891).

After complying with the suggested corrections, the final version of the questionnaire was applied in February 2021, after requiring the virtual filling of the respective authorization. It should be noted that the entire process was carried out virtually through the use of Google Forms and Messenger applications.

2.4 Statistical Analysis Procedures

The processing and analysis of the data collected was carried out through the statistical package SPSS, V. 23.0. In order to accurately analyze the responses of the study participants, descriptive statistics was applied to determine frequencies and percentages, as well as to calculate the mean and standard deviation.

Regarding the identification of differences in satisfaction according to gender and age, the Chi-square test was applied, for which 95% confidence intervals were determined with a significance level of $p < 0.05$.

2.5 Ethical Principles

Regarding the ethics of the research, it was complied with the timely presentation and approval of the research protocol by the Ethics Committee of the Santiago Antúnez of Mayolo National University, institution of affiliation of most of the authors of this study. In this way, in the development of the research, the ethical principles published by the World Medical Association [18] were scrupulously followed, especially those related to respect for the confidentiality of the data and the privacy of the participants.

Another aspect considered was the requirement of voluntary acceptance by registering data in an online form created with the Google Forms application, in which the respective declaration of informed consent was included.

3   Results

Table 1 shows that of the total of 290 people who answered the final version of the online questionnaire, most of them were young people (55.5%) of the female gender (62.4%) and whose main occupation was being housewives (38.6%).

Table 1. Characteristics of the population.

Characteristic	n	%
Gender:		
- Male	109	37.6
- Female	181	62.4
Age:		
- 18–39 years	161	55.5
- ≥ 40 years	129	44.5
Occupation:		
- Student	87	30.0
- Housewife	112	38.6
- Salaried worker	91	31.4

The averages of the satisfaction responses of the people who are members of the Facebook group managed by health professionals are reported in Table 2, where it is observed that the dimension that received the lowest rating was that of netiquette or rules of cordiality on Facebook (3.08), which means a position of indifference. However, despite the above, all the other dimensions received a satisfaction score, especially regarding the perception of the veracity of the information (4.52) and the quick response to inquiries (4.47), with a score overall average of 4.14 on a scale of 1 to 5.

Table 2. Averages of people's responses according to the dimensions of satisfaction.

Dimensions	Mean	Standard deviation
Diversity of topics covered	4.11	0.372
Thematic relevance	4.39	0.461
Application of information in daily life	4.25	0.497
Perception of the veracity of the information	4.52	0.584
Quick response to inquiries	4.47	0.506
Netiquette or rules of cordiality on Facebook	3.08	0.432

In order to identify the possible differences that could exist in people's satisfaction responses with respect to gender and age, these responses were grouped into 2 sets according to whether they expressed their satisfaction (scores of 4 and 5) or their indifference or dissatisfaction (scores of 1, 2 and 3).

In this sense, Table 3 shows that the female gender presented higher satisfaction values in all the dimensions evaluated, with the exception of the netiquette or rules of cordiality on Facebook, where the responses were mostly indifference or dissatisfaction. In relation to the statistical analysis, the existence of statistically significant differences was found between the satisfaction results of women and men in all dimensions (p < 0.05).

Table 3. Gender of people according to the dimensions of satisfaction.

Dimensions	Male		Female		Total		P-value*	IC 95%
	n	%	n	%	n	%		
Diversity of topics covered:								
- Satisfied	91	31.4	172	59.3	263	90.7	0.002	3.2–19.9%
- Indifferent or dissatisfied	18	6.2	9	3.1	27	9.3		
Thematic relevance:								
- Satisfied	89	30.7	170	58.6	259	89.3	0.002	3.5–21.1%
- Indifferent or dissatisfied	20	6.9	11	3.8	31	10.7		
Application of information in daily life:								
- Satisfied	94	32.4	171	58.9	265	91.3	0.028	0.2–16.2%
- Indifferent or dissatisfied	15	5.2	10	3.5	25	8.7		
Perception of the veracity of the information:								
- Satisfied	90	31.0	168	57.9	258	88.9	0.012	1.5–19.0%
- Indifferent or dissatisfied	19	6.6	13	4.5	32	11.1		
Quick response to inqucxiries:								
- Satisfied	92	31.7	175	60.3	267	92.1	< 0.001	4.3–20.3%
- Indifferent or dissatisfied	17	5.9	6	2.1	23	7.9		
Netiquette or rules of cordiality on Facebook:								
- Satisfied	46	15.9	52	17.9	98	33.8	0.026	1.4–25.6%
- Indifferent or dissatisfied	63	21.7	129	44.5	192	66.2		
Total	109	37.6	181	62.4	290	100		

* Chi square test
IC: confidence interval.

Regarding the age of the members of the Facebook group administered by health professionals, it is observed that the youngest people presented higher satisfaction values in 5 of the 6 dimensions evaluated; while in the netiquette the highest percentage corresponded to the responses of dissatisfaction or indifference (Table 4). The application of the Chi-square test allowed to identify the presence of statistically significant differences between the results of the youngest people and those with an age equal to or greater than 40 years ($p < 0.05$).

Table 4. Age of people according to the dimensions of satisfaction.

Dimensions	18–39 years		≥ 40 years		Total		P-value*	IC 95%
	n	%	n	%	n	%		
Diversity of topics covered:								
- Satisfied	156	53.8	107	36.9	263	90.7	< 0.001	6.2–21.7%
- Indifferent or dissatisfied	5	1.7	22	7.6	27	9.3		
Thematic relevance:								
- Satisfied	154	53.1	105	36.2	259	89.3	< 0.001	6.1–22.4%
- Indifferent or dissatisfied	7	2.4	24	8.3	31	10.7		
Application of information in daily life:								
- Satisfied	153	52.7	112	38.6	265	91.3	0.024	0.8–15.6%
- Indifferent or dissatisfied	8	2.8	17	5.9	25	8.7		
Perception of the veracity of the information:								
- Satisfied	155	53.4	103	35.5	258	88.9	< 0.001	8.2–24.6%
- Indifferent or dissatisfied	6	2.1	26	9.0	32	11.1		
Quick response to inquiries:								
- Satisfied	157	54.2	110	37.9	267	92.1	< 0.001	5.0–19.5%
- Indifferent or dissatisfied	4	1.3	19	6.6	23	7.9		
Netiquette or rules of cordiality on Facebook:								
- Satisfied	41	14.1	57	19.7	98	33.8	0.001	7.1–30.3%
- Indifferent or dissatisfied	120	41.4	72	24.8	192	66.2		
Total	161	55.5	129	44.5	290	100		

* Chi square test.
IC: confidence interval.

4 Discussion

The results found in the present research constitute evidence in favor of the usefulness and good use that can be given to social networks for the dissemination of valuable and important information for the lives of human beings. In that sense, the main objective of the study, aimed at determining satisfaction with respect to the information received about health care and the prevention of medical fake news on Facebook during the COVID-19 pandemic in Peru, has been fully met, having demonstrated the existence of high levels of satisfaction in a Facebook group managed by health professionals.

The aforementioned findings show similarity with the results reported by other research carried out in countries of America and Asia [15, 19], with the difference that in said research, the activities were oriented to other areas of knowledge other than care of health and the prevention of medical fake news [17, 19]. On the other hand, there are antecedents that highlight the usefulness of social networks, including Facebook, for the training of human resources in health and the publication of messages aimed at preventive campaigns for specific pathologies [3, 14]. However, the general care activities that can be developed through good guidance to people are left aside, together with the timely identification of harmful practices based on fake news [2, 8], aspects that, as has been found in the present study, received high percentages of satisfaction from the population.

On the other hand, an aspect that is interesting to highlight and on which the main contribution of this study falls is that it was carried out in a context of global health emergency caused by the COVID-19 pandemic. Therefore, it stands out the perception that people have regarding the most important dimensions that must be taken into account by health professionals when they carry out health promotion activities through Facebook. Knowledge of this perception is a contribution to the research area, which could later be compared in non-emergency contexts, or even to mean new care modalities based on information and communication technologies.

In this regard, the perception corresponding to the diversity of topics addressed, the thematic relevance and the application of the information in daily life, obtained satisfaction scores higher than 4 on a scale of 1 to 5. These results would be explained by the perceived usefulness by the members of the Facebook group, who could access a variety of information from different medical specialties [3, 15, 20]. Likewise, the theme developed arose from the prior planning carried out by consensus of the health professionals administrators of the Facebook group, who based on their own experiences and the prevalence of pathologies, established a schedule of activities, which were important for people and their families.

Regarding satisfaction with the aforementioned dimensions, other authors have found positive results when government authorities take part in the development of educational activities through, for example, their official Facebook pages. Therefore, the motivation and coordinated work of the authorities with community organizations is necessary for the dissemination of varied and relevant information for the population, as part of public health policies [14].

On the other hand, with regard to the perception of the veracity of the information and the quick response to inquiries, high satisfaction scores were also evidenced, which would be related to the positive effect of the participation and continuous monitoring of health professionals properly trained. The COVID-19 pandemic has meant restrictions on patient care; so many people have had to turn to sources of information whose origin cannot be verified. The knowledge of the identity and academic preparation of the responsible professionals allows the establishment of a relationship of greater trust [21, 22], which is valued positively as evidenced in the present study.

Research carried out in India and Australia [2, 23] has shown that people's trust in the administrators of social media pages is a very important factor not only to ensure participation, but also their permanence in the initiatives that may be proposed, together with the ability to be critical of the content that is shared [21]. The opposite can lead to mistrust, which can later turn into panic and severe mental health impairment [2].

Another aspect that is related to what is mentioned in the preceding paragraphs is that in many countries such as Peru, the participation of professionals has not been taken into account for the dissemination of truthful information through the use of information and communication technologies. Thus, to date in Peru there is no corresponding legal framework that effectively sanctions the dissemination of fake news, especially in areas as sensitive as medicine and health in general [24]. This situation has led health professionals to approach their patients independently and on their own initiative, through resources at their disposal such as social networks.

Special attention deserves the problem of training the general population with respect to information security and the timely identification of fake news, especially when until before the pandemic; people had not received sufficient training on such topics [1, 7, 8]. This reality is very common in Peru, where the digital divide is still very marked, especially the digital divide in technological skills, which increases the chances of being a victim of medical misinformation on the Internet.

The dimension corresponding to the Netiquette or rules of cordiality on Facebook, was the only one in which the majority of people expressed an indifferent position or dissatisfaction. These results undoubtedly show that this is an aspect that still needs to be worked on, not only by those who as in the present case, are in charge of the administration of a Facebook group, but also by the entire community on the Internet [25, 26]. In this way, new areas of research remain pending where intervention initiatives can be addressed to improve the rules of cordiality in social networks in general, for example through the participation of other professionals related to psychology.

Regarding the differences found in the satisfaction responses according to gender and age of the members of the Facebook group administered by health professionals; this is due to the fact that, according to what has been concluded in previous studies, women show greater interest in the health care issues [27, 28]. This behavior in turn, would be related to the fact that in many countries such as Peru, women are the ones who are mostly in charge of caring for the health of their children at home [27], as evidenced in the present research where the majority of participants were housewives.

About the differences found with respect to the age of the participants, which favored young people with higher satisfaction scores, this is due to the fact that it is easier for them to access and use social networks, which allows greater interaction and therefore better opportunities to satisfy their information needs [29]. Quite the opposite would happen in the case of older people, who despite the interest they may have in the issues raised about health care, show greater problems for virtual participation, which would affect their perception in general. Likewise, it is important to highlight that according to the findings made known in other studies, older people have better abilities to recognize and face medical fake news [29, 30], which could be considered in new research with certain age groups.

Finally, it is important to state the presence of several limitations in the development of this study, such as the non-identification of other aspects related to satisfaction with information on social networks and their variations according to the time of intervention, especially in a context of sanitary emergency, due to the cross-sectional design applied. Likewise, no external and internal factors were identified that could have affected the perception of the members of the Facebook group administered by health professionals, so the results could be different in other contexts and with professionals from other areas of knowledge. However, despite these limitations, it is important to highlight the importance and contributions of this research, which can serve as a basis for the development of new studies.

5   Conclusions and Future Steps

5.1   Conclusions

It was concluded the presence of high levels of satisfaction with respect to the information received on health care and the prevention of medical fake news on Facebook during the COVID-19 pandemic in Peru, after voluntary participation for 5 months in a group of said social network administered by health professionals. Likewise, it was concluded that there were statistically significant differences with respect to the gender and age of the participants, whose respect for netiquette or rules of cordiality on Facebook should be improved. What has been stated constitutes evidence in favor of the responsible use of social networks for the benefit of the population, through the participation of trained professionals.

5.2   Future Steps

The findings disclosed in this research can be taken into account for the realization of new studies that address the problem of medical fake news. In this way, it is suggested to address the influence of external and internal factors that could be affecting the dissemination of such fake news, as well as satisfaction with the information provided and its variations over time. The participation of other health professionals and specialists in other areas of knowledge could allow the study of other aspects and applications that make it possible to improve the dissemination of truthful information, especially in health emergency contexts.

Acknowledgements. To the people who voluntarily agreed to participate throughout the research process, for their trust and commitment. To the health professionals who contributed their knowledge and experience to the determination and development of the topics to be discussed in the Facebook group.

References

1. Mamak, K.: Do we need the criminalization of medical fake news? Med. Health Care Philos. **24**(2), 235–245 (2021). https://doi.org/10.1007/s11019-020-09996-7
2. Bhattacharya, C., et al.: The nature, cause and consequence of COVID-19 panic among social media users in India. Soc. Netw. Anal. Min. **11**(1), 1–11 (2021). https://doi.org/10.1007/s13 278-021-00750-2
3. Biancovilli, P., Makszin, L., Csongor, A.: Breast cancer on social media: a quali-quantitative study on the credibility and content type of the most shared news stories. BMC Womens Health **21**, 202 (2021). https://doi.org/10.1186/s12905-021-01352-y
4. Bender, J.L., et al.: Internet and social media use in cancer patients: association with distress and perceived benefits and limitations. Support. Care Cancer **29**(9), 5273–5281 (2021). https://doi.org/10.1007/s00520-021-06077-0
5. Pianese, T., Belfiore, P.: Exploring the social networks' use in the health-care industry: a multi-level analysis. Int. J. Environ. Res. Public Health **18**(14), 7295 (2021). https://doi.org/10.3390/ijerph18147295
6. Biancovilli, P., Makszin, L., Jurberg, C.: Misinformation on social networks during the novel coronavirus pandemic: a quali-quantitative case study of Brazil. BMC Public Health **21**, 1200 (2021). https://doi.org/10.1186/s12889-021-11165-1
7. Wawrzuta, D., Jaworski, M., Gotlib, J., Panczyk, M.: Characteristics of antivaccine messages on social media: systematic review. J. Med. Internet Res. **23**(6), e24564 (2021). https://doi.org/10.2196/24564
8. Waszak, P., Kasprzycka-Waszak, W., Kubanek, A.: The spread of medical fake news in social media – the pilot quantitative study. Health Policy Technol. **7**(2), 115–118 (2018). https://doi.org/10.1016/j.hlpt.2018.03.002
9. Zhang, X., Cozma, R.: Risk sharing on Twitter: Social amplification and attenuation of risk in the early stages of the COVID-19 pandemic. Comput. Hum. Behav. **126**, 106983 (2022). https://doi.org/10.1016/j.chb.2021.106983
10. Bozzola, E., et al.: Social media use to improve communication on children and adolescent's health: the role of the Italian Paediatric Society influencers. Ital. J. Pediatr. **47**, 171 (2021). https://doi.org/10.1186/s13052-021-01111-7
11. Pereira, A., Cabaços, C., Araújo, A., Amaral, A., Carvalho, F., Macedo, A.: COVID-19 psychological impact: the role of perfectionism. Personal. Individ. Differ. **184**, 111160 (2022). https://doi.org/10.1016/j.paid.2021.111160
12. Heuschen, A., et al.: Public health-relevant consequences of the COVID-19 pandemic on malaria in sub-Saharan Africa: a scoping review. Malar. J. **20**, 339 (2021). https://doi.org/10.1186/s12936-021-03872-2
13. Zhang, Q., Zheng, R., Fu, Y., Mu, Q., Li, J.: Mental health consequences during alerting situations and recovering to a new normal of coronavirus epidemic in 2019: a cross-sectional study based on the affected population. BMC Public Health **21**, 1499 (2021). https://doi.org/10.1186/s12889-021-11550-w
14. Al-Shakhanbeh, Z.M., Habes, M.: The relationship between the government's official Facebook pages and healthcare awareness during covid-19 in Jordan. In: Hassanien, A.-E., Elghamrawy, S.M., Zelinka, I. (eds.) Advances in Data Science and Intelligent Data Communication Technologies for COVID-19. SSDC, vol. 378, pp. 221–238. Springer, Cham (2022). https://doi.org/10.1007/978-3-030-77302-1_12
15. Shehab, N.A.: the dark side of social media: spreading misleading information during covid-19 crisis. In: Hassanien, A.-E., Elghamrawy, S.M., Zelinka, I. (eds.) Advances in Data Science and Intelligent Data Communication Technologies for COVID-19. SSDC, vol. 378, pp. 277–306. Springer, Cham (2022). https://doi.org/10.1007/978-3-030-77302-1_15

16. Wisk, L., Buhr, R.: Rapid deployment of a community engagement study and educational trial via social media: implementation of the UC-COVID study. Trials **22**, 513 (2021). https://doi.org/10.1186/s13063-021-05467-3

17. Green, H., Fernandez, R., MacPhail, C.: Social media as a platform for recruitment to a national survey during the COVID-19 pandemic: feasibility and cost analysis. JMIR Form Res. **5**(7), e28656 (2021). https://doi.org/10.2196/28656

18. World Medical Association: Declaration of Helsinki – Ethical principles for medical research involving human subjects. https://www.wma.net/policies-post/wma-declaration-of-helsinki-ethical-principles-for-medical-research-involving-human-subjects/. Accessed 28 June 2021

19. Lanius, C., Weber, R., MacKenzie, W.I.: Use of bot and content flags to limit the spread of misinformation among social networks: a behavior and attitude survey. Soc. Netw. Anal. Min. **11**(1), 1–15 (2021). https://doi.org/10.1007/s13278-021-00739-x

20. Ma, T., Lambert, K.: What are the information needs and concerns of individuals with polycystic kidney disease? Results of an online survey using Facebook and social listening analysis. BMC Nephrol. **22**, 263 (2021). https://doi.org/10.1186/s12882-021-02472-1

21. Goodyear, V.A., et al.: Social media use informing behaviours related to physical activity, diet and quality of life during COVID-19: a mixed methods study. BMC Public Health **21**(1), 1333 (2021). https://doi.org/10.1186/s12889-021-11398-0

22. Goodyear, V., Good, G., Skinner, B., Thompson, J.: The effect of social media interventions on physical activity and dietary behaviours in young people and adults: a systematic review. J. Behav. Nutr. Phys. Act **18**, 72 (2021). https://doi.org/10.1186/s12966-021-01138-3

23. Wallis, K., Prichard, I., Hart, L., Yager, Z.: The body confident mums challenge: a feasibility trial and qualitative evaluation of a body acceptance program delivered to mothers using Facebook. BMC Public Health **21**, 1052 (2021). https://doi.org/10.1186/s12889-021-11126-8

24. Przepiórka, A., et al.: Facebook intrusion as a mediator between positive capital and general distress: a cross-cultural study. Front. Psychiatry **12**, 667536 (2021). https://doi.org/10.3389/fpsyt.2021.667536

25. Mistretta, S.: The new netiquette: Choosing civility in an age of online teaching and learning. Int. J. E-Learn. Corp. Govern. Healthcare Higher Educ. **20**(3), 323–345 (2021)

26. Soler-Costa, R., Lafarga-Ostáriz, P., Mauri-Medrano, M., Moreno-Guerrero, A.: Netiquette: ethic, education, and behavior on Internet—a systematic literature review. Int. J. Environ. Res. Public Health **18**(3), 1212 (2021). https://doi.org/10.3390/ijerph18031212

27. Miani, C., Namer, Y.: Women's voices on social media: the advent of feminist epidemiology? Emerg. Themes Epidemiol. **18**, 7 (2021). https://doi.org/10.1186/s12982-021-00097-1

28. Smith, R., Alvarez, C., Crixell, S., Lane, M.: The food, feelings, and family study: Comparison of the efficacy of traditional methods, social media, and broadcast email to recruit pregnant women to an observational, longitudinal nutrition study. BMC Pregnancy Childbirth **21**, 203 (2021). https://doi.org/10.1186/s12884-021-03680-1

29. Pang, H.: Connecting mobile social media with psychosocial well-being: understanding relationship between WeChat involvement, network characteristics, online capital and life satisfaction. Soc. Netw. **68**, 256–263 (2022). https://doi.org/10.1016/j.socnet.2021.08.006

30. Sama, A., et al.: The impact of social media presence, age, and patient reported wait times on physician review websites for sports medicine surgeons. J. Clin. Orthop. Trauma **21**, 101502 (2021). https://doi.org/10.1016/j.jcot.2021.101502

Natural Language to Facilitate the Analysis of Statistical Evaluation of Educational Digital Games

Nayeth Solórzano Alcívar[1]([⊠]) [iD], Robert Zambrano Loor[2] [iD],
and Diego Carrera Gallego[3] [iD]

[1] Escuela Superior Politécnica del Litoral, ESPOL – FADCOM, Guayaquil, Ecuador
nsolorza@espol.edu.ec
[2] Escuela Superior Politécnica del Litoral, ESPOL – FIEC, Guayaquil, Ecuador
rjloor@espol.edu.ec
[3] UPM Universidad Politécnica de Madrid, UPM, Madrid, España
dcarrera@espol.edu.ec

Abstract. The application of educational digital games (EDG) requires multiple perspectives for an optimal adaptation. This study shows how relevant feedback is presented in simple outcome reports of EDG-based learning for teachers and parents in Natural Language (NL). NL as a Machine Learning process also can represent quantitative data sets in consumable Spanish language statements. The objective is to improve outcomes of EDG platforms using a cloud-based dashboard used to evaluate student EDG application behavioral efficiency. A novel tool is proposed to provide simple language explanations rather than statistical representations of feedback to parents and teachers in marginal areas of developing economies. With fuzzy logic, the researchers present verbatim explanations of student behavior towards educational EDG. Results reveal comprehensive, simple, or colloquial Spanish language information for parents and teachers to provide improved evaluation keys to enhance student learning via EDG related to the school curricula.

Keywords: Educational technology · Spanish language · Serious games · Artificial Intelligence · Machine learning · Learning Analytics · Fuzzy logic · MIDI-AM · PQM-Metrics · Game-based learning · Usability · Playability

1 Introduction

The growing acceptance of digital games or serious games brought the interest in its use for learning purposes [1]. Thus, multiple perspectives must be considered to apply educational digital games (EDG) and evaluate their usefulness and playability in learning environments in simple ways as is possible. The application of using common Spanish language or colloquial language as Natural Language (NL) to interpret EDG's statistical results is a challenge, primarily when dealing with a low academic level audience who requests to understand such results. Serious game platforms used as a teaching and learning process strategy can monitor statistically usage behavior and playability factors of EDG storing and monitoring data through a dashboard [2]. However, according to Bahi

© Springer Nature Switzerland AG 2021
J. P. Salgado Guerrero et al. (Eds.): TICEC 2021, CCIS 1456, pp. 127–141, 2021.
https://doi.org/10.1007/978-3-030-89941-7_10

and Necibi [3], many teachers stay skeptical regarding the objectivity of automatic scores given by computer applications, even with highly advanced scoring statistic methods. This observation, together with the matter that in developing economies like Ecuador, several teachers in low-income primary schools with only undergraduate degrees, statistical interpretation is a gap in knowledge among this population [4]. This study contributes to overcoming these limitations using fuzzy logic in developing a novel tool to provide written simple language explanations rather than a statistical representation for teachers' and parents' understanding.

The preliminary finding of this study [5], with an extended discussion of the outcomes in this article, indicates that in the past two decades, several studies have identified the importance of using ludic videogames (defined as serious games) or EDG for mobile applications as educational tools for children and adolescents. Computer advancement and mobile technologies have supported these games' development and dramatic learning growth [6, 7]. The games design with meaningful content and challenges accomplished an objective impacts social interaction, learning communities, and culture [8]. Some authors explain that EDG has great positive potential to address specific problems, educate about global issues, or teach particular skills [6, 7]. In addition to their entertainment value, these games provide a mental test for any consumer [6, 9]. Furthermore, observational studies have revealed that videogames or EDG are a preferred learning tool that effectively motivates and encourages proactivity among children [7].

However, a gap in the games market is evident regarding considerations of inclusion of educational values and academic content that follow and support the curricula for children. In addition, very few applications allow data exportation to track gaming results for measuring children's behavioral use and other usability factors, except for the game playability studies such as Playability Quality Model (PQM-Metric) research proposed González and Gutiérrez [10]. The possibility of measuring academic sense using EDG as teaching tools could provide useful information to demonstrate how EDG stimulates children's cognitive development [11].

Furthermore, academic experts in Learning Analytics (LA) explain applications' existence to build dashboards from data collected by users on the network (Siemens [12]. The dashboard helps monitor users to get the necessary data on their interests and obtain indicators for planning interactive games used in classes. The content is related to the data stored in a cloud and shown on the dashboard about children's behavioral use and playability. Usually, the dashboard administration option results show descriptive statistic values, graphics, and tables [13]. However, the problem arises when people who interpret the results have limited knowledge of statistics and graphs.

Natural Language (NL) process is the ability of a computer program to understand spoken and written human language. Computer machinery can develop a dataset of machine learning capabilities to carry out a cognitive structure that flares up in NL process tasks, both in data collection and annotation. According to Powers and Turk [14], for more than thirty years of research made with NL processing, smart programs demonstrate how it emulates the actual process of understanding a language as a concept of the Machine Learning (ML) method. NL application can be applied as an ML process using Artificial Intelligence (AI) for interpreting quantitative data produced and stored in a system. An AI technique that allows making decisions for handling imprecision is fuzzy logic [15]. The research question is how to apply fuzzy logic to interpret statistics EDG using simple Spanish language presented as a textual explanation suitable for understanding any audience lacking statistical knowledge?

The testing case used is the series of EDG "Children's Interactive Didactic Multimedia," MIDI (acronym in Spanish) applied to mobile devices, identified as the MIDI-AM series [2, 13]. The objective is to propose an alternative method of showing statistical data administered in a MIDI dashboard to be emulated in NL as qualitative assessments, more understandable for users. This work's focus involves using artificial intelligence through fuzzy logic to explain the statistical graphs results in the MIDI dashboard in colloquial or straightforward Spanish. The metrics determined allow analyzing the degrees of playability and usability of the MIDI-AM mobile application games series. According to Plass, Homer, and Kinzer [1], moving beyond simple play-by learning goals aims to prepare future learning measurable within games and incorporate playful learning principles as part of the design, rather than adding to existing structures.

1.1 Theoretical Framework

In Ecuador, academia has driven some initiatives to design and encourage monitored "serious game" with academic content for the primary school. Researchers have developed "Children's Interactive Didactic Multimedia" mobile applications with animated cartoons and EDG identified as MIDI-AM (Spanish acronym). This EDG generates control data for usability in a JavaScript Object Notation (JSON) stored in a database in a cloud for usability and playability measurements manage in a dashboard. The dashboard framework provides statistical feedback to parents and teachers about the content's progress and the game level [2, 13].

Nevertheless, teachers and parents who can use the dashboard as a tool to control the MIDI-AM series videogames outcomes may not have sufficient technical knowledge about statistics to interpret the metrics used to analyze playability and usefulness. For example, several low-income primary school teachers, subsidized by the government, have undergraduate degrees in Ecuador. Hence, statistical interpretation is a gap in knowledge among the population [4].

Concepts, Techniques and Fuzzy Logic Applied on NL Process

For this study, the researchers applied LA and used AI through fuzzy logic as a technique of AI that allows to make decisions [15] and to predict results base on the outcomes of the decisions of the game players [16]. Furthermore, this case aims to explain numeric values in NL, which were previously shown in statistical graphs and figures as the dashboard outcomes.

In the last decade, LA emerges as a growing area of Technology-Enhanced Learning (TEL) with a secure connection among various fields, including business intelligence, educational data mining, recommender systems, and web analytics [17]. LA is the collection, analysis, measurements, and presentation of data collected in learning sessions to understand and improve it from various perspectives. According to Elias [18], the typical phases of LA are four. These phases start with obtaining raw data. Secondly, the data obtained give meaningful information. Thirdly, information accomplishes knowledge from its analysis and synthesis, and finally, it achieves objectives from the use of knowledge considered a Wisdom stage.

The technology used in a dashboard is the rebirth of Executive Information Systems (EIS) to enhance a manager's ability to process information and act [19]. Its usefulness relies on aspects of business intelligence [20]. With dashboard use, the extent of specific data can be analyzed and measured to overview what is going on clearly and rapidly [20, 21]. Besides, the dashboards are rising in popularity, structured into different types according to their functional and visual features. However, they face the challenge of providing the right information to the right people at the right moment [18]. The dashboard structure chosen for the developed module is like the Klipfolio type, which facilitates comparisons and readings of large monthly or time-period data for knowing aspects that should or can be corrected in an analysis that visualizes all open issues for a specific project [22, 23].

Fuzzy logic is a technique of AI with the capacity to handle imprecisions to make decisions [15]. According to Bahi and Necibi [3], fuzzy logic promotes soft frontiers that would make more consensus between scores obtained, overcoming limitations related to the rating disparities that can make teachers more comfortable with automatic scores. This technique also provides a mechanism of inference that simulates human reasoning, imprecise by nature, based on a knowledge system [24]. The purpose is to systematically apply fuzzy concepts by considering human thought elements that do not manage numbers but concepts. For example, concepts expressed as fuzzy sets are: "brilliant," "very attractive," "more successful," "less successful," and more others intermediate rages such as "little less than hot" or "too cold" or "more or less warm" [24, 25].

In Fig. 1, the process starts with crisp numeric values entered as a discrete input. Next, these values go through the fuzzifier for providing a qualitative appreciation. Next, qualitative evaluation values are processed through the inference engine and the fuzzy or linguistic rules that compose the knowledge base. Hence, the result becomes another qualitative value, and it goes through the process of defuzzification that converts the qualitative values to quantitative [26].

Fig. 1. The general structure of fuzzy logic. Adapted from [26]

The fuzzy logic is related to fuzzy set theory, where a membership function provides the most appropriate level for an element and follows a human reasoning pattern [24, 26]. In this regard, it is possible to supply more element conditions including not only "low," "medium," and "high" but also "very low," "relatively high," "slightly low," among others [2]. Besides, different ranges of values between 0 to 1 can be assigned to identify, for example, "satisfactory," "unique," or "necessary" conditions for membership functions in a selection case [27].

Furthermore, these functions allow knowledge representation applies to Fuzzy Inference Systems (GIS) as human thought does. This system defines a non-linear correspondence between input variables and output variables from the determined fuzzy set. Thus, since creating fuzzy algorithms, there is a criterion for making decisions [24, 28]. The steps that comprise a fuzzy inference system summarized in Solorzano, Loor, Gonzabay, and Vintimilla [5] are:

- The definition of input and output variables with their linguistic values and their membership functions.
- The definition of the rules specifying the relationship between the input and the output variables.

  - The case of If–Then rules "specifies the relationship between the entry and output variables of the system. The diffuse relationships determine the degree of presence or absence of association or interaction among elements of 2 or more sets" [28].
  - The impersonation of IF–Then rules, usually defined from experts' knowledge through interviews, involves two steps. First, the researchers evaluate the antecedent by applying any diffuse operator. The second step is applying the antecedent result in the consequent [28], assuming the form as follows:

  - If X1 is A1 and X2 is A2 and… Xk is Ak, Then Y is B
  - Where A1, A2, …, Ak, and B are linguistic values defined in fuzzy sets for linguistic variables X1, X2, …, Xk, and Y, respectively.

- The outputs of the rules are combined to obtain a single fuzzy set with determined ranges. This process is commutative mining in that the order in each adding rule's output does not matter.

2 Materials and Methods

In a pragmatic and pluralistic approach, all the existing research methods and tools are relevant for guiding multidisciplinary research to solve a problem without compromising any specific method [27, 29]. This mix-method quantitative-qualitative research focuses on using artificial intelligence through fuzzy logic, explaining in NL the statistical graphs of a dashboard that show results about the level of efficiency, effectivity, flexibility, satisfaction, and playability EDG.

For the testing process, we obtain the data from the dashboard of the MIDI-AM games played by any children freely and for groups of children. The target children were those attending the first, and second-level classes in primary schools of low-income areas of Guayaquil monitored as pilot schools for this study. All the children were monitored with the corresponding ethical consent and permission from the school authorities and parents. The data obtained from the EDG played is sent through a JSON to the database tables, operated by a dashboard stored in the cloud. The dashboard's quantitative data is tested and alternatively processed using fuzzy analysis applied to NL. The outcomes written as simple statements are qualitative assessments more understandable for any user.

The MIDI Data Process. The raw data is obtained by employing previously developed games in research studies [2]. The data are collected through a JSON from four MIDI-AM series games created as beta applications. These games' objective is to examine the degrees of efficiency, effectivity, flexibility, and satisfaction and measure the games' use and playability levels. All the data collected are stored in a cloud database linked to an implemented dashboard [2, 13]. The EDG apps are available through the MIDI[1] a webpage or as a direct download from the Google Play Store.

When a child plays with these apps, related information is stored in a database. The information is related to the behavior and performance of the child using an EDG. The data reception structure designed shows the level of content by chapter related to a specific topic, animated story (content), and testing games by level. Then, the data recorded through a JSON is uploaded in a database implemented in PostgreSQL with the dashboard [2].

With the production of the MIDI-AM series, the process and structure used to develop EDG need to be documented to give continuity to support games for early childhood education in their different areas of knowledge. Thus, new games' creations can follow this methodology and use the same data structure to generate control data in JSON.

MIDI-AM games are specially instrumented to work with the proposed EDG games designed. If any other type of videogame applications need to be used to collect initial raw data, this could be done by including a JSON routine structured with the same design for MIDI-AM apps. A bridging connection can then be created to post generated data stored in a cloud database operated by the MIDI dashboard.

The required components for implementing a fuzzy interpretation system are the linguistic variable and the fuzzy sets. In an initial stage developed for this project, the technical researchers selected the linguistic variables from the metrics table. The quality table of metrics was obtained by combining the measure of quality in the development of the videogames or EDG, entitled Playability Quality Model (PQM-Metrics), and expanding the concept of Effectiveness and Efficiency with the Technology Acceptance Model (TAM) [2, 30].

A module to be implemented uses the same platform and tools previously applied for the existing dashboard. The dashboard is developed in Sailsjs with a section in Angular. The language that handles these frameworks is JavaScript [2]. The module converts the metrics or linguistic variables (Low, Medium, High) into NL using linguistic criteria. The meaning of each valuation is defined as a conclusion rule for pedagogical review. These rules added in a database table are part of the Postgresql database architecture used with a dashboard application.

The linguistic variables are the quality parameters measured in a fuzzy interpretation system, where fuzzy values define their valuations. The determining variables are Efficiency - Time that takes to complete the levels; Effectivity - Completed levels; Flexibility - player interaction in different scenarios; and Satisfaction - Preference of one level compared to others.

---

[1] http://midi.espol.edu.ec/.

3   Data Analysis and Results

3.1   Definition of Linguistic Input/Output Variables

The system model's implementation process, linked to the dashboard as a component of the current research, comprises the input variables used through the inference system to obtain the output variable results defined as follows:

Efficiency – As an input variable, represents the degree to which variables can accomplish the proposed goals by investing an appropriate number of resources to achieve effective use. It has five linguistic variables: a. Goal time; b. Target efficiency for correct answers; c. Target efficiency for incorrect answers; d. Efficiency relative to the best player results; e. Efficiency is relative to players with difficulties in the level. Finally, a. Efficiency is its output variable.

Effectivity – As an input variable represents the degree to which the variables can achieve the proposed goals precisely and completely. It has three linguistic variables: a. Effectiveness of the goal; b. Completeness of the goal; c. Frequency of attempts to reach the goal. B. Effectivity is its output variable.

Flexibility – As an input variable represents the degree to which the conditions can vary by test. It has two linguistic variables: a. Accessibility by goals; b. Accessibility by time. C. Flexibility is its output variable.

Satisfaction – As an input variable represents the degree to which players feel good when reaching a goal. It has only one linguistic variable: Preferences of use concerning the level versus the rest of the levels. D. Satisfaction is its output variable.

Playability – As an input variable, receive a set of properties that allow describing the player's game experience. This variable obtains its input of linguistic variables results from the outputs variables in the previous processes of A. Efficiency, B. Effectiveness, C. Flexibility, and D. Satisfaction. Therefore, the A, B, C, and D variable becomes the input variables for the final evaluation to measure Playability. Thus, E. Playability is the overall output variable of the entire process.

Finally, the list of values assigned for the fuzzy set and each variable's initials ranges describe the maximums and minimums obtained. Each input variable is necessary to provide a fuzzy set such as low, medium, and high (see Table 1). The values for each variable have a dynamic change concerning the data produced each time a user plays.

Table 1. Fuzzy input/output sets of linguistic variables with maximum and minimum

Inputs variables process		
Variables	Fuzzy set	Initial ranges (max. & min.)
Efficiency input	Low, medium, high	a. [70, 110], b. [5.45, 8.57], c. [0, 3.85], c. [0, 100], d. [0, 100]
Efficiency output	Low, medium, high	A. Efficiency
Effectivity input	Low, medium, high	a. [0, 100], b. [0, 100], c. [1, 4]
Effectivity output	Low, medium, high	B. Effectivity
Flexibility input	Low, medium, high	a. [0, 100], b. [0, 100]
Flexibility output	Low, medium, high	C. Flexibility
Satisfaction input	Low, medium, high	a. [0, 100]
Satisfaction output	Low, medium, high	D. Satisfaction
Outputs variables process		
Playability input	Low, medium, high	A. Efficiency, B. Effectiveness, C. Flexibility, and D. Satisfaction
Playability output	Low, medium, high	E. Playability

3.2 Fuzzy Rules and Linguistic

A table with interpretation criteria for each linguistic variable is coded, using composed statements for each variable's conclusion. In other words, the linguistic criteria are written as statements for Spanish speakers linking rules for combining cases. For coding the linguistic rules, the fuzzy set of numeric equivalences used are $0 = $ Low, $1 = $ Medium, $2 = $ High, and $3 = $ Inconsistent. For example, in a combination of the linguistic variables' value, as a conclusion rule determined for efficiency in a, b, c, d $= 0$ and e $= 2$. Then, the A-Efficiency outcome will be 3. Thus, for the linguistic criteria of a 'Conclusion Efficiency Rule,' the composed statement is stated as follows "Inconsistent results ($A = 3$). If the target efficiency for correct answers is low ($c = 0$), the incorrect answers' target efficiency should be high ($c = 2$) and never low ($c = 0$)."

A database table of conclusion variables rules statements is generally defined from their fuzzy set, considering the metrics and the parameters involved. Continuing with Efficiency values example, if the valuation that takes "a. (goal time)" is "low," it does not necessarily mean that this variable negatively affects the overall efficiency. On the contrary, it is convenient that the goal time or the average time children use to complete a level is low. In this case, to understand why the final efficiency assessment (A) receives the value it takes, it is first defined whether the valuations of a, b, c, d, e mean something good or bad, as described in Table 2.

In each case, the number of fuzzy rules is related to the number of inputted linguistic variables. The formula to obtain the total number of rules in A = Efficiency is 35 = 243; for B = Effectivity is 33 = 27; for C = Flexibility is 32 = 9, and for D = Satisfaction is 31 = 3. In playability as the output variable result, a total of rules is 34 = 81.

Table 2. The real contribution of the Efficiency example [5]

Variables	Assessment	Contributions	Assessment	Contributions	Assessment	Contributions
a	High	Bad (low)	Medium	Medium	Low	Good (high)
b	High	Good (high)	Medium	Medium	Low	Bad (low)
c	High	Bad (low)	Medium	Medium	Low	Good (high)
d	High	Good (high)	Medium	Medium	Low	Bad (low)
e	High	Bad (low)	Medium	Medium	Low	Good (high)

3.3 Outcomes Evaluation

Testing processes were carried out after implementing the proposed modules as simple Spanish language-translation tools of statistical results. The application processed data records stored in a previous stage of this study, and new data was collected. The data stored in the cloud included 699 children using the EDG freely at home and monitored by teachers at school. The EDG tested were used in the second semester of the year academic calendar between 2019–2020 to complement the learning process about the content of Natural Environment teaching to children between 4 to 7 years old who were attending the first and second level of primary school. With this data, we undertook several tests for analyzing favorable and unfavorable cases completed. For example, Fig. 2 shows a MIDI-dashboard view presenting the number of children monitored and statistic graphs of the Story game time view (yellow bars) and gaming completed and abandoned (Green bars) of the entire series 'Natural Environment.'

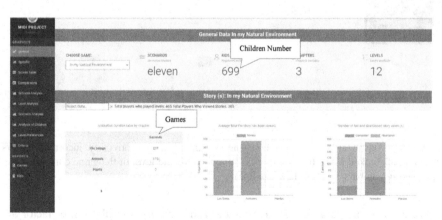

Fig. 2. MIDI-dashboard view -number of children monitored and EDG story statistic graphs- (Color figure online)

The testing was primarily done examining the data from the MIDI-dashboard about the game series "En mi Entorno Natural" (In my Natural Environment), with the chapters named in Spanish "Los Seres" (The Beings), "Animales" (Animals), and "Plantas"

(Plants) see Fig. 3. These game series are continually used in schools selected to be favored with this project as a pilot school in low-income sectors in Guayaquil, Ecuador, encouraging the use of technology and education using active learning. The EDG used in tablets and mobile phones as part of an active learning process complements the academic curriculum content in the Spanish language determined by the Ministry of Education of Ecuador for primary education. These EDG tested are part of the MIDI-AM apps available in beta versions in the Google Play Store.[2]

Fig. 3. MIDI-Dashboard statistic results (Using the games showing correct and incorrect answers (blue and pink stoked bars), time by games -yellow bars-, and level of the game completed and abandoned -green bars-). (Color figure online)

For each of the game levels, metrics of each usability and playability factor are calculated. Figure 4 is an example showing a Spanish results table with a qualitative valuation between low, medium, and high for each factor range obtained for the case of Natural Environment – Beings-Activity-4.

Finally, general evaluation statements of Playability metrics are shown to assess each factor evaluated through fuzzy analysis. See Fig. 5, presenting an example of assessment

---

[2] http://midi.espol.edu.ec/descargaproductos/.

outcome cases evaluated. The results can be favorable (high, medium), unfavorable (low), or inconsistency detected (when data identified was incomplete) to finally obtain the Playability outcomes from the metrics calculated. In this case, a low Playability result is shown. These factors help end-users to evaluate the dashboard outcomes, presenting more precise results based on the metric.

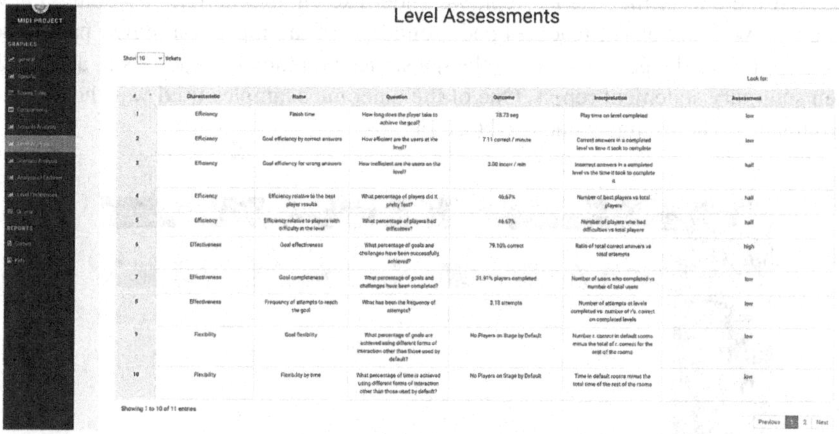

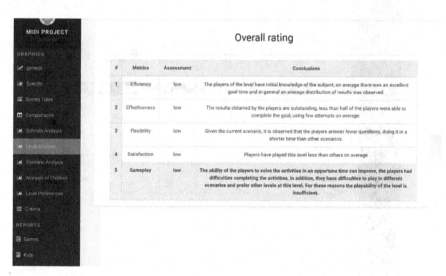

Fig. 4. MIDI-Dashboard screen showing n fragment assessing table of Efficiency, Effectivity, Flexibility, Satisfaction, and Playability metrics in Natural Language outcomes (translated).

Fig. 5. General evaluation of Metrics in Spanish Natural Language statements (translated).

4   Discussion Results and Conclusion

Teachers from the three selected schools and 130 parents (related to children who used the MIDI-AM games series in schools placed in low-income areas) were invited for focus groups and interviews for the undertaken tests. The first focus group began explaining to them the use of the games, how children can play the games on tablets and mobile phones. At the end of the scholar year, we undertake another activity by doing a new focus group with six of the teachers and around 30 of the most committed parents to monitor the use of the game, showing them a statics graphic outcome. Then, a Spanish written summary statement report. One of the outcome examples used was the Natural Environment – The Beings game used (see Fig. 6).

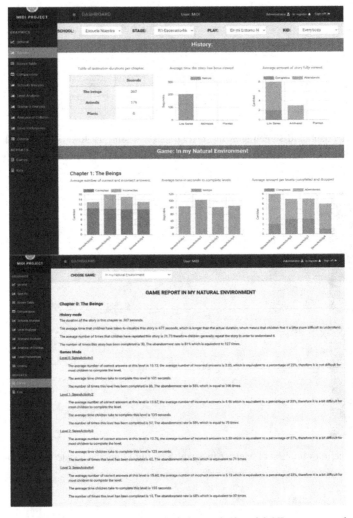

Fig. 6. MIDI-Dashboard results in a statistic graph (Spanish NL report translated)

We noted that all of them remain just observing the statistic graphic (Fig. 6, frame above), expecting us an explanation about them. However, Teachers and parents read the report when we showed them the information translated to NL using simple Spanish explaining the same graphic outcomes (Fig. 6, frame below). After reading the LN report, they gave us their opinion. Also, they provided feedback about what they think concerning the outcome obtained and what they can do to encourage the game to use better (if the reading results were not okay). Besides, the teachers were motivated to recommend improvements for the game to obtain better results.

Additionally, using the fuzzy NL application adapted to the MIDI dashboard and the teachers' evaluation based on the written Spanish report, we detected some inconsistencies in the data that need to be removed periodically. For example, the limit of time and abandoned games occurs because they leave the game open, causing inconsistencies in the time game. Parents and teachers also recommended more NL reports containing written information about children's game usage and playability individually and by level.

From the interviews and focus group observation results, we identify that primary school teachers and parents understood the Spanish NL information presented in the reports and, in some cases, on the screen. However, they did not make much comment about the possible understanding of statistical graphics. Thus, it was verified that fuzzy logic could be applied to interpret educational video games metrics statistics using simple Spanish language presenting results as a textual explanation, suitable for understanding any audience with a lack of statistics knowledge.

4.1 Conclusions

The proposed solution results meet the objective of moving beyond simple play by learning goals to prepare future learning measurable within games with feedback easy to understand to any audience, facilitating incorporating playful learning principles as part of the design. Fuzzy logic converts crisp numeric values of metrics obtained from mobile game applications into a narrated common Spanish language to NL easy-to-understand answer the research question. We conducted several qualitative tests using the developed module with observation techniques to gather adults' opinions on children's education. Also, a quantitative analysis of various cases was taken from 728 records of users playing the games, at home, or attending one of the three primary schools of low-income areas in Guayaquil, Ecuador (used as pilot groups). We extracted the minimum and maximum of each of the metrics used from the data.

Moreover, we identified the level and number of players who completed several games with their level to be played. Both favorable and unfavorable cases showing relevant information or inconsistency are presented in NL as written Spanish sentences that are easy to understand for parents and teachers at primary schools. Besides, unusual data uploaded and monitored in a dashboard can be debugged and corrected after any inconsistent review period. However, more evaluation from primary schools' teachers and parents needs to refine the NL results.

The outcomes and the developed tools provided more reliable results of EDG monitored in a dashboard, focusing on people without statistical knowledge. Thus, we have expanded the scalability concept of using any application to understand different users involved in primary education who might not have technical skills.

4.2 Future Work

The linguistic rules generated for EDG Spanish language feedback are static for three levels (low, medium, high). The improved tool to be developed to evaluate EDG, especially measuring their usefulness and playability in learning environments, should keep as simple as is possible but more flexible to increase the outcomes options for stakeholder's analysis. For games learning interpretation of outcomes feedback in NL intermediate conclusions, rules for the metric evaluated with the dashboard are recommended. However, conclusions must be more dynamic regarding the results in an expanded fuzzy system set of inferences. In this regard, it is also essential to consider revising the Spanish compositions statement's structure based on more experts' professional criteria in psychology, pedagogy, and copywriters to expand fundamental linguistic rules for the feedback's outcomes generated.

Acknowledgements. We wished to acknowledge ESPOL University for sponsoring the continuity of this research and publications. Particularly, we recognize the contribution of the group of researchers, academics, and students from the Art, Design, and Audiovisual Communication Faculty (FADCOM), the Electrical and Computer Engineering Faculty (FIEC), and the ESPOL Society Link Unit (UVS). Our Special thanks to Stalyn Gonzabay and Boris Vintimilla for their contribution to the technical bases of this work.

References

1. Plass, J.L., Homer, B.D., Kinzer, C.K.: Foundations of game-based learning. Educ. Psychol. **50**(4), 258–283 (2015)
2. Solorzano, N.I., Gallego, D.C., Quijije, L.S., Quelal, M.M.: Developing a dashboard for monitoring usability of educational games apps for children. In: 2nd International Conference on Computers in Management and Business - ICCMB, pp. 70–75 (2019)
3. Bahi, H., Necibi, K.: Fuzzy logic applied for pronunciation assessment. Int. J. Comput.-Assist. Lang. Learn. Teach. **10**(1), 60–72(2020)
4. Ponce, J., Bedi, A.S.: The impact of a cash transfer program on cognitive achievement: The Bono de Desarrollo Humano of Ecuador (The human development bond of ecuador). Econ. Educ. Rev. **29**(1), 116–125 (2010)
5. Solorzano, N.I., Loor, R., Gonzabay, S., Vintimilla, B.: Statistical representations of a dashboard to monitor educational videogames in natural language. In: The 2nd ACM Chapter International Conference on Educational Technology, Language, and Technical Communication - ETLTC, vol. 77, pp. 05003 (2020)
6. Gaudelli, W., Taylor, A.: Modding the global classroom? Serious video games and teacher reflection Contemp. Issues Technol. Teacher Educ. **11**(1), 70–91 (2011)
7. Griffiths, M.D.: The educational benefits of videogames. Educ. Health **20**(3), 47–51 (2002)
8. Squire, K.: Video Games and Learning. 1st edn. Teacher College Press, New York (2011)
9. Duval, E.: Open Learning Analytics: Erik Duval at TEDxUHowest'. In: Book Open Learning Analytics: Erik Duval at TEDxUHowest. https://www.youtube.com/watch?v=LfXDzpTnvqY. Accessed 18 June 2013

10. González, J.L., Gutiérrez, F.L.: Jugabilidad como medida de calidad en el desarrollo de video-juegos (Playability as a quality measure in video game development). CoSECivi, pp. 147–158 (2014)
11. Villacís, C.: Multi-player educational video game over cloud to stimulate logical reasoning of children. IEEE Computer Society Tolouse (2014)
12. Siemens, G., et al.: Open learning analytics: an integrated & modularized platform: society for learning analytics research. Open Learning Analytics (2011)
13. Solorzano, N.I., Sornoza, L.E., Carrera, D.A.: Adoption of children's educational video games monitored with dashboards in the cloud (Adopción de videojuegos educativos infantiles, monitoreada con tableros de control en la nube). Iberian J. Inf. Syst. Technol. RISTI (Revista Iberica de Sistemas e Tecnologias de Informacao) **19**, 146–160 (2019)
14. Powers, D.M., Turk, C.C.: Machine Learning of Natural Language. Springer, London (2012)
15. Monzonís, M.F.: Graphic adventure videogame using Fuzzy Logic algorithms to set the story's path. Technical report, Universitat Jaume I (2019)
16. De Araújo, S.A., Barros, D.F., De Silva, E.M., Da Cardoso, M.V.: Applying computational intelligence techniques to improve the decision-making of business game players. Soft Comput. **23**(18), 8753–8763 (2019)
17. Ferguson, R.: Learning analytics: drivers, developments and challenges. Int. J. Technol. Enhanced Learn. **4**(5/6), 304–317 (2012)
18. Elias, T.: Learning analytics, learning, pp. 1–22 (2011)
19. Bremser, W.G., Wagner, W.P.: Developing dashboards for performance management. CPA J. **83**(7), 62 (2013)
20. Yigitbasioglu, O.M., Velcu, O.: A review of dashboards in performance management: implications for design and research. Int. J. Acc. Inf. Syst. **13**(1), 41–59 (2012)
21. Few, S.: Information Dashboard Design, 1st edn. O'Reilly Media, Italy (2006)
22. Klipfolio Homepage. https://www.klipfolio.com/start-building. Accessed 17 July 2019
23. Storey, M.-A., Treude, C.: Software Engineering Dashboards: Types, Risks, and Future. Rethinking Productivity in Software Engineering, 1st edn. Springer, Berkley (2019)
24. Zadeh, L.A.: On Fuzzy Algorithms. Fuzzy Sets, Fuzzy Logic, and Fuzzy Systems: Selected Papers, 1st edn. World Scientific (1996)
25. Guzmán, D., Castaño, V.: La lógica difusa en Ingeniería: principios, aplicaciones y futuro (Fuzzy logic in engineering: principles, applications and future). Revista de Ciencia y Tecnología **24**(2) (2006)
26. Ibrahim, D.: An overview of soft computing. Procedia Comput. Sci. **102**, 34–38 (2016)
27. Solorzano, N.I.S., Sanzogni, L., Houghton, L.: Applying QCA with fuzzy logic to generate a refined set of factors for information systems adoption: the case of public Ecuadorian organization, an example of is adoption in emerging economies. Int. J. Online Biomed. Eng. **15**(3), 33–46 (2019)
28. Hurtado, S.M., Gómez, G.P.: Modelo de inferencia difuso para estudio de crédito. DYNA: Revista de la Facultad de Minas **75**(154), 215–229 (2008)
29. Mingers, J.: Combining IS research methods: towards a pluralist methodology. Inf. Syst. Res. **12**(3), 240–259 (2001)
30. Davis, F.D.: Perceived usefulness, perceived ease of use, and user acceptance of information technology. MIS Q. **13**(3), 319–340 (1989)

GIS for Decision-Making on the Gentrification Phenomenon in Strategic Territorial Planning

Jacinto Palma Zambrano[1]([✉])(iD), Tania Calle-Jimenez[1]([✉])(iD),
and Boris Orellana-Alvear[2]([✉])(iD)

[1] Escuela Politécnica Nacional, Quito, Ecuador
{jacinto.palma,tania.calle}@epn.edu.ec
[2] Universidad de Cuenca, Cuenca, Ecuador
boris.orellana@ucuenca.edu.ec
https://www.epn.edu.ec
https://www.ucuenca.edu.ec

Abstract. Gentrification is a worldwide phenomenon that generates population displacement due to various economic and social factors that change the way of life of residents in a geographical space. It also has a greater incidence in urban areas that have a Historic Center, as is the case for many Latin American countries that preserve these spaces as part of their cultural heritage. Quito stands out as an important case study of the gentrification phenomenon in its Historic Center. The increase in tourism and economic activity in the sector has generated the right environment for its development, elevating the cost of living by increasing the capital gain, thus promoting population displacement.

Currently, information on the gentrification phenomenon in Quito is scarce and it is not feasible to examine the phenomenon and how it has been developing over the decades. Therefore, the purpose of this research was to create a web system that employs geographic tools to analyze and visualize gentrification. The use of GIS in particular provides a better representation of the model used for the study and a different visualization of the data, making the user experience much more interactive. Based on this premise, the web system was created in such a way that it will allow the local government to better identify, visualize, and analyze the phenomenon. This will motivate the local government to generate public policies to reduce gentrification in the study area.

Keywords: Gentrification · Web application · GIS · Historical center · Decision-making

1 Introduction

The term 'gentrification' goes back decades. It was first proposed in 1964 by researcher Ruth Glass [10], who investigated the relationship between housing and social class problems in central London. These problems were caused by the

© Springer Nature Switzerland AG 2021
J. P. Salgado Guerrero et al. (Eds.): TICEC 2021, CCIS 1456, pp. 142–156, 2021.
https://doi.org/10.1007/978-3-030-89941-7_11

rapid changes and renovations taking place in Victorian buildings, leading to a substantial increase in price that meant these houses were now bought by people with a higher income, resulting in the eviction of the working class. Glass used the term 'gentry' as this was the name of the British landowning class [33]. In Latin American countries, the gentrification phenomenon has been observed and studied for several years. This phenomenon results in the displacement of the original residents of a specific neighborhood, who are usually on a low income and located in the center of the city due to a strong real estate investment in the sector [4]. Real estate investors look for cheap properties in central neighborhoods and purchase them with the aim of redeveloping and selling them to high-income consumers [18]. The government also gentrifies by rehabilitating public spaces, which generates an increase in capital gain in the area and therefore in the rent, forcing people to sell their properties due to the high cost of living [8,19]. Previous studies have demonstrated that the maintenance of historic centers makes the area a much more attractive space for gentrifying agents [20,27,32].

Latin American cities such as Buenos Aires, Santiago de Chile, and Mexico have undergone territorial modifications that have influenced population movements [2]. For instance, Cuenca's remodeling and relocation of informal jobs improved the visual appearance of the city, which opted for tourism development following its recognition as a world cultural heritage site [14,18,30]. In Quito's Historic Center, this is evidenced by the growth of tourism, which promotes the conservation and rehabilitation of antique buildings and urban spaces declared as part of the Cultural Heritage of Humanity by UNESCO [35].

This study aims to demonstrate the usability of Geographic Information Systems (GIS) in contributing to methodologies that permit the identification and analysis of gentrification. It also facilitates an exploration of socioeconomic characteristics associated with gentrification, with an emphasis on generating useful information for local governments.

To identify the phenomenon, a model based on similar studies conducted elsewhere in the world will be applied and adapted to the context of the Historic Center of Quito. Once the model and its results have been identified, they will be visualized and demonstrated through the use of GIS. In this way, the usefulness of these systems can be exhibited via the representation of data through maps, making them a useful tool to support decision making in the creation of policies that will help reduce the incidence of gentrification.

2 Related Works

Gentrification has previously been studied in other countries, which have evidenced the existing population displacement in the areas studied. In a global context, gentrification has different consequences according to the dimensions of the research. For instance, some researchers consider the phenomenon to be a social and economic issue [18] while others believe that gentrification is a result of the development of cities [2]. In either case, defining the phenomenon spatially for the purpose of urban planning is essential.

Proper urban planning takes into consideration the socioeconomic, territorial, environmental, transportation, and demographic factors that contribute to city planning, which is usually projected for future years. This planning relies on large amounts of data that can be collected through the use of GIS, and analyzed, represented, or modified to generate a spatial relationship through maps [23]. Therefore, GIS has become a tool for urban planners that enhances the value of the information they possess and utilize for decision making [17].

The ongoing changes in cities makes visible the presence of gentrification, especially when they have a colonial center, as is the case for many cities in Latin America. As an initial approach to the topic, a review was conducted of previous studies on the phenomenon that have identified similar characteristics between metropolitan cities. This served to identify an analytical model that allows gentrification to be identified in the Historic Center of Quito. Several studies have measured gentrification based on census data. For example, Galster and Peacock (1986) analyzed Philadelphia census variables using regression models [9], while other research has explored the relationship between eviction and gentrification; for example, Desmond and Gershenson in the USA in 2017, or Reades in London in 2019 [7,31].

The use of census data led to the use of the model proposed by Dr. David J. Hammel, which identifies gentrification based on population and housing censuses, thus facilitating its analysis [11]. An example of the analysis of gentrification is provided in a thesis developed by Dr. Li which explored the phenomenon from 1900 to 2000 in Chicago. This thesis used as its basis a model similar to that developed by Hammel and Wyly in 1996, Freeman in 2005, and Headlamp and Lucas in 2006. This provides an approximation of how the study should be developed, especially in terms of how the variables describe the phenomenon using a methodology that defines a neighborhood as gentrified through calculations based on census data.

Specifically, Hammel performed a Principal Component Analysis (PCA) of several individual income variables; tenant ratios; socioeconomic status based on employment; and percentage of artist residents. In addition, Freeman conducted work on the gentrification of New York using variables related to downtown location, low income, older homes, higher educational attainment, and a steeper rise in house prices [13].

Because an analysis involving GIS has been proposed for decision making, the online system developed by the University of California Berkeley for the study of gentrification was used as an example of prototyping. This identifies gentrification and its impact through the use of interactive maps, facilitating an understanding of the phenomenon over time and the variables that describe it [34]. This system aims to enhance knowledge and understanding of gentrification and neighborhood transformations (see Fig. 1).

Based on previous works, this research in the Historic Center of Quito uses the model proposed by Hammel [11]], drawing on census data to identify gentrification. The data were obtained through a collaboration with the National Institute of Statistics and Census (INEC), whose demographic data are publicly

Fig. 1. University of California Berkeley web system for the gentrification phenomenon visualization using GIS.

available on their website. To conduct the analysis, information from the 1990, 2001, and 2010 censuses was collected as this enabled a comparison to be made between several decades.

Subsequently, the data obtained for the statistical analysis in maps was collated to provide a better visualization of gentrification in the Historic Center using GIS. Such visualization was performed on a web application to ease access to and enhance comprehension of the information for users and competent governmental entities. This will help to motivate the creation of public policies that reduce gentrification.

3   Method

To perform this study, the following process was implemented. The first step was to select a method to calculate and quantify the gentrification phenomenon so that it could be visualized through the use of GIS. Once the method was selected, the data were collected – which involved obtaining census data – and the variables were selected in accordance with the method. Data analysis was then performed, which involved cleaning the data, obtaining map layers, and uploading them as a web service. Finally, the results were obtained and displayed in the web application and visualized using GIS tools, as depicted in Fig. 2.

3.1   Method Selection

The decision to select Hammel's method was based on a comparison of existing methods employed to study the phenomenon of gentrification.

For instance, Freeman's model [8] proposes the use of two methods: the first is to obtain data from the population and housing census to identify the area in

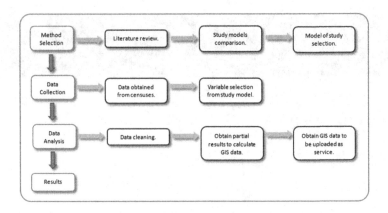

Fig. 2. Process used to develop the method.

which gentrification occurs and the second is a Panel Study of Income Dynamics (PSID), which consists of a longitudinal survey of a representative sample of U.S. individuals and the families with whom they reside [15]. The PSID has become a powerful tool as it contains geo-coded information on the same families since 1968. This model was not considered in the research as its primary source of information was the income of the family nucleus, which is not available in Ecuador.

An alternative model proposed by Nesbitt [28], was based on the collection of a large amount of data that provide indicators relating to the representation of gentrification through the use of GIS, adding geocoding so that the statistics can be visualized on maps. These indicators encompass multiple variables relevant to the study area, such as the average income, the number of occupied dwellings, the proximity of the dwellings to commercial sectors, and even the proximity to sectors of historical value. However, the Nesbitt model was not considered because the Ecuadorian government does not elicit all the information required within its census to develop the proposed variables, and some of the information necessary for its development is not publicly available.

The Hammel method [11], was derived as an alternative to the existing dichotomy between field work, using surveys of public officials [3] or surveys of published accounts [1], and population censuses. This method makes it possible to reduce the information gap in gentrified areas by using census data, which provides concise information on the local population. The method works by creating variables that help to identify gentrification by taking into consideration local changes in housing, a topic that has been proposed by several authors [6,12,21,22,24,29]. Therefore, the Hammel method was adapted to the data that exist within the population and housing censuses of Ecuador, thus allowing the variables to be matched.

3.2 Data Collection

The 13 neighborhoods that make up the Historic Center were selected as the study area as they are characterized by a high level of commercial activity, a high population density with wide age ranges, and the constant recovery and maintenance of historic sites. All the above-mentioned causes were added to factors such as tourist investment and urban improvement by the government, which has transformed the spatial aspect to attract real estate investment, generating an 'artificial landscape' [14, 26].

The census data analyzed in this study were taken from the years 1990, 2001, and 2010. This is because censuses in Ecuador are conducted every 10 years and INEC only possess digitized information from the 1990 census onwards. Table 1 compares the Hammel variables with the variables used for this study.

Table 1. Comparison of model and census variables.

Hammel variables	Selected variables
Socioeconomic	*Socioeconomic*
1. Median household income	Not considered
2. Change in median household income	Not considered
3. Percentage of workers in managerial, professional, or technical occupations	1. Percentage of workers in managerial, professional, or technical occupations
4. Change in percentage of workers in managerial, professional, or technical occupations	2. Change in percentage of workers in managerial, professional, or technical occupations
5. Percentage of persons age 25 and over with 4+ years of college	3. Percentage of persons age 25 and over with 4+ years of college
6. Change in percentage of persons age 25 and over with 4+ years of college	4. Change in percentage of persons age 25 and over with 4+ years of college
Housing	*Housing*
1. Median rent	Not considered; instead, the variable 'Improved Structures' was calculated
2. Change in median rent	
3. Change in median house value	
Population	*Population*
1. Persons	1. Total persons
2. Employed persons	2. Employed persons
3. Workers employed in managerial professional or technical occupations	3. Workers employed in managerial professional or technical occupations
4. Persons age 25 and over with 4+ years of college	4. Persons age 25 and over with 4+ years of college

The variable "Improved structures", was calculated on the basis of census questions about the structure and condition of the house, such as walls, roof, floor, water supply, connection to the sewage network, electrical connection, telephone connection, garbage collection, and other variables that have changed continually over the years such as internet connection.

Table 2 presents the population-type variables selected from the 2010 census. It presents the model variable, the census question code, the question content, and the score obtained for each question.

Table 2. Population questions selected for variable measurement in 2010 census.

Population[a]			
Selected variables from Hammel model	Census question code	Census question	Score
Total persons	TP1	Total persons 1	Number
Employed persons	TIPOACT	Activity type	Activities described on census
Workers employed in managerial, professional or technical occupations	RAMACT	Recoded branch of activity	Branches described on census
	GRUOCU	Recoded occupation group	Occupations described on census
	P23	Highest level of instruction	SUPERIOR
Persons age 25 and over with 4+ years of college	P24	Highest grade, course, or year	4
	P03	Age	≥25

[a]Data obtained from the 2010 INEC Population, Home and Housing Census - Population Section

In this particular case, the score obtained was calculated using a code developed in Python which takes the different values each question can yield and assigns a Boolean-type value that identifies the population that meets the characteristics of gentrification. This table also presents the socioeconomic information considered in the variables for the study; this was achieved by calculating the percentage changes between each census period.

According to INEC, a census housing is defined as: "*A structurally separate housing enclosure with an independent entrance built or arranged to be inhabited by one or more persons, provided that at the time of the census it is not used entirely for a different purpose.*". Similarly, INEC defines a census home as: "*... made up of one or more persons, who are not necessarily related, sleep in the same housing, cook their food together and share the same expenses for food, i.e., they eat from a common pot.*" [16].

Although the terms have different definitions, the set of questions in both sections allows the creation of the "Improved Structures" variable. For this variable, the research team calculated a score according to the response options the question may have; the higher the score obtained, the greater the change in the housing structures.

Tables 3 and 4 present information obtained for the housing and home sections of the 2010 census. These contain the census question, the question code, the different response options, and the score assigned depending on the type of response. It is important to specify that INEC's interpretations of census terms means several homes may be included in the same housing, i.e. when two families live in the same housing but they have separate expenses. When this was the case, an average of the "Improved Structures" variable was calculated. It should also be noted that the housing and home sections appear separately in the 2010 and 2001 censuses; whereas in the 1990 census they are represented as one single section.

Table 3. Housing questions selected for variable measurement in 2010 census.

Housing[a]			
Census question	Census question code	Census answer options	Score
Type of housing	VTV	1 = Home, 2 = Apartment in house or building, 3 = Rental room, 4 = Unfinished construction, 5 = Ranch,6 = Hovel,7 = Hut, 8 = Other private, 9 = Hotel/guesthouse/residential/hostel, 10 = Military barracks/police/firefighters, 11 = Jail/social rehabilitation center, 12 = Child/woman/indigent shelter, 13 = Hospital/clinic, 14 = Convent, 15 = Nursing home/orphanage, 16 = Other collective, 17 = No housing	1 = 17pts, 2 = 16pts, 3 = 15pts, 4 = 14pts, 5 = 13pts,6 = 12pts, 7 = 11pts, 8 = 10pts, 9 = 9pts, 10 = 8pts, 11 = 7pts, 12 = 6pts, 13 = 5pts, 14 = 4pts, 15 = 3pts, 16 = 2pts, 17 = 1pt
Predominant material of the roof or deck of the house	V01	1 = concrete(slab, cement), 2 = asbestos, 3 = zinc, 4 = roofing, 5 = palm leaf/straw/leaf, 6 = other materials	1 = 6pts, 2 = 5pts, 3 = 4pts, 4 = 3pts, 5 = 2pts, 6 = 1pt
Predominant material of the exterior walls of the house	V03	1 = concrete, 2 = brick/block, 3 = adobe, 4 = wood,5 = coated cane, 6 = uncoated cane, 7 = other materials	1 = 7pts, 2 = 6pts, 3 = 5pts, 4 = 4pts, 5 = 3pts, 6 = 2pts, 7 = 1pt
Predominant material of the housing floor	V05	1 = parquet/plank/floating floor, 2 = untreated wood, 3 = ceramic/vinyl/marble, 4 = brick/cement, 5 = rod, 6 = earth, 7 = other materials	1 = 6pts, 2 = 5pts, 3 = 7pts, 4 = 4pts, 5 = 3pts, 6 = 2pts, 7 = 1pt
Condition of the roof of the house	V02	1 = good, 2 = regular, 3 = bad	1 = 3pts, 2 = 2pts, 3 = 1pt
Condition of the walls of the house	V04	1 = good, 2 = regular, 3 = bad	1 = 3pts, 2 = 2pts, 3 = 1pt
Condition of the floor of the house	V06	1 = good, 2 = regular, 3 = bad	1 = 3pts, 2 = 2pts, 3 = 1pt
The water that the house receives is?	V08	1 = pipe inside the house, 2 = pipe outside the house but inside the building/batch/land, 3 = pipe outside the building/batch/land, 4 = no piped water	1 = 4pts, 2 = 3pts, 3 = 2pts, 4 = 1pt
Where the water that the house receives mainly comes from?	V07	1 = public network, 2 = well, 3 = river/spring, 4 = delivery cart, 5 = other(rainwater)	1 = 5pts, 2 = 4pts, 3 = 3pts, 4 = 3pts, 5 = 1pt
The toilet service of the house is?	V09	1 = connected to public sewage system, 2 = connected to septic tank, 3 = connected to cesspit, 4 = discharge to sea/river/lake, 5 = latrine, 6 = no toilet	1 = 6pts, 2 = 5pts, 3 = 4pts, 4 = 3pts, 5 = 2pts, 6 = 1pt
The service of electric light(energy) of the housing comes principally from?	V10	1 = utility grid, 2 = solar panel/light generator, 4 = other, 5 = no power	1 = 5pts, 2 = 4pts, 3 = 3pts, 4 = 3pts, 5 = 1pt
The house has an electricity meter?	V11	1 = exclusive use, 2 = common use to several houses, 3 = no meter	1 = 3pts, 2 = 2pts, 3 = 1pt
Primarily how is the garbage disposed?	V13	1 = collecting cart, 2 = waste ground, 3 = burn, 4 = bury, 5 = throw into river/canal, 6 = other	1 = 6pts, 2 = 5pts, 3 = 4pts, 4 = 3pts, 5 = 2pts, 6 = 1pt

[a]Data obtained from the 2010 INEC Population, Home and Housing Census - Housing Section

Table 4. Home questions selected for variable measurement in 2010 census.

HOME[a]			
Census question	Census question code	Census answer options	Score
Exclusive room for cooking	H02	1 = YES, 2 = NO	1 = 3pt, 2 = 0pt
Home hygiene service	H03	1 = exclusive use, 2 = shared with several households, 3 = does not have	1 = 3pts, 2 = 2pts, 3 = 1pt
Does this home have a space with facilities and/or shower for bathing?	H04	1 = exclusive use, 2 = shared with several households, 3 = does not have	1 = 3pts, 2 = 2pts, 3 = 1pt
What is the main fuel or energy this home uses for cooking?	H05	1 = gas (tank/cylinder), 2 = centralized gas, 3 = electricity, 4 = wood/carbon, 5 = vegetable and/or animal waste, 6 = other (gasoline, kerex), 7 = no fuel	1 = 5pts, 2 = 6pts, 3 = 7pts, 4 = 4pts, 5 = 3pts, 6 = 2pts, 7 = 1pt
Primarily, the water that the members of the home drink is?	H06	1 = drink it as it comes, 2 = boil it, 3 = chlorinate it, 4 = filter it, 5 = buy purified water	1 = 1pt, 2 = 2pts, 3 = 3pts, 4 = 4pts, 5 = 5pts
Does this home have a telephone service?	H07	1 = YES, 2 = NO	1 = 3pt, 2 = 0pt
Does any member of this home have cell phone service?	H08	1 = YES, 2 = NO	1 = 3pt, 2 = 0pt
Does this home have Internet service?	H09	1 = YES, 2 = NO	1 = 3pt, 2 = 0pt
Does this home have a computer?	H10	1 = YES, 2 = NO	1 = 3pt, 2 = 0pt
Does this home have cable television service?	H11	1 = YES, 2 = NO	1 = 3pt, 2 = 0pt

[a]Data obtained from the 2010 INEC Population, Home and Housing Census - Home Section

3.3   Data Analysis

Once the census questions related to the research were identified, Python code was developed to extract and clean the data obtained from the SPSS databases, and then transform it into CSV format. Once the data had been transformed, it was filtered and then separated according to the following census sections: population, housing and home. Each of these sections was cleaned using codes that removed the columns containing questions not considered and generated new columns with result information, such the sector code column that originates from the union of the following columns: province, canton, parish, and sector.

After obtaining the data for each neighborhood, we proceeded to perform the analysis with GIS. Each item of data was loaded into the GIS in order to match the sector codes obtained with the polygons containing the geographic coordinates. The polygons of the geographic layers contain the areas delimited for the census execution; these layers include the neighborhoods and sectors, representing the levels at which the study was carried out. Also, the geographic layers were acquired from various sources, including INEC, the Municipality of the Metropolitan District of Quito (MDMQ), and the Military Geographic Institute (IGM) in SHP format.

Once the population, housing, and home values were matched in the geographic layers, we generated the 'gentrification' attribute for each neighborhood. Subsequently, the final layers with the information were uploaded to the GIS cloud as a 'Feature Layer', transforming it into a web service that can be consumed by other applications. Figure 3 presents the architecture of this process.

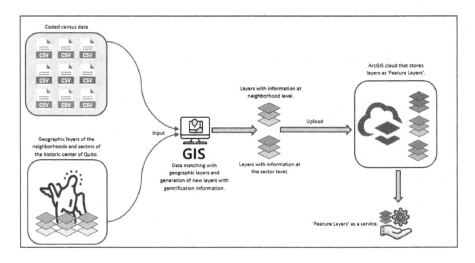

Fig. 3. Architecture of layer creation and deployment.

4   Results

The geographic layers are made up of the polygons of the census mapping of neighborhoods and sectors and the generated statistics as a result of the research. The scale is set by default to a zoom value of 15 at the coordinates $[-78.5155452, -0.2220584]$ that represent the set of neighborhoods and sectors that constitute the Historic Center. All layers stored in the cloud were created using INEC census cartography and the results obtained, so these are unique layers created by the authors and publicly available as a reference for future research.

The results obtained in the geographic layers stored in the cloud were used as a service for the web application created to visualize them. The web application allows the data to be visualized through interactive maps that display the information according to the conditions selected in the panel by the user. In addition, the user also selects which statistical information to present.

Figure 4 presents a screenshot of each of the panel options and the information displayed. The panel displays the following options:

- Census results: Contains the results obtained from the 2010, 2001, and 1990 censuses, respectively.
- Gentrification - Sectors: Presents a comparative map of the sectors and their gentrification status for 2 consecutive years.
- Gentrification - Neighborhoods: Presents a comparative map of neighborhoods and their gentrification status for 2 consecutive years.

Table 5 presents the results of the gentrification phenomenon for each neighborhood. Here we identify the neighborhood; the status of the phenomenon as: Gentrifiable (G), in the Process of Gentrification (GP), or Not Gentrifiable (NG); the percentages by which each of the variables that influence gentrification have changed for each period: the percentage of People aged 25 or above (%P25); People with employment (%EP); People with managerial, technical, or administrative employment (%MEP); People identified as gentrifiable (%GP); People with higher education (%PHE); and Changes in Infrastructure (%IC).

Positive values indicate an increase in the variable while negative values indicate a decrease.

The results obtained for the neighborhoods were calculated by averaging all the sectors that constitute each neighborhood. As explained previously, the distribution of sectors that form part of each neighborhood changes for each census measurement, therefore a generalized measure had to be used.

(a) Census results

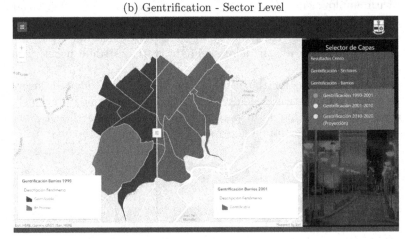

(b) Gentrification - Sector Level

(c) Gentrification - Neighborhood Level

Fig. 4. Display of information and results in the web application.

Table 5. Results of the gentrification phenomenon for each neighborhood.

Neighborhood	Period	Status		Gentrification variables					
		Y1	Y2	%P25	%EP	%MEP	%GP	%PHE	%IC
Gonzales Suarez	1990–2001	G	G	−19.15	146.68	117.56	32.91	−5.73	5.8
	2001–2010	G	G	−2	12.59	59.82	−37.14	−6.17	31.8
La Loma	1990–2001	G	G	0.48	172.47	99.04	−10.70	−3.04	7.03
	2001–2010	G	G	−12.27	0.48	45.26	−14.06	−0.46	28.24
La Merced	1990–2001	G	G	−2	195.4	178.43	−10.91	0.97	11.88
	2001–2010	G	G	−31.85	−14.92	18.31	−26.53	−14.7	35.03
La Recoleta	1990–2001	G	G	−1.94	265.05	146.94	57.69	−3.33	1.32
	2001–2010	G	G	19.97	41.53	65.29	−82.93	14.78	30.06
La Sena	1990–2001	G	G	−42.54	38.21	115.91	−21.98	−29.96	7.82
	2001–2010	G	G	1.76	13.2	43.68	−15.49	10.84	38.85
La Tola	1990–2001	G	G	35.84	283.65	230.49	52.59	27.46	8.66
	2001–2010	G	G	−22.95	−9.06	6.27	−31.07	−15.82	32.67
La Victoria	1990–2001	G	G	−33.81	83.39	130.85	19.51	−46.34	5.17
	2001–2010	G	G	19.20	49.63	54.38	26.53	16.91	29.14
Panecillo	1990–2001	NG	GP	−15.99	102.52	202.69	5.29	−13.92	8.24
	2001–2010	GP	G	−11.36	8.52	5.86	−2.51	1.64	36.87
San Blas	1990–2001	NG	GP	−22.04	129.8	114.34	−3.31	−18.37	9.72
	2001–2010	GP	G	−16.45	1.54	17.46	−6.29	−15.54	35.15
San Diego	1990–2001	G	G	4.58	169.76	170	41.67	−22.9	3.24
	2001–2010	G	G	21.22	53.14	69.84	55.88	47.37	40.26
San Marcos	1990–2001	G	G	−29.73	92.69	77.96	−20.47	−29.25	8.19
	2001–2010	G	G	−6.3	0.76	23.56	−26.73	−2.95	34.88
San Roque	1990–2001	G	G	17.11	267.21	272.34	113.59	−7.61	5.14
	2001–2010	G	G	−2.7	16.57	51.71	5	5.32	32.65
San Sebastián	1990–2001	G	G	−8.01	206.33	283.65	50	−4.63	7.68
	2001–2010	G	G	−4.85	18.29	41.6	−20.11	5.01	28

5   Discussion

In 2015, the Municipality of the Metropolitan District of Quito (MDMQ) published a document entitled the 'Metropolitan Plan for Development and Land Use Planning' that contains a section dedicated to 'Historic Areas' [25]. The explanation provided in the document regarding gentrification is based on the geographical phenomena observable at first sight, such as the scarce mobility that exists in the Historic Center because the space when it was created was not designed for the current volume of traffic and mobility. The document identifies the development of social and economic factors that have had an impact on the incidence of gentrification, such as drug micro-trafficking, prostitution, and homelessness, which are some of the causes of depopulation in this area.

The document proposed by the MDMQ recognizes the existence of gentrification in the study area, but does not quantify it because no research projects have been conducted to gather more information on the phenomenon and substantiate the social, cultural and economic factors mentioned. Therefore, the dimensions of the phenomenon and how it has or may affect the local population are unknown.

The use of a model such as Hammel's enables urban planners and local governments to visualize the current situation regarding gentrification and how it has changed over time. In this way, GIS is a support tool for strategic decision making in territorial planning that takes into consideration the development of gentrification and thus proposes policies to mitigate or halt its advance. Although the data used for the study were not all proposed by the model, the existence of gentrification in the study area was clearly demonstrated.

It is clear that the visualization through the use of GIS allows the process of change the area has undergone in terms of gentrification to be observed. It also provides the authorities with a way to identify the spaces that require greater attention to prevent depopulation in these areas. The conducted research allows observing the incidence of the gentrification phenomenon in the studied area over the years. In addition, it becomes a contribution to the development of digital documentation about the phenomenon through the use of a model, thus allowing the generation of a space for future research. A periodic study of the evolution of gentrification can be maintained as this investigation provides a model that allows it to be calculated over time and displayed using GIS.

6 Conclusions

Evidence for the continuation of gentrification over the years in the study area demonstrates how little information local governments have at their disposal to address the phenomenon. The MDMQ, despite having a dedicated section in the 'Metropolitan Plan for Development and Land Use Planning', has not been able to reduce the incidence of gentrification.

Territorial planning considers the economic development of the study area as a space with tourist potential, but at the same time has not taken into consideration the repercussions of the increase in the value of public space, which is one of the main causes of depopulation. As indicated in the results obtained from the research, these changes in structures play a fundamental role in determining the existence of gentrification in the study area.

The use of a model that quantifies gentrification ensures it is taken into consideration for subsequent territorial planning. Similarly, in the case of INEC, the census questions could cover more information, thus allowing studies carried out on the subject to be much more complete.

The contribution of GIS as a data visualization tool allows users to better understand the data. Using geo-coded information also facilitates the identification of a correlation between demographic data and the geographic position of these data, which gives added value to this information. It also enables demographic phenomena such as gentrification to be measured over time and thus generates new opportunities for research.

The application presents the information obtained as a result in the geographic layers, the reports generated from the information obtained, and a projection of the data for the year 2020. The projection was calculated using the methodology proposed by the University of California, Berkeley, taking into account the limitations of the data for the historic center of Quito [5].

References

1. Beauregard, R.A., Cousins, R.: The Spatial Distribution of Revitalizing Cities in the United States. Rutgers University, Department of Geography (1981)
2. Betancur, J.J.: Gentrification in Latin America: overview and critical analysis. Urban Stud. Res. **2014** (2014)
3. Black, J.T.: Private-market housing renovation in central cities: an urban land institute survey. In: Back to the City, pp. 3–12. Elsevier (1980)
4. Casgrain, A., Janoschka, M.: Gentrificación y resistencia en las ciudades latinoamericanas: El ejemplo de santiago de chile. Andamios **10**(22), 19–44 (2013)
5. Chapple, K., et al.: Developing a new methodology for analyzing potential displacement (2017)
6. Clay, P.L.: Neighborhood Renewal: Trends and Strategies. Lexington Books, Lexington (1979)
7. Desmond, M., Gershenson, C.: Who gets evicted? Assessing individual, neighborhood, and network factors. Soc. Sci. Res. **62**, 362–377 (2017)
8. Freeman, L.: Displacement or succession? Residential mobility in gentrifying neighborhoods. Urban Aff. Rev. **40**(4), 463–491 (2005)
9. Galster, G., Peacock, S.: Urban gentrification: evaluating alternative indicators. Soc. Indic. Res. **18**(3), 321–337 (1986)
10. Glass, R.: London: Aspects of Change, no. 3. MacGibbon & Kee (1964)
11. Hammel, D.J., Wyly, E.K.: A model for identifying gentrified areas with census data. Urban Geogr. **17**(3), 248–268 (1996)
12. Hamnett, C., Williams, P.: Social change in London: a study of gentrification. Lond. J. **6**(1), 51–66 (1980)
13. Han, L.: Modeling gentrification on census tract level in Chicago from 1990 to 2000. Ph.D. thesis, The University of Toledo (2012)
14. Hayes, M.: The coloniality of Unesco's heritage urban landscapes: heritage process and transnational gentrification in Cuenca, Ecuador. Urban Stud. **57**(15), 3060–3077 (2020)
15. Hill, M.S.: The Panel Study of Income Dynamics: A User's Guide, vol. 2. SAGE Publications, Incorporated (1992)
16. INEC: Evolución de las variables investigadas en los censos de población y vivienda del ecuador 1950, 1962, 1974, 1982, 1990, 2001 y 2010. Dirección de estadísticas sociodemográficas
17. Jankowski, P.: GIS for Group Decision Making. CRC Press (2001)
18. Janoschka, M.: Gentrificación, desplazamiento, desposesión: procesos urbanos claves en américa latina. Revista INVI **31**(88), 27–71 (2016)
19. Janoschka, M., Sequera, J.: Procesos de gentrificación y desplazamiento en américa latina, una perspectiva comparativista. Desafíos metropolitanos. Un diálogo entre Europa y América Latina, pp. 82–104 (2014)
20. Lang, M.H., Lang, M.B.: Gentrification Amid Urban Decline: Strategies for America's Older Cities. Ballinger Publishing Company (1982)
21. Ley, D.: Liberal ideology and the postindustrial city. Ann. Assoc. Am. Geogr. **70**(2), 238–258 (1980)

22. Lipton, S.G.: Evidence of central city revival. J. Am. Plan. Assoc. **43**(2), 136–147 (1977)
23. van Maarseveen, M., Martinez, J., Flacke, J.: GIS in Sustainable Urban Planning and Management: A Global Perspective. Taylor & Francis (2019)
24. Maher, C.: The changing residential role of the inner city: the example of inner Melbourne. Aust. Geogr. **14**(2), 112–122 (1978)
25. MDMQ: Plan Metropolitano de Desarrollo y Ordenamiento Territorial (2015)
26. Mínguez, C., Piñeira, M.J., Fernández-Tabales, A.: Social vulnerability and touristification of historic centers. Sustainability **11**(16), 4478 (2019)
27. Nelson, K.P.: Gentrification and Distressed Cities: An Assessment of Trends in Intrametropolitan Migration. University of Wisconsin Press (1988)
28. Nesbitt, A.J.: A model of gentrification: monitoring community change in selected neighborhoods of St. Petersburg, Florida using the analytic hierarchy process. Ph.D. thesis, University of Florida (2005)
29. O'Loughlin, J., Munski, D.C.: Housing rehabilitation in the inner city: a comparison of two neighborhoods in New Orleans. Econ. Geogr. **55**(1), 52–70 (1979)
30. Orellana-Alvear, B., Calle-Jimenez, T.: Analysis of the gentrification phenomenon using GIS to support local government decision making. In: Ahram, T. (ed.) AHFE 2020. AISC, vol. 1213, pp. 348–354. Springer, Cham (2021). https://doi.org/10.1007/978-3-030-51328-3_48
31. Reades, J., De Souza, J., Hubbard, P.: Understanding urban gentrification through machine learning. Urban Stud. **56**(5), 922–942 (2019)
32. Redfern, P.A.: What makes gentrification 'gentrification'? Urban Stud. **40**(12), 2351–2366 (2003)
33. Slater, T.: Gentrification of the City. The New Blackwell Companion to the City 1 (2011)
34. UDP: Los Angeles - gentrification and displacement—urban displacement project. https://www.urbandisplacement.org/los-angeles/los-angeles-gentrification-and-displacement
35. UNESCO: Centro del patrimonio mundial. https://whc.unesco.org/es/list/2

An Offline Educational Resources Access System for the Galapagos Islands

Darío Valarezo$^{(\boxtimes)}$, Gabriela Mendieta , Byron Maza ,
Manuel Quiñones-Cuenca , and Marco Morocho

Departamento de Ciencias de la Computación y Electrónica,
Universidad Técnica Particular de Loja, Loja, Ecuador
{djvalarezo,gvmendieta,bpmaza,mfquinonez,mvmorocho}@utpl.edu.ec

Abstract. The lack of Internet access increases the digital divide in the educational sector of developing countries, specifically in marginal and remote sectors, limiting universal access to Information and Communications Technology (ICT). This research aims to present a local educational resources access system for improving the Internet browsing experience, enhancing the user learning process (i.e., students, teachers, and administrative personnel) in the distance learning education system. Thus, this solution reduces the access time to digital content and broadband data consumption based on a low-cost web technology solution, affording two Internet browsing modes when there is a low or null Internet connection in the last mile. This proposal combines a multipurpose mini local server with a Learning Management System (LMS) platform of a higher education institution on the Internet, distributing educational resources (i.e., open e-books, videos, audios, images, among others) through secondary Uniform Resource Locators (URLs). Besides, the solution uses the existing small-scale Local Area Network (LAN) infrastructure available in a remote associate center in the Galapagos Islands. Finally, technical results submit the access system performance after the pilot test in the second term of an academic period (October 2019 - February 2020). The information provides evidence of the cached requests made by the devices (i.e., desktop computer, laptop, smartphone, or tablet) connected to the network.

Keywords: Educational resources access system · Low latency ·
Satellite link · Offline e-platform

1 Introduction

In an expanding digital age, Internet access promotes internationalization, transferring knowledge between societies [1]. The usage of different technological solutions encourages the economic performance of developing countries [1,8], making it possible to reduce the digital divide in remote areas [7,12]. The lack of Internet access is due to low investment, poor infrastructure, lower revenue, and

J. P. Salgado Guerrero et al. (Eds.): TICEC 2021, CCIS 1456, pp. 157–171, 2021.
https://doi.org/10.1007/978-3-030-89941-7_12

foreign location [2,4,8,18]. Therefore, the inequality access to an Internet connection increases the disparities in the education sector in remote zones [12,14,15], avoiding the development of digital territories [14,15]. These scenarios include all levels of education (i.e., primary, secondary, and higher education).

Universal access to ICT has to be promoted in marginal urban sectors, considering Internet access as a primary service [6]. The continuous digitalization process depends on the infrastructure and policies of each region [3], where telecommunication infrastructure is one of the pillars of pedagogical progress [7]. ICT inclusion reduces digital illiteracy, fomenting new learning and teaching methods. Therefore, ICT integration with society does not only depend on the Governments [3]. Other non-governmental organizations (i.e., foundations, companies, and universities) play a significant role, enhancing learning experiences [3]. Promoting new initiatives encourages the democratization of education based on web technologies [14,15], creating opportunities for vulnerable users that live in areas with low broadband speed [5].

There was a fixed and mobile Internet density of 66.18% per 100 inhabitants in Ecuador in the last quarter of 2019 [13]. Each city has a different broadband speed, depending on the location. However, there is a poor connection level in the Galapagos Islands [5]. Today, there is not yet an optical fiber connection with continental Ecuador. The telecommunications infrastructure is not homogeneous due to the poor investment projects in remote areas. In the same quarter, the islands used to have a fixed Internet accounts density of 0.20% per 100 inhabitants [13]. Besides, mobile Internet service depends on the technology and coverage area of the service providers. Therefore, broadband speed is deficient around the city. This service depends on the connection type to the Internet on the Internet Service Providers (ISPs).

In developing countries, ICT integration has a significant social impact, encouraging equality among minorities. This research presents a local educational resources access system that solves the low Internet connection issue to a high cost in distant zones. This work allows the strengthening of the distance learning education system in a remote associate center of the Universidad Técnica Particular de Loja (UTPL) [17]. The technological solution combines the access system that provides access to local educational resources through the LMS platform of the UTPL on the Internet, improving the Internet browsing experience of the users. Furthermore, the solution uses the existing small-scale LAN infrastructure available in the remote associate center of the Galapagos Islands. This study validates the access system performance after the pilot test in the second term of the academic period (October 2019 - February 2020). The information provides evidence of the cached requests made by the devices connected to the network. However, this research does not influence the conduct of the users on the Internet.

The remainder of this paper exhibits the following sections. Section 2 presents an overview of relevant literature. Then, Sect. 3 describes the access system design. Section 4 submits the technical results. Finally, Sect. 5 exhibits the conclusions and future research works.

2   Related Works

This section presents an overview of the relevant literature. These investigations reveal some implementations of different technologies in remote areas, showing the social impact on the community that permits the reduction of the inequalities.

In [4], the work presents a design of a radio link to promote Internet access in rural zones in Colombia. Besides, the authors deploy a telecommunication infrastructure between a broadcasting station and a radial production center. By focusing on indigenous people, ICT inclusion promotes cultural conservation through courses in the LMS platform. The results show that remote indigenous communities access e-learning web 2.0 tools based on Moodle as an LMS platform on the Internet, promoting the integration of minorities. Moreover, the LMS platform implementation uses cheap and open web applications.

In [9], the research presents some cases of ICT implementation in the last mile for the benefit of marginal communities. The solutions include productive sectors, such as governance, education, finance, and agriculture. ICT management reduces costs in the daily activities of the community. Therefore, technology kiosks decrease the digital divide, access costs, illiteracy, and lack of infrastructure. These solutions propose scenarios where private institutions can help marginal sectors. Consequently, different stakeholders in society have to participate in the ICT deployment, suggesting sustainable solutions that benefit all parties.

Furthermore, in [14], the author shows the findings of a user perspective study on the impact of ICT in rural India. Besides, the investigation explores ICT inclusion in the enhancement of opportunities in the rural sector. The research focuses on a computer network deployment to provide access to a remote zone, identifying the direct and indirect benefits of the ICT project. Consequently, ICT inclusion has a positive effect on the development process of a society. The results show that the reduction of the digital divide incentives equality. Moreover, ICT impacts the economy in remote sectors, fomenting new employment opportunities.

Finally, in [18], the investigation provides a survey of the literature of technologies for connectivity implementation in remote areas. The authors present different rural scenarios worldwide. Depending on the reality of each country, there is not a single solution to solve a connectivity problem. However, technological proposals have to be simple in rural areas. New projects have to reduce implementation costs, focusing on open-source. The connectivity schemes must consider the integration of fronthaul and backhaul networks. Besides, nongovernmental organizations have to support various connectivity initiatives.

Therefore, the relevant literature shows the feasibility of implementing a local educational resources access system for improving the Internet browsing experience.

3   Access System Design

This section describes the local educational resources access system for improving the Internet browsing experience that strengthens the distance learning education system in a remote associate center of the UTPL. Thus, this defines the background, architecture, and deployment of the developed device.

3.1   Internet Connection in the Galapagos Islands

Internet users in the Galapagos Islands have frustrating connections experiences due to low Internet service [5]. This barrier creates a learning disadvantage comparing with users in the urban sectors of continental Ecuador [1,4,12]. Therefore, broadband speed is an essential factor that influences the digital divide [5]. The UTPL provides tablets to all their students allowing them access to the Internet. However, due to the low Internet service, the UTPL incentives the innovation to enhance the Internet browsing experience in the remote associate centers, providing facilities to realize academic activities.

The UTPL has two remote associate centers in the Galapagos Islands [17]. In this case, the university administrates the small-scale LAN infrastructure available at each distant associate center. Each of them has a different network diagram and broadband speed. However, broadband speed depends on the availability installed by the national or international ISP. The ISP administrates a satellite link connection in the backhaul network that allows access to the Internet. Besides, the Internet service cost depends on the ISP plans and broadband speed.

In the Galapagos Islands, there are over 229 students in the Distance Learning Education Modality of the UTPL (MAD-UTPL, abbreviation in Spanish) [17]. However, the new modality of Law Degree in Spanish of the MAD-UTPL is one of the three careers with more than ten students, decreasing the sample to test the access system. In this career, there are 30 students distributed in 46 different courses. On the other hand, the university in the new curriculum uses the virtual learning environment canvasUTPL, powered by Instructure, as the new LMS platform, replacing the Moodle platform gradually. Besides, the UTPL administrates the canvasUTPL.

The existing deficiency in Internet access shows the need to implement innovative technologies based on low latency solutions, increasing ICT inclusion in the distance learning education system [3,6,9,18]. Hence, this work proposes a technological solution to improve Internet browsing at the UTPL remote associate centers located at the Galapagos Islands. This research focuses on the public policies recommended by the Ministry of Telecommunications and Information Society (MINTEL, abbreviation in Spanish) [10,11]. Besides, this work focuses on the Sustainable Development Goals (SDGs) four and nine proposed by the United Nations (UN) [16], reducing education inequality and promote telecommunication infrastructure in marginal urban sectors [2,18]. On the other hand, this investigation is an innovative initiative linking academia and entrepreneurship with society. This study stimulates the Research and Development (R&D) of new technology solutions in the country.

3.2 Architecture

There is no specific technology to provide a unique connectivity solution. Consequently, the technology proposal depends on the scenario and available supplies [18]. The local educational resources access system implements a developed device in the last mile, enhancing the LAN infrastructure capacity through an offline e-platform [4, 9, 18]. Therefore, the access system affords two Internet browsing modes when there is a low or null Internet connection [4]. The online mode permits users to browse using an acceleration system through a Domain Name System (DNS) caching server. In contrast, the offline method allows the user the local browse through a local web server. Both modes enhance the browsing perception of the users. Besides, the access system is a low-cost solution to solve connectivity problems only in the remote associate center of the UTPL [14, 18].

The access system solution uses a developed device known as the "KAMU Server" powered by the Research Group in Wireless Communications of the UTPL (GCOMIN-UTPL, abbreviation in Spanish) and the YAKOTT startup, as shown in Fig. 1. The KAMU Server uses universal hardware Next Unit of Computing (NUC) to create a multipurpose mini local server in the network. The technical characteristics of the motherboard, Random-access memory (RAM), and storage driver depend on the manufacture. On the other hand, the developed device uses a GNU/Linux distribution, providing a primary DNS caching server and a local web server for the small-scale LAN that improves the Internet browsing experience. Furthermore, the Operative System (OS) storages the different events of the services in several logs. All digital services are transparent to the users.

The developed solution comprises five major software components, as shown in Fig. 1:

- The DNS service that storages each DNS request made by the devices.
- The traffic manager service is in charge of forwards the network traffic between subnetworks.
- The Web service that implements the local web server.
- The network manager service is responsible for storing all the information related to the network traffic.
- And the Internet access service that affords access to the Internet.

DNS Service: The developed device works as a primary DNS caching server to resolve requests of the devices. The DNS Server resolves petitions to the Internet and the local web server. The DNS log storages each DNS request made by the users. Therefore, the access system first searches the domain names locally and then on the Internet. Moreover, the DNS server implements a local DNS cache to reduce Internet browsing time between recurrent requests. On the other hand, there is no content restriction to promote universal access to knowledge.

Traffic Manager Service: The KAMU Server forwards the network traffic using defined Internet Protocol (IP) table rules. The traffic manager provides Internet access to the devices connected to the LAN. Therefore, the developed device redirects the users between the two Internet browsing modes. In the online method, the users can access the educational resources available on the Internet. However, in the offline system, the users can access the local educational resources stored on the local web server.

Web Service: When the users select the offline mode, they access the main page of the local web server. Hence, the main page has the same corporate brand colors as the canvasUTPL. The developed device provides access to the local educational resources linked to the canvasUTPL through the local web server. The web service uses a specific URL for each subject and educational resource. The Web log storages information of the browser of the devices and claims to the local web server. The internal storage drive storages the educational resources, where the access system packages the local educational resources corresponding to each course. The users can download the educational resources. Moreover, each package is uploaded to the Internet to facilitate the massive installation process.

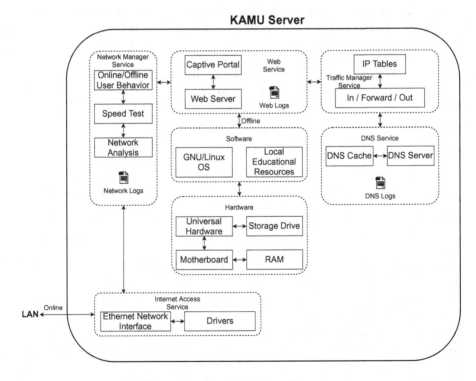

Fig. 1. Developed device architecture.

Network Manager Service: The KAMU Server has an automatic network management system with multiple real-time services. The execution of the different real-time services is every six hours. The Network log storages information related to in/forward/out network traffic. The online/offline user behavior service monitors when a user opens or closes an Internet connection. The speed test service watches the broadband speed of the Internet connection. The network analysis service continuously monitors the DNS request cached.

On the other hand, a remote access service facilitates the foreign management of the developed device. Furthermore, the access system has an update service that upgrades each packet corresponding to each course. However, the access system performs this process on weekends, avoiding interrupting Internet browsing.

Internet Access Service: The KAMU Server has one Network Interface Controller (NIC) that uses a Gigabit Ethernet (GbE) network interface, affording high-speed local services to the devices connected to the LAN. This network interface provides Internet access through a LAN connection, offering the online mode to the users. This service adapts to the available broadband speed of the Internet connection.

3.3 Deployment

As a scenario to implement the access system, this work used a remote associate center of the MAD-UTPL [17]. The remote associate center is located in Puerto Baquerizo Moreno, San Cristóbal Island, Galapagos Islands. On the other hand, the career selected was the new modality of the Law Degree in Spanish of the MAD-UTPL. There were 14 recurring students on the Island. The pilot test needed the current participation of the users [6,18]. All the users that visited the remote associate center had access to the access system, not only the 14 recurring students. Furthermore, there were 16 different subjects distributed in various courses.

The successful integration of the fronthaul and backhaul network enhances the connectivity initiatives [18]. Implementation of the local educational resources access system was possible thanks to the collaboration of the different departments of the MAD-UTPL [17]. The study took advantage of a small-scale LAN infrastructure available in the remote associate center of the UTPL, as shown in Fig. 2. A router, a switch, three desktop computers, a printer, and access points (APs) made up the LAN infrastructure. Hence, the Wireless Local Area Network (WLAN) coverage area depends on the power radiated of the APs, under the Institute of Electrical and Electronics Engineers (IEEE) 802.11 standard.

The KAMU Server used a free port of the switch, as shown in Fig. 2. The LAN ports are not available to the public. The developed device used a fixed IP address accessible in the IP addresses reserve range of the LAN. This option prevents the Media Access Control (MAC) filtering in the Dynamic Host Configuration

Protocol (DHCP). On the router, the primary DNS server sets the IP address of the KAMU Server. This configuration permits resolving the requests of the devices connected to the LAN.

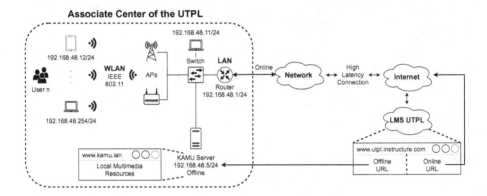

Fig. 2. Network design.

In the online mode, the access system resolves all the requests to the Internet. This method integrates the LMS platform with the local educational resources to reduce the access time, using a secondary URL for access to each educational resource, as shown in Fig. 2. The developed device is independent of the ISP network and the high latency satellite link connection to the Internet. This technological solution changes the meta course (template of each subject) in the virtual learning environment, independent of the number of virtual classrooms. Therefore, that permits linking the KAMU Server with the virtual learning environment canvasUTPL on the Internet.

In the offline mode, the access system only works within the WLAN coverage area. If there is no Internet connection available, the access to the local educational resources is independent of the LMS platform, as shown in Fig. 2. In this case, the users access directly to the local web server.

To make use of the access system, a user n has to connect his device to the WLAN. Then, the user n accesses his account in the virtual learning environment canvasUTPL with normality. On the main page of each course, the LMS platform presents an informative message indicating that if the user n is in the associate center, the user n can use another secondary URL to access the local educational resources linked throughout the course, as shown in Fig. 3a. On the weekly course distribution, the LMS platform presents another informative message indicating that if the user n is in the associate center, the user n can use another secondary URL to access the local educational resources linked in that week of study, as shown in Fig. 3b. In both scenarios, the access system redirects the user n to the local web server, as shown in Fig. 3c.

In this case, the users can choose how to access educational resources. The users perceive only one LMS platform with additional services. Furthermore, the

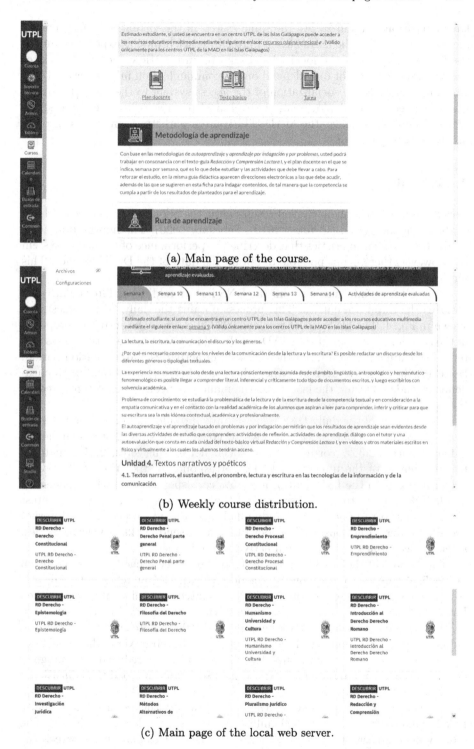

(a) Main page of the course.

(b) Weekly course distribution.

(c) Main page of the local web server.

Fig. 3. Combination of the local educational resources and LMS platform.

local educational resources are the same stored in the virtual learning environment canvasUTPL. The users have a better Internet browsing experience due to the browsing speed of the local educational resources. However, the ICT integration process does not only depend on telecommunication infrastructure [7,9]. This process needs the socialization of the access system to the users [18]. After the developed device deployment, the technical team socialized the access system to the users. Besides, the MAD-UTPL used marketing campaigns through institutional e-mail [18].

4   Results

This section submits the technical results after the pilot test in the second term of the academic period (October 2019 - February 2020). The information helps to identify the characteristics that describe the performance of the access system [7]. However, there is not possible to obtain the data of the DCHP service. This service is independent of the KAMU Server.

After filtering information from the DNS log, an additional filter counts and removes the duplicate entries. This process obtains the daily DNS requests, as shown in Fig. 4. The DNS server resolved 925330 claims. The activities proposed in the academic calendar of the MAD-UTPL relate to the usage of the access system. The claims increase when there is send of activities and evaluation period. However, the requests decrease when there is a holiday or a break in the academic calendar. During the last week, the mandatory containment generated by the global pandemic causes a continuous decrease.

The analysis of the daily DNS requests provides information on the behavior of the users. Where 3.08% corresponds to governance sites, 2.46% matches to e-mail services, 2.35% corresponds to social networking sites, 2.25% matches to subdomains of the university, 1.54% corresponds to the speed test service, 1.42% matches to the LMS platform, 1.35% corresponds to search engine sites, and 0.49% matches to the OS services of the access system. Therefore, the rest of the claims correspond to other individual searches. The users use the Internet access to different actions, such as download files, send works, review activities, attend video conferences, personal activities, and others.

The 18.25% of the DNS requests corresponds to the cached claims, as shown in Fig. 5. Where 14% corresponds to cloud services, 11% matches to Google services, 8% corresponds to governance sites, 7% matches to university services (i.e., LMS platform, e-mail service, academic services, and administrative services), 1% corresponds to social networking sites, and 0.05% matches to the local web server requests. The number of requests to the local web server is the variable to identify if the users browse through the offline mode. The reduced percentage of claims to the local web server is because the users can download the educational resources.

The speed test service monitors the state of the Internet connection. Satellite link latency average is over 500 milliseconds (ms), as shown in Fig. 6a. The latency of the Internet connection increases when the ground links between the

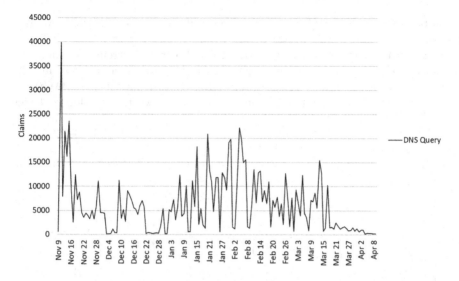

Fig. 4. DNS requests.

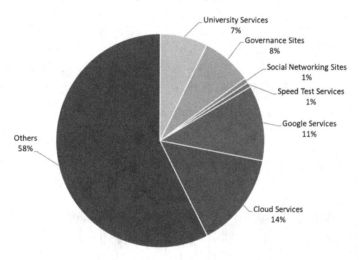

Fig. 5. DNS claims cached.

Galapagos Islands share the same satellite link connection. Although, the latency to access the local educational resources is less than 1 ms. On the other hand, broadband speed requirement increases, according to the simultaneous number of users [5]. Broadband speed depends on the plan contracted by the UTPL in the remote associate center, as shown in Fig. 6b. The Internet plan (2:1) acquired is 1 Megabit per second (Mbps) of Download and 512 Kilobit per second (kbps) of Upload. An online application on the Internet measures an approximation of broadband speed. The Upload speed is constant compared with the Download speed.

The power of the Alternating Current (AC)/Direct Current (DC) adapter determines the maximum electric energy consumption of the access system. The average monthly electric energy consumption is 47.45 Kilowatt-hour (kWh) per month. On the other hand, the memory service shows the developed device

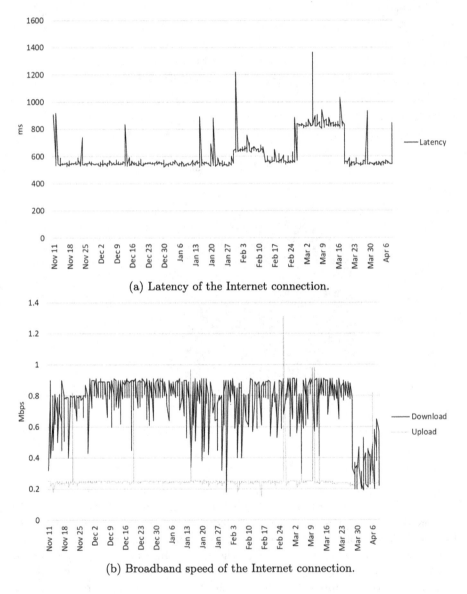

(a) Latency of the Internet connection.

(b) Broadband speed of the Internet connection.

Fig. 6. Speed test service.

performance, as shown in Fig. 7. The access system has 8032 Megabytes (MB) of RAM.

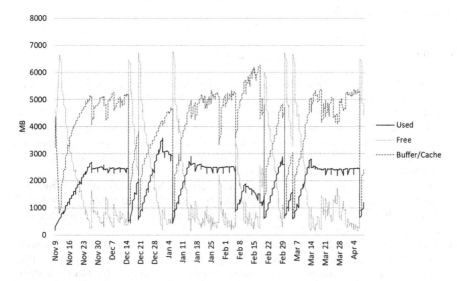

Fig. 7. RAM availability.

5   Conclusions

The access system presented in this paper provides access to local educational resources through the LMS platform of the UTPL, improving the Internet browsing experience of the users. An ICT solution in the last mile has to be simple, reducing cost using open source projects.

A primary DNS caching server and a local web server improve the Internet browsing experience, reducing broadband consumption. The organization of the access system and the virtual learning environment canvasUTPL avoids that the users have to enter two different platforms. This process is transparent to the users. However, the current broadband speed is not optimal for updating the packets through the Internet. This problem is noticeable when increasing the number of educational resources. On the other hand, the ICT integration process does not only depend on telecommunication infrastructure. Furthermore, this initiative reduces the digital divide between the insular and the continental users, enhancing the distance learning education quality.

In the long-term, this work proposes the deployment of the developed device in the local networks of the ISPs, providing access to educational resources to the users in their homes in the Galapagos Islands. On the other hand, the future study considers other remote associate centers of the UTPL with a low Internet connection to implement the access system. Later investigation suggests the access system expansion to other careers of the MAD-UTPL. Furthermore, future research could include the impact on the users.

Acknowledgments. The Research Group in Wireless Communications of the Universidad Técnica Particular de Loja supports this Research under project PROY_INNOV_2019_2598. The Universidad Técnica Particular de Loja provides the funds to develop this Work.

References

1. Bowen, R., Morris, W.: The digital divide: implications for agribusiness and entrepreneurship, lessons from wales. J. Rural Stud. **72**, 75–84 (2019). https://doi.org/10.1016/j.jrurstud.2019.10.031
2. Chiaraviglio, L., Liu, W., Gutierrez, J.A., Blefari-Melazzi, N.: Optimal pricing strategy for 5G in rural areas with unmanned aerial vehicles and large cells. In: 2017 27th International Telecommunication Networks and Applications Conference (ITNAC), pp. 1–7 (2017). https://doi.org/10.1109/ATNAC.2017.8215406
3. Dobrovská, D., Andres, P.: Digitization and current educational changes in Switzerland - inspiration for the Czech Republic? In: Auer, M.E., Hortsch, H., Sethakul, P. (eds.) ICL 2019. AISC, vol. 1135, pp. 402–408. Springer, Cham (2020). https://doi.org/10.1007/978-3-030-40271-6_40
4. Ferro, R., González, R., Cuartas, K., Díaz, Y.: Designing of a radio link to improve Web 2.0 and internet access in rural zones in Colombia. Case study: e-learning to the indigenous community of "Santander de Quilichao and Toribio Cauca". In: Uden, L., Liberona, D., Liu, Y. (eds.) LTEC 2017. CCIS, vol. 734, pp. 15–26. Springer, Cham (2017). https://doi.org/10.1007/978-3-319-62743-4_2
5. Gijón, C., Whalley, J., Anderson, G.: Exploring the differences in broadband access speeds across Glasgow. Telematics Inform. **33**(4), 1167–1178 (2016). https://doi.org/10.1016/j.tele.2015.11.003
6. Kim, S.: ICT and the UN'S sustainable development goal for education: using ICT to boost the math performance of immigrant youths in the us. Sustainability **10**(12), 4584 (2018). https://doi.org/10.3390/su10124584
7. Lim, C.P., Ra, S., Chin, B., Wang, T.: Leveraging information and communication technologies (ICT) to enhance education equity, quality, and efficiency: case studies of Bangladesh and Nepal. Educ. Media Int. **57**(2), 87–111 (2020). https://doi.org/10.1080/09523987.2020.1786774
8. Martínez-Domínguez, M., Mora-Rivera, J.: Internet adoption and usage patterns in rural Mexico. Technol. Soc. **60**, 101226 (2020). https://doi.org/10.1016/j.techsoc.2019.101226
9. Mathur, A., Ambani, D.: ICT and rural societies: opportunities for growth. Int. Inf. Libr. Rev. **37**(4), 345–351 (2005). https://doi.org/10.1016/j.iilr.2005.09.004
10. Ministry of Telecommunications and Information Society: Telecommunication and information and communication technology national plan 2016–2021 (2016). https://www.telecomunicaciones.gob.ec/
11. Ministry of Telecommunications and Information Society: Withe paper of information and knowledge society (2018). https://www.telecomunicaciones.gob.ec/
12. Mora-Rivera, J., García-Mora, F.: Internet access and poverty reduction: evidence from rural and urban Mexico. Telecommun. Pol. **45**(2), 102076 (2021). https://doi.org/10.1016/j.telpol.2020.102076
13. Telecommunications regulatory and control agency: accounts and users of the internet access service 2019 (2019). https://www.arcotel.gob.ec/

14. Tiwari, M.: ICTs and poverty reduction: user perspective study of rural Madhya Pradesh, India. Eur. J. Dev. Res. **20**(3), 448–461 (2008). https://doi.org/10.1080/09578810802245600

15. Tuteja, G.S.: Modernization in distance learning education system through BOOC's. In: Sharma, P., Rajput, S. (eds.) Sustainable Smart Cities in India. TUBS, pp. 721–730. Springer, Cham (2017). https://doi.org/10.1007/978-3-319-47145-7_43

16. United Nations: Final list of proposed sustainable development goal indicators (2016). https://sustainabledevelopment.un.org/

17. Universidad Técnica Particular de Loja: Homepage (2021). https://www.utpl.edu.ec/

18. Yaacoub, E., Alouini, M.: A key 6g challenge and opportunity–connecting the base of the pyramid: a survey on rural connectivity. Proc. IEEE **108**(4), 533–582 (2020). https://doi.org/10.1109/JPROC.2020.2976703

Hyperparameter Tuning over an Attention Model for Image Captioning

Roberto Castro[ID], Israel Pineda[ID],
and Manuel Eugenio Morocho-Cayamcela$^{(\boxtimes)}$[ID]

School of Mathematical and Computational Sciences,
Deep Learning for Autonomous Driving, Robotics, and Computer Vision Research
Group (DeepARC), Yachay Scientific Computing Group (SCG),
Yachay Tech University, Hda. San José s/n y Proyecto Yachay,
100119 Urcuquí, Ecuador
{roberto.castro,ipineda,mmorocho}@yachaytech.edu.ec
http://www.yachaytech.edu.ec

Abstract. Considering the historical trajectory and evolution of image captioning as a research area, this paper focuses on *visual attention* as an approach to solve captioning tasks with computer vision. This article studies the efficiency of different hyperparameter configurations on a state-of-the-art visual attention architecture composed of a pre-trained residual neural network encoder, and a long short-term memory decoder. Results show that the selection of both the cost function and the gradient-based optimizer have a significant impact on the captioning results. Our system considers the cross-entropy, Kullback-Leibler divergence, mean squared error, and the negative log-likelihood loss functions, as well as the adaptive momentum, AdamW, RMSprop, stochastic gradient descent, and Adadelta optimizers. Based on the performance metrics, a combination of cross-entropy with Adam is identified as the best alternative returning a Top-5 accuracy value of 73.092, and a BLEU-4 value of 0.201. Setting the cross-entropy as an independent variable, the first two optimization alternatives prove the best performance with a BLEU-4 metric value of 0.201. In terms of the inference loss, Adam outperforms AdamW with 3.413 over 3.418 and a Top-5 accuracy of 73.092 over 72.989.

Keywords: Image captioning · Visual attention · Computer vision · Supervised learning · Artificial intelligence

1 Introduction

Image captioning is a branch of computer vision whose main objective is the generation of accurate and organic text descriptions of any type of scenario portrayed in an image or frame [17]. Traditional approaches (i.e., before the neural network's era) tackled the image captioning problem using classical image processing methodologies that usually relied on the generation of templates together with object detection to produce the caption given an input image [10, 20].

© Springer Nature Switzerland AG 2021
J. P. Salgado Guerrero et al. (Eds.): TICEC 2021, CCIS 1456, pp. 172–183, 2021.
https://doi.org/10.1007/978-3-030-89941-7_13

As a consequence, joined to the usage of neural structures, visual attention has emerged as a high potential alternative, proposing to replicate human vision by enabling an emulation of attention by the neural network on the most relevant sections of an image [21]. Several researchers have replicated the benchmark implementation proposed by Xu et al. for further study [19]. The latter convolutional architecture can be broadly divided into two well-defined structures. On the one hand, a convolutional network, which takes as input the raw images to be processed, while it outputs a set of feature vectors, each of which represents a D-dimensional part of a section of the illustration. Thus, the decoding part of the model will be able to selectively focus on specific parts of the image by making use of subsets of the feature vectors. On the other hand, a long short-term memory (LSTM) network makes use of the previous output to generate a word at each time instant in dependence on a context vector, previously generated words, and the previous hidden state.

Modern artificial intelligence models provide promising results for the captioning problem. However, one of the remaining challenges is the optimization of hyperparameters which is far from trivial and remains a challenge for captioning and other applications [3].

In this paper, we study the performance impact of different hyperparameters of the model during the training and testing stages. More specifically, we conduct a comparative study to select the cost function that minimizes the training error over a certain number of epochs for our specific application. In addition, and using the leading cost function as an independent variable, we execute an optimizer sweep to appoint the best possible hyperparameter configuration for our captioning task. Based on our results, we can confidently claim that the arrangement of the cross-entropy as a cost function along with the gradient-based Adam optimizer, have led to superior results in terms of the top-5 accuracy and BLEU-4 metrics.

2 Related Works

According to the historical summary presented in Table 1, one of the pioneering research works incorporating an *attention* system is the one proposed by Larochelle & Hinton, based on a variant of the *restricted Boltzmann machine* (RBM) mainly used for digit classification. They used the benchmark MNIST dataset, where a limited set of pixels is provided from which the architecture collects both high- and low-resolution information about neighboring pixels [11]. Moving forward in the timeline, Bahdanau et al. reused the notion of attention applied to different convolutional architectures. In this case, a much more novel model such as an *encoder-decoder* makes use of a reduced but visible attention system to take into consideration certain parts of a sentence when performing the translation of a specific word [2]. The idea of taking advantage of the benefits offered by *recurrent architectures* was a common factor that persisted in later works, among which stand out research-oriented to digit classification such as that presented by Mnih et al. [14], and the one proposed by Ba et al. [1].

Table 1. Summary of visual attention related works.

Architecture	Data input	Cost Function	Optimizer	Performance metric	Reference
Multi-fixation Restricted Boltzmann Machine (RBM)	Images	Hybrid Cost Hybrid-Sequential Cost	SGD	Error rate and accuracy	Larochelle & Hinton (2010)
Encoder-Decoder	Source sentence of 1-of-K coded word vectors	N/A	SGD and Adadelta	BLEU	Bahdanau et al. (2014)
Recurrent Neural Network	Images	Cross entropy and Reinforcement	SGD with momentum	Error rate	Mnih et al. (2014)
Deep Recurrent Attention Model	Images	Log-Likelihood	SGD with the Nesterov momentum	Error rate	Ba et al. (2014)
Encoder-Decoder	Images and encoded captioning	Cross entropy	Adam	BLEU and METEOR	Xu et al. (2016)

Table 2. Summary of image captioning related works.

Architecture	Data input	Cost function	Optimizer	Performance metric	Reference
RNN	Image and sentence descriptions	Log-likelihood calculated by perplexity plus a regularization term	N/A	BLEU, Perplexity, Recall@K and Median rank	Mao et al. (2014)
LSTM	Image passes through a CNN	Sum of the negative log likelihood of the correct word at each step	SGD	BLEU, METEOR, CIDER, Recall@k and Median rank	Vinyals et al. (2014)
LSTM	Images or Text	Negative log likelihood	SGD	BLEU, METEOR, CIDER, Recall@k, Median rank and Rogue-L	Donahue et al. (2014)
Multimodal log-bilinear model	Images	Perplexity	N/A	BLEU, Perplexity	Kiros et al. (2014a)
Encoder-Decoder	Images	Pairwise ranking loss	SGD	Recall@k and Median rank	Kiros et al. (2014b)

In order to substantiate the evolution within the area of image captioning, a brief historical review of relevant works is presented in Table 2. Throughout this summary, we can find contributions such as the one proposed by Kiros et al., using a *multi-log bilinear model* for exploiting the characteristics of images to generate a biased version of this architecture [9]. Followed this research, the same author incorporated recurrent structures within an encoder-decoder model, a common factor among image captioning proposals. This fact is mainly due to the nature of human speech that is sought to be incorporated into the learning algorithm. Furthermore, authors such as Mao et al. [13], Vinyals et al. [18], and Donahue et al. [5] have reused this idea in their respective research efforts.

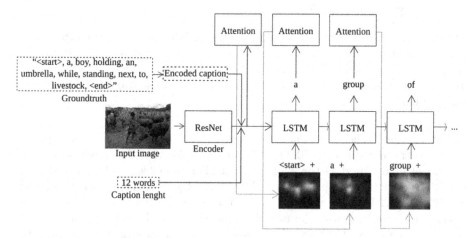

Fig. 1. Overall representation of the convolutional encoder-decoder architecture built to generate real captioning. The model uses a pre-trained ResNet architecture as the encoder backbone, along with recurrent LSTM operations for the decoder. The objects with discontinuous contours are only used during the training stage.

3   System Model and Design

The convolutional model employed for this study is built following an encoder-decoder architecture supported by a visual attention model. The proposed neural architecture is schematized in Fig. 1, where an instance of the dataset is outlined in order to show its operation.

On the one hand, the encoder makes use of transfer learning by borrowing the convolutional architecture of Resnet [6]. This incorporation aims to generate an encoded version of the input RGB image, with an output dimensionality of $2048 \times 14 \times 14$. On the decoder side, given the sequential nature of the problem to be solved, an LSTM recursive architecture is constructed [7]. Up to this point, the description of the input image is generated in a word-by-word basis. At each decoding step, the attention network uses the output generated by the encoder together with the previous hidden state, generating averaged weights for each pixel of the encoded image. Therein, the network is told "where" to look by assigning higher weights to pixels of upward relevance. Using this outcome and the previously generated word as references, the LSTM network generates a definitive caption for the input image.

On the other hand, the objects in Fig. 1 denoted with discontinuous contours are groundtruth components extracted from the dataset. Notwithstanding, those objects are only used during the training phase of the model. Their nature is described in the next section of the paper.

3.1 The Dataset Structure

The dataset used for training the network was the 2014 version of the MS COCO variant oriented to image captioning tasks [12]. Three inputs are structured in the dataset to be used by the neural network during the training stage. It should be noted that these three components are prepared for the training, testing, and validation sets.

Input Images. The set of images obtained from MS COCO must have pixels values in the domain $b \in \{0,1\}$ to be compatible with the pre-trained convolutional model used as the encoder block. For the effect, a normalization of the RGB channels is applied using the values of $\mu = [0.485, 0.456, 0.406]$ and $\sigma = [0.229, 0.224, 0.225]$, where μ and σ represent the mean and the standard deviation of the ImageNet dataset [4], respectively. Each image in the dataset is represented as $X^{(i)} \in \mathbb{R}^{256 \times 256}$, where $X^{(i)}$ is a matrix of 256×256 pixels. We let m be the total number of images on MS COCO dataset, and represent the entire dataset as $X\{X^{(1)}, \ldots, X^{(m)}\}$, where each image $X^{(i)}$ is mapped to a ground truth caption $Y^{(i)}$ that represents the corresponding ground-truth encoded caption.

Encoded Captions. In order to be able to manipulate the descriptions associated with each image in the dataset, the model uses a `.json` mapping file. Within this file, each word used in the captioning of the entire dataset has an identification number. Thus, the complete vocabulary supported by the network and its numerical equivalents can be visualized in this file. This new `.json` file will contain an array where each of its elements will correspond to the word-by-word captioning of each image using the numerical equivalences defined within the mapping file.

In addition, the inclusion of three special characters within the mapping file is required. On the one hand, the neural network requires a *start* and *end* signal to delimit the extension of the descriptions. On the other hand, since not all the descriptions occupy the same sentence size, it is required to fill the missing spaces of the encoded caption with a padding character. Consequently, taking the longest ground-truth as referral, the content of the rest of the captions is updated to match the reference length by incorporating the padding operator. The proposed methodology normalizes the MS COCO dataset in arrays of 52 elements.

Fig. 2. Image taken from the training set with an associated groundtruth caption: "a man with a red helmet on a small moped on a dirt road".

Table 3. Mapping system used to encode the caption the example image.

Original word	Encoded version
a	1
man	2
with	3
red	4
helmet	5
on	6
small	7
moped	8
dirt	9
road	10
...	...
<start>	9488
<end>	9489
<pad>	0

As an example, in Fig. 2 it can be seen an instance included in the validation group. This image is associated with a corresponding C description: "a man with a red helmet on a small moped on a dirt road". Referring to the file, which contains its encoded description E_C, one can find an encoding of the form:

$$E_C = [9488, 1, 2, 3, 1, 4, 5, 6, 1, 7, 8, 6, 1, 9, 10, 9489, 0, 0, ..., 0],$$

considering that it has been generated from the equivalences contained in the mapping file, the contents of which are presented in Table 3.

Caption Lenghts. Finally, the last file is generated whose purpose is to house an array, whose elements represent the number of words that make up the description associated with each of the images.

3.2   Hyperparameter Tuning

Cross-Entropy Loss Function. To describe the loss function of our attention model, we let a be the function parametrized by θ, the caption output of the network is represented as $C = a(X, \theta)$, where C is the collection of words inferred from the MS COCO dictionary. The loss function measures the inference performance of our attention model when compared with its respective ground truth. In order to measure the difference between the ground truth distribution and the distribution of the caption outcome, we define $J(\boldsymbol{\theta})$ as the *cross-entropy*. The cross-entropy loss function penalizes the attention model when it infers a low probability for a given caption. Our attention model works by updating the values of $\boldsymbol{\theta}$, moving the loss towards the minimum of $J(\boldsymbol{\theta})$ [15].

For our training set of $(\boldsymbol{X}^{(i)}, \boldsymbol{Y}^{(i)})$ for $i \in \{1, \ldots, m\}$, we estimate the parameters $\boldsymbol{\theta} = \{\theta^{(1)}, \ldots, \theta^{(n)}\}$ that minimizes $J(\boldsymbol{\theta})$ by computing:

$$
\begin{aligned}
J(\boldsymbol{\theta}) &= -\frac{1}{m} \sum_{i=1}^{m} L(\boldsymbol{X}^{(i)}, \boldsymbol{Y}^{(i)}, \boldsymbol{\theta}) \\
&= -\frac{1}{m} \sum_{i=1}^{m} \boldsymbol{Y}^{(i)} log\left(\hat{p}^{(i)}\right),
\end{aligned}
\tag{1}
$$

where $\boldsymbol{Y}^{(i)}$ represents the expected caption $\mathbf{C}$ of the ith image, and $\hat{p}^{(i)}$ constitutes the probability that the ith image outcomes the intended value of $\mathbf{C}$.

Adaptive Moment Optimizer. In order to optimize our attention model through a gradient-based optimization method, we express the gradient vector of (1) with respect to θ as

$$
\begin{aligned}
\mathbf{g} &= \nabla_{\theta} J(\boldsymbol{\theta}) \\
&= \frac{1}{m} \nabla_{\theta} \sum_{i=1}^{m} L(\boldsymbol{X}^{(i)}, \boldsymbol{Y}^{(i)}, \boldsymbol{\theta}) \\
&= \frac{1}{m} \sum_{i=1}^{m} \left(\hat{p}^{(i)} - \boldsymbol{Y}^{(i)}\right) \boldsymbol{X}^{(i)}.
\end{aligned}
\tag{2}
$$

To locate the minimum of $J(\boldsymbol{\theta})$, the proposed optimization algorithm moves to the negative direction of (2) iteratively. Our model computes individual adaptive learning rates for different parameters from estimates of first and second moments of $\mathbf{g}$ [8].

4 Experimental Settings

This work proposes two experimental scenarios. First, we maintain all the default hyperparameters of the model to study the impact of the different cost functions. Since the cross-entropy cost function was used to train the benchmark model, we contrasted the performance of the architecture using the negative log-likelihood, mean squared error, and the Kullback-Leibler Divergence cost functions.

Once the first experimental phase is completed, the aim is to keep the cost function as an independent variable to sweep different optimizers. Once again, in addition to the optimizer used in the benchmark implementation (Adam), we examined the effect of AdamW, RMSprop, SGD, and Adadelta optimizers.

Both experimental phases were applied over one training epoch, using a workstation with 8 GB of RAM and an NVIDIA GTX1650 graphical processing unit (GPU).

The criterion used to contrast the performance of the different hyperparameter settings consisted in the interpretation of the top-5 accuracy, loss value, and BLEU-4 as a way to compute the similarity between the predicted captions and the available ground-truths (based on 4-grams modified comparisons) [16]. In addition, and in a non-quantitative way, we have considered the quality of the generated captions for specific unseen images.

5   Results

From Table 4, it is possible to highlight an evident improvement in the performance of the model when using the cross-entropy as a loss function. Although the mean squared error (MSE) loss is positioned as the second-best alternative throughout the experimental process, a difference of 31.584 in the Top-5 accuracy indicator and 0.187 in BLEU-4 metric shows a large gap between the cross-entropy function and this alternative. Considering this significant difference, the results obtained by the Kullback–Leibler divergence (KLDIVLOSS) and the negative log-likelihood loss (NLL), position them as unsuitable alternatives for the model to be trained on.

Table 4. Experimental results using *Top-5* accuracy and the *BLEU-4* performance metric for each one of the loss functions under study.

	Top-5 Accuracy[†]	BLEU-4[†]
Cross-entropy	**73.092**	**0.201**
MSE	41.508	0.014
KLDIVLOSS	32.186	1.173e-155
NLL	32.186	1.173e-155

[†]Trained using a workstation with 8 GB of RAM and an NVIDIA GTX1650 GPU.

In addition to the quantitative results, Fig. 3 illustrates a captioning example generated using each one of the loss functions under study. The outcomes prove that the cross-entropy loss function is positioned not only as the one with the best results, but also the only loss function capable of generating a complete and meaningful description for an illustration that has never been seen by our model.

Proceeding with the second experimental scene, the results offered in Table 5 reveal a tighter situation when defining an optimal alternative. In the first instance, the optimizer Adam is positioned with the best results according to the three defined metrics. However, its variation, AdamW, not only returns the

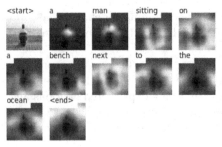

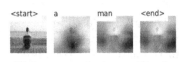

(b) Image captioning result using MSE loss.

(a) Image captioning result using cross entropy loss.

(c) Image captioning result using NLL loss.

(d) Image captioning result using KL-DIVLOSS.

Fig. 3. Image captioning results using an attention model with: (a) cross entropy loss, (b) MSE loss, (c) NLL loss, and (d) KLDIVLOSS. The results reveal an inadequate inference of MSE, NLL and KLDIVLOSS functions. By far, cross entropy is the only loss function that allows a proper training of our attention model.

same BLEU-4 value as Adam, but it is only 0.005 and 0.133 of difference in the loss and Top-5 Accuracy indicators, respectively. This closeness in terms of results can be visualized using Fig. 4. In this illustration, each optimizer is tested by predicting the captioning for an image consisting of a child in front of a laptop computer. When contrasting both variations of the Adam optimizer, it is observed that the predictions only differ when mentioning the gender of the person in the image. It is worth highlighting the performance of the root mean square propogation optimizer (RMSprop), which ranks as the third-best alternative, presenting a loss value of 3.663, along with 71.444 and 0.192 for Top-5 accuracy and BLEU-4, respectively. RMSprop shows promising results when comparing the output caption with the example image shown in Fig. 4. This optimizer is capable of generating a fully meaningful captioning by portrying to the content of the image. However, it missed minor details like not including a reference to the elderliness of the person in the illustration.

Finally, the stochastic gradient descent (SGD) and the Adadelta optimizers provided the worst results. Although both optimizers presented slightly different metrics, it is observed that neither of them were able to create a model capable of generating meaningful captions.

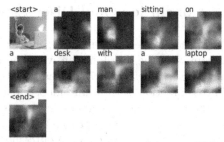

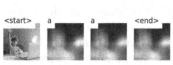

(a) Image captioning result using SGD and Adadelta optimizers.

(b) Image captioning result using RMSprop optimizer.

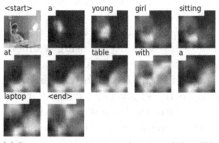

(c) Image captioning result using AdamW optimizer.

(d) Image captioning result using Adam optimizer.

Fig. 4. Image captioning results using: (a) SGD and Adadelta optimizers, (b) RMSprop optimizer, (c) AdamW optimizer, and (d) Adam optimizer. The image illustrates the inadequate inference results of SGD and Adadelta when compared with their alternatives. Also, note that Adam optimizer yields the finest result over the test image (a recurrent outcome obtained for further experiments using images from the test set).

Table 5. Experimental results using the training loss, the *Top-5* Accuracy, and the *BLEU-4* performance metrics for each one of the optimizers under study.

	Loss[†]	Top-5 Accuracy[†]	BLEU-4[†]
Adam	**3.413**	**73.092**	**0.201**
AdamW	3.418	72.989	**0.201**
RMSprop	3.663	71.444	0.192
SGD	7.011	33.606	1.273e-155
Adadelta	7.133	33.045	1.272e-155

[†]Trained using a workstation with 8 GB of RAM and an NVIDIA GTX1650 GPU.

6   Conclusions and Discussion

During the experimental stage, it was possible to determine that the cross-entropy was the loss function with the best results, returning Top-5 accuracy and BLEU-4 metrics of 73.092 and 0.201, respectively. On the other hand, once the loss function is set as an independent variable, the Adam optimizer returned the best indicators, completing the first training period with a loss value of 3.414, a Top-5 Accuracy of 73.092, and a BLEU-4 of 0.201. However, the results obtained are tight close to the outcomes obtained with the AdamW optimizer, sharing the same BLEU-4 value. The training time required for each epoch was six hours, i.e., a total of 48 h was required for the generation of all the results.

Although we have proved that the three optimizers offer feasible results for this architecture, future works can benefit from the individual training epoch to further study the convergence pace of the model under limited computational resources. In addition, future works can study the viability of using a different encoder architecture than ResNet, together with an extended investigation on the architectural framework. Finally, another alternative to foster this work would be to include further hyperparameters to the study (e.g., dropout rate, batch size, different types of stride and pooling, size of the kernels, weight initialization methods, model depth, weight decay, etc.), enabling an in-depth research of the attention architecture.

Acknowledgments. This research was partially supported by the Ecuadorian Corporation for the Development of Research and Academia (CEDIA), under the project "Divulga Ciencia 2021", grant No.: JLE-CN-2021-0105. This research was partially supported by NVIDIA Corporation under the program "NVIDIA Jetson Nano 2GB Developer Kit".

References

1. Ba, J., Mnih, V., Kavukcuoglu, K.: Multiple object recognition with visual attention. CoRR abs/1412.7755 (2014). http://dblp.uni-trier.de/db/journals/corr/corr1412.html#BaMK14
2. Bahdanau, D., Cho, K., Bengio, Y.: Neural machine translation by jointly learning to align and translate. In: 3rd International Conference on Learning Representations, ICLR 2015, 07–09 May 2015 (2015)
3. Carrión-Ojeda, D., Fonseca-Delgado, R., Pineda, I.: Analysis of factors that influence the performance of biometric systems based on EEG signals. Expert Syst. Appl. **165**, 113967 (2021) https://doi.org/10.1016/j.eswa.2020.113967. https://www.sciencedirect.com/science/article/pii/S095741742030748X
4. Deng, J., Dong, W., Socher, R., Li, L.J., Li, K., Fei-Fei, L.: ImageNet: a large-scale hierarchical image database. In: 2009 IEEE Conference on Computer Vision and Pattern Recognition, pp. 248–255 (2009). https://doi.org/10.1109/CVPR.2009.5206848
5. Donahue, J., et al.: Long-term recurrent convolutional networks for visual recognition and description. In: Proceedings of the IEEE Conference on Computer Vision and Pattern Recognition (CVPR) (2015)

6. He, K., Zhang, X., Ren, S., Sun, J.: Deep residual learning for image recognition. In: 2016 IEEE Conference on Computer Vision and Pattern Recognition (CVPR), pp. 770–778 (2016). https://doi.org/10.1109/CVPR.2016.90
7. Hochreiter, S., Schmidhuber, J.: Long short-term memory. Neural Comput. **9**(8), 1735–1780 (1997). https://doi.org/10.1162/neco.1997.9.8.1735
8. Kingma, D.P., Ba, J.: Adam: a method for stochastic optimization. In: 3rd International Conference for Learning Representations (2015)
9. Kiros, R., Salakhutdinov, R., Zemel, R.: Multimodal neural language models. In: Xing, E.P., Jebara, T. (eds.) Proceedings of the 31st International Conference on Machine Learning. Proceedings of Machine Learning Research, vol. 32, pp. 595–603. PMLR, Bejing (2014). https://proceedings.mlr.press/v32/kiros14.html
10. Kulkarni, G., et al.: Baby talk: understanding and generating simple image descriptions. IEEE Trans. Pattern Anal. Mach. Intell. **35**(12), 2891–2903 (2013). https://doi.org/10.1109/TPAMI.2012.162
11. Larochelle, H., Hinton, G.: Learning to combine foveal glimpses with a third-order Boltzmann machine. In: Lafferty, J., Williams, C., Shawe-Taylor, J., Zemel, R., Culotta, A. (eds.) Advances in Neural Information Processing Systems, vol. 1, pp. 1243–1251. Curran Associates, Inc. (2010)
12. Lin, T.-Y., et al.: Microsoft COCO: common objects in context. In: Fleet, D., Pajdla, T., Schiele, B., Tuytelaars, T. (eds.) ECCV 2014. LNCS, vol. 8693, pp. 740–755. Springer, Cham (2014). https://doi.org/10.1007/978-3-319-10602-1_48
13. Mao, J., Xu, W., Yang, Y., Wang, J., Yuille, A.L.: Deep captioning with multimodal recurrent neural networks (m-RNN). In: International Conference for Learning Representations (2015). http://arxiv.org/abs/1412.6632
14. Mnih, V., Heess, N., Graves, A., et al.: Recurrent models of visual attention. In: Advances in Neural Information Processing Systems, pp. 2204–2212 (2014)
15. Morocho-Cayamcela, M.E., Lee, H., Lim, W.: Machine learning to improve multi-hop searching and extended wireless reachability in V2X. IEEE Commun. Lett. **24**(7), 1477–1481 (2020). https://doi.org/10.1109/LCOMM.2020.2982887
16. Papineni, K., Roukos, S., Ward, T., Zhu, W.J.: Bleu. In: Proceedings of the 40th Annual Meeting on Association for Computational Linguistics - ACL 2002 (2001). https://doi.org/10.3115/1073083.1073135
17. Rennie, S.J., Marcheret, E., Mroueh, Y., Ross, J., Goel, V.: Self-critical sequence training for image captioning. In: Proceedings of the IEEE Conference on Computer Vision and Pattern Recognition (CVPR) (2017)
18. Vinyals, O., Toshev, A., Bengio, S., Erhan, D.: Show and tell: a neural image caption generator. In: Proceedings of the IEEE Conference on Computer Vision and Pattern Recognition (CVPR) (2015)
19. Xu, K., et al.: Show, attend and tell: neural image caption generation with visual attention (2016)
20. Yang, Y., Teo, C., Daumé III, H., Aloimonos, Y.: Corpus-guided sentence generation of natural images. In: Proceedings of the 2011 Conference on Empirical Methods in Natural Language Processing, pp. 444–454 (2011)
21. You, Q., Jin, H., Wang, Z., Fang, C., Luo, J.: Image captioning with semantic attention. In: Proceedings of the IEEE Conference on Computer Vision and Pattern Recognition (CVPR) (2016)

Quality Model for CloudIot Applied in Ambient Assisted Living (AAL)

María Caridad Cáceres[1] ⓘ, Daniel Peralta[1] ⓘ, Alexandra Bermeo[2] ⓘ,
Cristina Sánchez-Zhunio[2] ⓘ, and Priscila Cedillo[1,2(✉)] ⓘ

[1] Faculty of Engineering, Universidad de Cuenca, Cuenca, Ecuador
{caridad.caceres,daniel.peralta,priscila.cedillo}@ucuenca.edu.ec
[2] Computer Science Department, Universidad de Cuenca, Cuenca, Ecuador
{alexandra.bermeo,cristina.sanchezz}@ucuenca.edu.ec

Abstract. Nowadays, CloudIoT is used in several domains. Among them, AAL applications, where it can support the monitoring of certain variables related to the wellbeing of older adults at real-time. They store and manage personal information about users and vital signs, which are essential to be transmitted securely and reliably. Then, this paper presents a quality model focused on the CloudIoT layers in Ambient Assisted Living. It evaluates security, usability, and reliability, applied on the AAL domain, and focused on each of CloudIoT layers: Cloud Computing, Fog Computing, and Edge Computing. Also, an empirical evaluation of the AAL applications evaluation process in CloudIoT is presented. This method was evaluated using the Method Evaluation Model (MEM), 15 experts in computer science participated in the evaluation, the obtained results show that people find that the method is useful, easy to use, and allows to evaluate the viability of CloudIoT applications in AAL.

Keywords: Quality model · CloudIot · Ambient Assisted Living · ISO/IEC 25010 · ISO/IEC 25040 · Reliability · Usability

1 Introduction

Cloud Computing has become a new technology that improves information systems' computational complexity [1]. As stated by the National Institute of Standards and Technology (NIST), cloud computing is a model for enabling ubiquitous, convenient, on-demand network access to a shared pool of configurable computing resources. It can be rapidly deployed and shared with minimal administrative overhead, including flexibility, scalability, and dynamic provisioning [2, 3].

Moreover, the Internet of Things (IoT) is a computer environment that seeks the integration of several devices or sensors of the same infrastructure, using both public and private networks; also, they are capable of interacting with each other, while autonomous reactions are created [4–6]. The first implementation based on IoT was done with radio frequency identification systems; this transmission was performed so identification and management could be considered intelligent [7, 8]. Today, IoT is part of all aspects of people's lives, being applied in many domains [6].

© Springer Nature Switzerland AG 2021
J. P. Salgado Guerrero et al. (Eds.): TICEC 2021, CCIS 1456, pp. 184–198, 2021.
https://doi.org/10.1007/978-3-030-89941-7_14

Although IoT is a reliable technology, it also has some technological constraints like storage, processing, and energy. Therefore, it can benefit from the virtually unlimited capabilities and resources of cloud computing. Also, cloud computing can extend its scope within IoT [8]. To accomplish this, the integration of cloud computing with IoT, also known as CloudIoT or Cloud of Things, presents a flexible, less complex, and cost-effective solution [9].

The World Health Organization states that by using assistive technologies, like IoT, people with disabilities are equal beneficiaries of any development process [10]. Furthermore, as estimated by the same organization, 15% of the world's population live with some form of disability [10]. For this reason, the use of the CloudIoT paradigm in the healthcare field can bring several opportunities to medical information technology, and experts believe that it can significantly improve healthcare services and contribute to its continuous and systematic innovation [11].

Moreover, Ambient Assisted Living (AAL) also encompasses technical systems to support older adults and people with special needs in their daily routine; maintaining the autonomy of those people and, increasing safety in their lifestyle and home environment [12, 13]. Then, according to the ISO/IEC 12207 standard, quality is defined as the degree to which a system component or process meets the specified requirements and the users' needs or expectations [14].

According to [15], the usage of CloudIoT in AAL scenarios could potentially present problems that could quickly and dramatically cost lives. Therefore, it is important to emphasize the following quality characteristics: reliability, security, and usability, according to ISO/IEC 25010 [16].

These characteristics have been chosen because, the authors of [17] considered them as critical characteristics of the entire AAL domain. These properties can be evaluated in the layers of AAL, as presented by [18], they can be related to the CloudIoT structure presented by [19]. The structure of CloudIoT contains three principal layers: Cloud Computing, Fog Computing, and Edge Computing.

This work presents a quality model to evaluate the usability, portability and security of the CloudIoT applications. Also, a method to assess quality of CloudIoT applications in the AAL domain, which was presented by [28] and is based on the ISO/IEC 25040 standard [31]. Finally, the method was evaluated, through the use of the Method Evaluation Method (MEM). This was presented to 15 Computer Science students and professionals. After the application of the MEM, the results show that the method is feasible and can be used to evaluate any CloudIoT application.

This paper has the following structure: Sect. 2 discusses related work; Sect. 3 presents the proposed quality model. Section 4, presents the development of the method that was used to evaluate a CloudIoT application. Section 5 presents the experimental process applying MEM to validate the method. Section 6 presents the analysis of threats to validity, and Sect. 7 shows the conclusions and future work.

2   Related Work

In this section, contributions related to the study area are mentioned. Some of them present quality models to evaluate reliability, security, and usability. In terms of reliability, the authors of [20] present a quality model using characteristics from ISO/IEC

25010 and also based on ISO/IEC 25023. The performance and reliability are analyzed. Also, evaluations are carried out through simulators on IoT. They are tested in several applications since none can evaluate all the specified metrics. Otherwise, Zheng et al. [21] proposed CLOUDQUAL, a general model for cloud services. Six quality attributes are analyzed: usability, security, reliability, tangibility, responsiveness, empathy. The proposed model is an extension of the ISO/IEC 25010 model. Besides, the authors of [22] developed a quality model that studies the reliability of devices for mobile environments. They are based on the ISO 9126 standard and work with four external metrics that directly influence mobile devices. In addition, they carry out a study to measure the influence that this characteristic has concerning the other seven characteristics, according to ISO/IEC 25010, within these environments.

In the security environment, the authors of [23] present a quality model based on the ISO/IEC 25000 standards, specifically in 25010, 25021, 25023, to measure security in web applications during their design phase. They focus solely on the authenticity of protocols and rules. However, it is shown that it is possible to measure web applications' security characteristics in the early stages of the software development cycle using the presented metrics. Likewise, [24] present a quality model in encryption as a service domain, which can be considered a part of cloud computing. It is based on ISO/IEC 25010 to evaluate four characteristics: efficiency, reliability, security, and maintainability.

Security is one of the most critical attributes due to the confidentiality that data must have. In [25] and [26], the authors proposed evaluation methods based on the Goal Question Metric (GQM) approach [27], where it can be analyzed the quality of the software product in terms of its security. These two works are general methods that can be applied to software in any domain. Then, the authors of [28] propose a security quality model designed for CloudIoT, which is an extension of the model presented in the standard ISO/IEC 25010. This work employs a method of quality evaluation aligned with ISO 25040. A use case is used to test the approach in an e-health product that supports AAL.

Finally, a quality study is carried out, considering the usability as it is presented in [29], based on the ISO/IEC 25000 SQuaRE standard. A quality assessment for frameworks was created, which defined sixty-six quality measures for product quality and seventeen for quality in use. It presents that a higher functional adequacy score tends to indicate a lower usability score, and; a higher portability score tends to indicate higher usability scores. The authors of [30] present an excerpt of a usability model with the most related attributes and metrics associated with the social network sites domain when used by older people. It has been considered the SQUARE ISO/IEC 25010 for the quality model. The development of the quality model is presented by evaluating five sub-characteristics reliability, security, and usability, they focus only on one of them; instead, in this work, a joint study is carried out. Also, just one of them focused on the use of CloudIoT on the AAL domain but did not combine all the proposed characteristics.

3   Quality Model

A quality model of reliability, security, and usability is proposed, in order to evaluate the CloudIoT applications applied to AAL These characteristics have been chosen because, according to the literature review, they are pretty important within each CloudIoT layer: Cloud, Fog and Edge.

The main objective is to have attributes within each proposed characteristic, specific for each layer, therefore, each of the three characteristics are applied in the three mentioned layers. For this quality model, it has been considered the sub-characteristics aligned with the SQUARE ISO/IEC 25010 [31].

Then, the model is divided into three sections, each one corresponds to the CloudIoT layers:

1. *Metrics for Cloud Computing:* the security feature is made up of a sub-feature, confidentiality, which covers the handling of critical information and data, their classification and storage. Based on the values of the data, its storage location and the form of encryption used, security can be measured [32]. Regarding to the usability, the use of protection against user errors was proposed as a sub-characteristic. This included the recovery of said errors through the warning messages and troubleshooting forms that the system sends to the user [33]. On the other hand, the reliability characteristic has two sub-characteristics: fault tolerance and data recovery. The first sub-characteristic was sought to measure the handling of failures by detecting and resolving them, for which the formulas proposed in [8, 22] were used. Finally, the second sub-characteristic, data recovery, measures the recovery through the backups that are made in the system [2].

2. *Metrics for Fog Computing:* within this layer, security has two sub-characteristics: confidentiality and integrity. They are measured through the transmission of data and its synchronization or concurrency. It seeks to measure how secure these processes are within the layer, through the use of cryptographic algorithms, similar to the processes described by the authors of [32, 33]. The usability feature has the sub-features of the ability to recognize suitability and the ability to be used. The first one is measured by the user guides or the layer initiation messages, so it can be verified that the user does not have to memorize processes. The second sub-characteristic seeks to measure the portability of the system through the independence of the devices or platforms that are used. Finally, the reliability characteristics also has two sub-characteristics that are maturity and availability within this layer. This is done by measuring the validity and stability of the connections, and the availability of the devices. The forms presented in [3, 33, 34] were used for these values.

3. *Metrics for Edge Computing:* in this last layer, the security feature has two sub-features, which are confidentiality and accountability. They seek to measure password management and authentication, respectively. According to [32], they are based on the security of passwords and protocols for the authenticity of users. The usability feature has two sub-features: user interface and aesthetics interface [35]. The first focuses on the way the user is able to customize the system and if it has minimalist designs. On the other hand, the aesthetics of the interface focuses on the visual consistency and integrity of all its functions. Lastly, the reliability characteristic has maturity and recoverability as sub-characteristics. They focus on error prediction and device recovery, respectively. According to [2, 36] for its measurements, the way in which possible errors are dealt with and the persistence of the data after pauses will be verified.

After explaining the model and its characteristics and metrics, it should be mentioned that new sub-characteristics have been added due to the research carried out by the authors of [28, 29]. These authors define the importance of analyzing the monitoring of quality sub-characteristics, because the software must detect and record all attempts by the user and the program to modify unauthorized access [26].

Tables 1 and 2 present the information more detailed of the characteristics of mature and comprehensibility, that are part of security and usability respectively.

Table 1. Security quality model: mature sub-characteristic.

Attributes	Meaning
Audit level	What are the contains of audit trail record?
Security breach detection	How long does it take to report after any security violation?
Failed login attempts	How does fail login attempt count?
Malicious activity handle	How do virus, worms or other malicious code are detected, report and stop?

Table 2. Usability quality model: comprehensibility sub-characteristic.

Sub-Sub-Sub characteristic	Attributes	Meaning
Contrast between the text and the background	Brightness	Is there a brightness difference between text and background?
	Color	Is there a color difference between text and background?
Character set	Text font	Does the text have a simple font and allows the understanding of what is written?
	Text size	Does the size of texts limit their optical visibility, including disabilities that appear for the advanced age?
Need to scroll the text	Minimal scrollbars	Is it necessary to use scrollbars during the navigation?

4   Evaluation Method

It is necessary to consider that the evaluation will be multi-layered, working with the Cloud, Fog, and Edge Computing layers separately. In each layer, the corresponding metric to each characteristic will be evaluated, having reliability, security and usability.

The steps established in the evaluation method are suggested by the ISO/IEC 25040 [28, 31].

To establish a specific domain for the evaluation, it is important to use the method as proposed by [28]. Moreover, according to the established approach for the evaluation, additional steps have been added within the first four tasks of the method. These steps seek to separate the evaluation so it is easier to identify which is the quality characteristic that fails in each layer.

To establish the evaluation requirements, it is required to enter as new artifacts the specific application to evaluate, and the GQM guide which will be filled out during the establishment of the evaluation purposes, and the architecture of the application. Into this architecture, it will be explained the layers that were previously described.

Then, during the specification of the evaluation it is obtained the metrics' classification as a new artifact and one of the results of this step. This document contains the metrics that will be separated according to the layer in which they are applied.

The CloudIot Quality Model is used as a guideline on the evaluation design task; where two new artifacts were also added as an input to the constraint definition step: evaluation specification and the CloudIoT quality model. These provide the constraints to design the evaluation plan and obtain the evaluation design.

Finally, the evaluation execution task begins with the evaluation of the three traditional CloudIoT layers, where three evaluators are needed, who are an expert for each evaluated layer.

5 Empirical Evaluation

This section presents the experiment carried out to empirically evaluate the execution phase of the quality method. The Method Evaluation Model (MEM), proposed by [20] was applied. MEM measures two constructs which are:

- Current effectiveness based on User performance: Efficiency and effectiveness.
- Perceived efficacy based on user perceptions: Perceived Ease of Use (PEOU), Perceived Usefulness (PU), Intent to Use (ITU). These constructs are based on the Technological Acceptance Model (TAM) proposed by [37].

Then, the experimental process proposed by has been applied to evaluate the execution phase of the presented method. The process has the following phases: (i) definition of the scope, (ii) planning, (iii) operation, (iv) analysis and interpretation, and (v) presentation and packaging, which are described below:

5.1 Definition of the Scope

According to [27], the paradigm GQM seeks to define the goal of the evaluation. In this context, the goal of the evaluation has been defined as follows:

- Evaluate: execution phase of the method.
- With the purpose of: evaluate the method with respect to perceived efficacy.

- From the point of view of: Software quality professionals and/or students with enough quality and emergent technologies knowledge.
- In the context of: a group of students of the last year of systems engineering career of the Universidad de Cuenca, in Ecuador.

For this, the following research questions have been posed:

- RQ1: the method is perceived as easy to use and useful? If so, are users' perceptions the result of their performance when using the method to measure the quality of the Cloud, Fog and Edge Computing layers?
- RQ2: Is there an intention to use the method in the future? If so, are these usage intentions the result of the participants' perceptions?

To respond to RQ1, the hypotheses H1, H2, H3 and H4 have been proposed and to respond to RQ2, the hypotheses H5, H6, H7 and H8.

- $H1_0$: the method is perceived as difficult to use $H1_0 = \neg H1_1$.
- $H2_0$: the method is not perceived as a useful method, $H2_0 = \neg H2_1$.
- $H3_0$: Perceived ease of use cannot be determined by the current efficiency, $H3_0 = \neg H3_1$.
- $H4_0$: Perception of utility is not determined by effectiveness current. $H4_0 = \neg H4_1$.
- $H5_0$: There is no intention to use this method in the future, $H5_0 = \neg H5_1$.
- $H6_0$: Perceived utility is not determined by perceived ease of use, $H6_0 = \neg H6_1$.
- $H7_0$: Intent to use is not determined by perceived ease of use, $H7_0 = \neg H7_1$.
- $H8_0$: Intent to use is not determined by perceived utility, $H8_0 = \neg H8_1$.

5.2 Planning the Experiment

The experiment has the objective of evaluating the reliability, security, and usability, characteristics of LivingWith application. This application is described on [38], its purpose is to help manage some of the daily challenges faced by people living with cancer. In addition, it provides an attendance control panel to manage daily tasks and coordinate those of family and friends.

The execution phase of the method consists of two tasks:

- The first one consists on calculating the scores of the metrics of different quality attributes. It is carried out according to the quality model, the metrics of each layer, and the limitations included in the evaluation design for each of the layers.

In the second task, the scores are grouped by a characteristic of each layer, each score is multiplied according to the weight considered for the quality characteristic in the Evaluation Design phase. Here, a questionnaire was proposed that measures each MEM construct (See Table 3).

Table 3. Questionnaire used to measure MEM metrics.

Question	Positive declaration (5 points)
PEOU1	The method in the execution phase has seemed complex and difficult to follow
PEOU2	In general, the method in the execution phase is difficult to understand
PEOU3	The steps to follow to carry out the evaluation are clear and easy to understand
PEOU4	The execution phase is difficult to learn
PEOU10	I think it would be easy to use the execution guide in the method
PU5	In general, I find the evaluation phase in this method useful
PU6	I think that the process of weighting the quality characteristics of each layer is useful for the execution phase in the method
PU8	I think the method is NOT expressive enough to define how the formulas provided will be used in the execution phase
PU9	Using this method would help me evaluate the quality of CloudIoT products in AAL
PU11	In general, I think that with this method I can NOT properly quality assessment of CloudIoT applications in AAL
ITU7	If I were to use an evaluation method for CloudIoT oriented in AAL, I think I would consider this method
ITU12	I would not recommend using this method for quality assessment of CloudIoT applications in AAL

Then, to measure each MEM construct, in a similar way as [39] and [20], a questionnaire was proposed; it can be found on the URL: shorturl.at/jpPT6.

The answer to these questions is defined on a scale of 1 to 5, where one means totally agree and five, totally disagree, this depends on how the question was formulated. The variables are also based on the yield of interest and the measurement function used to determine their values. For this, effectiveness (1) and efficiency (2) are used.

$$Effectiveness = \frac{\sum_{i=1}^{n} Task_i \ successfully \ executed}{n} \tag{1}$$

$$Efficiency = \sum_{i=1}^{n} Task_i \ execution \ time \tag{2}$$

5.3 Operation

The evaluation was carried out on 15 students and professionals in Computer Sciences who participated in a previous training session. For both, training and evaluation, the description of the AAL application was explained to the participants. The proposed quality model was also shown, which presented the characteristics located in its corresponding layer. After that, they were asked to look for these characteristics in the description presented to perform their evaluation.

The characteristics presented were measured according to their metrics, being these subjective or by means of formulas.

This evaluation was made for each layer and finally weighted to find the quality measure for each layer. The formulas that were used were also presented to the participants along with the values or percentages necessary to use them.

5.4 Analysis and Interpretation

In this section, the analysis of user perceptions, performance analysis and analysis of causal relationships are carried out to verify compliance with the hypotheses.

Analysis of User Perceptions. Figure 1 shows the box plot of each variable, here it can be seen that the mean is higher than the number 3 value of the Likert scale.

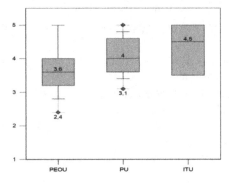

Fig. 1. Box plot for the PEOU, PU and ITU variables.

The Shapiro-Wilk test has been applied to determine if the sample has a normal distribution, this for hypotheses H1, H2 and H5. The results are shown in Table 4. For the variables with $p > 0.05$ (PEOU, PU) the t test has been applied, for the variable with $p < 0.05$ (UTI) the Wilcoxon test has been applied with a test value of 3 (neutral value of the Likert scale of 5 points). With this, the hypothesis has been rejected and the alternative hypothesis accepted.

Performance Analysis. The results obtained in the effectiveness and efficiency of the participants when using this method are: the total effectiveness was 70%, which indicates that a high percentage of participants were able to develop the method execution stage and calculate the quality of the different Cloud-IoT layers in AAL applications. On the other hand, it is shown that the participants' efficiency was 40 min.

Table 4. Shapiro-Wilk test for subjective variables.

Var	Min	Max	Mean	Std. Dev.	Shapiro–Wilk test p-value
PEOU	2.40	5.00	3.61	0.74	0.362
PU	3.10	5.00	4.05	0.56	0.751
ITU	3.50	5.00	4.37	0.64	0.004

Analysis of Causal Relationships. In this analysis, the causal relationships of the MEM constructs will be validated, in this context the hypotheses H3, H4, H6, H7 and H8 have been raised. For this, the significance levels mentioned in [40] were used.

H3 refers to the relationship between the variable's efficiency and PEOU, for this it was carried out in linear regression analysis where it was determined that the regression model is not significant with a value of $p = 0.181$ with 4.2% variance of the efficiency regarding PEOU. Hence, hypothesis H3 is accepted.

The regression model applied to the variables of effectiveness and PU was found to be non-significant with $p = 0.442$, the effectiveness is capable of explaining 4.6% of the variance with PU. With this, hypothesis H4 is accepted.

H6 is made up of the PEOU and PU variables. The regression model was determined to be of low significance with $p = 0.075$. PEOU can explain a 22.4% variance with PU. With this hypothesis H6 has been rejected.

The regression model related to the UTI and PU variables is of low significance with $p = 0.074$. UTI can explain the 22.5% variance with PU. This rejects hypothesis H7.

H8 has been rejected because the linear regression model of the UTI and PEOU variables is of medium significance with $p = 0.049$. UTI can explain the 26.5% variance with PEOU.

5.5 Presentation and Packing

The following global conclusions were obtained from each research question:

- RQ1: Most participants found that this method is very useful and easy to use at the time of the execution stage, which is directly related to user interaction due H1 and H2 have been rejected. This is supported by its effectiveness when directly related to user interaction, where it has a value of 70%. Furthermore, user perceptions are not determined by user performance because H3 and H4 have been accepted, that is, user perceptions do not depend on efficiency and effectiveness.
- RQ2: It was determined that users intend to use the method in the future because the H5 hypothesis was accepted with a mean value of 4.3 that is above the neutral value. Furthermore, the intention of use is determined by the user's perceptions since H6, H7 and H8 have been rejected with low significance. The result of the causal relationships of MEM are in Fig. 2.

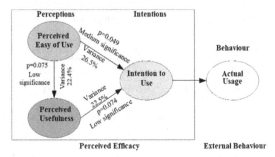

Fig. 2. Relationship between the PEOU, PU and ITU variables.

6   Threats to Validity

In this section, the main problems that can weaken the quasi-experiments' validity are explained, considering the four types of threats proposed by [41].

6.1   Internal Validity

The main threats to internal validity were: the experience of the participants, the author's biases, and the understandability of the material. To reduce the threat related to the participants' experience, a training session was prepared, which shows each step of the stage that was evaluated, and provides users with a high understanding of the method. Both the author's biases and those produced by the understandability of the material were reduced by working with a group of expert researchers in the area, where they evaluated the experimental material to reduce possible errors.

6.2   External Validity

Here, the main threat is the representativity of the results that may be affected by the design of the evaluation and the context of selected participants. An AAL application was chosen in the design of the evaluation that is available on different platforms oriented to a common domain where AAL is needed. Regarding the context of the participants, the quasi-experiment was conducted with students and professionals on Computer Sciences, who also attended the Software Quality course and have a good knowledge of quality models and metrics.

6.3   Construct Validity

The main threat to construct validity is the reliability of the questionnaire. The Cronbach's alpha test was applied to validate the questionnaire of the questions related to each variable. Values greater than the minimum accepted threshold were obtained $\alpha = 0.70$, where Cronbach's alpha of PEOU = 0.806, PU = 0.841 and ITU = 0.721. This means that the questionnaire was reliable.

6.4 Conclusion Validity

One of the statistical conclusions' main validity problems is the size of the sample in the quasi-experiment. A sample of 15 participants was taken, which could result in a problem of the validity of the conclusion. It can affect the issue of causality between the different variables; however, the participants were able to perform the tasks proposed in the experiment successfully. A homogeneous group of participants has been selected to control for the risk of variation due to individual differences.

7 Conclusions and Future Work

This work presented a quality method that aims to evaluate the different CloudIoT layers of AAL applications. Therefore, an experimentation was presented to evaluate the method in its execution phase, the results have made it possible to know that the method is easy to use, useful and that users intend to use it in the future. To carry out the experiment, the quality model and the experimental process of Wohlin et al. [42] had to be applied. Finally, the threats that could affect the validity of the experiment have been taken into account and these have been covered.

As future work, the validation of the quality method will be expanded with experts in the area and obtain a more significant sample with more participants. In addition, to validating the quality model, a case study will be carried out applying the proposed method to evaluate some AAL applications.

Acknowledgements. This work is part of the research projects: "Fog Computing applied to monitoring devices used in assisted living environments. Case study: platform for the elderly" and "Design of architectures and interaction models for assisted living environments for elderly people. Case study: ludic and social environments". Hence, the authors thank to DIUC of Universidad de Cuenca for its academic and financial support.

References

1. Tung, Y.-H., Tseng2, S.-S., Kuo1, Y.-Y.: Cloud Environment, pp. 97–100 (2017)
2. Liang, X., Yan, Z., Zhang, P.: Security, privacy, and anonymity in computation, communication, and storage. In: SpaCCS 2016, pp. 155–167 (2016). https://doi.org/10.1007/978-3-319-72395-2
3. Benabbes, S., Hemam, S.M.: An approach based on (Tasks-VMs) classification and MCDA for dynamic load balancing in the CloudIoT. In: Hatti, M. (ed.) Smart Energy Empowerment in Smart and Resilient Cities. ICAIRES 2019. LNCS, vol. 102, pp. 387–396. Springer, Cham (2020). https://doi.org/10.1007/978-3-030-37207-1_41
4. Kim, M., Park, J.H., Lee, N.Y.: A quality model for IoT service. In: Park, J., Pan, Y., Yi, G., Loia, V. (eds.) Advances in Computer Science and Ubiquitous Computing. UCAWSN 2016, CUTE 2016, CSA 2016. Lecture Notes in Electrical Engineering, vol. 421, pp. 497–504. Springer, Singapore (2017). https://doi.org/10.1007/978-981-10-3023-9_77
5. Khan, M.A., Salah, K.: IoT security: review, blockchain solutions, and open challenges. Future Gener. Comput. Syst. **82**, 395–411 (2018). https://doi.org/10.1016/j.future.2017.11.022

6. Gubbi, J., Buyya, R., Marusic, S., Palaniswami, M.: Internet of Things (IoT): a vision, architectural elements, and future directions. Future Gener. Comput. Syst. **29**, 1645–1660 (2013). https://doi.org/10.1016/j.future.2013.01.010
7. Sarma, S., Brock, D., Ashton, K.: The networked physical world.TR MIT-AUTOID-WH-001 MIT Auto-ID Centre, pp. 1–16 (2000)
8. Botta, A., de Donato, W., Persico, V., Pescapé, A.: On the integration of cloud computing and Internet of Things. In: 2014 International Conference on Future Internet of Things and Cloud, pp. 23–30 (2014)
9. Aazam, M., Huh, E.-N.: Fog computing and smart gateway based communication for cloud of things. In: Proceedings of the 2014 International Conference on Future IoT and Cloud, pp. 464–470. IEEE Computer Society, USA (2014)
10. World Health Organization: Disability and health (2020). https://www.who.int/news-room/fact-sheets/detail/disability-and-health
11. Darwish, A., Hassanien, A.E., Elhoseny, M., Sangaiah, A.K., Muhammad, K.: The impact of the hybrid platform of IoT and Cloud on healthcare systems: opportunities, challenges, and open problems. J. Ambient Intell. Hum. Comput. **10**, 4151–4166 (2019). https://doi.org/10.1007/s12652-017-0659-1
12. Dohr, A., Modre-Opsrian, R., Drobics, M., Hayn, D., Schreier, G.: The Internet of Things for ambient assisted living. In: 2010 Seventh International Conference on Information Technology: New Generations, pp. 804–809 (2010)
13. Cedillo, P., Sanchez, C., Campos, K., Bermeo, A.: A systematic literature review on devices and systems for AAL: solutions and trends from different user perspectives. In: ICEDEG 2018 (2018). https://doi.org/10.1109/ICEDEG.2018.8372367
14. ISO: International Standard ISO/IEC 12207: Systems and software engineering — Software life cycle processes (2008)
15. Saini, G.L., Panwar, D., Kumar, S., Singh, V.: A systematic literature review and comparative study of different software quality models. J. Discrete Math. Sci. Crypt. **23**, 585–593 (2020). https://doi.org/10.1080/09720529.2020.1747188
16. de Macedo, D.D.J., de Araújo, G.M., Dutra, M.L., Dutra, S.T., Lezana, Á.G.R.: Toward an efficient healthcare CloudIoT architecture by using a game theory approach. Concurr. Eng. Res. Appl. **27**, 189–200 (2019). https://doi.org/10.1177/1063293X19844548
17. Garces, L., Oquendo, F., Nakagawa, E.Y.: A quality model for AAL software systems. In: Proceedings - IEEE Symposium on Computer-Based Medical Systems, pp. 175–180 (2016). https://doi.org/10.1109/CBMS.2016.46
18. McNaull, J., Augusto, J.C., Mulvenna, M., McCullagh, P.: Data and information quality issues in ambient assisted living systems. J. Data Inf. Qual. **4** (2012). https://doi.org/10.1145/2378016.2378020
19. Araujo, V., Mitra, K., Saguna, S., Åhlund, C.: Performance evaluation of FIWARE: a cloud-based IoT platform for smart cities. J. Parallel Distrib. Comput. **132**, 250–261 (2019). https://doi.org/10.1016/j.jpdc.2018.12.010
20. Sanchez, C., Cedillo, P., Vazquez, A.: A memory game for elderly people: development and evaluation. In: ICEDEG 2020 (2020). https://doi.org/10.1109/ICEDEG48599.2020.9096862
21. Ashouri, M., Lorig, F., Davidsson, P., Spalazzese, R.: Edge computing simulators for IoT system design: an analysis of qualities and metrics. Future Internet **11**, 1–12 (2019). https://doi.org/10.3390/fi11110235
22. Zheng, X., Martin, P., Brohman, K., Xu, L.: Cloudqual: a quality model for cloud services. IEEE Trans. Ind. Inform. **10**, 1527–1536 (2014). https://doi.org/10.1109/TII.2014.2306329
23. Idri, A., Bachiri, M., Fernández-Alemán, J.L.: A framework for evaluating software product quality of pregnancy monitoring mobile personal health records. J. Med. Syst. **40**, 1–17 (2016). https://doi.org/10.1007/s10916-015-0415-z

24. Hakim, H., Sellami, A., Abdallah, H.: Evaluating security in web application design using functional and structural size measurements. In: Proceedings IWSM 2016 and Mensura 2016, pp. 182–190 (2017). https://doi.org/10.1109/IWSM-Mensura.2016.036
25. Calabrese, J., Muñoz, R., Pasini, A., Esponda, S., Boracchia, M., Pesado, P.: Assistant for the evaluation of software product quality characteristics proposed by ISO/IEC 25010 based on GQM-defined metrics. Commun. Comput. Inf. Sci. **790**, 164–175 (2018). https://doi.org/10. 1007/978-3-319-75214-3_16
26. Islam, S., Falcarin, P.: Measuring security requirements for software security. In: Proceedings of CIS 2011, pp. 70–75 (2011). https://doi.org/10.1109/CIS.2011.6169137
27. Basili, V., Caldiera, G., Rombach, D.: Goal question metric approach. Encycl. Softw. Eng. **1**, 528–532 (1994). ISBN: 0-471-54004-8, John Wiley & Sons
28. Cedillo, P., Bermeo, A., Piedra-García, D., Tenezaca-Sari, P.: CloudIoTSecurity: evaluating the security in cloud IoT applications (2020)
29. Komiyama, T., Fukuzumi, S., Azuma, M., Washizaki, H., Tsuda, N.: Usability of software-intensive systems from developers' point of view. In: Kurosu, M. (ed.) Human-Computer Interaction. Design and User Experience, HCII 2020. Lecture Notes in Computer Science, vol. 12181, pp. 450–463. Springer, Cham (2020). https://doi.org/10.1007/978-3-030-49059-1_33
30. Enriquez, E.M.L., Brito, J.F.B., Orellana, I.P.C.: Evaluating the usability of online social networks used by older people. In: Proceedings - 2017 International Conference on Information Systems and Computer Science, INCISCOS 2017, pp. 316–322 (2018). https://doi.org/10. 1109/INCISCOS.2017.40
31. ISO: ISO/IEC 25040. https://iso25000.com/index.php/normas-iso-25000/iso-25040
32. Shah, J.L., Bhat, H.F., Khan, A.I.: CloudIoT: towards seamless and secure integration of cloud computing with Internet of Things. Int. J. Digital Crime Forensics **11**, 1–22 (2019). https:// doi.org/10.4018/IJDCF.2019070101
33. Zhou, P., Wang, Z., Li, W., Jiang, N.: Quality model of cloud service. In: Proceedings - 2015 IEEE 17th International Conference on High Performance Computing and Communications, pp. 1418–1423 (2015). https://doi.org/10.1109/HPCC-CSS-ICESS.2015.134
34. Bagherzadeh, L., Shahinzadeh, H., Shayeghi, H., Dejamkhooy, A., Bayindir, R., Iranpour, M.: Integration of Cloud Computing and IoT (CloudIoT) in smart grids: benefits, challenges, and solutions. In: CISPSSE 2020 (2020). https://doi.org/10.1109/CISPSSE49931.2020.921 2195
35. Montagud, S., Abrahão, S., Insfran, E.: A systematic review of quality attributes and measures for software product lines. Softw. Qual. J. **20**, 425–486 (2012). https://doi.org/10.1007/s11 219-011-9146-7
36. Tzeng, J.R.; Li, S.H., Chen, C.H.: Applying QFD to improve the project management for cloud systems. Appl. Mech. Mater. **121–126**, 3185–3189 (2012). https://doi.org/10.4028/www.sci entific.net/AMM.121-126.3185
37. Hakim, H., Sellami, A., Abdallah, H.B., Cook, T.D., Campbell, D.T.: Quasi-experimentation: design and analysis issues for field settings. In: Proceedings IWSM 2016 and Mensura 2016, pp. 182–190 (2017). https://doi.org/10.1109/IWSM-Mensura.2016.036
38. Pfizer: LivingWith App—This Is Living With Cancer—Official Site. https://www.thisisliving withcancer.com/living-with-app
39. Insfran, E., Cedillo, P., Fernández, A., Abrahão, S., Matera, M.: Evaluating the usability of mashups applications. In: Proceedings - 2012 8th International Conference on the Quality of Information and Communications Technology, QUATIC 2012, pp. 323–326 (2012). https:// doi.org/10.1109/QUATIC.2012.28
40. Moody, D.L.: Dealing with complexity: a practical method for representing large entity relationship models (2001)

41. Cook, T.D., Campbell, D.T.: Quasi-Experimentation: Design and Analysis Issues for Field Settings. Houghton Mifflin (1979)
42. Wohlin, C., Runeson, P., Höst, M., Ohlsson, M.C., Regnell, B., Wesslén, A.: Experiment process. In: Experimentation in Software Engineering, pp. 73–81. Springer, Heidelberg (2012). https://doi.org/10.1007/978-3-642-29044-2_6

Industry 4.0

Design of an Electronic System
for the Exploration of Agricultural Parameters
in Solanum Lycopersicum Germination

Iván A. Cordero$^{(\boxtimes)}$, Hugo M. Torres$^{(\boxtimes)}$, and Francisco D. Salgado$^{(\boxtimes)}$

Escuela de Ingeniería Electrónica, Facultad de Ciencia y Tecnología, Universidad del Azuay,
Cuenca, Ecuador
icorderom@es.uazuay.edu.ec, {htorres,fdsalgado}@uazuay.edu.ec

Abstract. The development of this document is focused on the analysis of two types of soil: greenhouse substrate and earthworm humus mixed with the greenhouse substrate, which have been used to measure important factors, such as temperature, humidity, light, water irrigation, in the germination of Solanum lycopersicum (tomato) seeds, then stored this information in a database, the period of time for evaluation is the fifteen days. To acquire this information, sensors are used, capable of transforming variables such as temperature, environmental humidity, soil humidity, amount of ambient light, into electrical signals that are processed by an electronic microcontroller. This microcontroller is in charge of handling this data, it is also in charge of controlling the use of water irrigation pumps in a closed environment and later storing, in a database, its behavior. In the field of agriculture, the use of electronic hardware is implemented as a tool that helps in this area, presenting sensors to capture data and actuators that are useful for automating conditions such as water irrigation in closed environments.

Keywords: Tomato · Solanum lycopersicum · Germination · Soil moisture · Greenhouse substrate · Earthworm humus · Agricultural parameters · Sensors · Actuators · Microcontroller · Python · C++ · MySQL

1 Introduction

Within the area of agriculture, specifically in the measurement of variables such as temperature, humidity, light, the use of sensors has increased with greater frequency. In some cases, the same sensors have participated in more than one field of study, a clear example of this, Margret Sharmila shows us when using a temperature sensor (DHT11) as monitoring of an intelligent window [1], this window is combined with a stepper motor, it manages to open or close according to the behavior of the temperature, its action varies according to the temperature. Another example of this, it is presented by Fathima Dheena with the use in her intelligent system based on IoT for street lamps [2], she uses the DHT11 sensor as a complement to know the temperature of the environment, taking the data and store it. Demonstrating the utility and versatility provided by this type of sensor.

© Springer Nature Switzerland AG 2021
J. P. Salgado Guerrero et al. (Eds.): TICEC 2021, CCIS 1456, pp. 201–224, 2021.
https://doi.org/10.1007/978-3-030-89941-7_15

In the area of agriculture, temperature measurement is necessary to improve decision-making, because with this variable is a better solution to control of crop quality, for this Meili Liu proposes the use a set of sensors [3] that are combined with microcontrollers, its generate a better management of the information acquired. This is also present by Temesegan Waleling, he uses the DHT11 temperature sensor to make weather predictions using algorithms that employ long-term memory [4]. There is a high number of examples for this sensor, one of them in the area of agriculture, sensors are used to provide additional information such as soil moisture meters, Nagaraja in his research proposes the use of these two sensors complementing them in an intelligent agriculture system based on IoT [5], these systems are very useful because makes easier the maintenance of crops. Another example of this type of sensor is presented by Alessandra Dutra in the monitoring soil moisture using IoT [6], she used to get more accurately and extract the information provided by this sensor. Applications like these are carried out day by day and presented to contribute with tools of use either individually or together, as is the case of Prahlad Bhadani by using soil moisture, ambient temperature and ambient humidity together with a microcontroller [7], this microcontroller is in charge of managing the information and present it on a 16×2 lcd screen, making easier the understanding and visualization of the information.

The soil moisture sensor, like the rest of the sensors, can be produced from scratch, Matti Satish [8] has shown by using the resistivity of materials to obtain this information, it is also possible to use sensors that use capacitive reading methods, this is the case of Radi [9] that presents the calibration of the capacitive humidity sensor. With the information collected by the sensors, actions such as irrigation are taken, this example is presented [10–15], using automatic irrigation with smarts watering systems, many of this methods and algorithms use electronic components is as their hardcore.

The use of these sensors allows to development of electronic tools, which is the objective of this study, to implement these sensors in a closed environment to evaluate the behavior generated when are planted tomato seeds in two different types of soil, extracting information in variables such as temperature, thermal sensation and humidity of the closed environment, those variables are combined together with soil humidity. So with this information, the microcontroller will make irrigation decisions, using a submersible motor that will pump water to the seedbeds.

2   Research Framework

2.1   Characteristics of Tomato

The tomato known as Solanum lycopersicum is a food that contains a variety of nutrients, vitamins A, B and C, phosphorus, iron, calcium, potassium, lycopene among others. It is recommended in a balanced diet, in addition this type of vegetable has gone from being medicinal in the past, to being a culinary ingredient, since several dishes include tomato, for its color, flavor and versatility when is used to cook. The tomato seed has a diameter of 3 to 5 mm, the surface of the seed is covered by villi and small scales. The development time of these seeds varies between five to nine days depending on the temperature in which it is found, since it is considered a hot climate vegetable, having an ambient temperature range between 20 to 24 °C.

2.2 Sensor

The sensors are elements capable of measuring physical variables such as temperature, humidity, distance, amount of light, etc. They are used in industries, homes, large-scale or small-scale projects, depending on their use. The sensors can be classified into different types, depending on the physical magnitude to be measured, these can be temperature, force, distance, position.

2.2.1 Sensor DHT11

The DHT11 sensor (see Fig. 1) is a low cost temperature and relative humidity sensor, the sensor presents digital values ranging from 3.3 v to 5 v depending on the power supplied to the sensor, at its output it. This sensor has a capacitive component for humidity and a thermistor to measure the air that circulates through it.

Fig. 1. Sensor DHT11 (Color figure online).

The range is from 0 to 50 °C in temperature, while in relative humidity it has a range of 20% to 90%. Its presentation is in a blue encapsulation and the sensor can take a sample per second, having a maximum sampling frequency of 1 Hz.

2.2.2 Sensor Soil Moisture

The capacitive soil moisture sensor (See Fig. 2) generates changes in the capacitance according to its charge and discharge, this sensor has a copper plate in the center and another ground plate that surrounds the first plate.

Fig. 2. Sensor capacitive soil moisture.

The voltage that the sensor uses can be 3.3 v to 5 v, since the sensor has an internal regulator to operate with 3.3 v. When the sensor voltage decreases, it means that the soil around it is humid and when its voltage increases the soil has less humidity.

2.2.3 Sensor TCS34725

The TCS34725 sensor (see Fig. 3) has a voltage regulator, so it can use 3.3 v to 5 v to work with it, the sensor communicates through I2C communication. This sensor is used to acquire ambient light and transform it into a measure of color temperature, amount of lux and with measure in red, green and blue of the environment.

Fig. 3. Sensor TCS34725.

The sensor has a white light that exposes the surrounding light to a filter which detects the colors red, green and blue with better sensitivity.

2.3 Actuators

Actuators are those devices that make changes in the environment by interacting, these changes represent physical forces such as temperature, humidity, pressure, among others. The actuators are classified according to their operation, they can be electric, hydraulic and pneumatic.

2.3.1 Water Pump

This actuator is a submersible motor (see Fig. 4), it is designed to extract water from its exterior and pump it. This actuator works with voltages from 3 to 9 v, the fluid enters the motor and the internal propellers generate a circular movement, that pushes the water inside to its outlet, which is connected to a transparent hose in charge of directing the fluid to the space to be used. This method is the most efficient way to pump water.

Fig. 4. Water pump.

To control the motor voltage, it is complemented with the module IRF520 (see Fig. 5), this module has an electronic component call Mosfet which can use up to 100 v with a maximum of 9.7 A, if it is working with temperatures of 25 °C.

Fig. 5. Module IRF520.

The IRF520 module will be connected to a microprocessor to use pulse width modulation (PWM), in this way the water pump will be controlled.

2.4 Microcontrollers

2.4.1 Microcontroller ATMEGA2560

The 8-bit Atmega2560 microcontroller (see Fig. 6), is a low-power microcontroller whose manufacturer is Microchip, it contains 54 digital inputs and outputs for general purpose, in addition to having 6 timers, a 4Kbyte memory in its EEPROM and 8Kbytes in its SRAM, it also has 16 channels of 10bit ADC.

Fig. 6. Microcontroller Atmega2560.

This microcontroller has 11 ports that go from port A to port L that can be used bi-directionally with 8 bits and internal pull up and pull down resistors. It uses AVR structure which maximizes its speed and minimizes the power consumption.

2.5 Data Base

To understand the concept of a database, it is first necessary to know what is a piece of data, this can refer to a simple fact relating to any object that is considered, for example, a name, age, weight, height, etc. Images, files, audio that could be disorganized, can also be considered data. While a database is a systematized or organized collection of data that has entities, attributes. For the database management system (DBMS) is implemented MySQL (see Fig. 7), because its provide a free research platform for data storage.

The SQL language is known for being a structured query language, it is the standard language of relational databases, this language allows inserting, searching, updating and deleting information from database records.

Fig. 7. MySQL Data Base.

3   Implementation of the System

3.1   Structure Design

The dimensions of the structure are: 90 cm wide, 60 cm high and deep, it is made up of light and resistant material (see Fig. 8), its lower part is reinforced in this way it provides a wide space to observe the behavior of tomato seeds.

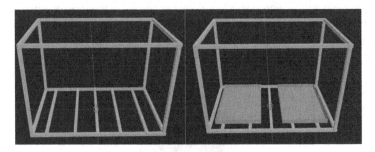

Fig. 8. Physic structure and seedbeds.

In this structure transparent material is placed around it, closing the environment against air currents that may interfere with the measurements, also seedbeds are placed inside, these seedbeds contain different types of soil, that contents one hundred seeds each, in this way the growth of the plants is evaluated through the passage of time.

3.2   Hardware Design

The hardware used is characterized by having of twelve temperature sensors, twelve soil moisture sensors, a light sensor, a motor actuator and a microcontroller, which form the electronic set for data extraction.

3.2.1   Sensors Design

The use of sensors for the acquisition of information has been used in various areas. This information is transformed into data, which is stored in the relational database for later analysis. A set of three DHT11 sensors has been placed on each pillar, of the structure, for the acquisition of ambient temperature, ambient humidity and sensation data. Forming a total of twelve DTH11 sensors divided into low, medium and high sections for each

Fig. 9. Sensors DHT11 on the Structure and Capacitive soil moisture sensors in seedbeds.

column. This acquisition is complemented with capacitive soil moisture meters (see Fig. 9).

These sensors are placed on the seedbeds to determine the humidity of the two types of soil for a period of fifteen days. Each type of floor has six sensors cataloged in three different front, middle and rear areas.

3.2.2 Actuators Design

The submersible motor, used to irrigate the seedbeds, is connected to the base of the trays using transparent hoses (see Fig. 10), these hoses are placement on the four sides of the structure of each seedbed.

Fig. 10. Hose irrigation mechanism in seedbeds.

The use of the irrigation is determined by two different studies, the first is an automatic irrigation every twenty-four hours, an irrigation will be on until the soil moisture sensors present values of 70%, and the second study is one irrigation every time the soil moisture sensor reaches values below 50%.

3.2.3 Microcontroller

The electronic components are connected to the ATmega2560 microcontroller (see Fig. 11), this microcontroller acquires the data from each sensor, saves them in momentary variables and sends them by serial communication to a computer, this computer will be the one in charge of storing the information in the database. The microcontroller is also in charge of irrigation for each seedbed.

A distribution of electronic components is made in the structure (see Fig. 12), dedicating three temperature sensors in each corner of the closed environment, a light sensor,

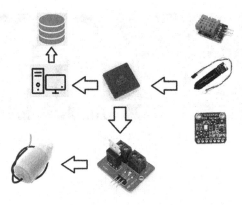

Fig. 11. Information flow graph.

six capacitive soil moisture sensors in each seedbed, in addition of an irrigation system that use an IRF520 module and a pumping water motor for each seedbed.

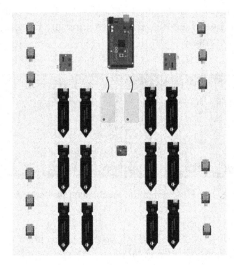

Fig. 12. Distribution of electronic components in a closed environment.

The connection of electronic components is carried out of four blocks (see Fig. 13), the first one uses the digital input pins that the microcontroller has for the temperature sensors, in this block twelve digital inputs were used. The second block is represented by the humidity sensors, these sensors are connected to the analog reading pins that the microcontroller has, using twelve capacitive soil humidity sensors in total.

The third block is represented by the light sensor, which uses I2C communication, connecting through the SCL and SDA pins of the microcontroller, and the last block uses the IRF520 module, which is in charge of controlling the speed of the propeller that pumps the irrigation motor.

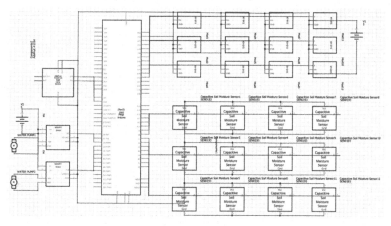

Fig. 13. Electronic scheme.

3.3 Software Design

3.3.1 Algorithm

Three types of algorithms are generated, the first two are focused on the ATMEGA2560 microcontroller and the last one for the computer. The first algorithm (see Fig. 14) for the microcontroller presents automatic irrigation every 24 h, this algorithm enters the variables of temperature, thermal sensation and humidity, continues with the process acquiring the values of the soil sensors, after this process its verified if the automatic irrigation time has reached to activate the pumping motor, otherwise it continues with the reading of the ambient light sensor to finish the loop sending data to the computer. If irrigation is activated this generates an active flag to send it to the computer until it reaches 70% humidity in the soil, once it reaches this percentage the flag is removed and automatic irrigation is configured for the next 24 h.

The second algorithm generated (see Fig. 15) is similar to the first with small changes, it could be observed after taking soil moisture information, by asking if the moisture variable is less than 50%. The same way as the first algorithm, activating a flag to send to the computer in charge of storing the information in the database.

The last algorithm is used by the computer (see Fig. 16), which takes the information from the microcontroller and inserts it into the database. For this, the information is received through text-type strings with initial, final and intermediate separators. Once the information is separated into short text strings, it is inserted into the database and stored it.

The experimental methods that are carried out below in the two types of soil are focused on checking ambient temperature, thermal sensation, humidity of the environment, in addition to measuring soil humidity in the greenhouse substrate and in the mixture of greenhouse substrate with earthworm humus. In them one hundred seeds are introduced, for each soil, this seeds are collected naturally from tomatoes that are distributed by local markets.

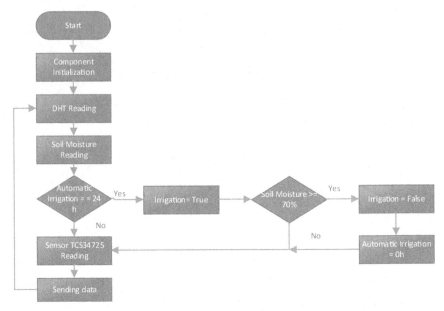

Fig. 14. Automatic watering algorithm every twenty-four hours.

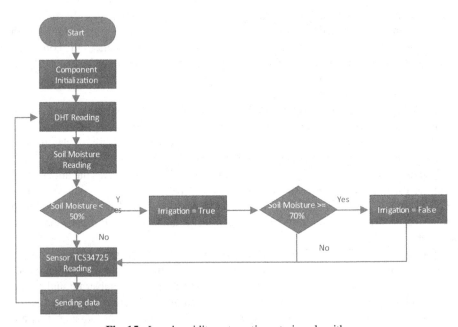

Fig. 15. Low humidity automatic watering algorithm.

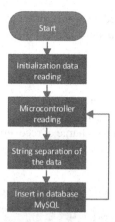

Fig. 16. Data insertion algorithm

4 Results

Data is extracted in a total time of fifteen days; in the seedbeds the tomato seeds are planted using the one hundred sample seeds in each tray. Data collection is separated into seven days with automatic irrigation every twenty-four hours and the second proposed algorithm is used for the remaining days.

4.1 Sending Data from the Microcontroller

The algorithm is implemented using the Arduino company's integrated development environment (IDE), because it is open source, to initialize the sensors and prepare the irrigation actuator under the conditions described by the algorithm (see Fig. 17).

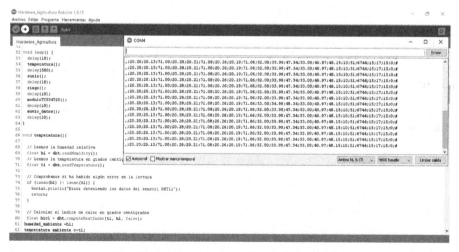

Fig. 17. Sending data through the microcontroller

The information from the closed environment is retrieved in a data chain, using serial communication between the microcontroller and the computer.

4.2 Data Reception

Using the data strings sent by the microcontroller, the data entry algorithm is generated in the computer, it is programmed using the Spyder IDE, this integrated development environment uses python language, in charge of recovering the information and dividing these strings data using the separators previously assigned in the chain (see Fig. 18).

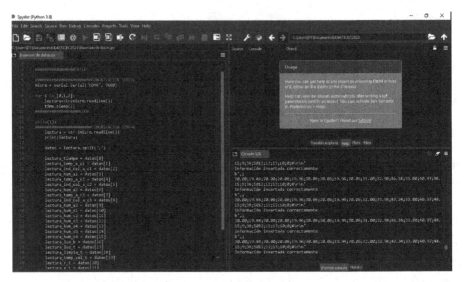

Fig. 18. Data extraction, string separation and storage

Once the data has been extracted and separated, the information obtained is inserted into the database.

4.3 Insertion Check in MySQL Database

The insertion of information for the computer is checked, to do so the integral development environment of MySQL Workbench is used (see Fig. 19).

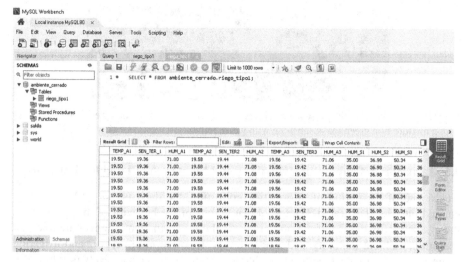

Fig. 19. Validation of insertion of information in MySQL Database

The total amount of data entered for the elapsed time reached 239,626 records sent by the microcontroller.

4.4 Seedbeds

At the end of the evaluation, it presents a total of one hundred seventy-four tomato plants (see Fig. 20), this represents 87% of the total sample, divided into the two types of soil used. In the greenhouse substrate, 95% of the sample germinated, starting with 6% on the sixth day and in the mixture of greenhouse substrate with worm humus, 79% was obtained at the end of the data collection time, starting with 3% after nine days.

Fig. 20. Closed environment after the evaluation period

The use of the second irrigation algorithm kept the two types of soil with higher humidity, producing a white layer on the greenhouse substrate (see Fig. 21).

While worm humus mixed with the greenhouse substrate absorbed more humidity without generating this layer of mold on its surface.

Fig. 21. Comparison of the presence of a layer of mold due to humidity in a greenhouse substrate with a mixture of a greenhouse substrate with worm humus

4.5   Behavior of Temperature, Humidity and Light in the Closed Environment

At the end of the period of information collection, the database, in CSV format, is entered into the IDE RapidMiner to obtain graphs of the behavior of the variables in the evaluation time. One of the first graphs is the set of ambient temperature, thermal sensation, ambient humidity, soil moisture type 1, soil moisture type 2 and irrigation using the colors orange, black, blue, light blue, green and red respectively (see Fig. 22). This graph shows the increase in temperature and decrease in humidity between the hours of 10am to 4 pm. Being the time in which the closed environment is exposed to a higher concentration of heat.

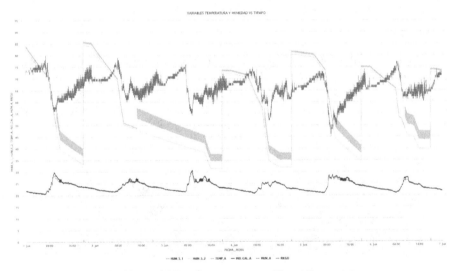

Fig. 22. Variables of temperature and humidity vs time

To better understand the graph, the records are taken from day three until day ten, since the behavior of the data presents a frequent pattern. The change between day and night is presented in the graph of humidity of the environment (see Fig. 23), lowering the humidity on sunny days and increasing it at night. In addition to this graph, the change in humidity of the environment is presented, together with the humidity presented in the two types of soils, for this graph light blue, green and orange colors are used to represent the variables of ambient humidity, soil humidity type 1 and soil humidity type 2 respectively.

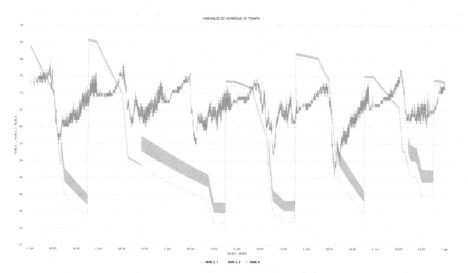

Fig. 23. Graphs ambient humidity and soil humidity vs time

In the same way, comparative graphs of temperature and thermal sensation are generated (see Fig. 24) with blue and green colors, observed show similarity between them, tending to increase their value in the hours of 10am to 12pm and decrease in the night reaching the minimum point of 20C before 8am to continue with their behavior pattern.

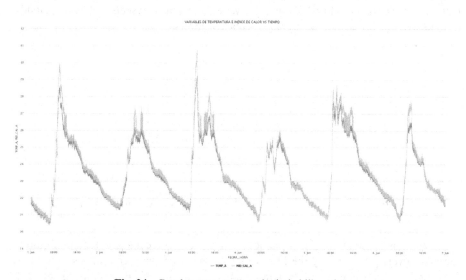

Fig. 24. Graph temperature and wind chill vs time

The set of lux variables, clean, color temperature, red, green and blue (see Fig. 25) are graphed, using the colors of light blue, green, orange, black, blue and red respectively. This graph, like the previous ones, presents a pattern of behavior; its intensity levels are high at the same times when there is lower humidity and higher temperature, as well as the temperature and humidity graphs.

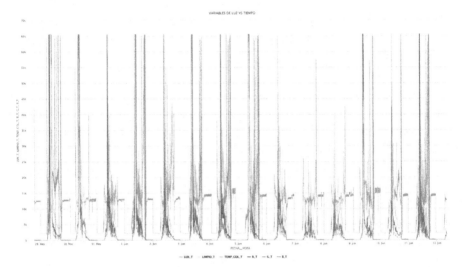

Fig. 25. Light vs time variables

Separating the graphs in luxe by time of blue color in the graph and the values of colors red, green, blue, represented by celestial, green and orange (see Fig. 26), the pattern of behavior tends to a daily frequency, the sunny days presents high levels, cloudy days its average levels and the night presents low levels.

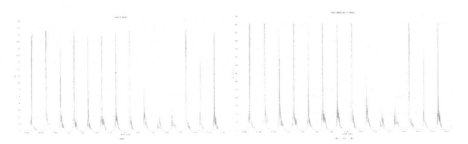

Fig. 26. Graphs of Luxe vs time and Red, Green, Blue vs time components

A zoom is made on the data obtained, between day three and day ten, highlighting the high levels presented by the luxe variable, which are very continuous with those presented by the blue color. By placing the two graphs in a single one, using celestial, green, orange and black colors for the lux components, red, green and blue (see Fig. 27), it is possible to observe the pattern that consists of greater light intensity that has had the day, it is represented as a sunny day, having a direct relationship with the temperature, since it has shown an increase in those periods of time.

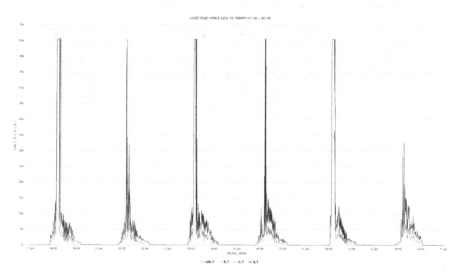

Fig. 27. Graph Luxe, Red, Green, Blue component vs approach time

The following graph represents the behavior of the closed environment in the evaluated period of time (see Fig. 28), representing each element such as temperature, humidity and light with its respective subcomponents.

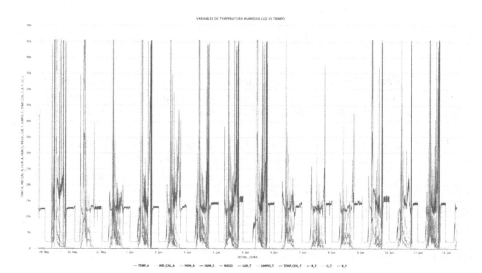

Fig. 28. Graph of global representation temperature, humidity, light vs time

These data have been processed and stored using electronic tools as well as hardware and software in the area of agriculture.

4.6 Comparative of Soil Types with Irrigation Algorithms

The behavior acquired using the first irrigation algorithm from the closed environment, shows that the humidity levels in the soil are maintained during the night until 8am, which presents an increase in the temperature of the closed environment until 10am. The humidity of the soil types drops drastically, showing the greenhouse substrate with a mixture of worm humus is the best to retain the humidity of the environment (see Fig. 29).

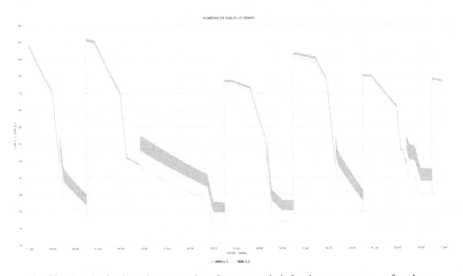

Fig. 29. Graph of soil moisture vs. time for automatic irrigation every twenty-four hours

When implementing the second irrigation algorithm, its activation occurs more frequently, especially in the greenhouse substrate represented in light blue (see Fig. 30), while the mixture of earthworm humus with greenhouse soil does not require a constant watering.

On the other hand, in the second algorithm the irrigation is shown active at the times when the closed environment has the highest temperature. Indicating a high waste of water by maintaining constant the level of humidity that is evaporated by the sun's rays, being the greenhouse substrate the one that retains moisture for the shortest time generating the greatest waste of water. To do this, a graph is generated, which indicates how many times the algorithm has been used in each type of soil (see Fig. 31). The graph showed the soil containing earthworm humus as green with 358 times and the greenhouse substrate as light blue with 439.

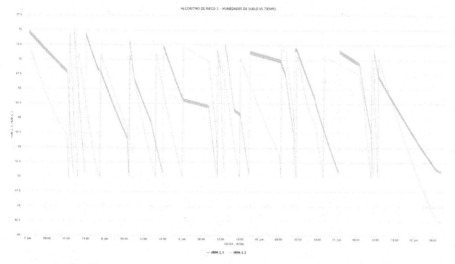

Fig. 30. Soil moisture vs time graph with second irrigation algorithm

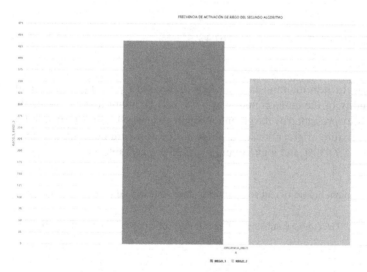

Fig. 31. Irrigation activation frequency graph of the second algorithm

The collected data are presented with the number of times that the algorithm was activated is shown (see Table 1), in the first case the algorithm had an activation of seven times in each soil while the second algorithm had an activation of a greater number of times, in the greenhouse substrate soil with 439 and in the greenhouse substrate mixture with earthworm humus of 358.

In the seven days, that the first algorithm was used, the minimum humidity of the environment was 45% and its maximum of 80%, while the minimum humidity presented by the greenhouse substrate was 31.36%, its maximum of 84.37% and the mixture of

Table 1. Activation count of the two types of algorithm.

	Greenhouse substrate	Greenhouse substrate mixture with earthworm humus
Irrigation Algorithm 1 count	7	7
Irrigation Algorithm 2 count	439	358

greenhouse substrate with earthworm humus presented was 34.52% and its maximum was 86.04% (see Table 2).

Table 2. Table of data of ambient humidity and soil humidity with first irrigation algorithm.

	Greenhouse substrate	Greenhouse substrate mixture with earthworm humus
Min ambient humidity	45%	45%
Max ambient humidity	80%	80%
Min soil moisture	31,36%	34,52%
Max soil moisture	84,37%	86,04%

On the other hand, in the remaining days in which the second algorithm was executed, the minimum humidity of the environment was 57%, its maximum to 85%, while the minimum soil humidity presented by the greenhouse substrate was 42,40%, its maximum of 74.26% and the mixture of greenhouse substrate with earthworm humus presented a minimum humidity of 50.50% and a maximum of 75.35% (see Table 3).

Table 3. Table of ambient humidity and soil humidity data with second irrigation algorithm.

	Greenhouse substrate	Greenhouse substrate mixture with earthworm humus
Min ambient humidity	57%	57%
Max ambient humidity	85%	85%
Min soil moisture	42,40%	50,50%
Max soil moisture	74,26%	75,35%

Once the humidity parameter has been evaluated, it is possible to analyze the ambient temperature and the thermal sensation presented in each algorithm, in the first algorithm, the minimum temperature presented in the closed environment was 20.40 °C with a thermal sensation of 20.45 °C and its maximum parameters appear at 29.20 °C of ambient temperature and 30.61 °C in thermal sensation (see Table 4).

Table 4. Table of ambient temperature and thermal sensation data with first irrigation algorithm.

	Greenhouse substrate	Greenhouse substrate mixture with earthworm humus
Min temperature environment	20,40 °C	20,40 °C
Max temperature environment	29,20 °C	29,20 °C
Min thermal sensation	20,45 °C	20,45 °C
Max thermal sensation	30,61 °C	30,61 °C

While in the time that the second algorithm was executed, it presents a minimum ambient temperature of 18.27 °C with a minimum thermal sensation of 18.30 °C, its maximum ambient temperature was 26 °C with a maximum thermal sensation of 26. 93 °C (see Table 5).

Table 5. Table of ambient temperature and wind chill data with second irrigation algorithm.

	Greenhouse substrate	Greenhouse substrate mixture with earthworm humus
Min temperature environment	18,27 °C	18,27 °C
Max temperature environment	26 °C	26 °C
Min thermal sensation	18,30 °C	18,30 °C
Max thermal sensation	26,93 °C	26,93 °C

With this, the data collected by the sensors of temperature, thermal sensation, humidity of the closed environment and the humidity presented in the two types of soil are reviewed.

5 Conclusions

Analyzing the two types of soils, the conclusion is the one that presents the greatest advantages is the earthworm humus soil with the greenhouse substrate mixture, since it presents greater moisture retention, this result can be verified in Fig. 29 in the irrigation established every twenty-four hours, in addition this soil presenting a lower amount of irrigation using the second algorithm. Another advantage that it presents is the high amount of nutrients for its high organic content and also the soil is compact, for that it is possible to control the growth of unwanted plants, a disadvantage that it has presented compared to the greenhouse substrate is the germination time of the seeds. Showing results three days longer than the greenhouse substrate. While the green house substrate presents a germination in less time, but a high content of germinated plants unwanted such as clovers, grass, among others, also presents less amount of nutrients.

The temperature generated in the closed environment is higher than 19 °C, being a suitable environment for sowing food plants such as tomato seeds. The number of germinated seeds was one hundred and sixty-four tomato plants, representing 87% of the two hundred seeds sown, these were divided in one hundred seeds for the greenhouse substrate with 95% reached starting with 6% on the sixth day and in the mixture of worm humus with greenhouse substrate 79% was obtained at the end of the data collection time, starting with 3% after nine days. Implementing electronic hardware for the acquisition of information is essential for this job, the records collected were 239,626 in fifteen days of storage, being the best way to store information and thus record larger amounts over long periods of time.

It is verified that the first proposed irrigation algorithm is adequate for closed environments, since it presents a better performance with respect to the second algorithm, in addition the irrigation time given in the first algorithm could be doubled, if worm humus is used per retain moisture for long periods of time. When the second algorithm is applied in the greenhouse substrate, it presents high humidity, generating a white layer of white mold, while the worm humus with greenhouse substrate retains more humidity without showing signs of excess like this white layer. However, the second algorithm will depend on the plant that is placed, the type of soil used and the environmental conditions.

A limitation to this experimental method is in the irrigation, being necessary to expand the variables analyzed, for example, ventilation conditions since it was development in a closed environment. Proposing as future work a greater number of sensors and actuators that measure the air quality of the environment according to the oxygen, carbon dioxide or other element that is found and in turn can intervene by improving the ventilation of the planted space. In addition, the irrigation algorithm has a lack of robust control, having this as a limitation, requiring a more precise control.

This work it is a preliminary work, it is proposed in the future to incorporate computer vision [16, 17], with these techniques it is proposed to generate an analysis to the seeds, to identify possible complications in their germination and select seeds with a greater probability of germination, also to use artificial intelligence techniques in conjunction with an automated system [18–20], with the future works a higher quality product can be obtained for export, favoring the agricultural sector of Ecuador.

Acknowledgment. This work has been possible thanks to the support of the Vice-Rectorate of Research of the University of Azuay, Cuenca - Ecuador.

References

1. Margret Sharmila, F., Suryaganesh, P., Abishek, M., Benny, U.: IoT based smart window using sensor Dht11. In: 2019 5th International Conference on Advanced Computing & Communication Systems (ICACCS), pp. 782–784 (2019). https://doi.org/10.1109/ICACCS.2019.8728426
2. Dheena, P.P.F., Raj, G.S., Dutt, G., Jinny, S.V.: IOT based smart street light management system. In: 2017 IEEE International Conference on Circuits and Systems (ICCS), pp. 368–371 (2017). https://doi.org/10.1109/ICCS1.2017.8326023

3. Liu, M., Zhang, C.: Design of hierarchical monitoring system for crop growth environment based on arduino yún development platform. In: 2019 2nd International Conference on Safety Produce Informatization (IICSPI), pp. 515–519 (2019). https://doi.org/10.1109/IICSPI48186. 2019.9095958

4. Ayele, T.W., Mehta, R.: Real time temperature prediction using IoT. In: 2018 Second International Conference on Inventive Communication and Computational Technologies (ICICCT), pp. 1114–1117 (2018). https://doi.org/10.1109/ICICCT.2018.8473209

5. Nagaraja, G.S., Soppimath, A.B., Soumya, T., Abhinith, A.: IoT based smart agriculture management system. In: 2019 4th International Conference on Computational Systems and Information Technology for Sustainable Solution (CSITSS), pp. 1–5 (2019). https://doi.org/ 10.1109/CSITSS47250.2019.9031025

6. Coelho, A.D., Dias, B.G., de Oliveira Assis, W., de Almeida Martins, F., Pires, R.C.: Monitoring of soil moisture and atmospheric sensors with Internet of Things (IoT) applied in precision agriculture. In: 2020 XIV Technologies Applied to Electronics Teaching Conference (TAEE), pp. 1–8 (2020). https://doi.org/10.1109/TAEE46915.2020.9163766

7. Bhadani, P., Vashisht, V.: Soil moisture, temperature and humidity measurement using Arduino. In: 2019 9th International Conference on Cloud Computing, Data Science & Engineering (Confluence), pp. 567–571 (2019). https://doi.org/10.1109/CONFLUENCE.2019. 8776973

8. Kumar, M.S., Chandra, T.R., Kumar, D.P., Manikandan, M.S.: Monitoring moisture of soil using low cost homemade Soil moisture sensor and Arduino UNO. In: 2016 3rd International Conference on Advanced Computing and Communication Systems (ICACCS), pp. 1–4 (2016). https://doi.org/10.1109/ICACCS.2016.7586312

9. Muzdrikah, F.S., Nuha, M.S., Rizqi, F.A.: Calibration of capacitive soil moisture sensor (SKU:SEN0193). In: 2018 4th International Conference on Science and Technology (ICST), pp. 1–6 (2018). https://doi.org/10.1109/ICSTC.2018.8528624

10. Mayuree, M., Aishwarya, P., Bagubali, A.: Automatic plant watering system. In: 2019 International Conference on Vision Towards Emerging Trends in Communication and Networking (ViTECoN), pp. 1–3 (2019). https://doi.org/10.1109/ViTECoN.2019.8899452

11. Bhardwaj, S., Dhir, S., Hooda, M.: Automatic plant watering system using IoT. In: 2018 Second International Conference on Green Computing and Internet of Things (ICGCIoT), pp. 659–663 (2018). https://doi.org/10.1109/ICGCIoT.2018.8753100

12. Siva, K.N., Kumar G.R., Bagubali, A., Krishnan, K.V.: Smart watering of plants. In: 2019 International Conference on Vision Towards Emerging Trends in Communication and Networking (ViTECoN), pp. 1–4 (2019). https://doi.org/10.1109/ViTECoN.2019.8899371

13. Kumar, J., Gupta, N., Kumari, A., Kumari, S.: Automatic plant watering and monitoring system using NodeMCU. In: 2019 9th International Conference on Cloud Computing, Data Science & Engineering (Confluence), pp. 545–550 (2019). https://doi.org/10.1109/CONFLU ENCE.2019.8776956

14. Divani, D., Patil, P., Punjabi, S.K.: Automated plant watering system. In: 2016 International Conference on Computation of Power, Energy Information and Commuincation (ICCPEIC), pp. 180–182 (2016). https://doi.org/10.1109/ICCPEIC.2016.7557245

15. Derisa, M., Mulyana, E., Sumaryo, S.: Designing a data logger monitoring system prototype on automatic PlantSprinklers. In: 2019 IEEE 5th International Conference on Wireless and Telematics (ICWT), pp. 1–7 (2019). https://doi.org/10.1109/ICWT47785.2019.8978250

16. Tombe, R.: Computer vision for smart farming and sustainable agriculture. In: 2020 IST-Africa Conference (IST-Africa), pp. 1–8 (2020)

17. Mukherjee, A., Jana, P., Chakraborty, S., Saha, S.K.: Two stage semantic segmentation by SEEDS and Fork Net. In: 2020 IEEE Calcutta Conference (CALCON), pp. 283–287 (2020). https://doi.org/10.1109/CALCON49167.2020.9106468

18. Chauhan, S., Agrawal, P., Madaan, V.: E-Gardener: building a plant caretaker robot using computer vision. In: 2018 4th International Conference on Computing Sciences (ICCS), pp. 137–142 (2018). https://doi.org/10.1109/ICCS.2018.00031
19. Islam, A., Saha, P., Rana, M., Adnan, M.M., Pathik, B.B.: Smart gardening assistance system with the capability of detecting leaf disease in MATLAB. In: 2019 IEEE Pune Section International Conference (PuneCon), pp. 1–6 (2019). https://doi.org/10.1109/PuneCon46936.2019.9105677
20. Correll, N., et al.: Building a distributed robot garden. In: 2009 IEEE/RSJ International Conference on Intelligent Robots and Systems, pp. 1509–1516 (2009). https://doi.org/10.1109/IROS.2009.5354261

Users Segmentation Based on Google Analytics Income Using K-Means

Alexandra La Cruz[1]([envelope]) [ID], Erika Severeyn[2][ID], Roberto Matute[3],
and Juan Estrada[3]

[1] Faculty of Engineering, Universidad de Ibagué, Ibagué, Tolima, Colombia
`alexandra.lacruz@unibague.edu.co`
[2] Dept. of Thermodynamics and Transfer Phenomena, Universidad Simón Bolívar,
Caracas, Venezuela
`severeynerika@usb.ve`
[3] Imolko.com, Panamá, Panama
`robertomatute@imolko.com`

Abstract. Business intelligence (BI) is a set of techniques and practices to extract, transform and handle large volumes of data from a business, for analyzing and turning them into actionable business insights, to improve the profit and the most important is getting to know the customers better. Market segmentation (MS) is one of the BI strategies which converts the heterogeneous market into homogeneous subgroups, with similar characteristics that will define the marketing strategies. There are machine learning techniques that allow the most efficient segmentation in the market. One of these techniques is the k-means, which is an unsupervised learning technique that allows the segmentation of a data set from the Euclidean distances between each data and the centroids established by the method. This research aims to segment the customers of a web service based on the behavioral characteristics of the users. A company dedicated to helping small businesses and new entrepreneurs increase their customer base through the use of digital marketing strategies provides a database, which registers user behavior through events on their web application. A k-means method was applied to segment our client's list based on their interactions with the application. The k-means performed segmentation of 15 clusters that were organized into four groups, the most important group reported a very varied behavior pattern of usage of the web service, the 64.38% of clients are within this group, which suggests that the client's profile could be attached to the characteristics of this group.

Keywords: Google analytic · User segmentation · K-means clustering

1 Introduction

Business intelligence (BI) is a set of techniques and practices to extract, transform and handle a large volume of data from a business. BI transforms unstructured information from internal and external sources into structured information for analyzing and turning them into actionable business insights, in order

J. P. Salgado Guerrero et al. (Eds.): TICEC 2021, CCIS 1456, pp. 225–235, 2021.
https://doi.org/10.1007/978-3-030-89941-7_16

to improve the profit and the knowledge of customers or possible customers [13]. One of the most used BI techniques is the market segmentation (MS) [10]. According to William Pride, "Market segmentation is the process of dividing a total market into groups of consumers who have relatively similar product needs" [24]. It can be summarized that segmentation consists of dividing a market made up of consumers with diverse characteristics and behaviors into homogeneous segments that contain people who respond in a similar way to the marketing effort of a company. E-commerce web pages have increased their market position in the last 20 years [15, 23].

The structures of e-commerce websites usually revolve around item listings, item characteristics, and online payment processes [6]. In this process of searching and purchasing items, users request to leave the usage or behavioral profile which may concern the type of customer that characterizes that user [16].

Therefore, market segmentation is possible based on these usage profiles [27]. Data mining is a set of techniques used for exploring datasets and extracting insights, also referred to as knowledge management or knowledge engineering in the past [9]. Machine learning is one of those techniques used for extracting information from large data sets or databases. Among the machine learning methods used in data mining are clustering methods. These methods take a set of data and divide it into groupings of the data elements based on similarity metrics or probability density models [12, 22]. The k-means is one of the most used data mining techniques in market segmentation [7, 28].

Kansal et al. [11] applied the k-means method to a database of 200 customers who reported the number of customer purchases and the frequency of customer visits to the store on an annual basis. By applying k-means it was possible to identify two more market segments that enriched the vision of potential customers of the business. Similarly, Ghosal et al. [3] used customer segmentation from data collected by a retail company that has many branches in Akwa Ibom State (Nigeria). The algorithm designed in MATLAB succeeded in segmenting 95% of the customers. The company then used this result to design a market strategy tailored to each customer segment, as well as to identify the products associated with each segment. Some studies have used k-means for segmenting the web users based on their browsing activities [20], the pattern of use for recognizing fraud users on a Bitcoin exchange platform [8] and clickstream information of the transaction-related shopping behavior [26].

This research aims to present a strategy to segment users of a website based on the clickstream information of the users when interacting with the website. For this, this work describes a performance of a k-means algorithm. Each identified group separates them according to the type of website interaction and recurrence in the use of the services.

2   Background

Imolko is a service company whose main purpose is to help businesses to increase their profits, keep clients, increase their sales, automatize the process of keeping the client well informed about the sale products in a smart way, and decreasing the Churn Rate. A Churn Rate is a term in marketing used as a measurement of customers who have abandoned or unsubscribed an entity. In order to improve their service, they would like to include in their process artificial intelligence techniques for better service for their clients. As a first task they want to know more about the behavior of their clients using their services, thus there are two mains tasks they want to analyze: i) segment the customer based on their behavior using the services offered, and ii) classification between recurring and non-recurring customers

3 Methodology

3.1 Database Preparation

The database used for this research came from a company involved in e-commerce marketing and e-mail service. The database consisted of customer interactions with the e-commerce site, which had 71,682 total action events recorded by users. The database was composed of 33,496 instances with six columns; the customer ID, the event category, the event action, the number of times the user performed the event action, and the time in months the user was connected and performed the event action. For all of these events, 846 different customers who interacted with the e-commerce company for a year registered the event.

The first transformation consisted of transforming a table whose instances are interactions by another whose instances are users and their interactions. The behavior of the user reflected in interactions was the object of our study [1].

The main idea is to segment the customer based on the action events they are performed. Therefore the data was to be transformed in a way where every instance represent a client ID and its correspondent number of event actions performed, and the time in month the user performed each event action. Then every column is formed by: ea_i, and tea_i, where ea_i correspond to the event action i and tea_i the time in month the customer performed x number of time the event action i.

3.2 Customer Market Segmentation

In this work, a behavioral segmentation will be carried out based on the inter-actions made by customers with the services page of a business that offers marketing and email services. For this, a methodology that consists of the following steps will be executed [29]:

- Step 1: The database will be pre-processed with the stipulations described in the previous section.
- Step 2: The pre-processed database was analyzed with k-means performed with different cluster numbers to determine the initial number of segments by the elbow method. A principal component analysis then helped to determine the variables that provide the most information [17].
- Step 3: A clustering analysis with the k-means algorithm was carried out with the chosen interactions and the initial number of determined segments to determine the final number of market segments [18].

3.3   K-Means Implemented

k-means [5] is a method that divides n observations into k clusters. In the k-means algorithm, each observation is assigned to the nearest centroid cluster by a distance function, and then the centroids of each cluster are recalculated. This process repeats until the centroids are equal at each step and until all possible clusters get formed.

This study applied a k-means method to the pre-processed database; the number of groups was set by the elbow method which uses the mean distance of the observations from their centroid [2,19]. The larger the number of clusters k, the intra-cluster variance tends to decrease [14]. The smaller the intra-cluster distance the better, since it means that the clusters are more compact. The elbow method searches for the value k that satisfies that an increase in k does not substantially improve the mean intra-cluster distance [30]. The Euclidean squared distance was used to calculate the distance between each variable of the data set with centroids, and the process was replayed 10 times to prevent local minima [4]. The silhouette coefficient (SC) was used to assess the assignment of the data set in the respective cluster [25].

4   Results

Fig. 1 shows the graph between the numbers of clusters (k) and the sums of the distances of each of the points or subjects and their centroid. The greater the number of clusters assigned, the smaller the distance from the points to each of the centroids. The number of optimal clusters will be found by the elbow method from Fig. 1. In this case, the point where the graph stops having significant differences in the sums of the distances to the centroids is when k = 15, that is the number of clusters chosen for the k-means analysis.

Additionally, Fig. 2 shows the contrast of the mean of the SC and elbow method. It exhibits that clustering with a k between 10 and 20 is acceptable for this data set [21] with a SC greater than 0.65.

In Tables 1, 2, 3 and 4 it is possible to see the percentage of events for each type of event, in addition to the mean and standard deviation of the number of events per person, the time in which these events took place, the number of clients in the cluster and the time taken for each interaction reported. The Table 1 shows the clusters with the highest number of events per person and having more than three subjects per cluster. The Table 2 shows the clusters with a lower number of events per person than the Table 1 and with more than three subjects per cluster. Table 3 shows clusters that have two or three subjects per cluster, and Table 4 shows clusters that have only one subject per cluster.

5   Discussion

Table 1 shows the clusters (clusters 1, 2, 14, and 15) that had several events per person between 10.039 ± 12.250 and $1,272.333 \pm 507.572$ and are also made

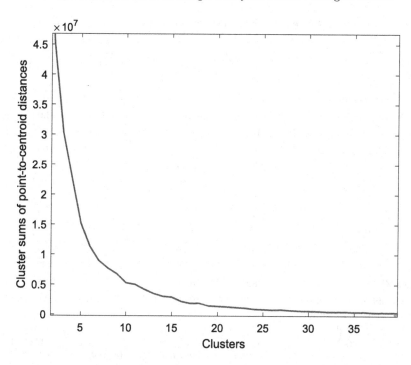

Fig. 1. Number of clusters vs. the sum of the distances from each of the points to the centroids (elbow method).

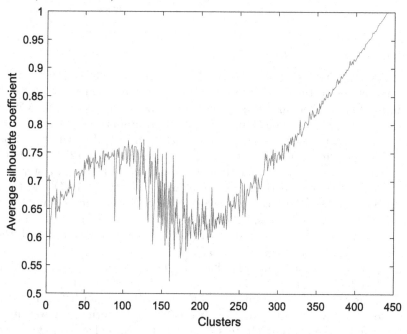

Fig. 2. Number of clusters vs. the average of the SC in that number of clusters.

Table 1. Percentage of the events of clusters 1, 2, 14 and 15.

Type of event	Cluster 1 n = 279	Cluster 2 n = 8	Cluster 14 n = 117	Cluster 15 n = 12
Approvals task done[%]	2.00	4.39	9.69	13.55
Complete profile[%]	3.71	0.07	0.47	0.01
Content task done[%]	8.25	4.71	10.78	13.99
Create Draft from Gallery[%]	11.25	1.49	8.68	8.86
Create Iform from Gallery[%]	10.00	0.57	0.82	0.05
Create Order[%]	2.21	6.36	8.84	6.82
Header task done[%]	10.46	6.18	13.78	16.03
Login[%]	27.81	35.66	14.68	7.07
Logout[%]	5.25	23.70	5.43	2.57
Order task done[%]	7.71	4.41	10.25	13.44
Publish Draft[%]	6.07	4.20	9.45	12.80
Save profile[%]	0.46	2.50	3.85	1.93
Others[%]	4.82	5.76	3.27	2.88
% of clients in the cluster/% of clients according of total amount of clients in dataset	12.30/5.37	91.67/9.02	47.86/45.90	62.5/4.09
Average of events	10.039 ± 12.250	705.625 ± 284.649	126.068 ± 144.960	1,272.333 ± 507.572
Event time [month]	1.448 ± 1.695	10.875 ± 3.944	4.932 ± 4.664	12.000 ± 1.809
Hours per event	109.867 ± 24.691	13.499 ± 9.657	37.835 ± 16.988	7.845 ± 3.082

up of more than two subjects. These clusters are characterized by having a varied interaction in types of events, the types of events that are repeated the most in the four clusters are: Approvals Task Done, Complete Profile, Content Task Done, Create Draft from Gallery, Create Iform from Gallery, Create Order, Header Task Done, Login, Logout, Order Task Done, Publish Draft and Save Profile. Cluster 1 has a higher percentage of events in Login (27.81%), Create Draft from Gallery (11.25%) and Header Task Done (10.46%). Cluster 2 has a higher percentage of events in Login (35.66%), Logout (23.70%) and Create Order (6.36%). Cluster 14 has a higher percentage of events in Login (14.68%), Header Tasks Done (13.78%) and Content Task Done (10.78%). Cluster 15 has a higher percentage of events in Header Task Done (16.03%), Content Task Done (13.99%) and Approvals Task Done (13.55%).

The subjects in Table 1 (n = 416) have a time between events of 7.845 h per event and 109.867 h per event. The percentages of every event type are lower than 36%, suggesting that the subjects of these clusters do not have a particular preference for an event type and have a varied usage pattern of the website.

Table 2 shows the clusters (clusters 3, 4, and 11) that had an average between 1.459 ± 1.531 and 5.006 ± 6.045 events per person and that have more than two

Table 2. Percentage of the events of clusters 3, 4 and 11.

Type of event	Cluster 3 n = 109	Cluster 4 n = 171	Cluster 11 n = 136
Complete Profile[%]	3.77	5.14	2.16
Content task done[%]	0.63	3.86	0.48
Create Draft from Gallery[%]	1.89	13.55	13.67
Create Iform from Gallery[%]	5.03	15.19	15.11
Create Order[%]	–	4.44	1.68
Header task done[%]	1.26	6.89	0.96
Login[%]	78.62	38.08	51.32
Logout[%]	3.14	4.56	7.43
Others[%]	5.66	8.29	7.19
% of clients in the cluster/% of clients according of total amount of clients in dataset	2.75/2.45	5.84/8.20	8.08/9.02
Average of events	1.459 ± 1.531	5.006 ± 6.045	3.066 ± 3.830
Event time [month]	1.486 ± 1.636	1.538 ± 1.944	1.544 ± 1.873
Hours per event	725.670 ± 72.221	220.549 ± 28.756	363.144 ± 22.787

subjects per cluster (between 109 and 171 subjects). In general, these clusters are characterized by having a higher percentage of events in a reduced group of types of events such as Complete Profile, Content Task Done, Create Draft from Gallery, Create Iform from Gallery, Create Order, Header Task Done, Login, and Logout. Cluster 3, 4, and 11 have a higher percentage of events in Login (78.62%, 38.08%, and 51.32%) and Create Iform from Gallery (5.03%, 15.19% and 15.11%).

The subjects in Table 2 (n = 416) have a time between events of 363.144 ± 22.787 h per event and 725.670 ± 72.221 h per event. The subjects of Table 2 use the website with a limited amount and type of events and have a very high preference for some particular event.

Table 3 shows the clusters (6, 7, 9, 10 and 12) that had an average of events per person between 767.000 ± 203.647 and 3,181.667 ± 579.532 and a time between events of 12.649 ± 3.359 h per event and 2.259 ± 1.229 h per event, but only less than three subjects per cluster. In these clusters, two groups with a different patterns of website usage are identified. The groups that had a high percentage of events in a reduced type of events such as cluster 7, 10, and 12, whose higher event percentages are Send Email (78.06%) and Save Profile (9.19%) for the case of cluster 7; Save Profile (49.84%) and Header task done (8.57%) in the case of cluster 10; and Create Order and Delete flow in the case of cluster 12.

Table 3. Percentage of the events of clusters 6, 7, 9, 10 and 12.

Type of event	Cluster 6 n = 2	Cluster 7 n = 2	Cluster 9 n = 3	Cluster 10 n = 2	Cluster 12 n = 2
Approvals task done[%]	6.90	0.96	12.93	6.84	0.85
Content task done[%]	6.86	0.90	13.19	7.33	0.85
Create Order[%]	11.21	0.37	22.16	2.04	70.08
Delete Flow[%]	–	0.03	1.95	–	10.82
Header task done[%]	7.62	1.24	16.34	8.57	0.98
Login[%]	26.19	4.81	6.33	5.86	5.28
Logout[%]	22.88	0.68	2.26	4.62	2.02
Order task done[%]	6.90	0.96	11.47	7.20	0.52
Publish Draft[%]	6.70	0.96	11.05	6.66	0.52
Save Profile[%]	3.40	9.19	–	49.84	0.20
Send Email[%]	–	78.06	0.01	–	–
Others[%]	1.34	1.84	2.30	1.02	7.89
% of clients in the cluster/% of clients according of total amount of clients in dataset	100/1.63	50/0.82	66.67/1.63	100/1.63	100/1.63
Average of events	1,529.500 ± 203.647	1,768.500 ± 526.795	3,181.667 ± 579.532	1,125.500 ± 178.898	767.000 ± 731.8564
Event time [month]	9.000 ± 5.657	13.000 ± 0.000	9.333 ± 3.512	13.000 ± 0.000	13.000 ± 0.000
Hours per event	4.065 ± 0.718	5.538 ± 1.650	2.259 ± 1.229	8.423 ± 1.339	12.649 ± 3.359

These groups seem to have a usage pattern like the clusters of Table 2. And the clusters 6 and 9 that have not a high percentage of events in a particular type of event, these clusters have similarities of usage like clusters of Table 1.

Table 4 shows clusters with a single person, these are subjects that have a very high average of events (between 3,790 and 4,101). These subjects have a limited variety of types of events, as is the case of cluster 5 (Send Email) and cluster 8 (Create Order and Save Profile). In cluster 13, there are varied types of events with a high percentage.

Out of 846 users, 122 users are customers, of which 5.37% are in cluster 1, 9.02% are in cluster 2, 45.90% are in cluster 14, and 4.09% are in cluster 20, indicating that 64.38% of the customers are in the Table 1, which are users who use the platform with a variable pattern. Cluster 3 has 2.45%, cluster 4 has 5.84%, and cluster 11 has 9.02%, indicating that users who tend to use a small group of event types, which are those in the Table 3 have 19.67% of the customers. Only 15.95% of the clients are in the clusters of Tables 3 and 4.

Table 4. Percentage of the events of clusters 5, 8, and 13.

Type of event	Cluster 5 n = 1	Cluster 8 n = 1	Cluster 13 n = 1
Approvals task done	–	7.05	15.62
Content task done[%]	–	7.02	15.57
Create Draft from Gallery[%]	–	0.12	4.46
Create Order[%]	–	22.99	–
Header task done[%]	–	8.68	16.65
Login[%]	0.20	3.51	0.37
Order task done[%]	–	6.17	16.23
Publish Draft[%]	–	5.83	15.51
Save Profile[%]	2.44	32.04	13.85
Send Email[%]	97.33	–	–
Others[%]	0.03	6.58	1.74
% of clients in the cluster/% of clients according of total amount of clients in dataset	–	100/0.82	100/0.82
Average of events	3,969.000	4,101.000	3,790.000
Event time [month]	13.000	13.000	13.000
Hours per event	2.358	2.282	2.470

6   Conclusions

The results obtained suggest that the k-means method performs clustering based on event uniformity and event mean. The k-means performed segmentation of 15 clusters organized into four groups. Cluster 1 has the subjects who reported events with the page every 7 to 109 h, being subjects with a very varied website usage behavior pattern. It is worth noting that 64.38% of the customers are within this cluster, suggesting that the customer profile could stick to the characteristics of this group.

Cluster 2 reported events with the website every nine days, two weeks, or one month. The usage pattern of this group is limited to a few types of events with a very high percentage of the mean number of such events. Cluster 3 reported events with the website every 2.26 h to 12 h. In cluster 3 there were two different usage patterns identified. Clusters 7, 10, and 12 are similar to cluster 2, and clusters 6 and 9 are similar to cluster 1. The main activities of cluster 3 are focused on sending emails and saving the profile. Cluster 4 has only one subject this is due to the subject have an exaggerated amount of events.

As future work supervised machine learning techniques will be explored to enable the design of algorithms that predict the probability of customer engagement or customer churn based on website clickstream information.

Acknowledgment. IMOLKO C.A. financed a part of this research work, as did the Research and Development Department of the Simón Bolivar University (DID-USB) and the Research Department of the Ibagué University.

References

1. Alasadi, S.A., Bhaya, W.S.: Review of data preprocessing techniques in data mining. J. Eng. Appl. Sci. **12**(16), 4102–4107 (2017)
2. Cui, M., et al.: Introduction to the k-means clustering algorithm based on the elbow method. Account. Audit. Financ. **1**(1), 5–8 (2020)
3. Ghosal, A., Nandy, A., Das, A.K., Goswami, S., Panday, M.: A short review on different clustering techniques and their applications. In: Mandal, J.K., Bhattacharya, D. (eds.) Emerging Technology in Modelling and Graphics. AISC, vol. 937, pp. 69–83. Springer, Singapore (2020). https://doi.org/10.1007/978-981-13-7403-6_9
4. Gupta, M.K., Chandra, P.: An empirical evaluation of k-means clustering algorithm using different distance/similarity metrics. In: Singh, P.K., Panigrahi, B.K., Suryadevara, N.K., Sharma, S.K., Singh, A.P. (eds.) Proceedings of ICETIT 2019. LNEE, vol. 605, pp. 884–892. Springer, Cham (2020). https://doi.org/10.1007/978-3-030-30577-2_79
5. Hartigan, J.A., Wong, M.A.: Algorithm as 136: a k-means clustering algorithm. J. R. Stat. Soc. Ser. C (Appl. Stat.) **28**(1), 100–108 (1979)
6. Hernandez, S., Alvarez, P., Fabra, J., Ezpeleta, J.: Analysis of users' behavior in structured e-commerce websites. IEEE Access **5**, 11941–11958 (2017)
7. Hung, P.D., Ngoc, N.D., Hanh, T.D.: K-means clustering using ra case study of market segmentation. In: Proceedings of the 2019 5th International Conference on E-Business and Applications, pp. 100–104 (2019)
8. Jain, N., Ahuja, V.: Segmenting online consumers using k-means cluster analysis. Int. J. Log. Econ. Glob. **6**(2), 161–178 (2014)
9. Joseph, S.I.T., Thanakumar, I.: Survey of data mining algorithm's for intelligent computing system. J. Trends Comput. Sci. Smart Technol. (TCSST) **1**(01), 14–24 (2019)
10. Kamthania, D., Pawa, A., Madhavan, S.S.: Market segmentation analysis and visualization using k-mode clustering algorithm for e-commerce business. J. Comput. Inf. Technol. **26**(1), 57–68 (2018)
11. Kansal, T., Bahuguna, S., Singh, V., Choudhury, T.: Customer segmentation using k-means clustering. In: 2018 International Conference on Computational Techniques, Electronics and Mechanical Systems (CTEMS), pp. 135–139. IEEE (2018)
12. Li, C., Kulwa, F., Zhang, J., Li, Z., Xu, H., Zhao, X.: A review of clustering methods in microorganism image analysis. In: Pietka, E., Badura, P., Kawa, J., Wieclawek, W. (eds.) Information Technology in Biomedicine. AISC, vol. 1186, pp. 13–25. Springer, Cham (2021). https://doi.org/10.1007/978-3-030-49666-1_2
13. Liang, T.P., Liu, Y.H.: Research landscape of business intelligence and big data analytics: a bibliometrics study. Expert Syst. Appl. **111**, 2–10 (2018)
14. Liu, F., Deng, Y.: Determine the number of unknown targets in open world based on elbow method. IEEE Trans. Fuzzy Syst. (2020)
15. Liu, J., Liao, X., Huang, W., Liao, X.: Market segmentation: a multiple criteria approach combining preference analysis and segmentation decision. Omega **83**, 1–13 (2019)

16. Lu, L., Reardon, T.: An economic model of the evolution of food retail and supply chains from traditional shops to supermarkets to e-commerce. Am. J. Agric. Econ. **100**(5), 1320–1335 (2018)
17. Maneno, K.M., Rimiru, R., Otieno, C.: Segmentation via principal component analysis for perceptron classification: a case study of kenyan mobile subscribers. In: Proceedings of the 2nd International Conference on Intelligent and Innovative Computing Applications, pp. 1–8 (2020)
18. Manero, K.M., Rimiru, R., Otieno, C.: Customer behaviour segmentation among mobile service providers in kenya using k-means algorithm. Int. J. Comput. Sci. Issues (IJCSI) **15**(5), 67–76 (2018)
19. Nainggolan, R., Perangin-angin, R., Simarmata, E., Tarigan, A.F.: Improved the performance of the k-means cluster using the sum of squared error (SSE) optimized by using the elbow method. In: Journal of Physics: Conference Series, vol. 1361, p. 012015. IOP Publishing (2019)
20. Nasser, M., Salim, N., Hamza, H., et al.: Clustering web users for reductions the internet traffic load and users access cost based on k-means algorithm. Int. J. Eng. Technol. **7**(4), 3162–3169 (2018)
21. Nawrin, S., Rahman, M.R., Akhter, S.: Exploreing k-means with internal validity indexes for data clustering in traffic management system. Int. J. Adv. Comput. Sci. Appl. **8**(3), 264–272 (2017)
22. Oktar, Y., Turkan, M.: A review of sparsity-based clustering methods. Signal Process. **148**, 20–30 (2018)
23. Pomarici, E., Lerro, M., Chrysochou, P., Vecchio, R., Krystallis, A.: One size does (obviously not) fit all: using product attributes for wine market segmentation. Wine Econ. Policy **6**(2), 98–106 (2017)
24. Pride, W.M., Ferrell, O., Lukas, B.A., Schembri, S., Niininen, O., Casidy, R.: Marketing Principles with Student Resource Access 12 Months. Cengage AU (2017)
25. Rousseeuw, P.J.: Silhouettes: a graphical aid to the interpretation and validation of cluster analysis. J. Comput. Appl. Math. **20**, 53–65 (1987)
26. Schellong, D., Kemper, J., Brettel, M.: Generating consumer insights from big data clickstream information and the link with transaction-related shopping behavior (2017)
27. Sondhi, N.: Segmenting & profiling the deflecting customer: understanding shopping cart abandonment. Procedia Comput. Sci. **122**, 392–399 (2017)
28. Syakur, M., Khotimah, B., Rochman, E., Satoto, B.: Integration k-means clustering method and elbow method for identification of the best customer profile cluster. In: IOP Conference Series: Materials Science and Engineering, vol. 336, p. 012017. IOP Publishing (2018)
29. Tleis, M., Callieris, R., Roma, R.: Segmenting the organic food market in lebanon: an application of k-means cluster analysis. Br. Food J. (2017)
30. Yuan, C., Yang, H.: Research on k-value selection method of k-means clustering algorithm. J-Multidiscip. Sci. J. **2**(2), 226–235 (2019)

Evaluating the Precision and Security of Data in Middleware Applications

Priscila Cedillo$^{(\boxtimes)}$ (ID), Edwin Narvaez-Miranda, Mauricio Calle-Morales, Wilson Valdez (ID), and Paul Cardenas-Delgado (ID)

Universidad de Cuenca, Av. 12 de abril s/n, Cuenca, Ecuador
{priscila.cedillo,edwin.narvaez,mauricio.calle,wilson.valdezs,
paul.cardenasd}@ucuenca.edu.ec

Abstract. A Middleware is a software product that constitutes a fundamental part of distributed systems since they facilitate the development and integration of applications in those heterogeneous environments. Besides, distributed systems consider the quality of data in terms of precision and security. As Middlewares are essential for many solutions, developing a quality model that meets the essential characteristics of accuracy and security and creating an efficient evaluation method since there are no models in the current literature solutions that specifically evaluate their characteristics. Thus, this paper presents a quality model for Middleware oriented to the precision and security of the data based on specific characteristics and sub-characteristics of ISO 25012 and a method to evaluate said quality, aligned with the ISO 25040. In addition, a case study is presented to demonstrate the feasibility of the evaluation method.

Keywords: Quality of software · Data quality · Middleware

1 Introduction

Internet of Things (IoT) is an emerging paradigm that provides an intelligent environment for the communication and interconnection of various devices (sensors and actuators) [1, 2]. IoT provides new services to citizens, companies, and public administrations in general areas such as smart cities, transport, industry, healthcare, and farming. Here, a significant challenge is coordinating the synchronism and connection between devices which sometimes is a slow and delicate, errable process [3, 4].

In this sense, Middleware has become a necessary component in any distributed system, such as the wireless sensor networks typical of IoT. It unifies the data collection, processing, and showing to users by integrating heterogeneous devices, software, and services [3, 5].

Due to the importance of an efficient operation of Middlewares in any of their application fields, determining the quality of these components and primarily those related to data becomes essential to achieve it; however, the view of quality presents different perspectives. For instance, when talking about data-centric Middlewares, reference is made to decide to deliver and store the data where the data quality is intrinsically found [6].

© Springer Nature Switzerland AG 2021
J. P. Salgado Guerrero et al. (Eds.): TICEC 2021, CCIS 1456, pp. 236–249, 2021.
https://doi.org/10.1007/978-3-030-89941-7_17

Nevertheless, several studies, such as [6–8], treat data quality from a ubiquitous computing point of view. On the other hand, others address it from the Quality of Service (QoS) [9–14].

Consequently, this paper presents a data-centered quality model aligned to the ISO/IEC 25,012 data quality standard to support the evaluation of Middlewares [15]. The model primarily addresses precision and safety features, breaking them down into sub-features and attributes. Furthermore, an evaluation method is presented based on the ISO/IEC 25,040 [16] evaluation guidelines. Finally, to assess the proposed method, a study case is applied to a Middleware oriented to the healthcare field that gathers several data sources [17].

The remaining of this document is structured as follows: Sect. 2 analyzes the related work, considering the previous quality models used for evaluating Middlewares. Section 3 presents the quality model; Sect. 4 presents the precision and security-focused evaluation model on Middleware; Sect. 5 presents a study case applied to the Healthcare domain. Finally, Sect. 6 the conclusions and future work.

2 Related Work

This section briefly addresses some studies related to the quality of the data applied in Middleware through proposals and applications of various quality models and others that apply the use of quality standards.

First of all, the research presented in [6] focuses on a comprehensive development process based on models for distributed applications enabled for quality of service on Middleware platforms enhanced with QoS. This paper relies upon the importance of quality models for assessing Middlewares. Nevertheless, it does not address the data quality but the quality of service.

Giough et al. [7] present a technique for evaluating quality features in an RFID Middleware based on ISO/IEC 9126 standard. The study uses the Analytic Hierarchy Process (AHP) technique to simplify the metric selection. Also, it presents an interesting evaluation method to assess quality criteria. However, although the study uses a quality standard and an evaluation method, it does not assess the data quality.

Besides, Kim Yung et al. [8] present the COSMOS Middleware platform. The study is made within the Ubiquitous Sensor Networks (USN) domain and addresses some quality features for the Middleware, such as accessibility and data quality. However, this paper does not present any quality model aligned to a standard.

Moreover, the QoS is one of the most valuable characteristics of Middleware. In this sense, the studies presented in [9–14] address it differently, such as frameworks, tolerance to a fault, publication/subscribe. However, most of them lack research because they do not address it to a standard or present an organized evaluation model.

Concerning IoT applications, Rausch et al. [18] propose EMMA Middleware of publication/subscription enabled for Edge Computing. It can address the challenges presented by the Cloud Computing approach, such as customer mobility and high availability, without neglecting QoS. However, it does not address the data quality.

Regarding data quality in data-centralization platforms. Moraga C. et al. [19] present a data quality model for web portals derived from ISO/IEC 25,012 standard and the data quality model for portals (PDQM). The model aims to provide quality to data generated in web portals; it is focused on 42 characteristics aligned with the mentioned standards and covers many features. However, a very general model is obtained, which can hardly be applied in specific contexts.

In [20], a basis for the detection of characteristics and sub-characteristics is presented in the definition of the quality model focused on security. Therefore, the study serves as a guide to define the characteristics considered more suitable to generate the data quality model. This study is aligned with the ISO/IEC 25,012 standards and obtained the metrics from the ISO/IEC 25,024.

Consequently, after reviewing several investigations, it is verified that many of these are focused on creating quality models for supporting the evaluation of quality for Middlewares. However, no research was found that focuses on both simultaneously; that is, no study deals with data quality in Middleware.

3   Quality Model

In this section, a quality model is presented. It is focused mainly on the precision and security characteristics of data for Middleware applications assessment.

A quality model is a guide between the implemented applications and the end-users to identify if the product in question complies with the agreed quality standards [21]. ISO proposes the ISO/IEC 25,012 standard to define the characteristics of a data quality model. This quality model was designed with two main characteristics in mind: precision and data security.

3.1   Precision Model

Precision is the degree to which data have accurate attributes or provide insights in a specific context [22]. Hereof, the domain-relevant sub-characteristics analyzed by the proposed model were extracted from the ISO/IEC 25,012 standard (see Table 1).

Table 1. Precision model: sub characteristics and definition

Sub characteristics	Definition
Accuracy	The degree to which the information is reliable in the sense of being free from errors
Credibility	Degree to which the data has attributes that are considered true and credible in a specific use context. Credibility includes the concept of authenticity (the veracity of data sources, attributions, commitments)
Actuality	Degree to which the data has attributes that are the correct age in a specific usage context
Traceability	Degree to which the data has attributes that provide an audited path to the data or any other changes made to the data in a specific use context

3.2 Security Model

ISO/IEC 25,012 proposes several characteristics for data quality assurance in terms of security, which is why several of these characteristics have been analyzed to propose the security model. Security is defined as: "The degree to which a product or system protects information" [22]. Besides, to complement the attributes from the standard, it has been considered the trust module algorithm in order to enhance the authentication to verify that the data source is correct [23]; this was considered in the responsibility sub characteristic. In this context, the sub-characteristics of the proposed quality model are shown in Table 2 as follows.

Table 2. Security model: sub characteristics and definition

Sub characteristics	Definition
Confidentiality	The data is accessible only to those who have authorized access
Integrity	Prevent unauthorized access or modification of computer programs or data
Responsibility	Actions taken by any given entity can be traced back to the entity itself

4 Evaluation Method

As presented in the quality model, a Middleware is an application that brings importance to several quality characteristics such as precision and data security [7]. Here, those characteristics have a subset of quality factors or attributes that influence the Middleware performance. On the other hand, ISO/IEC 25,040 standard shows a process divided into five activities to evaluate a software product [16]. Therefore, this section presents an adaptation of this process into the Middleware evaluation domain and the use of the quality model within it (Fig. 1). The process is represented by using SPEM (Software Process Engineering Metamodel) specification [24]. Besides, to correctly obtain the evaluation requirements, it is necessary to determine the Middleware application domain (e.g., Smart Cities, Health, Industry, etc.) as defined in the ISO/IEC 25,040; this is addressed through the input remarked in a red square (Fig. 1) where the selection of the Middleware application domain is the first step before starting the process.

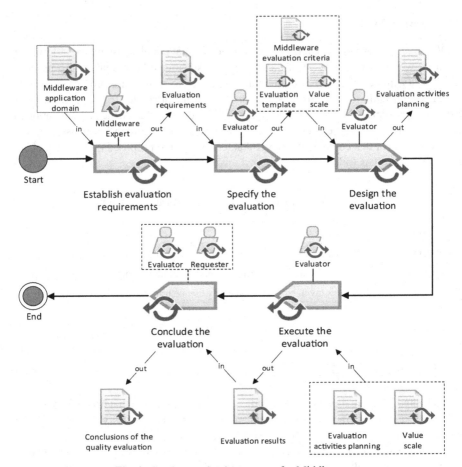

Fig. 1. Product evaluation process for Middlewares

4.1 Establish Evaluation Requirements

The first stage is to *establish the evaluation requirements*. As shown in Fig. 2, the first step is to establish the purpose of the evaluation; here, it is essential to know about the Middleware application domain to make comparisons and review required documents such as ascertain service level agreements. Second, the product quality requirements are obtained from the ISO/IEC 25,010–25,012 standards [25, 26], and specific requirements from the Middleware domain.

Afterward, the product components to be evaluated must be identified, especially the entity-relationship diagrams (ERD) and any data model diagram that makes up the Middleware. Also, the quality model proposed (Sect. 3) is considered.

Finally, the rigor of the evaluation is defined based on determining aspects such as security and economic risk. Then, it is possible to establish which techniques must be applied and thus the evaluation requirements document.

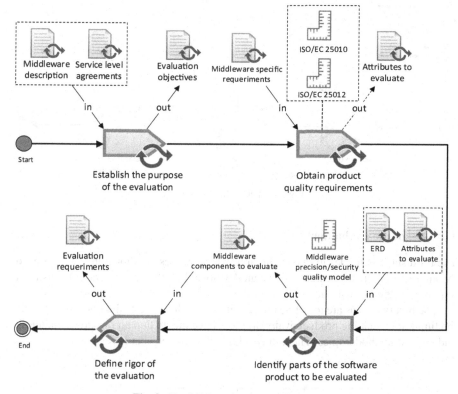

Fig. 2. Establish evaluation requirements

4.2 Specify the Evaluation

The second stage of the process is to *Specify the evaluation*. Figure 3 indicates this sequence, where the first step is to select and define the metrics used for the evaluation; for this, the ISO standards [10] and [15] are used, together with the evaluation and quality requirements, in addition to considering precision and security of data.

Secondly, is to define the decision criteria for the metrics, which were selected from the ISO/IEC-25024 standard [27], which are summarized in the quality model proposed in this paper. The result of this is a document with the thresholds for the assessment, along with their metrics.

Finally, the decision criteria for the evaluation are defined by using metrics and documents previously defined. The outputs of this stage are, on the one hand, the quite complete evaluation criteria, which includes the attributes, characteristics, and sub-characteristics proposed by this method, and on the other hand, the template for evaluating security and precision in Middlewares.

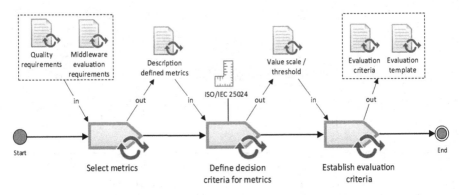

Fig. 3. Specify the evaluation

4.3 Design the Evaluation

The third stage is to Design the evaluation, whose process is shown in Fig. 4. it needs the intervention of the "evaluation designer" who defines the parameters and constraints required for the evaluation.

The first two steps are to define the activities to address the evaluation and to specify the limitations that the product evaluation will have due to human resources, materials, budget, and methodologies. Then, the evaluation activities plan is designed.

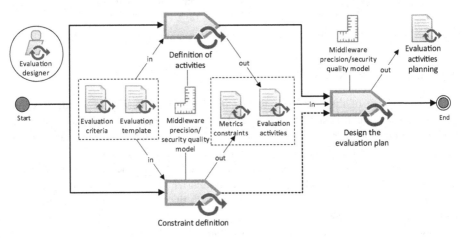

Fig. 4. Design the evaluation

4.4 Execute the Evaluation

After defining the activities and processes necessary for the evaluation, the next stage is to Execute the evaluation. This process consists of 4 activities (Fig. 5).

The evaluation is executed by the evaluator, who performs the measurements with the indicators previously established for each metric, characteristic and sub-characteristic defined in the scope of the evaluation. Besides, the data generated in each step is recorded and stored for analysis. After obtaining all the values, the metrics and decision criteria are applied. The final results are compiled in a document with the results of the evaluation.

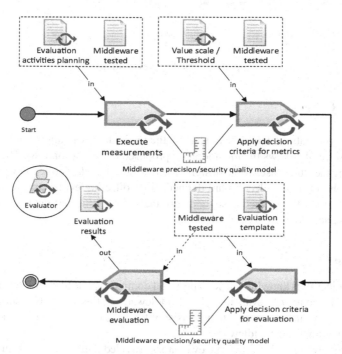

Fig. 5. Execute the evaluation

4.5   Conclude the Evaluation

The evaluation process ends at Conclude the evaluation stage, which is shown in Fig. 6. This process needs the intervention of the evaluator and the requester, who reviews the results of the evaluation.

Then, it is created the evaluation report using the data obtained from the previous steps; Additionally, this report must have the specification of the requirements, problems encountered, limitations or restrictions present, and the data of the evaluator. It is recommended a review of this report by a domain expert, to guarantee its validity.

Finally, all data must be processed properly. The report and data must be stored, returned, archived or deleted as appropriate and then it is obtained the final evaluation results document.

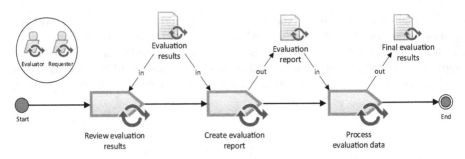

Fig. 6. Conclude the evaluation

5 Study Case

This section presents a study case to analyze the methodology to apply a quality model for Middleware. It follows the methodology proposed by Runneson [28]. The activities for executing the study case are: (i) design, (ii) preparation for data collection: procedures and protocols for data collection are defined, (iii) collecting evidence: execution with data collection on the studied case, and (iv) analysis of collected data and reporting. Below, these activities are described.

5.1 Design

The main objective is knowing the perceptions of domain experts like Middleware quality engineers. The context to evaluate is IoT Middleware. In this sense, two subjects were chosen as a convenience sample; they consist of two software engineer who are experts in IoT applications and Middleware.

The Middleware under which the evaluators provided their criteria within the precision and security about data characteristic consisted of one for managing the heterogeneity of data provining from IoT devices in Ambient Assisted Living (AAL) Environments [17]. The domain experts were able to assess the Middleware by following both the evaluation model and the quality model. For it, the evaluators used Node-Red to simulate sensors and an AAL scenario both sending data to the Middleware.

The evaluation's objectives and scope were established with Goal Question Metric (GQM) approach proposed by Basili et al. [29], who proposes a paradigm that defines the evaluations' scope and objectives. The proposed GQM is presented in Table 3.

In this context, the research questions are:

- Does the quality model evaluate the precision and security of Middleware?
- What is the perception of Middleware experts on the usefulness of a methodology that allow evaluate the precision and security of Middleware?

According to Runneson et al. [30] recommendations, this case study method is holistic-unique, and the units of analysis are presented in Fig. 7.

Table 3. Goal question metric (GQM) scope

Sub characteristics	Definition
Analyze	The evaluation analyzes the inputs for the methodology proposed by the quality engineers
Whit the propose of	The objective is evaluating the perceptions of Middleware experts regarding the usefulness of the information resulting from the methodology
From the point of view of	Informatics engineer
In the context of	The study is carried out in an IoT Middleware

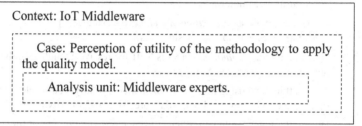

Fig. 7. Holistic-unique method

5.2 Preparation of Data Collection

In order to collect data about the domain experts experience by using the evaluation method and quality model, one survey has been designed based on the technology evaluation model (TAM) proposed by Davis [31]. This model consists of evaluating three constructors: the Perceived Ease of Use (PEOU), the Perceived Usefulness (PU), and the Intention to Use (ITU) [31]. The questionnaire is presented in Table 4.

5.3 Collecting Evidence

After using both the Middleware tool for sending data from several IoT devices and the evaluation method to assess the data precision and security in two hours, the questionnaire presented in Table 4 was applied to the domain experts. Each question was evaluated on a Likert scale from 1 to 5 to gather the impressions, as proposed by Bangor et al. System Usability Scale (SUS) [32]. Here, the key is how to present the questions since when using the Likert scale, a rating of 5 in a cheerful question is not the same as in a negative question. For this reason, SUS weights the results of each query as follows:

- Positive questions score: (obtained score) - 1
- Negative questions score: 5 - (obtained score)

Table 4. Technology acceptance model (TAM) questionnaire

Constructor	Question
PEOU1	Has been the *evaluation model* complex and difficult to use?
PEOU2	Would *evaluation model* reduce time and effort to evaluate data precision and security quality in Middleware?
PEOU3	Overall, do you consider the *evaluation model* difficult to understand?
PEOU4	Are the steps to follow the *evaluation model* clear and easy to understand?
PEOU5	Overall, do I find the *evaluation model* useful?
PU1	Is the *evaluation model* difficult to learn?
PU2	Do you think that the *evaluation model* is useful to evaluate the data precision and security in Middlewares?
PU3	If you need to use an *evaluation model* for assessing data precision and security in Middlewares, would you consider this?
PU4	Do you think the *evaluation model* is NOT expressive enough to evaluate data precision and security in Middlewares?
PU5	Do you think that using the *evaluation model* regularly, you would improve your performance when evaluating the data precision and security in Middlewares?
PU6	Do you think you could be proficient using the *evaluation model* for assessing data precision and security in Middlewares?
ITU1	Overall, do you think that with *evaluation model*, you can NOT evaluate data precision and security in Middlewares?
ITU 2	If you need to evaluate data precision and security in Middlewares, would you consider this *evaluation model*?
ITU 3	Would you NOT recommend using the *evaluation model* to assess data precision and security in Middlewares?

Where "obtained score" is the score assigned by the participant for each question. Hence, the same process is applied within evidence collection process. The questionnaire has 14 questions, where questions 3, 6, 9, 12, 14 are negative and questions 1, 2, 4, 5, 7, 8, 10, 11, 13 are positive. Then, the next stage is analyzing and report the data.

5.4 Data Analysis and Results Reporting

As presented in SUS [32]. the result is assessed over 100. With this, the following results are obtained (Table 5):

Since the presented results (Table 5), the mean is an indicator of the subject's satisfaction with using the proposed task method; therefore, the obtained value allows verifying the validity of the method with 70.35. On the other hand, the minimum value obtained is 43.45. Thus, overall, the perceptions of the two domain experts about the evaluation method and quality model are satisfactory.

Table 5. Experimental results.

Metric	Obtained values
Mean	70.3586752145
Minimun	43.4565848
Maximun	100
Standard deviation	16.86508457
Mode	75

6 Conclusions and Future Work

Although there are quality models used in Middleware, there is no one that focuses particularly on the precision of the data; Hence, the model generated in this research works for a wide range of Middleware regardless of their domain. In addition, the proposed evaluation method is a tool to assess data quality characteristics since it provides a structured mechanism, both in terms of data precision and safety characteristics, and thus, a complete understanding of the domain.

The study case section was determinant to prove the model's applicability because domain experts addressed it by following an organized sequence of steps to use the tool adequately. Results determined a 70.35 of validity since the assessor's satisfaction. Hereof, it was found that the method allows identifying certain shortcomings in terms of security characteristics in the early stages. In more mature stages of development, it allows checking that the data meets certain precision levels.

Finally, as future works, experimentation with groups with more domain experts is needed to expand feedback and enhance the model to the Middleware quality assessment.

Acknowledgements. This work is part of the following research projects: "Fog Computing applied to monitor devices used in assisted living environments; case study: a platform for the elderly people" and "Design of architectures and interaction models for assisted living environments aimed at older adults. Case study: playful and social environments". Therefore, we thank the Research Department of Universidad de Cuenca (DIUC) for its support.

References

1. ITU: The Internet of Things. Itu Internet Rep. **2005**, 212 (2005). https://doi.org/10.2139/ssrn.2324902
2. Rayes A., Salam S.: The things in IoT: sensors and actuators. In: Internet of Things from Hype to Reality, pp. 57–77. Springer, Cham (2017). https://doi.org/10.1007/978-3-319-44860-2_3
3. Palade, A., Cabrera, C., Li, F., White, G., Siobhán, M.A.R.: Middleware for Internet of Things : an evaluation in a small-scale IoT environment. J. Reliab. Intell. Environ. 4(1), 3–23 (2018). https://doi.org/10.1007/s40860-018-0055-4

4. Miorandi, D., Sicari, S., De Pellegrini, F., Chlamtac, I.: Internet of Things: vision, applications and research challenges. Ad Hoc Netw. **10**(7), 1497–1516 (2012). https://doi.org/10.1016/j. adhoc.2012.02.016

5. Al-Jaroodi, J., Mohamed, N.: Middleware is STILL everywhere!!!. In: Concurrency Computation Practice and Experience, vol. 24, no. 16, pp. 1919–1926 (2012). https://doi.org/10. 1002/cpe.2817

6. G. Chen, M. Li, y D. Kotz: Data-centric middleware for context-aware pervasive computing. Perv. Mob. Comput. **4**(2), 216–253 (2008). https://doi.org/10.1016/j.pmcj.2007.10.001

7. Gioug, O., Dooyeon, K., Sangil, K., Sungyul, R.: A quality evaluation technique of RFID middleware in ubiquitous computing. In: Proceedings - 2006 International Conference on Hybrid Information Technology, ICHIT 2006, vol. 2, pp. 730–735 (2006). https://doi.org/10. 1109/ICHIT.2006.253690

8. Kim, Y.B., Kim, M., Lee, Y.J.: COSMOS: a middleware platform for sensor networks and a u-Healthcare service. In: Proceedings of the ACM Symposium on Applied Computing, pp. 512–513 (2008). https://doi.org/10.1145/1363686.1363812

9. Li, B., Nahrstedt, K.: A control-based middleware framework for quality-of-service adaptations. IEEE J. Sel. Areas Commun. **17**(9), 1632–1650 (1999). https://doi.org/10.1109/49. 790486

10. Weis, T., Ulbrich, A., Geihs, K., Becker, C.: Quality of service in middleware and applications: a model-driven approach. In: Proceedings - IEEE International Enterprise Distributed Object Computing Workshop, EDOC, pp. 160–171 (2004). https://doi.org/10.1109/EDOC.2004.134 2513

11. Zeng, L., Benatallah, B., Ngu, A.H.H., Dumas, M., Kalagnanam, J., Chang, H.: QoS-aware middleware for Web services composition. IEEE Trans. Softw. Eng. **30**(5), 311–327 (2004). https://doi.org/10.1109/TSE.2004.11

12. Zheng, Z., Lyu, M.R.: A QoS-aware middleware for fault tolerant web services. In: Proceedings - International Symposium on Software Reliability Engineering, ISSRE, pp. 97–106 (2008). https://doi.org/10.1109/ISSRE.2008.17

13. Tang, M., Dai, X., Liu, J., Chen, J.: Towards a trust evaluation middleware for cloud service selection. Future Gener. Comput. Syst. **74**, 302–312 (2017). https://doi.org/10.1016/j.future. 2016.01.009

14. Corsaro, A., et al.: Quality of Service in publish/subscribe middleware (2006)

15. Systems and Software Engineering—Systems and software Quality Requirements and Evaluation (SQuaRE)—Evaluation process. ISO/IEC 25012:2008 (2008)

16. Systems and Software Engineering—Systems and software Quality Requirements and Evaluation (SQuaRE)—Evaluation process. ISO/IEC 25040:2011 (2011)

17. Cedillo, P., Riofrío, X., Orellana, M.: A middleware for managing the heterogeneity of data provining from IoT devices in ambient assisted living environments

18. Rausch, T., Nastic, S., Dustdar, S.: EMMA: distributed QoS-aware MQTT middleware for edge computing applications. In: Proceedings - 2018 IEEE International Conference on Cloud Engineering, IC2E 2018, May 2018, pp. 191–197 (2018). https://doi.org/10.1109/IC2E.2018. 00043

19. Moraga de la Rubia, C., Moraga, Á., Caro, A.: Evaluación de Calidad de Datos en Portales Web. Universidad de Castilla-La Mancha (2013)

20. Cedillo, P., Bermeo, A., Piedra-Garcia, D., Tenezaca-Sari, P.: CloudIoTSecurity: evaluating the security in cloud IoT applications. In: dic 2020, pp. 1–6 (2020). https://doi.org/10.1109/ andescon50619.2020.9272054

21. Bevan, N.: Los nuevos modelos de ISO para la calidad y la calidad en uso del software. In: Calidad del producto y proceso software, Cap: 2, pp. 5–75. Editorial Ra-Ma, España (2010)

22. Fernández Sáenz, M.A., Dávila Ramón, A.E., García García, C.Y.: Desarrollo de un modelo de calidad de datos aplicado a una solución de inteligencia de negocios en una institución educativa: caso lambda, Lima (2018)
23. Abbasi, M.A., Memon, Z.A., Durrani, N.M., Haider, W., Laeeq, K., Mallah, G.A.: A multi-layer trust-based middleware framework for handling interoperability issues in heterogeneous IOTs. Cluster Comput. **24**(3), 2133–2160 (2021). https://doi.org/10.1007/s10586-021-032 43-1
24. Object Management Group: Software & Systems Process Engineering Meta-Model Specification. Disponible en (2008). http://www.omg.org/spec/SPEM/20070801/Infrastructure.cmof. Accessed 13 Apr 2021
25. International Organization For Standardization: Software engineering - Software product Quality Requirements and Evaluation (SQuaRE) – System and software quality models. ISO/IEC 25010:2011, vol. 2, no. 937 (2011)
26. ISO/IEC, ISO/IEC 25012 - Quality of Data Product Standard (2019)
27. ISO - ISO/IEC 25024:2015 - Systems and software engineering—Systems and software Quality Requirements and Evaluation (SQuaRE)— Measurement of data quality (2021). https://www.iso.org/standard/35749.html. Accessed 13 Apr 2021
28. Runeson, P., Höst, M.: Guidelines for conducting and reporting case study research in software engineering. Empir. Softw. Eng. **14**(2), 131–164 (2009). https://doi.org/10.1007/s10664-008-9102-8
29. van Solingen, R., Basili, V., Caldiera, G., Rombach, H.D.: Goal question metric (GQM) approach. In: Encyclopedia of Software Engineering. Wiley (2002)
30. Runeson, P.: Introduction to Case Study Research Case study Case Studies in SE, pp. 1–23 (2007)
31. Davis, F.: A technology acceptance model for empirically testing new end-user information systems : theory and results, p. 291 (1989). http://dspace.mit.edu/handle/1721.1/15192
32. Bangor, A., Kortum, P.T., Miller, J.T.: An empirical evaluation of the system usability scale **24**(6), 574–594 (2008). https://doi.org/10.1080/10447310802205776

Detection of Incipient Faults in Three-Phase Motors Through Analysis of Stator Currents

Fausto Méndez[1] , Luis Calupiña[1]([⊠]), Marcelo V. García[2] , and Gustavo Caiza[1,3]

[1] Universidad Politécnica Salesiana, UPS, 170146 Quito, Ecuador
{fmendezc2,lcalupina}@est.ups.edu.ec, gcaiza@ups.edu.ec
[2] Universidad Técnica de Ambato, UTA, 180103 Ambato, Ecuador
mv.garcia@uta.edu.ec
[3] Universidad Politécnica de Madrid, UPM, 28006 Madrid, Spain

Abstract. The detection of incipient faults in three-phase induction motors is a fundamental pillar in the preventive maintenance at the industrial level. Three-phase motors are used in most industrial processes, and thus it is essential to know in advance the fault being generated by the motor, with the objective of avoiding a production stop, there are in the market equipment that help to detect incipient faults, but their cost is very high and it is necessary to process in a computer the information obtained from the equipment to determine the fault. The proposed prototype is a low-cost and easy to use system which detects two types of electric faults, broken bars and short circuits in the windings. Authors describe the general architecture of the prototype, parameters for determining the fault and give details about the implementation and tests of the prototype in WEG W22 High Eff motors. The results obtained show that when the amplitude of the power spectrum in the sidebands varies at particular frequencies, an incipient fault is determined.

Keywords: Incipient faults · Preventive maintenance · Three-phase motors · Low-cost system

1 Introduction

The world as it is known today would not exist without one of the most important technological advances of the nineteenth century, the electric motor, the technological development experienced during all these decades, would not be possible without the electric motor, which can be found in small, medium and large applications. In industry, the electric motor has always been and will be fundamental since it transforms electrical energy into mechanical energy [1], which means specific and significant production force. However, as any type of mechanism they are susceptible to different types of faults. In recent years, research studies about fault monitoring and prevention have arisen as a challenging topic in the scientific community [2]. The different research studies have focused in the diagnosis of faults of induction motors, mainly due to the economic and technical consequences that may appear if problems are not detected in time. The "squirrel cage" three-phase induction motors are the machinery mostly used in industry, representing about 85% of the energy consumption in industrial plants [3].

© Springer Nature Switzerland AG 2021
J. P. Salgado Guerrero et al. (Eds.): TICEC 2021, CCIS 1456, pp. 250–263, 2021.
https://doi.org/10.1007/978-3-030-89941-7_18

This type of motors may present different types of faults, there are about 50 faults that may affect the operation of electric motors [4], but the most common faults are: mechanical unbalances, asymmetry in the stator or rotor windings, overload faults, bearing faults, among others [5]. Nevertheless, the most frequent problems are breakdown of the bars in the rotor cage and short circuit in the motor windings. A motor with broken bars will apparently work well, but this fault may produce overheating, undesired vibrations or may force the breakdown of the healthy bars of the motor [6].

At present, most small and medium size companies that use three-phase electric motors do not have processes for detecting incipient faults in these motors, which may generate production losses in the companies [7]. Nowadays, there are mathematical analyses that use the stator current of the motor [8], the instruments employed for monitoring such currents often have an extremely high cost, are of invasive nature or require a process for extracting information using current sensors, and a subsequent analysis of harmonics by means of a numerical computation software [9]. The development of the non-invasive prototype will enable fixing these problems, by performing an analysis with a low-cost device accessible to small and medium size companies, without requiring additional elements such as a computer and a specific software.

Today, low-cost devices are called to carry out experimentation, training at various levels and developing prototypes of different nature; due to the wealth of information, user support and versatility [10], they are preferred by researchers and educational institutions for teaching different subjects, their importance day to day is taking more relevance due to the ease for acquiring them and for the technological advance implemented by the newest low-cost devices.

The main objective of this research is the development of a prototype for detecting incipient faults in three-phase squirrel cage induction motors, using a non-invasive probe and a single-board computer. The first step is to determine the power spectrum of the motor, by means of the fast Fourier transform (FFT) using the "Flattop" window function, then define the sidebands of frequencies that will show the faults caused by broken bars or short circuit between loops of the same phase, further analyze the amplitude of the variation in the sidebands and, finally, the incipient fault is determined based on the band where the variation and the amplitude difference occur. In the tests performed, a variation greater than 10 dB in the first sideband is detected as an incipient fault due to short circuit in loops of the same phase, and for the case of broken bars the fault will be determined by a variation of 15 dB in the first general band.

The document is organized as follows: Section 2 presents a brief literature review about faults in motors, Section 3 describes the concepts and methodology used in the research, Section 4 illustrates the hardware and software components that constitute the prototype, Section 5 shows the implementation and the results obtained, and finally Section 6 establishes some conclusions and future work.

2 Literature Review

Induction electric motors are the base of industrial processes: low cost, easy maintenance and robustness among other features, have made them fundamental for any process. As any machine they have limitations, and if these are exceeded an early fault will occur in the stator or in the rotor [11].

Table 1. Chance of faults occurrence in induction motors [13, 14]

Studied by	Bearing Fault (%)	Stator Fault (%)	Rotor Fault (%)	Other (%)
IEEE	42	28	8	22
EPRI	41	36	9	14

Table 1 shows the main faults in induction motors, found in a study sponsored by the IEEE [Institute of Electrical and Electronics Engineers] and the EPRI [Electric Power Research Company], and carried out by the General Electric Company. According to this study, faults may be categorized as follows: Electrical faults, mechanical faults and faults related with the environment. Electrical faults include supply of unbalanced voltage or current, overvoltage, grounding fault, internal short circuit, phase fault. Within the classification of mechanical faults there are broken bars, unbalanced load, bearings damage, faults in the rotor and stator windings. At last, the faults related with the environment are due to external factors such as temperature, a bad installation of the machinery, which may produce vibrations, a manufacturing defect, among others [13].

In an induction motor, multiple faults may occur simultaneously, and in such a case determining the initial problem may be difficult. These faults may increase the magnitude of particular harmonic components in the voltage and current signals [15]. Any of the aforementioned faults may alter the efficiency of the motor, and here lies the importance of a timely detection [16]. This document will focus in the diagnosis of two types of faults: short circuit in the loops of the same phase and broken bars.

For detecting faults in induction motors, it may be applied different analytical tools such as motor current signature analysis (MCSA), vibration analysis, temperature analysis, among others [17]. This document is based on the detection of faults from the analysis of currents, this technique has an advantage with respect to other tools previously mentioned, since for other processes it was necessary to connect transducers or elements that may interrupt the motor operation, not to mention their high cost.

The authors of [18] conclude that the motor current signature analysis (MCSA) is a non-invasive detection method and the information of the current signal may be acquired in real time, if necessary, which also implies that it is not necessary to stop the motor to perform the diagnosis tests. The method comprises three main steps, the data acquisition through non-invasive sensors such as Hall effect or a current transformer, monitoring the three phases is not necessary, and this is the reason why in this research work it was chosen to analyze only one phase. The information obtained is digitized and filtered to remove undesired components, these data are stored for further analysis. The second step is processing the information by means of any mathematical tool, namely fast Fourier transform (FFT), Wavelet transform (WT), Hilbert transform (HT), discrete Fourier transform (DFT), etc. [19].

The aforementioned mathematical tools detect the presence of harmonic components, which are generated by faults in the motor. The last step is fault diagnosis, which is generally performed comparing the frequency spectrum of a healthy motor with the motor under study, it is necessary a precise knowledge of the motor to be analyzed [20].

The MCSA technique is applicable for detecting some faults such as (i) broken bars, (ii) load unbalance, (iii) short circuit in the stator winding. The current analysis in the state is non-invasive, precise, low-cost and is a highly efficient technique. The data necessary may be obtained from a running motor at any moment, and various studies have successfully used this method for the diagnosis of motors, such as Bonnet [21] who detected damage in bearings by monitoring the stator current. Thomson and da Silva [22, 23] detected broken bars and short circuit in the stator windings using the MCSA through online current monitoring.

3   Materials and Methods

3.1   Analysis of Stator Current of the Motor

The analysis of stator current of the motor, also known as Motor Current Signature Analysis (MCSA), is based in the waveform consumed by the motor, which is subjected to the Fast Fourier Transform to obtain the power spectra, where the amplitude of the different frequencies is evaluated [24, 25].

The MCSA is capable of detecting faults such as: short circuit in windings, broken bars, eccentricity and bearing faults, this method uses mathematical processes; besides the fast Fourier transform, it may be carried out using: Hilbert transform, new techniques that have a high computational cost have been developed, for example: Wavelet, Wigner-Ville, MUSIC, Empirical Mode Decomposition, Hilbert, Hilbert-Huang, to name only a few [6].

3.2   Main Faults in Three-Phase Motors

Faults caused by broken bars, most of which start with a small crack in one rotor bar, in the short circuit ring or close to it; due to the continuous operation, this produces faults in multiple bars, a broken bar produces magnetic and electric asymmetry in the rotor, which introduces components in the lower sideband in the stator current, and for this reason the stator current signal undergoes changes because it reflects the harmonics of the fundamental component of the fault together with the noise. When the motor has a broken bar fault, asymmetric or unbalanced conditions are created that generate a delayed rotating magnetic field, which turns at the slip speed and produces short circuits in the stator windings, and consequently a voltage and a current are induced with the same frequency of the rotating field, the frequency at which the fault is perceptible is given by Eq. (1) [25].

$$f_{sb} = f_1(1 \pm 2ks) \tag{1}$$

Where:

fsb = Frequency of sidebands due to broken bars
f1 = Frequency of the supply network connected to the motor
k = Integer value (1, 2, 3 ...), which depends on the frequency band obtained
s = slip of the motor

Faults caused by short circuit between loops of the same phase, is one of the most critical faults in three-phase motors, because it starts with a small imperceptible short circuit, which becomes more severe over time and may cause a severe damage to the motor; the short circuit between the loops cause a modification of the electric circuit of the motor, which changes the flux density since a coil different to the original is created that has a small resistance, the current generated tends to be very high and to produce heat. The harmonics of interest for this fault at frequencies below 400 Hz are given by Eq. (2) [25].

$$f_{cc} = f_1\left(\frac{m}{p}(1-s) \pm k\right) \tag{2}$$

Where:

fcc = frequency of sidebands due to short-circuited loops
f1 = Frequency of the supply network connected to the motor
m = Integer value (1, 2, 3 ...), which depends on the frequency band obtained
p = number of pair of poles of the motor
s = slip of the motor
k = Integer value (1, 2, 3 ...), which depends on the frequency band obtained

4 Proposed System

This section presents the design of the proposed system at two levels, hardware and software. All elements can be observed in Fig. 1, the components used are described as well as their function in the prototype; diagrams of unified modeling language have been used for the description.

4.1 Hardware Architecture

The Hardware architecture consists in the design of a system that enables obtaining the data of current from one of the phases of the motor, and sends them to a single board computer, a Raspberry Pi, to be processed by means of software. For the interaction with the user, it is employed a touchscreen that enables showing the graphical interface with which the device will operate and will provide the user the control, as well as the information of the analysis and the diagnosis of the motor. The screen communicates with the Raspberry single board computer through the DSI (Display Serial Interface) port, which groups the video, supply and communication elements in a single connector [26]. The Arduino is connected to a conditioning circuit through a YHDC model 3TA17-200 three-phase transformer, which is in charge of obtaining the current signal from one of the phases of the motor, when there is a current in the primary winding, a time-varying magnetic field is created that induces a current in the secondary winding. This current is proportional to the current in the primary winding according to the transformer ratio, for the case of the prototype this ratio is 1000/1 [27].

The current signal is subjected to a correction by means of the conditioning circuit, which consists of a set of capacitors and resistances, such that three tasks are carried

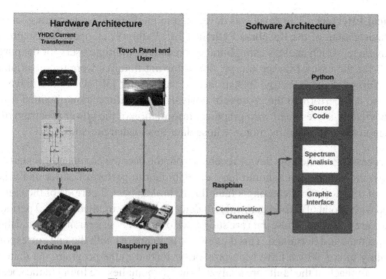

Fig. 1. Architecture of the prototype

out: convert the current signal into a voltage signal, enable the reading of the voltage signal increasing the values acquired to only positive values to eliminate reading errors in the Arduino, and protect against noise.

4.2 Software Architecture

Consists of two levels, the first is made in the Arduino IDE which uses an adaptation of the C++ programming language, for reading and sending the data acquired to the single board computer. Data reading should be carried out at a high speed such that it has enough information to be subject to Fourier analysis. The proposed device has a sampling frequency of 50000 Hz. At this level it is also configured to send the data constantly through the serial port of the development board. The second level was developed in the Raspbian Python IDLE, which is a development environment for the Python language in which the instructions for receiving information, Fourier analysis, comparison of spectra, diagnosis and graphical interface were programmed.

Data Reading. This level was developed in an adaptation of the C++ programming language in the Arduino IDE, due to the requirements of the device, such as a high sampling rate, it is necessary to change the default configuration of the ATMEGA microcontroller, to perform a change in the ADCSRA register, specifically in its last 3 bits which determine the division factor between the frequency of the AVR clock and the frequency of the ADC clock. The data samples acquired are stored in a data vector of size 3900 data, considering the SRAM memory of the microcontroller; a vector of this size uses 97% of such memory, and extending the use of this memory of the device may result in false readings or in an inappropriate behavior [29].

Graphical Interface. This level was developed in the Python programming language, in the environment of the Raspbian Python IDLE. Python is an open license programming language, which enables using libraries created by multiple users for the purposes required; for the case of the prototype, the following libraries were used: serial, Matplotlib, Numpy, Pandas, Scipy, PyAstronomy and Tkinter [30]. Once the diagnosis is started and it is performed the process of analysis of the information obtained from the phase, a window is presented with graphical information of the power spectrum of both the test motor and the healthy motor, whose data was loaded previously.

Data Processing. When the device receives from the user the command for starting the diagnosis, the signal found should have enough data to perform Fourier analysis. For the case of diagnosis for detecting a fault due to broken bars, 2 periods of the signal are analyzed with a total of 1024 data, while for detecting short-circuited loops, 3 periods and 2048 data are analyzed. These data are subjected to the fast Fourier transform and then the power spectrum is determined. This data vector is compared with the one corresponding to a healthy motor, which have been previously loaded to the program, the data of the sidebands for each of the faults are analyzed, and if anomalies are found in the spectrum, significant differences in amplitude, a flag is raised to indicate the diagnosis depending on the anomaly detected (Fig. 2).

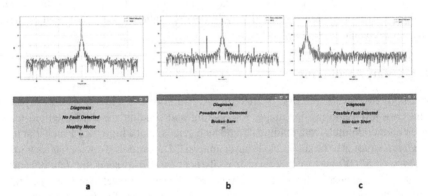

Fig. 2. Different diagnosis windows available in the prototype together with the power spectrum for each test. a) Windows for the healthy motor, b) Windows for broken bars fault, c) Windows for short-circuited loops fault

Figure 3 shows the UML (Unified Modeling Language) diagram of the classes of the main program written in the Python programming language; there is the main program that executes the graphical interface and all the existing subprocesses, besides there are 4 classes, each representing a window existing in the program, which will superimpose to the others depending on the conditions of the execution.

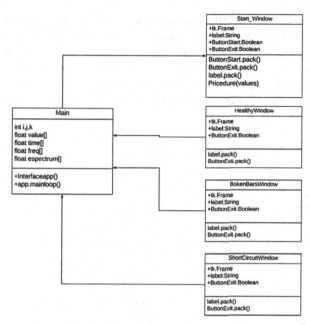

Fig. 3. Class diagram of data analysis

5 Implementation and Analysis of Results

For the implementation of the prototype, a test bench was used where the tests of incipient faults were applied and analyzed, as can be seen in Fig. 4.

Fig. 4. Implementation of the prototype

The test bench consists of: a magnetic power braking unit and a controller to configure the torque required to test motors up to 10 Nm, a current transducer up to 20 A, a differential probe from 3 V to 500 V, an oscilloscope for acquiring the current signal to contrast it with the one obtained by the prototype, and finally two WEG W22 High Eff squirrel cage asynchronous motors with features illustrated in Table 2. The motors used for the tests are new, i.e., they have 0 h of service, and thus they fulfill the international standard IEC 60034 of the International Electrotechnical Commission for rotating electrical machines and standard IEC 60072 about dimensions and output series for rotating electrical machines [31].

Table 2. Features of the motors.

Type	Data
Number of Phases	3
Power	0.37 Kw-0.5 Hp
Rated Voltage	220/380–440 v
Rated Current	1.87/1.08–1.12 A
Speed	1700/1725 rpm
Frequency	60 Hz
Number of poles	4

For the fault by broken bars, it was made a perforation of approximately 7 mm of diameter and 13 mm of depth, for the fault by short circuit in the loops of the same phase, the insulation of the coils was removed and a short circuit was produced by means of tin welding in four points. For validating the prototype, tests were conducted on a motor without fault, in all tests the motor was configured at nominal current and nominal speed, at 1.87 A and 1700 RPM; two tests were performed of the motor without faults, it was determined the power spectrum and the relative amplitude at all frequencies, resulting in a variation of 2.84 dB (decibels) in the 1024 samples, which may be due to the time-varying noise component of the signal analyzed. Once a reference signal is determined and taking into account the average variation of the readings, the test is conducted on a motor without fault, the prototype does not detect any variation in the sidebands for broken bars (53.33 Hz and 66.66 Hz) or short circuit in loops of the same phase (74.18 Hz and 148.35 Hz), and thus the system detects it as a healthy motor; the results of the tests are observed in Fig. 5, showing the power spectrum, where it can be seen that there is no alteration in the sidebands analyzed, and determines that the motor examined by the prototype does not have any fault. For validating the results, the power spectrum was compared with the one obtained in the oscilloscope, it may be observed in Fig. 6 the power spectrum where it is not distinguished a considerable variation at the frequencies under analysis.

When carrying out tests to the motor with short circuit in loops of the same phase, it was observed that the nominal speed and current are different, and consequently tests were first carried out at nominal speed, which had a current of 1.2 A at 1700 RPM, and then at nominal current, in which it was reached 1619 RPM at 1.87 A. In order to determine a fault by short circuit there should be a variation greater than 10 dB [25] in

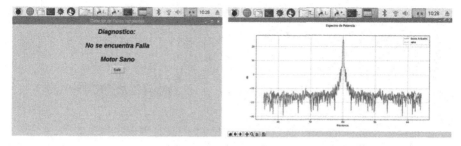

Fig. 5. Tests to the healthy motor

the first sideband (74.18 Hz) and a difference of at least 8 dB in the second sideband (148.35 Hz), which was determined experimentally, the frequencies at which the peaks appeared were: 95 Hz and 130 Hz, the variation of the sidebands is due to the slip of the motor [32], Fig. 7 displays the results of the test showing the power spectrum, where it can be observed that there is an alteration in the first and second sideband analyzed, and determines that the motor examined by the prototype has a fault due to short circuit in loops, for validating the results the power spectrum was compared with the one obtained in the oscilloscope, it may be observed in Fig. 8 the presence of sidebands in the oscilloscope.

For the failure of broken bars, several measurements were taken, at nominal current and nominal speed, a failure due to broken bars being determined when there is a variation greater than 15 dB, in the side bands of 53.33 Hz and 66.66 Hz, the frequency where the peaks were presented were: 53 Hz and 67 Hz, this small displacement of the lateral bands occurs due to the sliding of the motor [32], having a relative error of less than 0.66%, in the Figs. 9 and 10, shows the power spectrum of three tests carried out on the motor, it

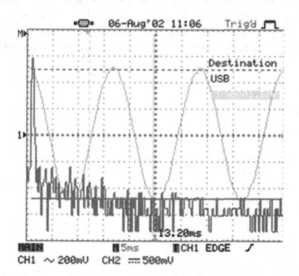

Fig. 6. Power spectrum obtained in the oscilloscope of the healthy motor

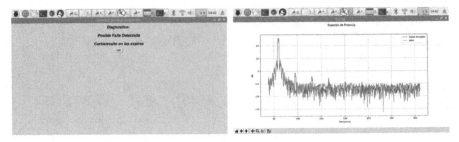

Fig. 7. Tests to a faulty motor with short-circuited coils.

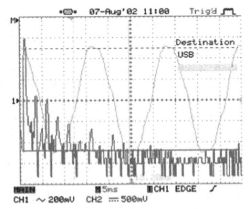

Fig. 8. Power spectrum obtained in the oscilloscope of the faulty motor with short-circuited coils.

can be clearly seen that in the side bands in the analysis there is a variation greater than 15 dB, in addition it is observed that 46 Hz and 74 Hz, there is a considerable peak due to the second sideband, the average variation in the first sideband is 17.73 dB over the reference reading of a healthy motor, which establishes that the three tests detected that the failure was due to bars broken in the motor rotor.

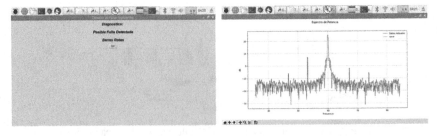

Fig. 9. Test of a faulty Motor with broken bars in the rotor.

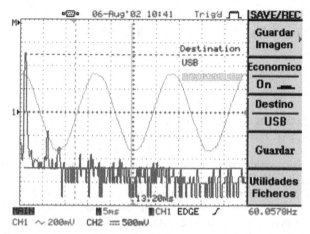

Fig. 10. Power spectrum obtained in the oscilloscope of the faulty motor with broken bars in the rotor.

6 Conclusions and Future Works

The prototype for detecting incipient faults in three-phase motors through the analysis of stator currents, is capable of detecting two faults, which are the most common in industrial environments. For detecting broken bars, the sidebands of 53 Hz and 67 Hz are analyzed, and for detecting short circuit in loops of the same phase the first and second sidebands, 95 Hz and 130 Hz, respectively, are analyzed; it is necessary a variation of 15 dB with respect to the measurement in the frequencies of the sidebands for a fault by broken bars, and a variation of 10 dB in the first band and 8 dB in the second to determine a fault by short circuit in loops of the same phase.

For conditioning the signal sent by the current transformer, it was used the principle of Shunt resistance, to determine the current that goes through the transformer, and a coupling circuit that filters the DC component and conditions it from 0 to 5 V, which is the voltage allowed by the Arduino; this was achieved with an arrangement of resistances and capacitors, the input signal is analyzed by the Arduino ADC, which stores in engineering units, and sends it in a buffer to the Raspberry through the serial interface.

The prototype is capable of detecting faults by broken bars and short circuit in loops of the same phase, and motor without faults, various tests of the different fault conditions were conducted, detecting in all of them the fault to which the motor was subject; for validating the results it was compared the frequency spectrum obtained with the prototype with the one of an oscilloscope, verifying that amplitude variations are generated in the two elements, in the sidebands expected for each case.

The Raspberry Pi single board computer is one of the most developed in different projects today, for this reason for future researchers it is feasible to implement wireless communications in the prototype, to achieve remote communication through a smartphone. There are also sensors with better performance than the current transformer, such as the Rogowski probe or Rogowski coil, its main advantage compared to other types of transformers is its design, which is open and flexible, allowing measurements without disturbing the conductor cable, given Since the Rogowski coil does not have an iron core, but an air core, this allows it to have a low inductance and response to rapidly varying currents.

References

1. Salguero, F.: Máquinas eléctricas, Primera Ed. Buenos Aires (2013)
2. Guerreo Castro, O.: Prevención de las fallas de los motores trifásicos de inducción mediante una adecuada selección. Tecnol. en Marcha **23**(1), 78–93 (2015)
3. García, J.: Deteccion de fallas en motores trifásicos de inducción utilizando análisis de componentes independientes (2018)
4. Congreso de Mantenimiento & Confiabilidad Latinoamericana: Los 50 modos de falla de los motores eléctricos. Congreso de Mantenimiento & Confiabilidad Latinoamérica (2016). https://cmc-latam.com/los-50-modos-falla-los-motores-electricos/. Accessed 05 Sept 2019
5. Díaz, D.: Diagnóstico de fallas en motores de inducción tipo jaula de ardilla mediante la aplicación de métodos híbridos. Universidad del Valle (2013)
6. Gardel Sotomayor, P.E.: Aportaciones al mantenimiento predictivo de motores de inducción mediante una metodología de diagnóstico basada en el uso combinado de técnicas estadísticas y redes neuronales artificiales (2013)
7. Piñol, A., Ortega, J., Romeral, J.: Mantenimiento predictivo de motores de inducción, pp. 1–4 (2013). http//www.
8. Poncelas López, O.: Diagnóstico de motores de inducción mediante la adquisición de corrientes de estator con sonda Rogowski. Universidad Politécnica de Catalunya (2014)
9. Diwatelwar, K.P., Malode, S.K.: Fault Detection and Analysis of three-phase induction motors using MATLAB Simulink model, pp. 1643–1649 (2018)
10. Salcedo Tovar, M.L.: Minicomputador educacional de bajo costo Raspberry Pi: Primera parte, vol. 7, Venezuela, pp. 28–45 (2015)
11. Krause, S.P., Wasynczuk, O., Sudhoff: Analysis of Electric Machinery and Drive Systems, 2nd Edn. Wiley InterScience, New Jersey
12. Mitra, M.: Induction Motor Fault Diagnosis
13. Singh, G.K., Saleh, A., Kazzaz, A.: Induction machine drive condition monitoring and diagnostic research a survey, vol. 64 (2003)
14. Mccoy, R.M., Owen, E.L.: Boissurlng, no. 1, pp. 39–46 (1986)
15. Bonnett, A.H., Soukup, G.C.: Analysis of rotor failures in squirrel-cage induction motors. IEEE Trans. Ind. Appl. **24**, 1124–1130 (1988)
16. Verma, A.K., Nagpal, S., Desai, A., Sudha, R.: An efficient neural-network model for real-time fault detection in industrial machine. Neural Comput. Appl. **33**(4), 1297–1310 (2020). https://doi.org/10.1007/s00521-020-05033-z
17. Ahamed, S.K., Karmakar, S., Sarkar, A., Mitra, M., Sengupta, S.: Diagnosis of broken rotor bar fault of induction motor through envelope analysis of motor startup current using Hilbert and wavelet transform. Innov. Syst. Des. Eng. **2**, 163–176 (2011)
18. Taylor, P., Kliman, G.B., Stein, J.: Electric Machines & Power Systems Methods of Motor Current Signature Analysis, no. December 2012, pp. 37–41 (2007)
19. Toma, R.N., Kim, J.: Applied Sciences Bearing Fault Classification of Induction Motors Using Discrete Wavelet Transform and Ensemble Machine Learning Algorithms (2020)
20. Bologna, U., Risorgimento, V., Parma, U., Scienze, V.: Development of expert system knowledge base to online diagnosis of rotor electrical faults of induction motors
21. Bonnett, A.H., Soukup, G.C.: Cause and analysis of stator and rotor induction motors. IEEE Trans. Ind. Appl. **28**(4), 921–937 (1992)

22. Thomson, W.T., Barbour, A.: Predict the level of static airgap eccentricity in three-phase induction motors. IEEE Trans. Energy Convers. **13**(4), 347–357 (1998)
23. Silva, A.M., Povinelli, R.J., Demerdash, N.A.O.: Induction machine broken bar and stator short-circuit fault diagnostics based on three-phase stator current envelopes. IEEE Trans. Ind. Electron. **55**(3), 1310–1318 (2008)
24. Antonino-Daviu, J.A., Quijano-Lopez, A., Rubbiolo, M., Climente-Alarcon, V.: Advanced analysis of motor currents for the diagnosis of the rotor condition in electric motors operating in mining facilities. IEEE Trans. Ind. Appl. **54**(4), 3934–3942 (2018)
25. Oñate, W., Perez, R., Caiza, G.: Diagnosis of incipient faults in induction motors using MCSA and thermal analysis. In: Botto-Tobar, M., León-Acurio, J., Díaz Cadena, A., Montiel Díaz, P. (eds.) ICAETT 2019. AISC, vol. 1067, pp. 74–84. Springer, Cham (2020). https://doi.org/ 10.1007/978-3-030-32033-1_8
26. OSOYOO: Instruction for Raspberry Pi 3.5″ DSI Touch Screen (2017). https://osoyoo.com/ 2020/05/29/instruction-for-raspberry-pi-3-5-dsi-touch-screen/. Accessed: 24 July 2020
27. YHDC: YHDC 3TA17-100 Characteristics, p. 1 (2006)
28. Godoy Calderon, A.J., Pérez, I.G.: Microcontrolador arduino como sistema de adquisición de datos. In: XXXIX Jornadas de Automática, Badajoz, pp. 546–553 (2018)
29. Mendoza Galindo, J.O.: Implementación de un sistema de adquisición de datos con la interfaz de Arduino Mega para el estudio de fenómenos físicos. Universidad Nacional Mayor de San Marcos (2018)
30. Lundh, F.: An Introduction to Tkinter (1999). http://www.pythonware.com/library/tkinter/int roduction/index.htm. Accessed 20 July 2020
31. WEG S.A.: Motores Eléctricos Guía de Especificación (2016)
32. Castelli, M., Andrade, M.: Metodología de monitoreo, detección y diagnóstico de fallos en motores asíncronos de inducción. Mem. Trab. Difusión Científica y Técnica **5**, 65–76 (2007)

Technology and Environment

Variation of Drinking Water Consumption Due to the Health Emergency of SARS-CoV-2 Through Dynamic Modeling in Macas City, Amazon from Ecuador

David Carrera-Villacrés[1,2(✉)], Iván Palacios[1,3], Tatiana Albán[2], Johanna Barahona[2], Doménica Calderón[2], Andrés Castelo[2], and Michael Vega[2]

[1] Departamento de Ciencias de la Tierra y la Construcción, Universidad de las Fuerzas Armadas ESPE, 171103 Sangolquí, Ecuador
dvcarrera@espe.edu.ec

[2] Facultad de Ingeniería en Geología, Minas, Petróleos y Ambiental (FIGEMPA), Universidad Central del Ecuador, 170521 Quito, Ecuador

[3] Gobierno Municipal del Cantón Morona, 140101 Macas, Ecuador

Abstract. The consumption of drinking water in the populations in the last 20 years has varied for different reasons, thus, it is necessary to determine its behavior for sustainable use of the resource. The objective of this work was to present the variation in drinking water consumption during the Sars-Cov-2 health emergency through dynamic modeling in the city of Macas in the Amazon region of Ecuador. The integrated moving average autoregressive model was used for the study (ARIMA), predicting the behavior of drinking water consumption for the year 2021 in the different neighborhoods of the city and relating this result with socioeconomic variables. The prediction for the year 2021 presented a decrease of 0.21% in the volume consumed compared to 2020, in April 2021 an increase of 85.21% was observed compared to the consumption of 2019, which can be attributed to the effects of the pandemic. The highest water consumption occurred in the cluster of neighborhoods with the highest population density, medium-high socioeconomic status, and high availability of basic services. The study aims to provide a valid alternative for decision-making in the framework of a health crisis, as well as possible conflicts in vulnerable areas in the face of the pandemic that affects the entire world.

Keywords: Water consumption · ARIMA · Pandemic · Forecast · Socioeconomic variables

1 Introduction

The stable supply of drinking water plays an important role in ensuring the public health of a population [1], especially during the outbreak of epidemic diseases, when security measures that require the use of water, such as constant hand washing, food cleaning, among others, are essential to prevent the spread of a virus [2]. In the context of the

© Springer Nature Switzerland AG 2021
J. P. Salgado Guerrero et al. (Eds.): TICEC 2021, CCIS 1456, pp. 267–280, 2021.
https://doi.org/10.1007/978-3-030-89941-7_19

SARS-CoV-2 pandemic (COVID-19), several ways of mitigating the spread of the virus have emerged, such as UV light to disinfect surfaces [3], ionized air [4], among others; but the vast majority of prevention actions make use of water resources.

Drinking water and sanitation services are essential in society as a human right; however, in a pandemic situation, its importance and necessity become more evident [5].

The impact of water consumption by the population during the time of pandemic has been studied in several cities worldwide, where it is pointed out that actions such as government restrictions on population displacement, the adoption of telework, activities cleaning and feeding, influence the demand for residential water [6]. There have been few studies in the Amazon region of Ecuador that analyze the dynamics of water consumption in the population, giving greater emphasis only to the spatial modeling of consumption [7], however, the possible underlying relationships of this water use with socioeconomic variables that may help to understand and explain the reason for the aforementioned event have not been considered. In addition, there has been little interest in investigating the behavior of water consumption in relatively small cities and municipalities, although these represent the highest percentage of those existing in Ecuador and South America in general, therefore, the proposed study also aims to supply that shortage of experiences on the subject.

On March 11, 2020, the State of Sanitary Emergency was declared in Ecuador in the National Health System, where six days later a State of Exception was decreed due to Public Calamity throughout the national territory due to COVID [8]. Despite this, the Autonomous Decentralized Municipal Governments (GADM) had to guarantee by law, the provision and maintenance of the drinking water system permanently, complying with the National Constitution of Ecuador and according to the necessary protection measures.

The adoption of an integrated approach to water resources management, combined with spatialized cartographic information from socio-economic data and dynamic models of water consumption, can help the countries of the region, especially the small GADMs, to improve the allocation of water resources in these times of pandemic [9]. Understanding the impact of disease containment actions on water consumption provides a solid foundation for policymakers to plan and prioritize to successfully overcome this challenge [7]. In addition, it is important to take into account that the growth of the human population has created a constant demand for the supply of drinking water in all the cities of the planet [10].

In the context of the COVID-19 pandemic, some works have modeled water consumption through various methods, such as water demand models [11], or regression models [12]. The present study proposes the use of an unconventional technique, such as the model ARIMA for the dynamic study of water consumption. This technique is considered one of the most used approaches for studies of climatic and hydrological variability since it considers non-stationary data records [13]. ARIMA allows the modeling of the recent and remote values of the variable and also includes terms for the recent and remote noises, which guarantees that all the components of the series can be included and analyzed integrally [14].

The objective of this study was to analyze and predict drinking water consumption in the city of Macas, Ecuador's Amazon region by the year 2021, through the dynamic model ARIMA based on data from 2018 to 2020, and contrast with socio-economic information to identify underlying relationships of consumption levels during the health crisis of COVID-19 and the characteristics of its population, as a tool in the sustainable management of the water resource of the city.

2 Methods

2.1 Study Area

The city of Macas has geographically located 2°18′12″ of South Latitude and 78°07′03″ West Longitude. It is the capital of the Morona canton and in turn of the Morona Santiago province in the Amazon region of Ecuador [15, 16]. It sits on the left bank of the Upano River, surrounded by lush vegetation that is conserved by several natural reserves [17, 18].

The urban area of the city has an area of 1054 ha, adjacent to the parishes of General Proaño to the North, Río Blanco to the South, Sevilla Don Bosco to the East, and 9 de Octubre to the West [19] (Fig. 1). Macas city has an urban population projected to 2021 of approximately 28035 inhabitants, distributed in 23 neighborhoods that make up the urban land of the city, where the highest concentration of facilities and services is concentrated in the center of the city [20].

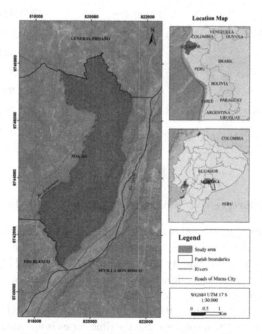

Fig. 1. Location of the study area, Macas City

2.2 Information About the Study Area

The drinking water consumption data and the geographic information necessary to spatialize the consumption were provided by the Directorate of Potable Water and Sewerage Management of the GADM of Macas, in the period from January 2018 to December 2020, through the information of water consumption for the city.

This consumption information was tabulated and classified according to the month, year, and neighborhood to which they belong, through the meter code and measurement route established in the cadastre (Table 1). With the help of a GIS, the values of water consumption in each neighborhood were represented, in which it was possible to identify the dynamics of use during the three periods of time.

Table 1. Monthly-annual drinking water consumption of Macas city

Month	2018 Consumption (m^3)	2019 Consumption (m^3)	2020 Consumption (m^3)
January	171,488	203,688	178,981
February	215,081	171,753	168,991
March	117,432	167,638	168,991
April	137,694	134,880	249,950
May	243,507	178,601	195,803
June	170,139	158,403	161,325
July	163,221	173,554	138,518
August	199,750	173,292	201,844
September	151,516	154,623	137,441
October	181,156	204,889	180,131
November	176,231	156,249	163,839
December	133,606	159,832	172,982
Total	2,060,821	2,037,402	2,118,796

2.3 Integrated Autoregressive Moving Average Model, ARIMA

In this study, a script of the model was developed ARIMA in the free software R, with the use of the tseries libraries, MASS, mlogit, stats, astsa, among the most prominent. To apply a model ARIMA, a stationarity test must be performed first [21], since the model works on data with normal behavior. In this case, the test was used de Dickey-Fuller which seeks to determine the existence or not of unit roots in a time series [22].

Once the test of Dickey-Fuller, the data for most neighborhoods have an initial p-value greater than 0.05, which suggests that the time series is not stationary [23], Therefore, to achieve the stationarity of the time series of water consumption, it was necessary to replace by the difference between the current observation and that corresponding to the previous seasonal period to obtain a regular differentiation or differentiation of order 1. With the second difference, a p-value of less than 0.05 was reached in the neighborhoods that exceeded this threshold, so that the prediction of the time series could continue [14, 24] (Table 2).

Table 2. Annual consumption by neighborhoods

Neighborhood	Dickey-Fuller test		
	Normal	Diff	Diff2
	(p-value)	(p-value)	(p-value)
27 de febrero	0.08023	0.01	–
5 de Octubre	0.2783	0.06347	0.03373
Amazonas	0.4501	0.03594	–
Centro	0.06543	0.01	–
El Mirador	0.02793	–	–
El Rosario	0.4386	0.1145	0.0161
Jardín de Upano	0.3644	0.04578	–
Juan de la Cruz	0.06103	0.02164	–
La Alborada	0.03881	–	–
La Barranca	0.03158	–	–
La Florida	0.2085	0.01	–
La Loma	0.01	–	–
La Unión	0.2709	0.03833	–
Los Canelos	0.6315	0.02152	–
Los Vergeles	0.06319	0.01	–
Naranjal	0.09942	0.01334	–
Norte	0.01	–	–
Remigio Madero	0.143	0.02722	–
Sangay	0.118	0.01683	–
Tinguichaca	0.309	0.01326	–
Universitario	0.1111	0.01	–
Valle Upano	0.3687	0.01	–
Yambas	0.1237	0.01	–

The models ARIMA were created by adjusting different parameters for each neighborhood, such as the number of autoregressive, number of differences used, and the number of moving averages for the time series. Finally, to guarantee that the prediction of the values of the new water consumptions in the city to the year 2021 is correct and does not present anomalous quantities, the test was performed Ljung – Box, to show the presence of white noise in the time series [25].

2.4 Relationship with Socioeconomic Variables

The socioeconomic variables that were considered are: population density, level of access to basic services, and socioeconomic level of the population These data were collected by the Ecuadorian Space Institute (IEE) for the project "Generation of geospatial information at a scale of 1: 5000 to determine the physical fitness of the territory and urban development through the use of technologies", which were spatialized at the neighborhood level in the city. The data of the variables were converted to heat maps, to graphically represent the various ranges of values in territorial units (neighborhoods), and in this way visually relate and contrast with the prediction models of water consumption.

3 Analysis, Results, and Discussion

Using the model ARIMA was possible to predict the behavior of drinking water consumption in the urban area of the Macas city for the year 2021. One of the advantages of using this method is that it generates confidence ranges of the predicted values, both at 90% and 95%; In addition, a graph of the error of the time series is generated with which the behavior of the data can be graphically analyzed, in which it is mean must be close to zero (white noise), (Fig. 2) for the neighborhood 27 de Febrero.

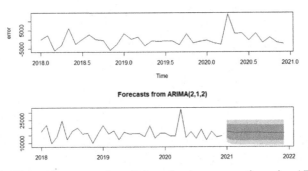

Fig. 2. Time series error and prediction of water consumption using ARIMA

The presence of white noise in the resulting series is checked with the standardized residuals, as well as the values of the coefficients of the autocorrelation function that do not exceed the tolerance threshold, and which are finally evidenced by the results of the test of Ljung – Box whose p-value values are greater than 0.05 in all cases. As an example, Fig. 3 shows the information from neighborhood 27 de Febrero.

The values obtained by the model ARIMA for the year 2021 are presented in Table 3 for each neighborhood, in which it is evidenced that for the 5 de Octubre neighborhood there will be an increase of 39.8% compared to the previous year, while for the Rosario neighborhood a reduction in consumption of 49.8% is expected compared to 2020.

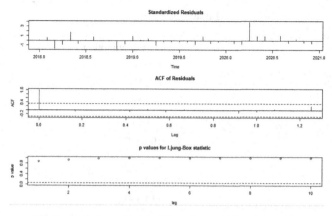

Fig. 3. Statistics calculated from the resulting time series

Table 3. Annual consumption by neighborhoods 2021

Neighborhood	2021 Consumption (m^3)
27 de Febrero	200,273.79
5 de Octubre	54,200.24
Amazonas	142,074.83
Centro	396,243.40
El Mirador	56,899.18
El Rosario	11,495.75
Jardin de Upano	88,521.57
Juan de la Cruz	120,867.61
La Alborada	21,318.03
La Barranca	113,197.09
La Florida	105,814.36
La Loma	184,833.35
La Unión	23,319.40
Los Canelos	48,911.63
Los Vergeles	60,016.16
Naranjal	51,397.01
Norte	94,546.09

(*continued*)

Table 3. (*continued*)

Neighborhood	2021 Consumption (m^3)
Remigio Madero	2,106.03
Sangay	67,587.85
Tinguichaca	41,119.95
Universitario	100,158.99
Valle Del Upano	11,182.94
Yambas	118,313.98
Total	2,114,399.246

If the variation in water consumption in the city between the years 2018, 2019, 2020, and 2021 is analyzed graphically (Fig. 4), It is observed that between the months of March and April 2020 there was an increase in consumption of 0.81% and 85.31% respectively about the months of March and April of the year 2019, and 43.91% and 81.53% compared to March and April of 2018, evidencing an unusual behavior in consumption patterns within the study area. Comparing March and April 2018 to 2019, years that were not affected by the pandemic, there was an increase of 29.9% and a decrease in water consumption of 2.09% respectively. The United Nations World Water Development Report states that global water demand continues to increase at an annual rate of 20–30%, driven by a combination of population growth, socio-economic development, and the economic and social development of the world's poorest and most vulnerable populations [26].

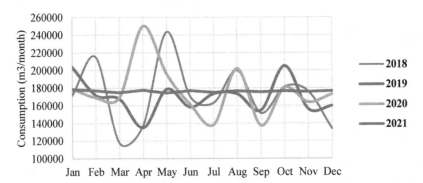

Fig. 4. Variation of drinking water consumption, period 2018–2021

The increase in water consumption in the homes of the population coincides temporarily with the appearance of COVID-19 cases in the city of Macas, since the outbreak in March and which continues to increase in the following months [27] (Fig. 5), and that to date it continues with certain restrictions to avoid crowds of people dictated by the national authority [8]. This change in the normal behavior of water consumption can be attributed to the practice of protection measures against the coronavirus, as well as to activities within homes (disinfection, personal hygiene, food, telework, among others), which lead to an increase in the use of water per household [28] and [29].

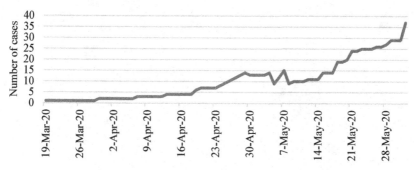

Fig. 5. Number of positive COVID-19 cases in Macas City

Despite this, according to the results of the prediction ARIMA, for 2021 a decrease of 0.21% is expected over the average consumption of the previous year, while in 2020 there was an increase of 4% over the average consumption of drinking water in 2019. This may be related to the fact that after a year of pandemic, the population is adjusting to the "new normal" and normalizes its consumption after the first months of total restriction (March–August 2020) (Table 4).

Table 4. Mean water consumption

Year	Mean water consumption (m³/year)
2018	171,735.08
2019	169,783.50
2020	176,566.33
2021	176,199.94

Additionally, the spatialization of consumption allowed to represent the volume of water at the level of the 23 neighborhoods within the urban area of the city of Macas, where it is observed that the neighborhoods present a greater increase in the consumption of drinking water during the month of April of 2018 – 2021 (Fig. 6). In this way, it was possible to identify that the neighborhood Centro, La Loma, 27 de Febrero, and Amazonas have a higher consumption compared to the rest of the neighborhoods (Table 2).

When comparing the values of water consumption in April 2020 for April 2019, it was identified that the neighborhoods: La Loma, 27 de Febrero, Centro, Yambas, Juan de

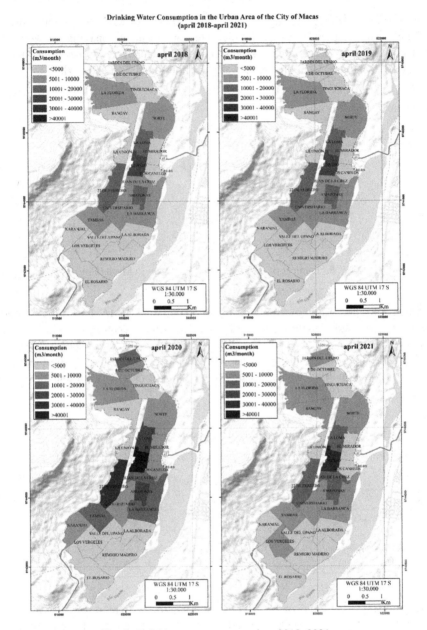

Fig. 6. Drinking water consumption, 2018–2021.

la Cruz, and La Barranca, increased their consumption of vital fluid by 54%, 166%, 91%, 87%, 130%, and 125% respectively. This can be attributed to the fact that the pandemic modified the drinking water consumption patterns in the population, thus having an increase in its use due to issues of personal hygiene, domestic activities, disinfection, and others carried out within the confinement of the population in their homes. On the other hand, in April the Centro neighborhood recorded the highest consumption of drinking water in the city throughout, with a value of 46,211 m^3, whose values gradually decrease until the end of May, and which correspond to the beginning of the confinement of the pandemic.

In several studies, it has been determined that the main dimensions that influence the vulnerability of the population to COVID19 are demography, socioeconomic conditions, and health [30, 31], which denotes an underlying relationship between the characteristics of the population and its behavior during the times of the SARS-CoV-2 pandemic, and therefore, the importance of its analysis in the population of the study case.

The population density is related to the agglomeration of people, and therefore a greater risk of contagion due to the intrinsic mobility of the population in these sectors [32]. Regarding access to basic services, it is directly related to the population's contagion prevention efforts, mainly with the clean water service, which is a challenge faced by several countries during the COVID-19 pandemic [33]. On the other hand, the socioeconomic level of the population has made it possible to relate the housing conditions and even the relationship with the degree of education of its inhabitants, with the lower strata being the ones that tend to be more vulnerable to the current pandemic [34].

In the city of Macas, the population density is located in the central neighborhoods (Amazonas and Centro principle, followed by Juan de la Cruz, El Mirador, and La Loma). Regarding basic services, the peripheral neighborhoods of both the North and South sectors present limitations to access these services, and therefore, they would be more vulnerable to COVID-19, with 39.13% of neighborhoods in average availability to basic services, 56.52% have high availability of basic services, and only 4.34% (1 neighborhood) show a low availability, so it can be inferred a good state in the provision of basic services in the entire urban area of the city.

Finally, according to the information on the socioeconomic level of the population, it suggests that 69.57% of the neighborhoods of Macas have middle and lower class conditions, which could lead to a greater risk of contagion due to the characteristics of the population itself (characteristics of housing, educational level, economic sectors) [35]. In Fig. 7 the socioeconomic variables of each neighborhood are presented, in which it can be identified that the central neighborhoods of the city encompass a cluster expressed in a medium-low and medium-high socioeconomic level, a concentrated population density, a high economic stratum where finds the highest economic capacity, which is also related to higher drinking water consumption [36].

If the neighborhoods that have greater availability of basic services are contrasted, with a medium-high socioeconomic level and high population density, there is a direct relationship with the history of high water consumption values in the neighborhoods considered central, such as La Loma, Amazonas, Centro, and Juan de la Cruz; However, according to the results of the prediction to 2021, the neighborhoods Jardín del Upano, La Florida, Sangay, and Los Vergeles maintain significant water consumption, which

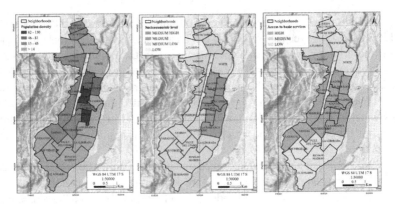

Fig. 7. Socioeconomic variables

could suggest a vulnerability of the population to COVID-19, and that goes hand in hand with the socioeconomic conditions of these sectors.

4 Conclusions

The model ARIMA allowed modeling a non-linear behavior of water consumption in the city of Macas at the level of each neighborhood, whose prediction results for 2021 suggest a decrease of 0.21% in the volume consumed to the average consumption of 2020 on the other hand, It was also determined that between 2019 and 2020 there was an increase of 4% in the consumption of drinking water.

When analyzing the variation in the monthly consumption of drinking water in the study area, it was concluded that the month of April 2020 presented an increase of 85.21% compared to the consumption of April 2019, which can be attributed to the effects of the pandemic.

By comparing the socioeconomic variables and the spatialization of the results of the prediction of water consumption in the different neighborhoods of the city, a persistent behavior was evidenced in the time studied, where the cluster of neighborhoods with the highest density population, medium-high socioeconomic level, and high availability of basic services, present the highest water consumption.

The results of this study provide a valid alternative for decision-making in the framework of the health crisis that the city is going through, as well as to identify possible conflicts in vulnerable areas in the face of the pandemic that is going through the whole world, and mainly Ecuador.

Climatic variables: temperature, humidity, precipitation, can also generate changes in drinking water consumption, and it would be of great importance to study them in the future so that water resource management is comprehensive.

References

1. Sorenson, S.B., Morssink, C., Campos, P.A.: Safe access to safe water in low income countries: Water fetching in current times. Soc. Sci. Med. **72**(9), 1522–1526 (2011). https://doi.org/10.1016/j.socscimed.2011.03.010

2. World Health Organization: Facilities Across the Country. WMO Bulletin, November 2015
3. Kitagawa, H., et al.: Effectiveness of 222-nm ultraviolet light on disinfecting SARS-CoV-2 surface contamination. Am. J. Infect. Control **49**(3), 299–301 (2021). https://doi.org/10.1016/j.ajic.2020.08.022
4. Liu, D.T., Philips, K.M., Speth, M.M., Besser, G., Mueller, C.A., Sedaghat, A.R.: Portable HEPA purifiers to eliminate airborne SARS-CoV-2: a systematic review. Otolaryngol. - Head Neck Surg. (US) (2021). https://doi.org/10.1177/01945998211022636
5. Babiano, L.: COVID-19 Manual Urgente para Operadores de Gestión Urbana de Agua (2020)
6. Shang, Y., et al.: Management of critically ill patients with COVID-19 in ICU: statement from front-line intensive care experts in Wuhan, China. Ann. Intensive Care **10**(1), 1–24 (2020). https://doi.org/10.1186/s13613-020-00689-1
7. Kalbusch, A., Henning, E., Brikalski, M.P., de Luca, F.V., Konrath, A.C.: Impact of coronavirus (COVID-19) spread-prevention actions on urban water consumption. Resour. Conserv. Recycl. **163**, 105098 (2020). https://doi.org/10.1016/j.resconrec.2020.105098
8. Presidencia de la República del Ecuador: Decreto Presidencial No 1017 (2020)
9. Banco Interamericano de Desarrollo – BID: De estructuras a servicios (2020)
10. Fernández, A., Du Mortier, C.: Evaluación de la condición del agua para consumo humano en Latinoamérica. In: Blesa, M., Blanco, J. (eds.) Tecnologías solares para la desinfección y descontaminación del agua, pp. 17–32 (2012)
11. Li, D., et al.: Stay-at-home orders during the COVID-19 pandemic reduced urban water use. Environ. Sci. Technol. Lett. **8**(5), 431–436 (2021). https://doi.org/10.1021/acs.estlett.0c00979
12. Brauer, M., Zhao, J., Bennitt, F., Stanaway, J.: Global access to handwashing: implications for COVID-19 control in low-income countries. Environ. Health Perspect. **128**(5), 1–6 (2020). https://doi.org/10.1289/EHP7200
13. González Álvarez, D., Pérez Guerra, J.: La estadística de paseo con la estilística, o el estado de la cuestión en el análisis textual multidimensional. In: Revista canaria de estudios ingleses, no. 46, pp. 131–160. Dialnet (2003)
14. Coutin Marie, G.: Utilización de modelos ARIMA para la vigilancia de enfermedades transmisibles. Rev. Cuba. Salud Pública **33**(2) (2007). https://doi.org/10.1590/s0864-34662007000200012
15. Palacios, I., Toulkeridis, T.: Evaluation of the susceptibility to landslides through diffuse logic and analytical hierarchy process (AHP) between Macas and Riobamba in Central Ecuador. In: 2020 7th International Conference on eDemocracy eGovernment, ICEDEG, pp. 201–207 (2020). https://doi.org/10.1109/ICEDEG48599.2020.9096879
16. Palacios, I., Arellano, K.: Modelo predictivo del cambio de cobertura forestal en el área de conservación Municipal Quílamo-Cantón Morona. Rev. Geoespacial **18**(1), 1–13 (2021). https://doi.org/10.24133/geoespacial.v18i1.2201
17. Palacios, I., Castro, S., Rodriguez, F.: Almacenamiento de carbono como servicio ambiental en tres reservas naturales del Ecuador. Rev. Geoespacial **16**(1), 1–14 (2019). https://doi.org/10.24133/geoespacial.v16i1.1275
18. Palacios, I., Rodríguez, F.: Economic valuation of environmental goods and services of the Protector Forest Kutukú – Shaimi, SE Ecuador. Int. J. Energy Environ. Econ. **27**(2), 117–132 (2021)
19. Palacios, I.: Evaluación multicriterio para la ubicación de un relleno sanitario en la ciudad de macas, a través de la ponderación de sus variables con el proceso analítico jerárquico, AHP. Rev. Ciencias Segur. Def. **III**(3), 83–94 (2018)
20. Palacios, I.: Generación de un modelo de crecimiento tendencial urbano de la ciudad de Macas (Ecuador) al año 2030, mediante técnicas de modelación espacial multivariable. Universitat de Barcelona, Barcelona (2020)

21. Yosipovitch, G., Schneiderman, J., Van Dyk, D.J., Chetrit, A., Milo, G., Boner, G.: Impairment of the postural venoarteriolar response in young type 1 diabetic patients - a study by laser Doppler flowmetry. Angiology **47**(7), 687–691 (1996). https://doi.org/10.1177/000331979 604700708

22. De Arce, R., Mahía, R.: Modelos ARIMA. Programa CITUS: Técnicas de Variables Financieras (2003)

23. Montero, R.: Variables no estacionarias y cointegración. Doc. Trab. en Econ. Apl. Univ. Granada, España, pp. 1–8 (2013)

24. Arvanitis, S.: A note on the limit theory of a Dickey-Fuller unit root test with heavy-tailed innovations. Stat. Probab. Lett. **126**, 198–204 (2017). https://doi.org/10.1016/j.spl.2017. 02.032

25. Moreno, M.: Una modelización para los accidentes de trabajo en España y Andalucía. Rev. Digit. Segur. y Salud en el Trab., no. 1, pp. 1–9 (2007)

26. The United Nations World Water Development Report, NO DEJAR A NADIE ATRAS. París – Francia (2019)

27. Comité de Operaciones de Emergencia: Informe de Situación COVID-19 Ecuador (2020)

28. Villar, L., Ledo, M.: Aplicación de Herramientas Estadísticas Para El Análisis De Indicadores. Ing. Ind. **37**(2), 138–150 (2016)

29. Sowby, R.B.: Emergency preparedness after COVID-19: a review of policy statements in the U.S. water sector. Util. Policy **64**, 101058 (2020). https://doi.org/10.1016/j.jup.2020.101058

30. Ressl, R., et al.: Mapping Mexican COVID-19 vulnerability at municipal scale. Terra Digit. **4**(2), 1–8 (2020). https://doi.org/10.22201/igg.25940694e.2020.2.79

31. Avila, D., Flores, C., Gómez, D.: An index of municipality-level vulnerability to COVID-19 in Mexico. Terra Digit. **4**(2), 1–11 (2020). https://doi.org/10.22201/igg.25940694e.2020.2.73

32. Ortega Díaz, A., Armenta Menchaca, C., García López, H., García Viera, J.: Índice de vulnerabilidad en la infraestructura de la vivienda ante el COVID-19 en México. Notas Poblacion, pp. 2010–2018 (2021). https://200.9.3.182/bitstream/handle/11362/46559/20-00528_ LDN111_07_Diaz.pdf?sequence=1&isAllowed=y

33. Freeman, M., Caruso, B.: Comment on 'Global access to handwashing: implications for COVID-19 control in low-income Countries.' Environ. Health Perspect. **128**(9), 1–2 (2020). https://doi.org/10.1289/EHP7852

34. Sánchez, P., Zamora, G.: El impacto de la pandemia Covid-19 en ciudades de desarrollo geográfico desigual. Guayaquil

35. Hernández, H.: COVID-19 en México: un perfil sociodemográfico. Notas Poblacion **47**(111), 105–132 (2021)

36. Montenegro, D., Tapia, J.: Indicadores de cantidad y calidad del agua consumida en la ciudad de Macas. Universidad Nacional de Chimborazo (2014)

Predicting Ozone Pollution in Urban Areas Using Machine Learning and Quantile Regression Models

Fernando Cueva[1,2](✉) , Victor Saquicela[1] , Juan Sarmiento[1] ,
and Fanny Cabrera[1]

[1] Universidad de Cuenca, Av. 12 de Abril s/n, Cuenca, Azuay, Ecuador
wfc9474@rit.edu, {victor.saquicela,juan.sarmiento,
fanny.cabrerab16}@ucuenca.edu.ec
[2] Rochester Institute of Technology, One Lomb Memorial Drive, Rochester, NY, USA

Abstract. Ozone is the most harmful secondary pollutant in terms of negative effects on climate change and human health. Predicting ozone emission levels has therefore gained importance within the field of environmental management. This study, performed in the Andean city of Cuenca, Ecuador, compares the performance of two methodologies currently used for this task and based on machine learning and quantile regression techniques. These techniques were applied using cross-sectional data to predict the ozone concentration per city block during the year 2018. Our results reveal that ozone concentration is significantly influenced by nitrogen dioxide, sedimentary particles, sulfur dioxide, traffic, and spatial features. We use the mean square error, the coefficient of determination, and the quantile loss as evaluation metrics for the performance of the ozone prediction models, employing a cross-validation scheme with a fold. Our work shows that the random forest technique outperforms gradient boosting prediction, neural network, and quantile regression methods.

Keywords: Ozone · Pollutants · Ensemble models · Neural networks · Quantile regression

1 Introduction

The quality of life in any city is strongly linked to environmental and health conditions, such as air quality, water, waste treatment, and the environmental noise that citizens regularly experience [1]. The impacts of these factors are reflected in people's physical and mental health. In particular, health is highly exacerbated by air pollution, causing chronic and fatal diseases such as pneumonia, lung cancer, ischemic heart disease, and others [2]. Air pollution has increased considerably in recent years. Worldwide, fossil fuel consumption rose significantly and NO_2 emissions increased by 0.9% each year between 1996 and 2012 [1]. When NO_2 is combined with radiation and other components, ozone (O_3) is created [3], forming one of the most important secondary pollutants in the atmosphere [4]. Ozone not only causes severe damage to human health [5] but also

© Springer Nature Switzerland AG 2021
J. P. Salgado Guerrero et al. (Eds.): TICEC 2021, CCIS 1456, pp. 281–296, 2021.
https://doi.org/10.1007/978-3-030-89941-7_20

contributes to global warming [4]. Therefore, it is not surprising that the global number of deaths attributed to low air quality reaches 7 million people annually [6].

Nowadays, air pollution affects large metropolises and many other cities considered to be medium or small in size; this is due to rapidly increasing urbanization [7], vehicles on the road [8], and greater industrialization [9]. Moreover, the problem worsens with flawed environmental regulatory systems and institutional frameworks, government corruption, and greater population purchasing power, issues commonly observed in many Latin American, Asian, and African countries. Therefore, monitoring and measuring pollutant emissions is highly relevant [9] for sustainable city planning and policy generation. Furthermore, the prediction of the levels of these pollutants plays a fundamental role in environmental management [10] and health [11] decision-making. Several methods have been used to predict pollutant concentrations, including machine learning techniques, time-series models, linear and non-linear regression, and principal component analysis, among others [12]. Currently, machine learning methods (e.g., artificial neural networks) and quantile regression [13] have gained importance because of the non-linear characteristics of contaminant behavior [14].

In this context, this article's main objective is to test and compare several techniques widely used in the literature for ozone (O_3)-level prediction, such as quantile regression and machine learning, using data from the city of Cuenca, Ecuador. The Municipal Public Company for Mobility, Transit, and Transportation of Cuenca (EMOV by its acronym in Spanish) collects information on ozone levels and other pollutants in the city through the Air Quality Monitoring Network. This study focuses on estimating the average ozone level per block during 2018, using a cross-sectional dataset that contains information on pollutant covariates, vehicle traffic, and spatial characteristics. The article is organized into six sections. The next section presents background information on the city of Cuenca and the current problems concerning pollution, as well as related work. In the third section, we describe our data and variables. The fourth and fifth sections specify the methods for forecasting and evaluating the predictions—including the training criteria—and the main findings regarding the evaluation and comparison of these methods. Finally, the conclusions derived from the results and future research are discussed.

2 Background and Related Work

This section is divided into two parts. The first offers some context regarding pollution in the city of Cuenca, Ecuador, and the second presents a brief review of studies addressing contamination analysis and the methods they employ.

2.1 The City of Cuenca, Ecuador

Cuenca is the third most populated city in Ecuador, with 625,775 inhabitants in 2019 according to INEC (Instituto Nacional de Estadísticas y Censos); and around 65% of the population inhabits the Cuenca canton's urban area [15], an area of 72.23 km^2; this implies a density of 5,654 inhabitants per square kilometer, compared to 72 inhabitants/km^2 in the rural area.

In Ecuador, the number of vehicles increased from 1.0 to 2.4 million between 2008 and 2018 [16]. Azuay province has 18.1 vehicles per 100 inhabitants, higher than other provinces with higher population density [16]. In Cuenca (the capital of Azuay province), the annual growth rate for the non-commercial vehicle fleet since 1975 is almost 12% [17]. The relatively small size [18] of roads has led to significant traffic congestion and, potentially, more concentrated noise and air pollution, especially within and around the city center. Moreover, the colonial architecture found in this city, featuring two- to four-story buildings, in addition to particular topographic characteristics with high reliefs, do not allow the flow and dispersion of contamination. As a result of these factors, the architectural, topographic, geographic, demographic, and mobility characteristics exacerbate the contamination problem in Cuenca.

The most dangerous secondary pollutant for the ecosystem and for human health is tropospheric ozone (O^3), the concentration of which depends on meteorological and climatic conditions, transportation or vehicular traffic [19], land use, the spatial distribution of the population, and emissions that influence the greenhouse effect, which in turn increases the temperature because of solar radiation absorption. O^3 arises from nitrogen oxide (NOx) and volatile organic compounds (VOCs) when these components react to solar radiation [20].

The spatial distributions of O_3 and its precursor NO_2 in Cuenca are shown in Fig. 1. High levels of O_3 are concentrated in three main areas. The first is the historical center towards the south, where high commercial activity is evident (Fig. 1b), the second is a region ranging from a residential area to the commercial and health area, and the third zone extends to the northern border and includes an industrial park and residential areas. NO_2 emissions (Fig. 1a) are concentrated in three main areas: the historical center, the industrial park, and the public market, called Feria Libre (Free Market). The latter is the largest commercial supply area in the city, with a high flow of public transportation. Smaller contamination levels are evident in the rest of the historic center, where there are shopping centers and various services. Finally, the peripheral urban area exhibits low or moderate pollution.

When O_3 and NO_2 emissions are compared, the areas where NO_2 is concentrated do not necessarily overlap with the areas where O_3 is high. O_3 formation and transport complexity are observed because high emissions can occur in areas located far away from where emissions are generated [20].

2.2 Related Work

In the empirical literature, several techniques have been applied to measure various pollutants, including traditional methods such as linear regression models, machine learning techniques, or combinations of these methods. For example, Arsić et al. [21] applied traditional methods such as a multiple linear regression model to measure ozone concentrations in Zrenjanin, Serbia. They compared the results against those of a neural-network-based method, which demonstrated better predictions since it considers non-linear relationships and does not make assumptions such as normality and linearity.

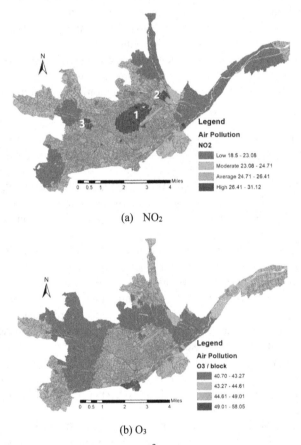

(a) NO$_2$

(b) O$_3$

Fig. 1. Spatial distribution of mean NO$_2$ (μg/m^3) and O$_3$ concentrations in Cuenca's urban area in 2018. Zone 1 is the historical center, zone 2 is the industrial park, and zone 3 is the *Feria Libre*.

Arce et al. [10] proposed an approach to identify the incidence of and correlations among five harmful air pollutants in the Andean region using the time moving correlations method. Experiments were conducted using x-means and k-means algorithms [22, 23] over a dataset obtained from an air quality monitoring and measuring station in Cuenca, Ecuador. Samples were taken every second, acquiring O$_3$, CO, SO$_2$, NO$_2$,

PM2.5, and temperature data, in addition to other variables such as precipitation level, radiation, wind direction and speed, temperature, and humidity. Results showed that O_3 has more significant repercussions on other pollutants.

Different studies have attempted to estimate air pollutant concentrations using pure statistical and machine-learning-based techniques and different sets of environmental or temporal features. For example, Singh et al. [6] aimed to predict air quality indices (AQIs) in a city Lucknow in India using air quality and meteorological databases, with measurements taken over five years and containing a total of 1,407 air quality features: SO_2, NO_2, SPM, RSPM, as well as meteorological parameters such as air temperature, relative humidity, wind speed, evaporation, and daily sunshine period. The authors identified vehicular emissions and fuel combustion as significant air pollution sources and proved that ensemble-based models are good urban ambient air quality estimators.

Bashir et al. [7] experimented with different machine learning models such as support vector machines (SVMs), model trees (M5P), and artificial neural networks (ANNs) to predict average concentrations of urban air pollutants (e.g., SO_2, NO_2, O_3). Different timeframes in a three-month (uni/multi) variate time series data set containing different features (air pollutants, temporal features, temperature, humidity, and wind speed) were collected from multi-gas sensing devices. The results showed that the M5P model outperformed other approaches for all gases in all horizons, whereas a shallow ANN model showed the worst performance due to overfitting.

Kamińska [8] proposed a probabilistic model for NO_2 concentration prediction using approximately 26,000 h of records containing traffic flow, wind speed, temperature, air, and temporal features captured on the main intersection of a city Wrocław in Poland. Zhu et al. [9] predicted the hourly air pollution concentration based on meteorological data from previous days using a multi-task learning (MTL) model. The dataset comprised air quality data (O_3, PM2.5, SO_2) and 10-year meteorological data (air temperature, relative humidity, wind speed and direction, wind gust, precipitation accumulation, visibility, dew point, wind cardinal direction, pressure, and weather conditions) from a monitoring station. Rybarczyk et al. [11] carried out a systematic literature review of the field, concluding that air quality estimation problems tend to implement ensemble learning and regression, whereas forecasting uses ANN- and SVM-based models. Furthermore, these studies aim to predict the amounts of pollutants and identify non-linear relationships between meteorological, atmospheric, and temporal features as relevant predictors.

In Xu and Lin [12], the authors used quantile regression to explore the driving forces of the difference in PM2.5 levels using features such as total population, economic growth, energy efficiency, urbanization level, industrialization level, and energy structure. Faced with the problems of non-linear associations common in pollutant behavior, Xu and Lin [12] applied the quantile regression approach to analyzing the determinants of PM2.5 concentrations in China. Finally, hybrid techniques have also emerged to model pollutants; for example, Flores-Vergara et al. [3] apply recurrent neural nets (RNNs) and the quantile regression method to forecast O_3 in Chile. Unfortunately, RNNs led to underestimates of the concentration peaks of O_3. This bias was reduced by using the quantile-regression-based learning method.

There are no previous studies pertaining to the city of Cuenca that allow predicting health-threatening pollutant levels and could thus serve as a basis for a regulatory policy with preventive measures. Moreover, the articles reviewed above cannot determine if O_3 prediction is more accurate using machine learning methods or quantile-regression-based methods. This article aims to provide decision-makers with a basis for implementing actions seeking to improve environmental quality.

3   Process for Pollutant Data Prediction

This section presents the data and the explanatory variables used in the models to predict O_3, the information sources, and data processing. We describe the machine learning processes and the quantile regression technique that used the above data to predict air pollution via O_3. Moreover, we describe the process used to evaluate the performance of the prediction methods through the calculation of the root mean squared error (RMSE) and the (pseudo) coefficient of determination (R^2) obtained through cross-validation.

3.1   Dataset and Preprocessing

The data set considered in this study pertains to the city of Cuenca (Ecuador) and contains cross-sectional empirical evidence from 4,172 different city blocks, captured during 2018. City blocks are generally heterogeneous in size and are defined by the local government based on human settlement or city planning. However, in the center of the city the blocks are more homogeneous, with a size of approximately 100 m^2. Data include traffic, pollutants, population, and space-based features. The data originate from several sources, as explained below.

To predict air pollution, we use data on ozone (O_3) emissions obtained from the Air Quality Monitoring Network, which currently has 20 monitoring points at different city locations (Fig. 2). The natural logarithm of O^3 is used as a dependent variable to measure air pollution in the city. O^3 concentrations are expected to be higher in the late afternoon and lower in the morning [24].

The model also considers noise valley and noise peak indices, built by applying principal component analysis (PCA). The noise valley index includes the decibel level at times of 10 am, 3 pm, and 9 pm. The noise peak index includes the decibel level at times of 7 am, 13 pm, and 6 pm.

Characteristics of the Space. Other elements of the city of Cuenca may influence ozone concentrations. For example, higher pollution levels are expected when block i is located in the city's historic center (HC) since this area experiences the highest level of travel. Similarly, a positive relationship is expected when block i is located in or around an industrial zone (IZ) because industrial activity is considered the second most polluting activity in the city. In addition, studies performed in the neighboring country of Colombia found that the acceleration, deceleration, and displacement for starting and stopping vehicles in traffic-light-controlled areas also leads to an increase in air pollution [25]. Therefore, the variable traffic light (S) is also incorporated into the model. HC and IZ were provided by the local government and S by EMOV.

Pollution intensifies with population density [26]. In this study, the job density per block is used since, for example, only 7.5% of the population lives in the historic center

[18] but this is an area with high travel intensity. Therefore, job density (JD) is considered appropriate to capture the effect of both population and business intensity. This variable was constructed based on the number of companies and the number of Cuenca employees in an area, information provided by the Internal Revenue Service (SRI). Data extraction is carried out in two steps: (1) companies are located on a map of the city, and (2) the number of employees in each block is obtained by summing the workers of all companies that are located in the same block.

Temperature and wind speed are meteorological variables widely used in the empirical literature since they are positively and negatively related to the level of O_3, respectively [8]. In addition, humidity and solar radiation have negative and positive effects, respectively [4]. However, these are not used in the current study because the data are difficult to access and could not be obtained.

Variables are listed in Table 1. All features are considered as predictors for our models. Prior to model definition, an exploratory data analysis of the continuous variables was performed. Table 1 shows a summary of the descriptive statistics for the variables included in the dataset. Almost 99% of the records correspond to non-industrial urban areas; one out of ten are located in the city center, whereas 4% of all blocks have a park within their area. In terms of traffic rates, 50% of blocks registered low traffic during a complete day. Table 2 shows the correlations between variables. As previous studies indicate, a negative correlation is observed between ozone (O_3) and its precursor, NO_2. The relationship between O_3 other pollutants, namely PS and SO_2, is positive and negative, respectively. Noise pollution and work density are positively correlated with O_3 levels. Finally, there is no evidence of high correlations between the explanatory variables, except for noise at off-peak and peak hours.

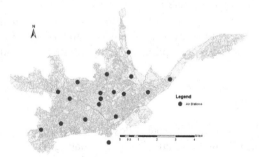

Fig. 2. Locations of monitoring stations

3.2 Estimation and Forecast Methods

The present study explores different techniques to estimate the concentration of O_3 pollution per $block_i$; that is, we focus on finding a regression function $f(y_i)$ capable of predicting the pollutant concentration as the logarithm of O_3 levels. We experimented with two approaches: machine learning models (random forest, gradient boosting, and a neural network model) [27–29] and quantile regression, described in the following paragraphs.

Quantile Regression. A quantile regression model is considered an extension of the classical least-squares estimation of conditional mean models [30]. This model is more robust as it does not require fulfillment of the strict assumptions of ordinal least squares (OLS) regression (e.g., normality and no heteroskedasticity) [3]. Additionally, it can reveal the effects of the explanatory variables at different quantiles of the explained variable. Therefore, it allows considering the non-linear associations between the variable response and explanatory variables [31]. The quantile regression model is presented in Eq. 1.

$$y_i = x_i \beta^{(q)} + \varepsilon_i^{(q)}; \ q = 0.25, 0.5, 0.75, \tag{1}$$

where y_i is the response variable (O_3 concentration) in city block i, x_i is the explanatory variable, $\beta^{(q)}$ is the coefficient that measures each covariate's effect on the qth quantile of ozone, and $\varepsilon_i^{(q)}$ represents the error term for qth quantile [31].

Ensemble Learning Approaches. Ensemble learning models use multiple algorithms (e.g., decision trees) to obtain better performance and more generalizable results than using a single instance of such algorithms. Techniques such as bagging and boosting are usually used during ensemble construction [32].

Artificial Neural Networks. Inspired by the human nervous system, artificial neural networks (ANNs) can learn non-linear relationships between input variables and outcomes. The most straightforward neural network (NN) architecture is called the multilayer perceptron, usually considered a shallow network that consists of at least three layers (input, hidden, output layer), with a smooth activation function applied at the output of each layer (except the layer that feeds the model). The model is then trained using a stochastic gradient descent optimization algorithm with backpropagation [14].

3.3 Validation Method

The predictive performance of the models described above is evaluated through indicators commonly used in the literature [3, 33]. Evaluating a model's fit and predictive ability using the complete sample set would probably lead to an overly optimistic assessment of its performance. A cross-validation technique is usually applied to avoid the overestimation problem and is commonly employed in non-linear models with some complexity. Although authors such as Watson et al. [34] use a leave-one-out cross-validation technique, this usually involves very high computational costs for relatively large sample sizes. However, this method does not provide significantly better results than other cross-validation methods (e.g., K-fold cross-validation).

The K-fold cross-validation method divides the data into K groups of the same size after a random mixing of the data. Subsequently, one group is taken as a test set and the remaining (K–1) groups comprise the training set. The performance of the model estimated with the training set is evaluated with the test set. The process is repeated K

Table 1. Dataset metadata description and statistics

Variable	Data type	Units of measurement	Description	Mean	St.d	Min	50%	Max
Pollutant covariates								
NO_2	Real	$\mu g/m^3$	Nitrogen dioxide	24.384	1.567	18.508	24.375	31.127
PS	Real	$\mu g/m^3$	Sedimentary particles	0.202	0.038	0.111	0.194	0.398
SO_2	Real	$\mu g/m^3$	Sulfur dioxide	4.847	0.721	3.240	4.608	7.562
Vehicular traffic								
Bus weight	Ordinal	0–4	Index of bus traffic	1.955	1.162	0	2	4
RushHourMorning	Ordinal	0–4	Index of traffic in the morning	1.408	0.729	1	1	4
RushHourNoon	Ordinal	0–4	Index of traffic at noon	1.457	0.774	1	1	4
RushHourNight	Ordinal	0–4	Index of traffic at night	1.468	0.805	1	1	4
Noise valley	Score	Index PCA	Noise factor in valley hours (10 am, 3 pm, and 9 pm)	0	1	−7.441	0.236	2.042
Noise peak	Score	Index PCA	Noise factor in peak hours (7 am, 1 pm, 6 pm)	0	1	−4.876	0.157	2.582
Spatial characteristics								
HC	Boolean	0–1	If block is located within the city center	0.114	0.318	0	0	1
IZ	Boolean	0–1	If block is located in an industrial zone	0.004	0.063	0	0	1
S	Boolean	0–1	If a semaphore is installed	0.024	0.154	0	0	1
JD	Real	number of workers	Job density. The $log1p$ function is applied	−5.380	7.192	−11.512	−11.512	8.121
Park	Boolean	0–1	If block is located in a park	0.0439	0.204	0	0	1

Table 2. Dataset metadata description and statistics

Variables	[1]	[2]	[3]	[4]	[5]	[6]
[1] O_3	1.0000					
[2] NO_2	−0.0044	1.0000				
[3] PS	0.0276	−0.2812	1.0000			
[4] SO_2	−0.2981	−0.5321	0.3182	1.0000		
[5] Noise valley	0.1284	0.3160	−0.0718	−0.4735	1.0000	
[6] Noise peak	0.2100	0.1985	−0.0055	−0.4217	0.9285	1.0000
[7] JD	0.0254	0.2435	−0.0723	−0.2630	0.1227	0.1204

times to finally obtain a global measure of fitting and the model's predictive capacity with new data. The value K = 10 was used because this number allows each test–train data to be large enough to be statistically representative. Given the sample of 4,172 elements, there were 3,755 observations in each training set and 417 in each test set.

The model's predictive performance was evaluated using three measures: the root mean squared error (RMSE), the (pseudo) coefficient of determination (R^2), and finally, the quantile loss. The latter corresponds to an optimization function for all models, defined as the loss associated with a specific quantile q.

$$lossquantile = max(q * e, (q - 1) * e) \mid q \Rightarrow quantile, e = (y_i - f_i) \qquad (2)$$

Where f_i represents the estimate ozone level. Table 3 lists the hyperparameter settings used in the experiments. To avoid bias in the experiments, each model was run ten times and results were averaged.

Table 3. Hyperparameter configuration for each model

Model	Quantile Regression	Random Forest	Gradient Boosting	Neural Network
Hyperparameters	Quantiles: [0.25, 0.5, 0.75]	n_estimators = 100 min_samples_leaf = 1 random_state = 42 max_features = 0.5	n_estimators = 1000 max_depth = 40 learning_rate = 0.01 min_samples_leaf = 1 min_samples_split = 2 max_features = "log2"	learning_rate = 0.001 patience = 20 epochs = 100 batch_size = 128 hidden_layers = 2 hidden_units = 512 validation_split = 0.2 activation function = ReLU

4 Results and Discussion

This section presents O_3 concentration results on an explanatory and a predictive level. The first includes the coefficients estimated by quantile regression and aims to explain the factors influencing ozone variation. Next, we describe four techniques we used to predict O_3 concentrations, evaluated in terms of the RMSE, R^2, and quantile loss at the predictive level.

4.1 Influencing Factors for Differences in O_3 Concentrations in Cuenca

The results of the quantile regression model are presented in Fig. 3. The O_3 quantiles are shown on the abscissa axis, whereas the ordinate axis contains the value of the effect of the explanatory variable on O_3 levels. The dashed line in the center represents a constant effect of the explanatory variable on the average value of O_3 concentration, obtained with OLS. The result shows that the explanatory effect of variables is different depending on the O_3 quantile level analyzed; consequently, the constant effect exhibited by OLS does not adequately explain the non-linear effects of factors.

The quantile regression results are shown in Fig. 3, which provides the 25th, 50th, and 75th quantile results. It can be seen that O_3 air pollution decreases as NO_2 concentrations increase. However, higher NO_2 levels imply an increase in O_3; thus, a U-shaped relationship between O_3 and NO_2 is evidenced. Awang et al. [24] state that this is explained by the differences between the NO_2 photolysis rate and NO titration rate; when the former is higher than the latter, variation in the chemical reaction rate, then O_3 increases. This U-shaped relationship was observed in the 50th and 75th O_3 concentration quantiles but not at low O_3 levels (i.e., in the 25th quantile).

Other pollutant covariates such as SPs positive influence O_3 levels when there is low contamination (quantile 25th, though they have the opposite effect when there is high contamination (quantile 75th). We also note that SO_2 negatively influences O_3 levels in all quantiles analyzed, with a p-value < 0.001. The positive or negative effects depend on phenomena such as photolysis and the catalyzing process [35]. Additionally, while environmental noise in valley hours induces a decrease in O_3, noise in peak hours increases this type of pollution when ozone concentrations are already high (quantile 75th), with a p-value < 0.001 in both cases.

Regarding the traffic variables, the model indicates that bus and motorized vehicle traffic decrease and increase the levels of O_3, respectively (with a group of significance of 1% or 5%). Furthermore, the historic center and areas subject to traffic lights control have higher ozone levels, mainly when pollution is low (quantile 25th), with a p-value < 0.001. Finally, maintaining everything else constant, with a higher density of workers and in areas cataloged as industrial, pollution levels decrease.

4.2 Prediction of O_3 Concentrations and Evaluation

The performance indicator results for the four models in q quantiles (0.25, 0.5, and 0.75) are summarized in Table 4 and Fig. 4. Cross-validation is developed with ten folds using a training dataset. The three measures that assess the model's predictive performance are calculated as the average result for the ten-fold cross-validation. The random forest technique shows the best performance for predicting ozone concentration, with a smaller RMSE value and a higher R^2 coefficient (Table 4) than the other techniques. In terms of accuracy, gradient boosting exhibits the second-best performance, followed by the neural network and quantile regression.

The quantile loss indicator confirms the accuracy of the random forest model (Fig. 4). Furthermore, ensemble-based models outperformed the other models, and all models report better results than the quantile regression. These results are congruent with the research of Watson et al. [34], who concluded that the gradient boosting and random forest models are the best models for ozone-level prediction, compared to elastic net regression, linear model, neural network, support vector machine (SVM), and other approaches. In addition, Jumin et al. [36] found that boosted decision trees outperform linear regression and neural network algorithms for ozone concentration prediction.

These results were expected because most of the features included in the input dataset X are categorical (ordinal). The gradient boosting (GB) model results can be improved by applying a further grid search on the hyperparameters; this is true for the shallow NN model, as a larger number of hidden layers and different numbers of hidden units could lead to better empirical results. Nevertheless, these models could suffer from overfitting and not generalize well. This can occur for the following reasons: a) the dataset used does not include enough examples; b) there are not enough continuous variables to capture the non-linear relationship between the concentration of air pollutants and their sources of emission and dispersion.

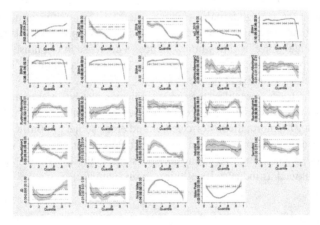

Fig. 3. Effects of the determinants of air pollution according to quantiles

Table 4. Results of 10-fold cross-validation in terms of mean RMSE and coefficient of determination, R^2

Method	Gradient Boosting			NN			Quant. Reg			Random forest		
q	0.25	0.50	0.75	0.25	0.50	0.75	0.25	0.50	0.75	0.25	0.50	0.75
RMSE	0.0095	0.0073	0.0073	0.0312	0.0285	0.0316	0.0376	0.0337	0.0358	0.0058	0.0029	0.0063
R2	0.9359	0.9531	0.9526	0.2399	0.3987	0.2552	0.1401	0.2268	0.2549	0.9739	0.9739	0.9739

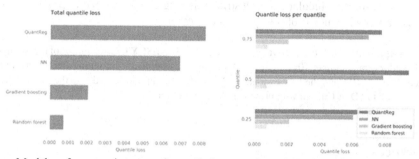

a. Model performance in terms of quantile loss   b. Model performance per quantile

Fig. 4. Model performance in terms of quantile loss

5 Conclusions and Future Work

The predictive performance of the random forest model is the best in terms of RMSE and R^2 indicators, compared to the other models. The model exhibits high precision, with an R^2 greater than 0.97 and an RMSE smaller than 0.007 for all quantiles. In explanatory terms, the ozone concentration in Cuenca during 2018 is explained by its precursor, NO_2, and other pollutants. There are particular chemical reactions that can explain its positive or negative effects on the ozone. Furthermore, the traffic and spatial characteristics of the analyzed city blocks also influence ozone concentrations. However, additional studies are needed to improve the model proposed in this research.

As a limitation to this study, certain input parameters such as meteorological factors commonly used in the literature have not been used in the models, we considered to predict ozone concentrations since access to such information is very restricted. In addition, we conclude that the spatial relationships of pollution should be excluded from any future research, as it shows a significant correlation with the spatial distribution of ozone. This result can help policymakers identify areas of the city with harmful ozone levels. Note that new hybrid techniques may be an interesting avenue for future research as they make it possible to take advantage of the particular benefits of distinct methods, for example, by combining neural networks with quantile regression. We leave this type of analysis for subsequent investigation. Our results show that spatial characteristics, such as industrial land, particular features of the historic center of the city, and labor-population density, may significantly influence ozone concentrations. This suggests that environmentally sustainable city planning must take into account these aspects in order to generate strategies that reduce environmental pollution.

We believe that this and related future research results are useful for policymakers to achieve two fundamental environmental objectives: 1) an early warning mechanism that allows identifying the moment and the geographical area where high levels of ozone pollution can occur, and 2) scientific proof to motivate citizen support for environmental policy proposals aimed at reducing pollution levels. Within these policies, we can mention the following: a) improvements in transport planning, such as the regulation of the entry of highly polluting vehicles to certain areas of the historic center, b) improvements in planning for the use of public spaces and specific spaces designated as industrial zones, c) stricter control of vehicular and industrial polluting emissions, and c) promotion of the use of alternative means of transport, among others.

Acknowledgments. This research was supported by the SENESCYT, Government of the Republic of Ecuador [grant number 704-2012]. We thank the Department of Computing and Information Sciences Ph.D. of RIT and the Universidad de Cuenca for the support provided to the researchers. We also thank GAD of Cuenca who provided the information.

References

1. Geddes, J.A., Martin, R.V., Boys, B.L., van Donkelaar, A.: Long-term trends worldwide in ambient NO2 concentrations inferred from satellite observations. Environ. Health Perspect. **124**, 281–289 (2016). https://doi.org/10.1289/ehp.1409567
2. WHO Regional office for Europe (2013) Data and statistics. https://www.euro.who.int/en/hea lth-topics/environment-and-health/noise/data-and-statistics. Accessed 5 Sept 2020
3. Flores-Vergara, D., Ñanculef, R., Valle, C., et al.: Forecasting ozone pollution using recurrent neural nets and multiple quantile regression. In: 2019 IEEE CHILEAN Conference on Electrical, Electronics Engineering, Information and Communication Technologies (CHILECON), pp. 1–6 (2019)
4. Ezimand, K., Kakroodi, A.A.: Prediction and spatio temporal analysis of ozone concentration in a metropolitan area. Ecol. Ind. **103**, 589–598 (2019). https://doi.org/10.1016/j.ecolind.2019. 04.059
5. Feng, Z., Hu, E., Wang, X., et al.: Ground-level O3 pollution and its impacts on food crops in China: a review. Environ. Pollut. **199**, 42–48 (2015). https://doi.org/10.1016/j.envpol.2015. 01.016
6. Singh, K.P., Gupta, S., Rai, P.: Identifying pollution sources and predicting urban air quality using ensemble learning methods. Atmos. Environ. **80**, 426–437 (2013). https://doi.org/10. 1016/j.atmosenv.2013.08.023
7. Bashir Shaban, K., Kadri, A., Rezk, E.: Urban air pollution monitoring system with forecasting models. IEEE Sens. J. **16**, 2598–2606 (2016). https://doi.org/10.1109/JSEN.2016.2514378
8. Kamińska, J.A.: Probabilistic forecasting of nitrogen dioxide concentrations at an urban road intersection. Sustainability **10**, 4213 (2018). https://doi.org/10.3390/su10114213
9. Zhu, D., Cai, C., Yang, T., Zhou, X.: A machine learning approach for air quality prediction: model regularization and optimization. Big Data Cogn. Comput. **2**, 5 (2018). https://doi.org/ 10.3390/bdcc2010005
10. Arce, D., Lima, J.-F., Orellana, M., et al.: Discovering behavioral patterns among air pollutants: a data mining approach. Enfoque UTE **9**, 168–179 (2018). https://doi.org/10.29019/enf oqueute.v9n4.411

11. Rybarczyk, Y., Zalakeviciute, R.: Machine learning approaches for outdoor air quality modelling: a systematic review. Appl. Sci. **8**, 2570 (2018). https://doi.org/10.3390/app812 2570
12. Xu, B., Lin, B.: What cause large regional differences in PM2.5 pollutions in China? Evidence from quantile regression model. J. Clean. Prod. **174**, 447–461 (2018). https://doi.org/10.1016/j.jclepro.2017.11.008
13. Yang, H., Ma, M., Thompson, J.R., Flower, R.J.: Waste management, informal recycling, environmental pollution and public health. J. Epidemiol. Commun. Health **72**, 237–243 (2018). https://doi.org/10.1136/jech-2016-208597
14. Rumelhart, D.E., Hinton, G.E., Williams, R.J.: Learning Internal Representations by Error Propagation. California University San Diego, La Jolla Institute for Cognitive Science (1985)
15. INEC: Censo de Población y Vivienda 2010 (2010)
16. INEC: Transporte. In: Instituto Nacional de Estadística y Censos (2019). https://www.ecuadorencifras.gob.ec/transporte/. Accessed 5 Sept 2020
17. Sander, K., Mira-Salama, D., Feuerbacher, A.: The cost of air pollution - a case study for the city of Cuenca, Ecuador. In: World Bank report (2015). https://documents.worldbank.org/en/publication/documents-reports/documentdetail/458511468189273908/The-cost-of-air-pollution-a-case-study-for-the-city-of-Cuenca-Ecuador. Accessed 8 Jun 2021
18. GAD de Cuenca: Plan de Movilidad y espacios públicos. Municipalidad de Cuenca, Cuenca (2015)
19. Gupta, A., Gupta, A., Jain, K., Gupta, S.: Noise pollution and impact on children health. Indian J. Pediatr. **85**(4), 300–306 (2018). https://doi.org/10.1007/s12098-017-2579-7
20. EMOV: Informe de calidad del aire Cuenca 2018. Empresa Pública de Movilidad, Tránsito y Transporte (EMOV-EP), Cuenca (2018)
21. Arsić, M., Mihajlović, I., Nikolić, D., et al.: Prediction of ozone concentration in ambient air using multilinear regression and the artificial neural networks methods. Ozone: Sci. Eng. **42**, 79–88 (2020). https://doi.org/10.1080/01919512.2019.1598844
22. Yadav, J., Sharma, M.: A review of k-mean algorithm. Int. J. Eng. Trends Technol. (IJETT) **4**, 2972–2976 (2013)
23. Kingsy, G.R., Manimegalai, R., Geetha, D.M.S., et al.: Air pollution analysis using enhanced K-Means clustering algorithm for real time sensor data. In: 2016 IEEE Region 10 Conference (TENCON), pp. 1945–1949 (2016)
24. Awang, N.R., Ramli, N.A., Yahaya, A.S., Elbayoumi, M.: Multivariate methods to predict ground level ozone during daytime, nighttime, and critical conversion time in urban areas. Atmos. Pollut. Res. **6**, 726–734 (2015). https://doi.org/10.5094/APR.2015.081
25. Daniels, F., Martínez López, E., Quinchía, R., et al.: Contaminación atmosférica y efectos sobre la salud de la población Medellín y su área metropolitana. Medellín (2007)
26. Martínez-Bravo, M., Martínez-del-Río, J.: Urban pollution and emission reduction. In: Leal Filho, W., Azul, A., Brandli, L., Özuyar, P., Wall, T. (eds.) Sustainable Cities and Communities. Encyclopedia of the UN Sustainable Development Goals, pp. 1–11. Springer, Cham (2019). https://doi.org/10.1007/978-3-319-71061-7_30-1
27. Zhou, Z.-H.: Ensemble learning. In: Zhou, Z.-H. (ed.) Machine Learning, pp 181–210. Springer, Singapore (2021). https://doi.org/10.1007/978-981-15-1967-3_8
28. Maleki, H., Sorooshian, A., Goudarzi, G., Baboli, Z., Tahmasebi Birgani, Y., Rahmati, M.: Air pollution prediction by using an artificial neural network model. Clean Technol. Environ. Policy **21**(6), 1341–1352 (2019). https://doi.org/10.1007/s10098-019-01709-w
29. Cabaneros, S.M., Calautit, J.K., Hughes, B.R.: A review of artificial neural network models for ambient air pollution prediction. Environ. Model. Softw. **119**, 285–304 (2019). https://doi.org/10.1016/j.envsoft.2019.06.014
30. Sousa, S.I.V., Pires, J.C.M., Martins, F.G., et al.: Potentialities of quantile regression to predict ozone concentrations. Environmetrics **20**, 147–158 (2009). https://doi.org/10.1002/env.916

31. Munir, S., Chen, H., Ropkins, K.: Characterising the temporal variations of ground-level ozone and its relationship with traffic-related air pollutants in the United Kingdom: a quantile regression approach. Int. J. SDP **9**, 29–41 (2014). https://doi.org/10.2495/SDP-V9-N1-29-41

32. Yang, P., Yang, Y.H., Zhou, B.B., Zomaya, Y.A.: A review of ensemble methods in bioinformatics. Curr. Bioinform. **5**, 296–308 (2010)

33. Alimissis, A., Philippopoulos, K., Tzanis, C.G., Deligiorgi, D.: Spatial estimation of urban air pollution with the use of artificial neural network models. Atmos. Environ. **191**, 205–213 (2018). https://doi.org/10.1016/j.atmosenv.2018.07.058

34. Watson, G.L., Telesca, D., Reid, C.E., et al.: Machine learning models accurately predict ozone exposure during wildfire events. Environ. Pollut. **254**, 112792 (2019). https://doi.org/10.1016/j.envpol.2019.06.088

35. IDEAM: Formación y destrucción del ozono estratosférico (2015). http://www.ideam.gov.co/web/tiempo-y-clima/formacion-y-destruccion-del-ozono-estratosferico. Accessed 29 May 2021

36. Jumin, E., Zaini, N., Ahmed, A.N., et al.: Machine learning versus linear regression modelling approach for accurate ozone concentrations prediction. Eng. Appl. Comput. Fluid Mech. **14**, 713–725 (2020). https://doi.org/10.1080/19942060.2020.1758792

Design of Operational Radiation Protection in Compact Proton Therapy Centers (CPTC)

Gonzalo F. García-Fernandez[1]([✉]), Lenin E. Cevallos-Robalino[2],
Karen A. Guzmán-García[3], Héctor R. Vega-Carrillo[3], Alejandro Carabe-Fernández[4],
José M. Gómez-Ros[5], and Eduardo Gallego[1]

[1] Dep. Ing. Energética (DIE), Universidad Politécnica de Madrid (UPM), 28006 Madrid, Spain
gf.garcia@upm.es
[2] NANOTECH, Universidad Politécnica Salesiana (UPS), Guayaquil, Guayas 090108, Ecuador
[3] UA Estudios Nucleares, Univ. Autónoma de Zacatecas (UAZ), 98060 Zacatecas, México
[4] Hampton University Proton Therapy Institute (HUPTI), Hampton, VA 23666, USA
[5] CIEMAT, 28040 Madrid, Spain

Abstract. Proton therapy, an external radiotherapy using proton beams to treat some type of tumours with outstanding benefits, is in continuous ever evolving to improve its performance. Some prominent current trends involve cutting-edge delivery methods or raise compact building. Compact centers take in specific features to reduce their size while achieving more affordable facilities and new developments have direct impact in radioprotection. This work is framed into the research project *Contributions to operational radiation protection and neutron dosimetry in compact proton therapy centers (CPTC),* which is focused on designing, assessing, and commissioning their operational radiation protection. The main goal is to present and collect the activities developed from 2018 in fields as checking shielding, comparing ambient dose yielded by neutrons in several facilities, analyzing activation in shielding with different types of concrete, characterizing wide range Rem-meters to measure neutron fields, studying new proton delivery techniques and their neutron fields, or assessing personal dosemeters suitable for these centers, among others. The results reached show that future highly compact centers will have a relevant impact on the radiation protection.

Keywords: Compact proton therapy centers · Neutron radiation area monitoring · Neutron dosimetry

1 Introduction

The advantages of proton therapy (PT) in some treatments against cancer have led to a significant expansion of proton therapy centers around the world, with almost one hundred in operation and over fifty at different stages of development. Current trends in PT are to build small compact and standard facilities, along with the renovation of large multiple room proton therapy centers (MPTC), laid down in the early stages of PT [1].

Based on International Basic Safety Standards and Regulatory Principles [2], main radiological risks in proton centers (PTC) have been widely stated and summarized [3]:

© Springer Nature Switzerland AG 2021
J. P. Salgado Guerrero et al. (Eds.): TICEC 2021, CCIS 1456, pp. 297–312, 2021.
https://doi.org/10.1007/978-3-030-89941-7_21

1. External exposure to secondary radiation (neutrons and photons) from beamline.
2. External exposure from activated equipment, materials of the facility, water and air.
3. Internal exposure for inhalation of radioisotopes in activated air.

Nevertheless, proton therapy is in continuous ever evolving to improve its performance, and some prominent current trends involve cutting-edge delivery methods or building compact proton centers [4]. New developments have a direct impact in radiation protection of proton facilities and actions should be continuously developed to update the new requeriments of centers [5]. Remarkable works about operational radiation protection design in MPTC are collected elsewhere [6–10]. Compact Proton Therapy Centers (CPTC), act out latest advances in particles therapy and have specific features to reduce their size while achieving more affordable facilities [11]. Consequently, from the point of view of operational radioprotection, CPTC face significant challenges [12]:

1. Usually these centers have one single room (sometimes two) and small footprint.
2. They have a higher radiation density in Sievert per square meter (Sv/m^2).
3. They have a standard geometry and configuration worldwide.
4. There is an intensive use of new materials and technology.
5. They use the most advanced equipment and machinery to reduce their size.
6. The usual delivery mode of protons is Pencil Beam Scanning (PBS).
7. There is a narrow mix of professional exposed workers (clinical and technical staff).

The present work is framed into the project *Contributions to operational radiation protection and neutron dosimetry in compact proton therapy centers (CPTC)*, which is focused on assessing the impact of these innovations on the operational radiation protection and commissioning of the compact proton facilities [13]. Thus, several tasks have been carried out over the last three years, as checking and evaluation of shielding [14], comparing ambient dose equivalent of several CPTC [15], analyzing activation with different types of concrete, and activation in machinery, air and water of the facility [16], characterizing wide range rem-meters and neutron area monitors to measure neutron fields [17], studying new proton delivery techniques and their neutron fields [18], or assessing personal dosemeters [19], among others. The aim of the work is to present outcomes achieved in the aforementioned areas. As a result, a commissioning process of the operational radiation protection in CPTC will be suggested, lined up with the requirements by the Spanish Regulatory Body [20].

2 Material and Methods

2.1 Compact Proton Therapy Centers (CPTC) Considered in the Work

Although there are a wide range of commercial models of CPTC developed by different vendors, CPTC considered in this work are the standard version of the two centers in the first years of operation in Spain, being compact size both [13]. The first one, working from December 2019, has a cyclotron accelerator with extraction energy at 230 MeV and a footprint close to 360 m^2. The second one, working from May 2020, has a synchrotron accelerator, with extraction energy adjustable between 70 and 230 MeV and a footprint near 800 m^2. The standards CPTC modelled are made up of accelerator room (AR), treatment room with a compact rotating gantry (GTR) and the maze. Lay-out of the CPTC are shown in Fig. 1 for synchrocyclotron (SC), and Fig. 2 for synchrotron (SY). Further details are collected in [14, 15].

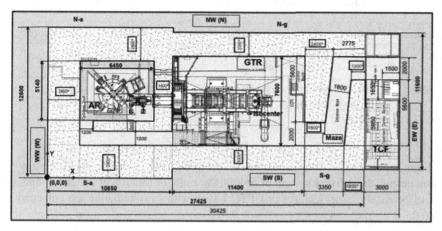

Fig. 1. Main features of CPTC with synchrocyclotron (SC)

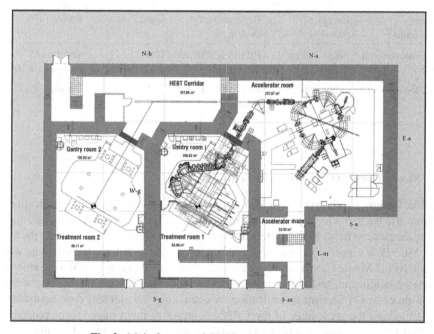

Fig. 2. Main features of CPTC with synchrotron (SY)

Both centers have three key elements: firstly, the accelerator, secondly the beamline (BL), and finally the Gantry Treatment Room (GTR). The general features of CPTC studied in this project are collected in Table 1.

Table 1. General features of CPTC considered in this work

Manufacturer	Model	Type of accelerator	Number of rooms	Footprint (m^2)
IBA	ProteusOne®	Synchrocyclotron (SC)	1	400
Hitachi	Expandable One Gantry System (EOGS)	Synchrotron (SY)	1 + (1)	800

From a point of view of generation of neutrons fields, considering the energy of proton beams, the delivery system of proton, the angle of rotation of the gantry and the type of beam, the main features or CPTC linked with stray radiation are collected in Table 2.

Table 2. Main features of CPTC with influence in neutron fields

Type of accelerator	Energy of protons	Beam delivery system	Gantry rotation	Proton field
Synchrocyclotron (SC)	Fixed 230 meV	PBS Pencil Beam Scanning	220°	Continuous (virtually, KHz)
Synchrotron (SY)	Adjustable 70 to 230 meV	PBS Pencil Beam Scanning	360°	Pulsed (Hz)

2.2 Monte Carlo (MC) Codes and Settings

Facility Design, Equipment, and Materials. The study of shielding verifications, activation in barriers, characterization of rem-meters and personal dosemeters, and comparing the neutron fields with different delivery methods, were carried out using the MC code MCNP6® versions 6.1 and 6.2 [21, 22]. The process to validate the shielding with the MCNP6.2 Monte Carlo code was developed in three main stages [23]: (1) Defining geometry, equipment, and radiation sources; (2) Modelling sources through a condensation process; (3) Shielding verification by estimating the ambient dose equivalent, H*(10) behind the enclosures of the CPTC. Features of main materials employed in MCNP6 were collected from [24]. In enclosures with influence in the shielding (walls and roofs), regular concrete, density, 2.3 g/cm^3 was tested. Calculation and hypothesis were based in data and information published in research works about synchrocyclotron systems [25] and synchrotrons systems [26]. Modelling all the components of the facility is neither viable nor useful from the point of view of the radiation sources. The method followed was the point neutron-equivalent in which the radiation sources are the points where proton beam losses interacting with matter [9]. A water phantom, with dimension of $40 \times 40 \times 40$ cm^3, was considered as a patient, irradiated with a beam proton equal to the global efficiency at each energy [27]. The workload was estimated in agreement with data, in nA·h per year in each energy, at the exit of accelerator, assuming a conservative approach of 16-h workday in two 8-h shifts, six working days per week, and fifty weeks per year, 450 patients/year, 17.000 sessions, with 2 Gy/session, considering the clinical data about number of patients and typical treatment plans [28]. Occupancy factors were obtained from international recommendations by choosing the most conservative options [29]. The MCNP6 physics models chosen were the default options, the CEM03.03 model for intranuclear cascade (INC) followed by the GEM model for evaporation process (EVP), because the computation time is shorter, and the results are more conservative [30].

Area Monitoring Magnitude and Personal Dosimetry Magnitude. In agreement with ICRU/ICRP, the operational quantity chosen was the ambient dose equivalent, H*(10), along the enclosures of the center, because is a conservative magnitude [31]. H*(10) was obtained through the convolution of neutron fluence, $\Phi(E)$, in cm^{-2}, and the ICRU fluence to ambient dose equivalent conversion function, h(E), in Sievert per square centimetres, Sv·cm^2 [32], and its expansion above 201 MeV [33]. These coefficients vary strongly with neutron energy as shown in Fig. 5, because of the differences between the interactions that dominate for different energy regions: dose deposition by fast neutrons is mainly by elastic scattering whereas capture reactions dominate dose deposition for lower energies.

In personal dosimetry, the operational quantity used for external irradiation is the personal dose equivalent, Hp(d), which provides a reasonable overestimation of the limiting quantities and can be measured with relatively simple instrumentation. Hp(d), is the soft tissue equivalent dose at an appropriate depth, d, below a specified point in the human body. For strongly penetrating radiation, as neutrons, the assumed value of d is 10 mm. Personal equivalent dose strongly depends on both, neutron energy and angle [31].

MCNP6 Settings and Calculations. Simulations were carried out considering 20 energy groups (from 10^{-9} to 230 MeV), with a number of histories quite enough to achieve statistical uncertainties under 3%, verifying the ten statistical checks in MCNP [22]. ENDF/B (version VII.1), evaluated nuclear data libraries, La150n library, were used up to 150 meV [34, 35], and nuclear models above that energy. GEM03.03 Model for INC reactions, and GEM Model for EVM process. To study the sensitivity of simulations and results to nuclear data, some works have been reached using three further libraries: (1) JEFF (version 3.3), which is jointly managed by the Joint European File (JEF) and the European Fusion File (EFF) groups [36]. (2) TENDL 2017 and 2019 libraries, Talys Evaluated Nuclear Data Library [37]. Thermal treatments, designed by $S(\alpha, \beta)$ in the MCNP code, have been used in all the simulations for all neutron energies [38]. All rooms were considered air-filled and void in the proton beam. The results were computed using superposed mesh tallies inside the facility, along the walls and roofs and outside the enclosures. As variance reduction in cells of the walls, roof and air in vaults, biasing methods and weight factors were used based on geometry splitting and Russian roulette [22].

3 Results

3.1 Shielding Design and Ambient Dose Equivalent, H*(10)

Effectiveness of shielding in CPTC was verified by calculating the ambient dose equivalent, H*(10) in uSv/year, due to secondary neutrons, outside the enclosures and walls. The facilities modelled had a standard configuration, and width of walls based on dimensions proposed a priori by the vendors. Results are collected in Fig. 3.

In all cases, assuming the worst scenario, the values reached in both facilities were well below 1 mSv/year (millisievert per year), which is the legal limit internationally accepted for the general public. Although in both facilities, using different accelerators, the ambient dose equivalent to the public reached with the shielding considered is less than 0,5 mSv/y, a 50% under the maximum limit, the results are achieved with different wall thickness, approximately 2.8 m in Synchrocyclotrons, while in Synchrotrons the thickness of typical wall is 2 m. Several models of radiation sources and type of concrete in walls were simulated, starting from a conservative assumption (radiation sources in accelerator, energy selection system and phantom), followed by more realistic hypothesis. The simulations were carried out using Monte Carlo (MC) code MCNP6® version 6.2, computing the fluences of secondary neutrons produced by interaction of the beam of protons in different points of the facilities. Full details of study in CPTC with synchrocyclotron are set out in [14], while details of the study in compact center with synchrotron, and benchmarking of both facilities, are collected in [15].

3.2 Neutron Activation and Materials in Barriers

The next task was to carry out a comparative analysis of neutron activation in CPTC facilities with synchrocyclotron, using the MCNP6 code [16]. Five different types of concrete were studied: conventional Portland concrete, hormirad® (high density concrete with magnetite), colemanite (concrete with a high percentage of hydrogen), and finally two new different low activation concretes (LAC), called LAC1® and LAC2®, respectively. Attenuation plot reached with different concretes is shown in Fig. 4.

Characteristics and composition of the materials studied are collected in [14–16] and [39, 40]. Considering the energy reached by neutrons, up to 230 meV, four different neutron cross-section libraries were used, ENDF/B VII.1, JEFF-3.3 and TENDL2017/19, in order to study the sensitivity of results to nuclear data.

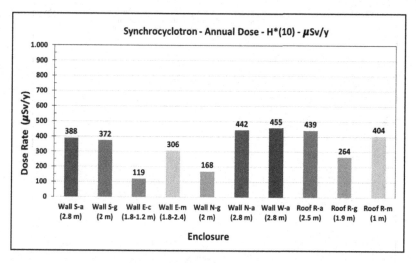

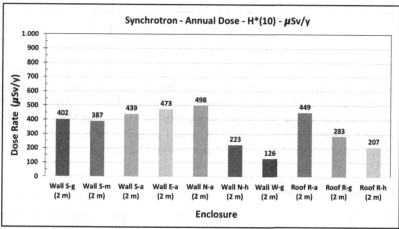

Fig. 3. H*(10) behind walls of CPTC, (a) Top, with SC, (b) Bottom, with SY

From the point of view of activation, the most recommended concretes are those with the lowest content of impurities that can be activated and generate radioactive waste. From an attenuation point of view, however, concretes of high density (with magnetite) or with high hydrogen content (with colemanite) are more efficient. Conventional Portland-type concrete has an intermediate activation and attenuation behaviour, and its building cost is more profitable than with special concretes. The comparative summary of performance with different type of materials are collected in Fig. 5.

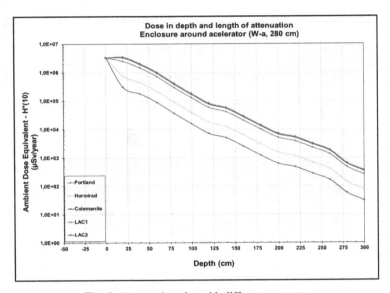

Fig. 4. Attenuation plot with different concretes

In summary, it would be advisable to use different concretes for each area, depending on the neutron fluence expected neutron fluence in each wall, optimizing the selection with criteria based on attenuation, activation and the cost of building. The barriers with the highest fluence are those around the accelerator and the wall in front of the beam, in the treatment room. Further results, and studies of activation in metallic parts and mechanical elements of the facility, water and air are reported equally in [16].

3.3 Rem-Meters and Neutron Area Monitors

The radiological monitoring of proton therapy centers requires using appropriate neutron measurements instruments of extended energy range. The analysis and response evaluation of several extended range neutron rem-meters and neutron area monitors were carried out, and WENDI-II, LUPIN-II and PRESCILA devices were characterized through the Monte Carlo code MCNP6, for their application in shielding and radiation area monitoring in CPTC facilities.

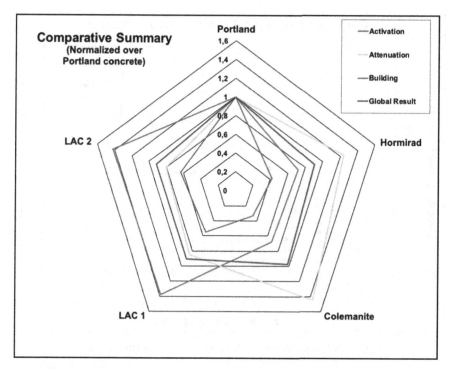

Fig. 5. Comparative summary of global performance with different concretes

WENDI-II [41], Wide Energy Neutron Detection Instrument, is a rem-meter, type Anderson-Braun (A-B). LUPIN-II [42], Long Interval, Ultra-Wide dynamic, Pile-up free, Neutron rem-counter, is also a rem-meter, type Anderson-Braun (A-B). Finally, PRESCILA, Proton recoil Scintillator-Los Alamos [43], is a device, type scintillator, developed by los Alamos National Laboratory. Further details of the process are included in [17, 18]. The fluence-to-Ambient dose conversion coefficients, h(E), and the Ambient dose equivalent responses of these rem-meters are shown in Fig. 6.

Once characterized, these monitors were used in several proton therapy facilities [17, 18]. Likewise, to characterize the neutron spectrum is such facilities, it would be useful to use extended-range Bonner Sphere systems (BSS); the response of one of such BSS was carried out as described in [44].

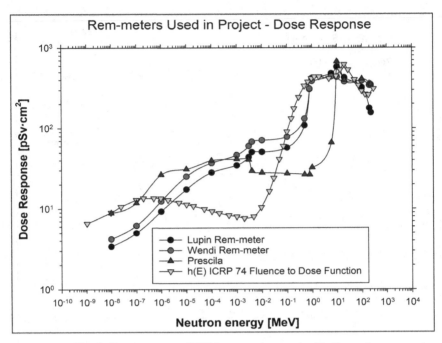

Fig. 6. Dose response of REM-meters characterized in the work

3.4 Comparing Neutron Fields of New Delivery Methods in Proton Therapy

Proton monoenergetic arc therapy (PMAT) is a new delivery modality, currently at development stages by Prof. Carabe-Fernández [45], which aims to take advantage of irradiation of the tumour volume under fields with a full 360° angle, using monoenergetic protons and optimizing the LET (Linear Energy Transfer) inside the target [46].

Experimental measurements, using a PRESCILA detector, of neutronic fields yielded with PMAT were compared with those generated with the conventional intensity-modulated proton therapy (IMPT) treatment, at different distances and angles of the circular phantom used in the radiobiological experiment [46]. The measurements were carried out at the Fixed Beam Treatment Room (FBTR) of the Roberts Proton Therapy Center (RPTC) in the Hospital of the University of Pennsylvania (UPenn). The experimental set-up is shown in Fig. 7, with fully details collected in [18].

Results show that inside the treatment room, H*(10) with both modalities is within the same order of magnitude, however, the dose with PMAT is almost three times lower than with IMPT. Likewise, simulations carried out with MCNP6.2 code were compared with experimental measurements. To conclude, PMAT would have dosimetric advantages and optimization of LET, at the same time that would achieve a not negligible reduction of secondary neutrons [18].

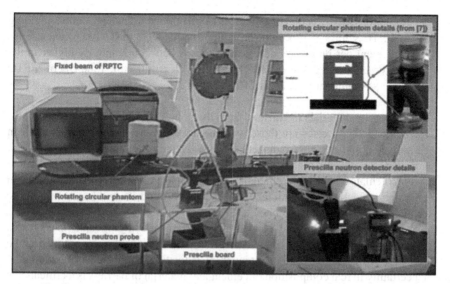

Fig. 7. Experimental set-up at FBTR (Fixed Beam Treatment Room) of RPTC

4 Discussion and Conclusions

Despite of the large and exhaustive studies developed in the implementation of radiological protection measures in proton therapy facilities, some of them mentioned in this project, proton therapy discipline is constantly evolving and incorporating new developments that pose a great challenge for radiation protection of patients, medical staff, exposed workers and the general public.

Therefore, when it is come to speak about the design of the operational radiation protection in moderns CPTC, based on the main results achieved in the several tasks mentioned above throughout this survey, some basic premises could be established, as a summary of the work, collected below in ten recommendations:

1. Suitable barriers and shielding against neutron and gamma stray radiation are essential in both, accelerator and treatment room (or rooms in facilities with compact synchrotron), and control rooms, to limit doses to staff and general public. Although gamma radiation is also yielded, its order of magnitude is much lower than neutron radiation.

2. The design of the mandatory shielding could be based on Monte Carlo simulations, however, validation and estimation of doses of exposed workers by measurements with portable neutron and gamma devices should be carried out in commissioning stages. The results, achieved in several task of this work tied with checking of shielding in CPTC, show:

   a. Uncertainty in physics models and nuclear data library in MCNP could vary from 1.3 to 1.9, depending on the physic model and the nuclear data library employed.

b. Radiation density achieved in the works mentioned in the paper corresponding to CPTC with synchrocyclotron is approximately 2 mSv/Gy (Ambient dose equivalent per biological dose), what means between 2 and 5% higher in the benchmark carried out with MPTC. This is clear, since the footprint of MPTC centers is quite larger than in CPTC.

3. Regarding the materials in barriers, from the point of view of activation, the most recommended concretes are those with the lowest content of impurities that can be activated and generate radioactive waste. From an attenuation point of view, however, concretes of high density (with magnetite) or with high hydrogen content (with colemanite) are more efficient. Conventional Portland-type concrete has an intermediate activation and attenuation behaviour, and its building cost is more profitable than with special concretes.

4. Considering that the flux and the neutron spectrum varies significantly in each area of the installation, it would be advisable to use different concretes, optimizing the selection with criteria based on attenuation, activation, and the cost of building.

5. Uncertainty in real composition of cement and material of barriers is a critical data in calculation both, attenuation, and activation. Evenly, results achieved in this work linked with the study of activation in CPTC show:

   a. Percentage of hydrogen in conventional cement could vary between 0.4% to 2.1%. To estimate both, features of attenuation and activation of the barriers, it is essential to know, as accurate as possible, the real composition of the cement supplied in the building of the facility.

   b. Density of conventional concrete varies between 2.3 and 2.4 g/cm^3. In this case, the density should be also tested at different stages of the building of center, at the laboratory of materials. These checks could be carried out at the same time as mandatory tests to verify the bearing strength of concrete.

   c. Hence, collect data of main materials, cement and concrete, along the building of center is a key task in commissioning process of these facilities.

6. It would be necessary to place neutron and gamma detectors at critical points of the facility (near the accelerator and isocenter), to monitor dose rates, mainly neutrons stray fields from protons interactions in beamline and the patients, and gamma radiation from activation in shielding and metallic parts of the facility (accelerator and ancillary structures). As collected along this work, results achieved in several task characterizing the response of monitors and carried out experimental measurements in proton centres, show that uncertainty in monitors and REM-meters response could vary from 3 to 10%, depending on energy of neutrons and orientation of the monitor relative to the source of radiation.

7. In addition to the fixed monitors mentioned, it would be absolutely essential to have and handle portable devices for gamma, neutron and contamination detection, in order to check several equipment and materials liable of being activated during the operation of the facility, as ground water, heating and air conditioned (HVAC) water, air or metallic elements.

8. Personal neutron dosemeters should be used for both, medical and technical staff. There are different types, but gamma dosemeters and neutron dosemeters would be mandatory. For some operations of technical staff in the accelerator room it would be advisable to wear ring dosemeters and active devices (APDs).
9. Considering the distinctive spectrum of the proton centers, both, ambient monitors and personal dosemeters, should be able to measure neutrons in a large range spectrum, from thermal, 10^{-9} MeV, to high energies, 230 MeV. Currently there are no devices with a suitable response for all energy ranges, so it is recommended to use complementary monitors, with efficient responses in different ranges.
10. Because of the previous point, neutron field characterization of the facility, both, energy spectra and angle, should be carried out and regularly updated, in order to state specific facility and local correction factors (LCF), using proper devices and wide range equipment as Bonner spheres, slab phantoms or ambient monitors, among others.

There is a current general trend to reduce the size of proton therapy centers and make them increasingly compact. This strategy seeks on the one hand, to cut down the direct costs of deployment, since the smaller the center is, the lower the price should be. On the other hand, if extremely small proton equipment were achieved, it would be possible to place them in rooms with the same size as conventional radiotherapy (using photons), which would also produce an indirect reduction in the cost of implantation. In this hypothetical limit scenario, a space for conventional radiotherapy with photons could be replaced by a facility with protons [47]. The final goal is to achieve more affordable proton therapy facilities so that if there are more proton centers, proton treatments can reach more patients, since it is estimated that currently only 1 % of patients receive proton therapy, when, if they could have access, between 15 and 50% could benefit from these treatments. The reason for this discrepancy is the high capital cost and the size of the proton therapy equipment [48]. Apparently, the main factor impacting in the high cost of the proton centers is the rotating gantry, whose missions are, on the one hand, to support the beamline from the accelerator to the patient, and on the other, to drive the current with the most efficient angle to treat accurately the tumour. The gantry is made up of a large metallic structure weighing several tons, with large size and height of several floors. Consequently, some new developments limit the angle of rotation of the gantry to reduce the size and cost of the proton facilities [49].

Some research based on the follow-up of treatments dispensed in proton therapy centers for ten years, conclude that only certain orientations of the gantry are necessary for most cases. In other words, using a fixed gantry, a stretcher with a more versatile patient positioning system, more efficient immobilization systems, and more precise image guidance systems, smaller and cheaper proton therapy facilities would be possible, thus more proton therapy centers could be built, and more patients could have access to proton treatments [50]. However, even if technological advances in medical treatments and tools, could lead to reduce the size of proton therapy centers as conventional radiotherapy rooms, the operational radiological protection of these super-compact proton facilities would be an even more demanding challenge.

Currently, compact proton therapy centers are in full expansion throughout the world, therefore the study of the impact of these new developments on operational radiation protection, proposed in this work, is an important task that must be considered. Although the study of radiological protection in multi-room centers has been widely studied elsewhere, however, compact centers have specific features that pose a challenge in radiation protection, therefore the present work makes different contributions to the body of knowledge in these compact facilities. Considering the new methods of application of dose in development (flash therapy with proton, for example), future works must be carried out to study their impact on operational radiation protection.

In short, the results reached in the activities of the project, show that new CPTC have a relevant impact on the operational radiological protection and must be shaped to the challenges of these facilities. The contributions of radiological protection to achieve affordable proton centers and more patients benefit from these highly effective treatments should not be overlooked.

References

1. PTCOG. Proton Therapy Facilities: Homepage of Particle Therapy Co-Operative Group (2021). https://www.ptcog.ch. (Accessed March 2021)
2. International Atomic Energy Agency: Regulatory control of the safety of ion radiotherapy facilities, IAEA-TECDOC-1891. IAEA, Vienna (2020)
3. Yonekura, Y., et al.: Radiological protection in ion beam radiotherapy: practical guidance for clinical use of new technology. Ann. ICRP **45**(1_suppl), 138–147 (2016)
4. Bortfeld, T., Loeffler, J.: Three ways to make proton therapy affordable. Nature **549**, 451–453 (2017)
5. Depuydt, T.: Proton therapy technology evolution in the clinic: impact on radiation protection. Ann. ICRP **47**(3–4), 177–186 (2018)
6. Makita, Y., et al.: Radiation shielding design of a cancer therapy facility using compact proton synchrotron. J. Nucl. Sci. Technol. **41**(Supp. 4), 18–21 (2004)
7. NCRP: Radiation protection for particle acceleration facilities. Recommendations of the National Council, Report 144, Revision. NCRP (2005)
8. Ipe, N.E.: Shielding design and radiation safety of charged particle therapy facilities. PTCOG Report 1. Particle Therapy Cooperative Group (2010)
9. Urban, T., Kluson, J.: Shielding calculation for the Proton-Therapy-Center in Prague, Czech Republic. Radioprotection **4**, 583–597 (2012)
10. De Smet, V.: Secondary neutrons inside a proton therapy facility: MCNPX simulations compared to measurements performed with a Bonner Sphere Spectrometer and neutron H*(10) monitors. Radiat. Meas. **99**, 25–40 (2017)
11. Lomax, A.: What will the medical physics of proton therapy look like 10 years from now? A personal view. Med. Phys. **45**(11), e984–e993 (2018)
12. Hernalsteens, C., et al.: A novel approach to seamless simulations of compact HT for self-consistent evaluation of dosimetric and RP quantities. EPL **132**, N 5 (2020)
13. García-Fernández, G.F., Gallego, E., Nuñez, L.: Los nuevos Centros de Protonterapia en España. Radioprotección Magazine. **94**, 19–28 (2019). Publication of Spanish Society in Radiation Protection (SEPR)
14. García-Fernández, G.F., et al.: Neutron dosimetry and shielding verification in commissioning of CPTC using MCNP6.2 Monte Carlo code. Appl. Radiat. Isot. **169**, 109279 (2021)
15. García-Fernández, G.F., et al.: Intercomparing of stray neutron fields produced by synchro-cyclotrons and synchrotrons used in Compact Proton Therapy Centers. In: Nuclear España, J. Spanish Nuclear Society (SNE), online publication of better presentations at 45ª annual meeting of SNE (2020).

16. García-Fernández, G.F., et al.: Study of neutron activation in shielding of CPTC with different types of concrete using the MCNP6 code. Oral Presentation at Annual Meeting of Nuclear Spanish Society (2020). Online
17. García-Fernández, G.F., et al.: Monte Carlo characterization and benchmarking of extended range REM-meters for its application in shielding and radiation area monitoring in CPTC. Appl. Radiat. Isot. **152**, 115–126 (2019)
18. García-Fernández, G.F., et al.: Impact of new delivery techniques (PMAT, flash-therapy) in the commissioning of operational radiation protection in Compact Proton Therapy Centers (CPTC). In: Proceedings of 59th PTCOG 2021 Online. Oral presentation (2021)
19. García-Fernández, G.F., et al.: Assessment of individual neutron dosemeters in the design of the operational radiation protection in CPTC using MCNP6.2 and GEANT4 Monte Carlo Code. In: Proceedings of ISSSDXX. Oral Presentation (2020)
20. García-Fernández, G.F., et al.: A proposal to carry out the process of commissioning of the operational radiation protection in Compact Proton Therapy Centers (CPTC) summarized in ten recommendations. In: Proceedings of ISSSDXXI. Oral Presentation (2021)
21. Goorley, T.: Initial MCNP6 release overview. Nucl. Technol. **180**, 298–315 (2012)
22. Werner, Ch.J.: MCNP® User's manual, code Version 6.2. Report LA-UR-17–29981. National Laboratory, Los Alamos US (2017)
23. Ferraro, D., Brizuela, M.: Tests & benchmarking methodology for 230 MeV proton accelerator calculations. In: Conference Proceedings. AATN, XLLI Reunión Annual (2015)
24. McConn Jr., R., et al.: Compendium of material composition data for radiation transport modeling. Report PNNL-15870 Revision 1. PNNL. US (2011)
25. Tesse, R.: Quantitative methods to evaluate the radioprotection and shielding activation impacts of industrial and medical applications using particle accelerators. Doctoral thesis. ULB-EPB (2019)
26. Umezawa, M.: Development of compact proton beam therapy system for moving organs. Hitachi Rev. **64**(8), 86–93 (2015)
27. Han, S.E., Cho, G., Lee, S.B.: An assessment of the secondary neutron dose in the passive scattering proton beam facility of the National Cancer Center. Nucl. Eng. Technol. **49**, 801–809 (2017)
28. Verma, V., Shah, C., Rwigema, J.C.M., Solberg, T., Zhu, X., Simone II, C.B.: Cost-comparativeness of proton versus photon therapy. China Clin. Oncol. **5**(4), 56 (2016)
29. IAEA: Radiation protection in the design of radiotherapy facilities. International Atomic Energy Agency, Safety Reports Series 47, Vienna (2006)
30. Solc, J.: Comparison of proton interaction physics models and cross section libraries for proton therapy Monte Carlo simulations by MCNP6.2 code. Radiat. Meas. **125**, 57–68 (2019)
31. ICRP: Conversion coefficients for use in radiological protection against external radiation. Ann. ICRP **26**, (3–4). ICRP Publication 74 (1996)
32. Gallego, E., Lorente, A., Vega-Carrillo, H.R.: Characteristics of the neutron fields of the facility at DIN-UPM. Radiat. Prot. Dosim. **110**, 73–79 (2004)
33. Sannikov, A.V., Savitskaya, E.N.: Ambient dose equivalent conversion factors for high energy neutrons based on the ICRP 60 recommendations. RPD **70**, 383–386 (1997)
34. Chadwick, M.B., et al.: ENDF/B-VII.1 nuclear data for science and technology: cross sections, covariances, fission product yields and decay data. Nucl. Data Sheets **112**, 2887 (2011)
35. Conlin, J.L.: Listing of available ACE data tables. Report LA-UR-13–21822, Rev. 4. Los Alamos National Laboratory, US (2014)
36. Plompen, A.J.M., Cabellos, O., et al.: The joint evaluated fission and fusion nuclear data library, JEFF-3.3. Eur. Phys. J. A **56**, 181 (2020)
37. Koning, A.J., Rochman, D.: Modern nuclear data evaluation with the TALYS code system. Nucl. Data Sheets **113**, 2841–2934 (2012)

38. Shultis, J.K., Faw, R.E.: An MCNP primer. Kansas State University, KS, 66506 (2011)
39. Gallego, E., Lorente, A., Vega-Carrillo, H.R.: Testing of a high-density concrete as neutron shielding material. Nucl. Technol. **162**, 399–404 (2009)
40. Vega-Carrillo, H.R., Guzmán-García, K.A., Rodríguez-Rodríguez, J.A.: Photon and neutron shielding features of quarry tuff. Ann. Nucl. Energy **112**, 411–417 (2018)
41. Olsher, R.H., et al.: WENDI: an improved neutron rem meter. Health Phys. **79**, 170–181 (2000)
42. Caresana, M., et al.: A new version of the LUPIN detector: improvements and latest experimental verification. Rev. Sci. Instrum. **85**(2014). https://doi.org/10.1063/1.4879936
43. Olsher, R.H., et al.: PRESCILA: a new, lightweight neutron rem-meter. Health Phys. (6), 603–612 (2004)
44. García-Baonza, R., García-Fernández, G.F., Cevallos-Robalino, L.E., Gallego, E.: Analysis by Monte Carlo methods of the response of an extended-range Bonner Sphere Spectrometer. Appl. Radiat. Isot. **163**, 109196 (2019)
45. Carabe-Fernández, A., Bertolet, A., Karagounis, I., Huynh, K., Dale, R.G.: Is there a role for arcing techniques in proton therapy? Br. J. Radiol. **93**, 1107 (2019)
46. Carabe-Fernández, A., et al.: Radiobiological effectiveness difference of proton arc beams versus conventional proton and photon beams. Phys. Med. Biol. **65**, 165002 (2020)
47. Yan, S.: Compact gantry-less proton therapy system to increase the availability to patients. Int. Organ. Med. Phys. IOMP online (2020)
48. Bortfeld, T., Viana, M., Yan, S.: The societal impact of ion beam therapy. Zeitschrift fur medizinische Physik (2021)
49. Mazal, A., et al.: Biological and mechanical synergies to deal with proton therapy pitfalls: minibeams, FLASH, Arcs, and Gantryless Rooms. Front. Oncol. **10**, 613669 (2021)
50. Yan, S., et al.: Reassessment of the necessity of the proton gantry: analysis of beam orientations from 4332 treatments at the Massachusetts General Hospital proton center over the past 10 years. Int. J. Radiat. Oncol. Biol. Phys. **95**(1), 224–33 (2016)

Management System Using Fuzzy Logic for Reference Governors in Solar Field Systems: A Case Study in Hospitals

Cristhian García Acosta[1], Gary Ampuño Avilés[1]([✉]) [iD], and Francisco Jurado[2] [iD]

[1] Universidad Politécnica Salesiana, Chambers 227 y 5 de junio, 090109 Guayaquil, Ecuador
cgarcia@est.ups.edu.ec, gampuno@ups.edu.ec
[2] Department of Electrical Engineering, EPS Linares, University of Jaén, 23700 Jaén, Spain
fjurado@ujaen.es

Abstract. This paper describes implementing models of a solar-assisted heat generation system for preheating water at the inlet of boilers in hospitals, which they used for both simulation and control. The following models are developed based on static and dynamic energy, mass balances, and step response methods (experimental tests). The main objective of the heat generation system is to supply the boilers in hospitals with hot water within a specific temperature range, using thermal storage tanks as input buffers to the system. The main achievement of this work was to add a hierarchical controller based on fuzzy logic that provides an adequate balance between complexity and performance. As a result, at startup, generator decision-making is very close to human oversight in the face of significant disturbances caused by passing clouds and large setpoint changes.

Keywords: Dynamic simulation · Solar energy · Hospital boilers · Fuzzy logic controller · Automatic setpoint generator · Solar field systems

1 Introduction

According to global development indicators, one of the main challenges to be reversed is the high concentration of greenhouse gases (GHG) due to fossil fuels in electricity generation applications and industrial processes [1, 2]. One of the means to achieve GHG reduction is the use of technologies to convert solar energy into electricity. Among the leading technologies are photovoltaic (PV) [3] and concentrating solar thermal (CST).

The most commonly used solar collectors [4, 5] for fluid heating at temperatures up to 200 °C are flat plate, parabolic compound, and vacuum tube; while for fluid heating at temperatures up to 400 °C, parabolic collectors, Fresnel lenses, parabolic dishes, and heliostat fields are used.

© Springer Nature Switzerland AG 2021
J. P. Salgado Guerrero et al. (Eds.): TICEC 2021, CCIS 1456, pp. 313–325, 2021.
https://doi.org/10.1007/978-3-030-89941-7_22

In works such as [6], the authors reviewed the use of solar energy in industries and indicated the various situations in which it is possible to use solar energy. On the other hand, [7] evaluated the potential of applying different collectors for hot water demand in industry and used life cycle savings as a decision criterion.

Research where the technical and financial evaluation of a heating and cooling system is developed as in [8, 9] and used solar energy as a hospital source. We used the TRN-SYS program for the development of the simulation model. The work investigated the influence of cooling water temperature and temperature on the performance coefficient of the absorption chiller and proposed alternatives for the heat sink.

In Ecuador, an example of solar thermal energy is the project implemented at the Roberto Gilbert Children's Hospital of the Junta de Beneficencia de Guayaquil in Guayaquil [10]. It was considered the 2016 Green Latin America Award winner for implementing a field of solar panels that preheat the water for the boiler system. The boilers feed hot water to the hospital for laundry and steam generation. Due to the changing weather conditions, it is important to have reference temperature set point generators that allow for the optimal start-up of the solar collector plants. It is considering the temperature demands and constraints that will affect the plant, the setpoint.

The novelty of the present work is in the design and simulation of a hierarchical control using fuzzy logic to maximize the benefits of hot water production [11, 12].

This paper is structured as follows. After the introduction, Sect. 2 presents the modeling of the solar collector field. Section 3 shows the testing of the solar thermal. Section 4 studies the implementation of a PI controller and a predictive controller based on the model. Section 5 implements the fuzzy logic reference generator. Finally, there are the results and conclusions of the paper.

2   Description of the Solar Field System

The facility located at the Roberto Gilbert Hospital (see Fig. 1) has a flat solar field supplying process heat to an industrial system, in this case, the boiler. This plant aims to preheat the water entering the boiler using the large-aperture static solar-resistive collectors coupled with to steam generation processes. Figure 1 also shows the layout of this plant which consists of two main circuits; the primary circuit is the heat generation system. The secondary circuit is the consumption system composed of the boiler.

This work deals with the modeling and simulation of the primary circuit, the heat generation system based on solar energy, composed of the solar field, a heat exchanger, and the connecting pipes. The static solar field (Distributed Collector System, DCS) comprises 72 collectors distributed among three loops connected in parallel. Each loop consists of 24 flat collectors. Each bottle has its pumping system so that it can work independently. Solar radiation is the primary source of energy. Solar radiation is not manipulable and acts as a disturbance from the point of view of control. The fluid flow controlled by the pump determines the output temperature of the solar field [13–15]. Depending on the operation requirements (characterization of the solar field, the process heat for the boiler), the hot fluid of the solar field goes directly to a heat exchanger. Later, in the secondary circuit, the water increases its temperature and accumulates in the thermal storage tanks. Table 1 describes the nomenclature used in this work.

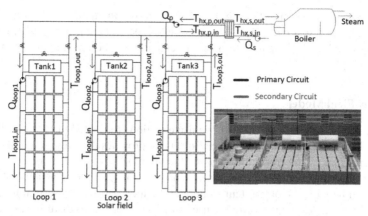

Fig. 1. Solar collector system located at the Roberto Gilbert Children's Hospital in the city of Guayaquil.

3 Model of the Solar-Assisted Heat Generation System

This section presents the mathematical models based on the differential equations of the system. In studies such as [16], the authors perform tests and validate the distributed parameter model. In turn, works such as [17, 18] ratify the functioning of the distributed parameter model through current investigations.

As will be explained in Sect. 3.1, given that the solar field model is a model of concentrated parameters, some of the inputs delay reproducing the actual plant's dynamic behavior. The model provides the outlet temperature of each loop. Depending on the mode of operation, the desired output can be $T_{hx,in}$, which is the input of the heat exchanger model.

Table 1. Nomenclature

Symbol	Description	Unit
Q_{loopj}	Volumetric flow in the loop j ($j = 1..3$)	L min^{-1}
Q_p	Volumetric flow in the primary circuit	L min^{-1}
Q_s	Volumetric flow in the secondary circuit	L min^{-1}
$T_{loopj,in}$	Inlet temperature in the loop j ($j = 1..3$)	°C
$T_{loopj,out}$	Outlet temperature in the loop j ($j = 1..3$)	°C
$T_{hx,p,in}$	Input temperature in the primary circuit	°C
$T_{hx,p,out}$	Outlet temperature in the primary circuit	°C
$T_{hx,s,in}$	Input t temperature in the secondary circuit	°C
$T_{hx,s,out}$	Outlet temperature in the secondary circuit	°C
Q_{loopj}	Volumetric flow in the primary circuit	L min^{-1}

It is essential to mention that, in the primary circuit, the temperature sensors used for the validation are at the end of each solar field loop and the heat exchanger's input and output (see Fig. 1). Due to the transport delay in the tubes, a delay in the model is incorporated [15].

3.1 Solar Field Model

To model each loop of the solar field, we use equations presented in [13, 14, 19]. It is a model of concentrated parameters (see Eq. 1) that provides the evolution of the outlet temperature, $T_{loopj,out}(t)$ (for the case of the loop number j ($j = 1..3$)), considering that a hypothetical equivalent flat collector tube has the same behavior as any solar field loop. As can be seen, the output temperature of the loop depends on several inputs; the manipulated one, $Q_{loop}(t)$ is the volumetric flow. The others act as disturbances: $Tl_{oopj,n}(t)$ is the inlet temperature, $T_a(t)$ la room temperature, y $I(t)$ es la solar irradiation. The equations that model the dynamics of the output temperature of the loops are:

$$\rho C_p A_{cs} \frac{\partial T_{loopj,out}(t)}{\partial t}$$
$$= \beta I - \frac{H}{L_{eq}}(T_m(t) - T_a(t)) \qquad (1)$$
$$- \frac{\rho}{C_f} C_p Q_{loopj}(t) \frac{T_{loopj,out}(t) - T_{loopj,in}(t - d_{tout-tin})}{L_{eq}},$$

$$\tilde{T}(t) = \frac{T_{loopj,out}(t) + T_{loopj,in}(t - d_{tout-tin})}{2} \qquad (2)$$

Where ρ is the density of water, c_p is the specific heat capacity. A_{cs} is the cross-sectional area of the flat collector tube. Leq is the length of the equivalent flat collector tube. H is the coefficient of thermal losses $J \cdot s^{-1} \cdot {}^\circ C^{-1}$. β is a parameter that modulates the solar radiation component, $\tilde{T}(t)$ is the average temperature of the equivalent plane collector tube and equivalent flat plate collector tube, and c_f is a conversion factor to have the number of modules connections and conversion L min^{-1} [19].

3.2 Comparison Between Controllers

This section shows the results obtained from the simulations of the proposed models and compares them with the actual data of solar collector fields in works by authors such as [13] and [20].

To compare the performance of the implemented controllers, we used the same irradiation conditions, ambient temperature, and inlet temperature, considering 5 h duration presented by Vergara [20]. The irradiance profiles are in Fig. 2 and the inlet temperatures in Fig. 3.

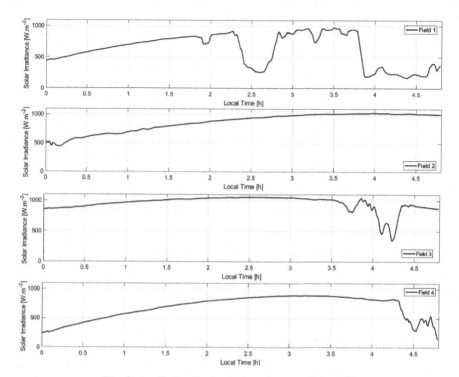

Fig. 2. Irradiation for the different sectors of the field

Using scenarios with different irradiances, we compared the PID, MPC, and PNMPC controllers. To quantify the results, we analyze the system's efficiency, the amount of heat available from the layout, and the resulting total flux, as presented in Fig. 4.

In addition, the root means square error (RMSE) and mean absolute error (MAE) has been calculated for the simulation time to analyze the control effort and reference tracking, respectively, as shown in Table 2.

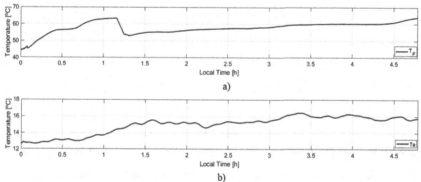

Fig. 3. (a) Inlet temperature at the solar collectors and (b) ambient temperature

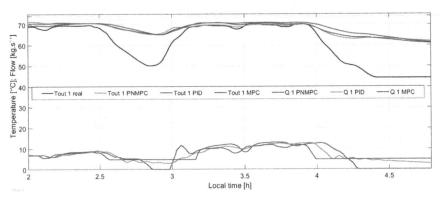

a) Results of the outlet temperature and flow in sector 1 of the solar collector field

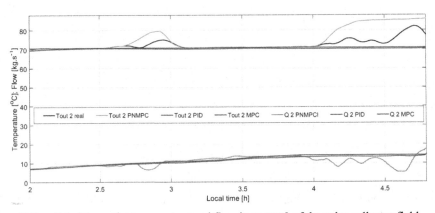

b) Results of the outlet temperature and flow in sector 2 of the solar collector field

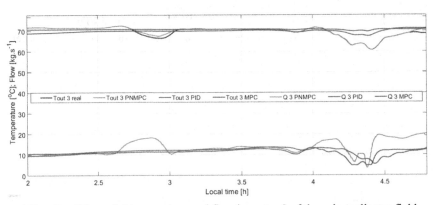

c) Results of the outlet temperature and flow in sector 3 of the solar collector field

Fig. 4. Outlet temperature in solar collectors with different controllers

Table 2. MAE and RMSE error results

	MPC		PID		PNMPC	
	RMSE	MAE	RMSE	MAE	RMSE	MAE
Field 1	2,46 °C	6,42 °C	3,02 °C	7,35 °C	8,83 °C	17,99 °C
Field 2	0,79 °C	0,91 °C	0,32 °C	0,62 °C	5,95 °C	15,15 °C
Field 3	0,69 °C	0,82 °C	0,73 °C	2,57 °C	2,67 °C	9,25 °C
Field 4	0,67 °C	0,77 °C	0,18 °C	0,49 °C	2,78 °C	6,66 °C

4 Reference Generators

The reference generators are part of a two-layer hierarchical control structure, which allows the ideal setpoint to be calculated automatically and reasonably based on a series of constraints identified in the design analysis. Figure 5 presents the structure of a multi-layer control, where the first layer is the regulation layer (controllers) and a second layer consisting of the setpoint generator.

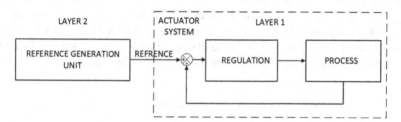

Fig. 5. Multi-layer hierarchical control scheme

In the solar collector field, layer 2 aims to find the reference temperature according to meteorological conditions such as irradiation and ambient temperature. Among the main objectives of a setpoint, the generator provides a start and stop of the plant that safely avoids critical points.

4.1 Fuzzy Logic Generator Development

One of the techniques employed in the development of fuzzy logic-based setpoint generators is fuzzy logic. Furthermore, it is widely used due to its similarity with human reasoning. FLCs do not use complex mathematical equations but rather apply experience and knowledge (acquired by a process operator). In solar collector fields, the two most influential variables when determining the appropriate setpoint are the solar radiation I and the fluid temperature at the solar field inlet T_{in}. The input I indicate the maximum possible increase in the fluid temperature inside the solar field. In contrast, the input T_{in} indicates the fluid's temperature at the start of the process. The above ensures that the maximum possible value to be achieved is within the safety limits ΔT.

For both I and Tin, it is necessary to construct the universes of discourse covering the minimum and maximum ranges of solar radiation levels and the inlet temperature of the fluid to the solar collector field (15 °C to 70 °C). The membership functions are triangular, being on the left side of type L and the right end of type Gamma as seen in Fig. 6; where the sets are based on three levels with linguistic values "very low" (VL), "Low" (L), "medium-low" (ML), "Medium" (M), High (H), "very high" (VA).

Figure 6 shows the resulting surface with the data entered in the Fuzzy logic design tool of Matlab, where the radiation levels range from 0 W.m^{-2} to 1100 W.m^{-2} with intervals of 27 W.m^{-2} and from 15 °C to 70 °C in 1.8 °C intervals. The reference temperature T_{ref} increases as I and T_{in} increase. If there is a large amount of solar energy, it is possible to increase the temperature at the output of the solar field. Table 3 shows the implemented knowledge base that relates the linguistic values of the input temperature and solar radiation to those of the reference temperature.

Table 3. Tref - Knowledge base linking linguistic values.

	Inputs: Solar irradiation and inlet temperature		Output: Reference temperature
Rules	I	Tin	Tref
1	L	VL	VL
2	L	L	VL
⋮			⋮
17	H	H	H
18	H	MH	VH

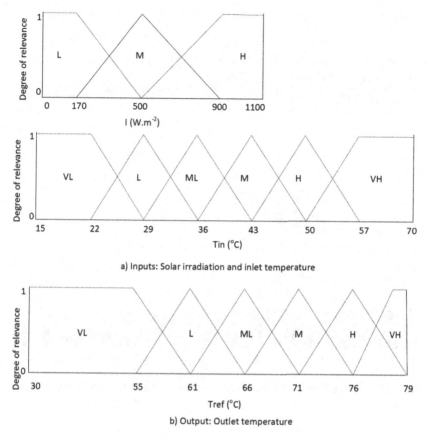

a) Inputs: Solar irradiation and inlet temperature

b) Output: Outlet temperature

Fig. 6. Fuzzy sets of input and output.

We set up a control algorithm representing layer 1 (regulation) to test the fuzzy logic-based reference generator (Fig. 7). Figure 8 shows the multilayer hierarchical control scheme applying the fuzzy logic setpoint generator (Layer 2) and the MPC control tested above. The setpoint changes automatically according to the solar radiation levels and the input temperature of the solar field. The setpoint is input to the MPC control algorithm, which calculates the required flow rate to have the minimum error between T_{out} and T_{ref}.

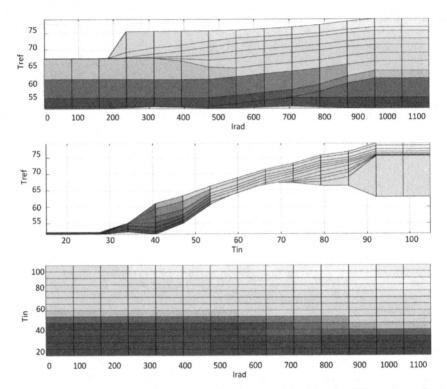

Fig. 7. T_{ref} surface generated by the speech universes of I and T_{in} for different intervals.

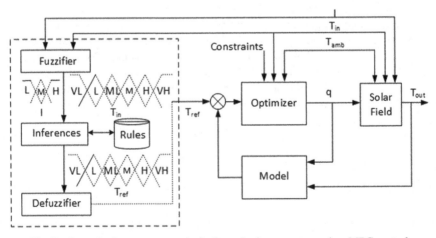

Fig. 8. Control scheme composed of a fuzzy logic generator and an MPC control.

4.2 Simulation Results

The experiments shown in the following section are variations of the experiments carried out with actual data entered into the model and implemented in the scheme composed of the fuzzy logic generator with MPC control of the solar field. The objective of these tests is to verify that the algorithm correctly generates a T_{ref} whose behavior is by the safety constraints of the plant.

Figure 9 shows a test where the solar radiation is at maximum, and therefore the system start-up starts at maximum. We observe how T_{ref} evolves as a function of increasing T_{in}. In this case, the field sets the minimum flow rate of the inlet pump (4.8 kg.s^{-1} safety range), intending to keep the fluid longer in the field and raise the temperature immediately.

At the end of the test, we notice a drop in solar radiation I and observe how the fuzzy logic generator calculates a T_{ref} taking into account the change in I, thus keeping the temperature increase levels within the safety limits. When solar radiation decreases, the Tref does not increase and remains at levels below 67 °C.

The test in Fig. 10 shows a test on a cloudy day. The generator's response is to make a smooth decrease (steps) in T_{ref} if it detects that solar radiation has varied considerably for a considerable time. For some time (about 25 min, around 11 o'clock), the radiation drops below 300 W.m^{-2}. Regardless of the flow rate generated, since there is no thermal energy, T_{out} drops due to thermal losses. The setpoint generator sets the setpoint to the minimum set above T_{in}. As the solar energy increases, the control algorithm recovers the track without oscillations from the accumulation of the error.

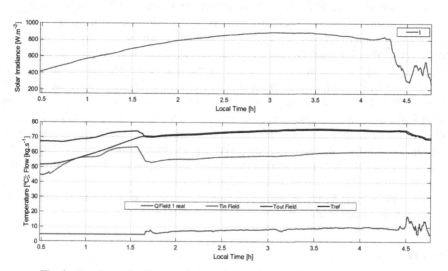

Fig. 9. Results of the fuzzy logic-based slogan generation for a cloudless day

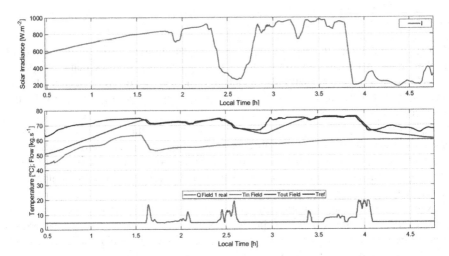

Fig. 10. Results of the fuzzy logic-based setpoint generation for a day with passing clouds

5   Conclusions

The presented work shows the development of three controllers for the proper use of fluid temperature at the outlet of solar fields. The development of the controls requires the incorporation of restrictions. These restrictions are considered minimum and maximum values that ensure the useful life of the equipment and avoid accidents in the plant.

The developed algorithms test different operating conditions on the plant model to contrast which three controllers demonstrate acceptable behavior. The results show that predictive control is reasonable even in situations with significant disturbances caused by cloud passages, great setpoint changes, or plant start-up. The results are verified visually and numerically, using mean square error rates (RMSE) and mean absolute error (MAE). We also describe the use of an automatic setpoint generator based on fuzzy logic. The generator implemented in the plant is a two-layer hierarchical control scheme. We performed several tests under various operating conditions. As a result, at start-up, the generator decision-making is very close to human supervision, ensuring the life time of the solar field components because of the temperature limit constraints and actuator limits that are input to the hierarchical control.

An improvement to the setpoint generator is to add the energy production costs incurred during plant operation.

References

1. Bonissone, P.P., Badami, V., Chiang, K.H., Khedkar, P.S., Marcelle, K.W., Schutten, M.J.: Industrial Applications of fuzzy logic at general electric. Proc. IEEE **83**(3), 450–465 (1995). https://doi.org/10.1109/5.364490
2. Pezeshki, Z., Mazinani, S.M.: Comparison of artificial neural networks, fuzzy logic and neuro fuzzy for predicting optimization of building thermal consumption: a survey. Artif. Intell. Rev. **52**(1), 495–525 (2019). https://doi.org/10.1007/s10462-018-9630-6

3. Killian, M., Kozek, M.: Implementation of cooperative Fuzzy model predictive control for an energy-efficient office building. Energy Build. **158**, 1404–1416 (2018). https://doi.org/10.1016/j.enbuild.2017.11.021
4. Singh, J., Singh, N., Sharma, J.K.: Fuzzy modeling and control of HVAC systems - a review. J. Sci. Ind. Res. (India) **65**(6), 470–476 (2006)
5. Qin, S.J., Badgwell, T.A.: A survey of industrial model predictive control technology. Control Eng. Pract. **11**, 733–764 (2003)
6. Mekhilef, S., Saidur, R., Safari, A.: A review on solar energy use in industries. Renew. Sustain. Energy Rev. **15**, 1777–1790 (2011)
7. Kalogirou, S.: The potential of solar industrial process heat applications. Appl. Energy **76**, 337–361 (2003)
8. Tsoutsos, T., Aloumpi, E., Gkouskos, Z., Karagiorgas, M.: Design of a solar absorption cooling system in a Greek hospital. Energy Build. **42**, 265–272 (2010)
9. Monne, C., Alonso, S., Palacín, F., Serra, F.: Monitoring and simulation of an existing solar powered absorption cooling system in Zaragoza (Spain). Appl. Therm. Eng. **31**, 28–35 (2011)
10. Hospital Roberto Gilbert: Iniciativa sustentable es reconocida en Premios Latinoamérica Verde. Rev. médica la Junta Benefic (2016). https://www.hospitalrobertogilbert.med.ec/noticias/17-noticias/1522-iniciativasustentable-premios-latinoamerica-verde
11. Cirre, C.M., Berenguel, M., Valenzuela, L., Klempous, R.: Reference governor optimization and control of a distributed solar collector field. Eur. J. Oper. Res. **193**(3), 709–717 (2009). https://doi.org/10.1016/j.ejor.2007.05.056
12. Ampuño, G., Agila, W., Cevallos, H.: Implementación y analisis de rendimiento de un control industrial de nivel para tanques con fluidos, basado en lógica difusa. MASKANA I+D+ingeniería **5**, 27–36 (2015)
13. Roca, L., Guzmán, J., Normey-Rico, J., Berenguel, M., Yebra, J.: Robust constrained predictive feedback linearization controller in a solar desalination plant collector field. Control Eng. Prac. **17**, 1076–1088 (2009)
14. Ampuño, G., Roca, L., Berenguel, M., Gil, J.D., Pérez, M., Normey-Rico, J.E.: Modeling and simulation of a solar field based on flat-plate collectors. Sol. Energy **170**(May), 369–378 (2018)
15. Ampuño, G., Roca, L., Gil, J.D., Berenguel, M., Normey-Rico, J.E.: Apparent delay analysis for a flat-plate solar field model designed for control purposes. Sol. Energy **177**(November), 241–254 (2018). https://doi.org/10.1016/j.solener.2018.11.014
16. Guney, M.S.: Solar power and application methods. Renew. Sustain. Energy Rev. **57**, 776–785 (2016)
17. Khan, J., Arsalan, M.H.: Solar power technologies for sustainable electricity generation—A review. Renew. Sustain. Energy Rev. **55**, 414–425 (2016)
18. Carmona, R.: Análisis Modelado y Control de un Campo de Colectores Solares Distribuidos con un Sistema de Seguimiento de un eje. Ph.D. thesis, Universidad de Sevilla, Sevilla, Spain (1985)
19. Gil, J.D., Ruiz-Aguirre, A., Roca, L., Zaragoza, G., Berenguel, M.: Solar membrane distillation: a control perspective. In: 23th Mediterranean Conference on Control and Automation, MED-2015, Málaga, Spain (2015)
20. Vergara, J.: Contribuicoes ao controle preditivo e otimizacao com aplicacoes. Universidade Federal de Santa Catarina (2019)

Biomedical Sensors and Wearables Systems

Liquid-Based Pap Test Analysis Using Two-Stage CNNs

Oswaldo Toapanta Maila[✉][iD] and Oscar Chang[iD]

School of Mathematical and Computational Sciences, Yachay Tech University,
100650 Urcuquí, Ecuador
bryan.toapanta@yachaytech.edu.ec

Abstract. According to the World Health Organization (WHO) cervix cancer is a real threat for women at earthly level. A practice to avoid those losses is an early diagnosis of the disease, generally done with the Papanicolaou or Pap test. This requires for a pathologist to check pap smear images in an arduous assignment, to determine the existence of suspicious or cancer cells. In third world countries doctors checks pap smear manually with microscopes, creating an enormous deficit of service. This paper proposes a TensorFlow ambient where the analysis of digital pap smears is carry out as a two-stage process. First, the sample is scanned using a ROI of 150×150 pixels and two versions of the resulting image are stored in separated lists; one of low resolution (20×20 pixels) and one of high resolution (250×250 pixels). Then for the analysis, the first stage quickly evaluates the low-resolution images using a neural network that detects cells shapes saving their index (coordinates). In the second stage a specialized deep network uses this index to locate the high resolution images of the detected cells for zooming and recognition, being finally able to make high-resolution classifications. The software uses liquid-based pap smear equivalent to 460 patients with a 40x magnification. The trained system successfully classifies cells into normal and abnormal and could be big help to overloaded pathologists.

Keywords: Neural network · Pap smear · Cell · Cervix cancer · Screen · Two-stage

1 Introduction

Of all the types of cancer, cervical cancer has one of the most significant death rates, being in the fourth position worldwide and mostly affecting less developed areas like Latin America and Africa. There are two methods to prevent cervical cancer, HPV vaccine and screening (Pap smear). Since most cervical cancer cases develop from HPV infections, providing HPV vaccines to women at young ages is crucial to reduce cervical cancer risk. Also, cervical cancer takes years to develop; that is why periodical screening is essential to detect this disease at early stages, incrementing possible treatments' effectiveness [2,23]. Both mentioned methods

J. P. Salgado Guerrero et al. (Eds.): TICEC 2021, CCIS 1456, pp. 329–344, 2021.
https://doi.org/10.1007/978-3-030-89941-7_23

have shown high efficacy, reducing mortality and incidence rates; for example, since the USA implemented widespread screening, cervical cancer cases have dropped more than 50% [20]. However, that is not the reality for all the countries; by 2008, the Institute for Health Metrics and Evaluation at the University of Washington showed countries with the highest global wealth decile achieved a 64% of women getting effective cervical screens, while countries with the lowest global wealth just reached a 9% [3]. Additionally, a projection made in 2019 shows that countries with low and medium human development indexes (HDI) will achieve just 10% and 20% of screening coverage by 2023; this could be the case of Ecuador, which was scored with a medium HDI of 0.759 by the United Nations in 2019 [17,21]. In particular in Ecuador, cervix cancer is the second with the most prominent incidence and mortality [4]. One of the obstacles in Latin America to improve the number of cervix cancer screens is the amount of time needed to give results. In Ecuador, laboratories take up to one month to give pap smear analysis results, and in other third world countries, this time can increase up to 3 months [1]. This problem with delayed results opened a new field where technologies can help to accelerate the process, especially Artificial Neural Networks (ANN) [11,18]. In particular, neural network classification systems are optimal tools to speed up the screening process since cervical cancer screening is a matter of cell classification.

This paper presents a fast cell recognition system with two stage classification using convolutional networks in TensorFlow ambient. Two main processes are involved in the proposed method: a low-resolution scanning for quick cell detection and location and a second high-resolution one, for detailed classification. The program categorizes cells into two types: Negative for intra-epithelial malignancy or Normal Cells and Abnormal Cells (which includes low and high squamous intraepithelial lesion and squamous cell carcinoma). The usefulness of this classification is that pathologists can save time by meticulously evaluating just those samples declared with abnormal cells, incrementing the number of patients that can be attended. The proposed classifier system uses a database of 963 liquid-based pap smear digital images, corresponding to 460 patients with a 40x magnification using a Leica ICC50 HD microscope [6]. This challenging set of images are classified covering from the most abnormal cell found in it to completely healthy ones, so all cells fit inside this broad range. For training purposes it was necessary to create a database of isolated, individual cells and manually labeled them to train the used deep neural networks. To improve the performance this work introduces an evaluation method that avoids robust categorization across all sample image sections and focuses its effort on essential areas, being the final objective to reduce the overall processing time.

2   Related Work

Su et al. implemented a system for cervical cancer cell classification in samples of liquid-based cytology. The primary purpose of the presented method by the authors was to create a high-accuracy sort. To achieve the wanted accuracy, they used a cascade implementation with two different classification systems, one applied after another. Each system classifies evaluating distinct features like roundness, area, diameter, etc., all extracted with pixels counting and calculation rather than using neural networks, like other existent methods [19]. Although applying the cascade structure showed high accuracy because the classification systems complement each other, the proposed method focuses on manually isolated cells. Therefore, adding an extra technique to automatize cell extraction for later classification would be feasible.

Kumar et al. presented a framework for cancer detection and classification in 2015. The mentioned framework consisted of four processes: enhancing microscope images, segmenting background cells, extracting features, and classifying them. Kumar et al. used histogram equalization to modify image contrast in the image enhancement stage; K-means algorithm to perform segmentation; pixels calculations using their intensity, presence, and distribution to determine morphological features; and neural networks, random forest, among others for the classification stage [9]. This method differs from the previously mentioned because it works on the image as a whole instead of working in specific sections or elements.

Hussain et al. presented a cell classifier method based purely on nucleus analysis. The authors used convolutional networks and auto-encoder for nuclei segmentation and later classification. The technique works on the whole cervical sample by predicting nuclei pixels and highlighting their contour to differentiate them when evaluating clustered nuclei. This project works directly in the given cervix sample, avoiding image preprocessing techniques, common in automated cell classification. According to their evaluation, the method's accuracy was 96% for categorization in normal and abnormal cells. However, it is worth mentioning that this method does not consider any other cell feature than the nuclei [7].

Shanthi et al. proposed a cervix cell classification system based on a neural network. The proposed model uses the pap smear Herlev databases and a convolutional neural network to extract cell image characteristics like edges, size, etc. [8]. The authors used image processing techniques like Bi-histogram equalization, Sobel operator, brightness changes, etc., to highlight essential cell features like the nucleus and cytoplasm contour. The project uses supervised neural networks to classify cells into a minimum of two classes (normal and abnormal) and a maximum of five (normal, mild, moderate, and carcinoma), with high accuracies of above 92%. Experimental results were obtained by testing the neural networks in a group of isolated cell images [15].

William et al. presented an analysis method for pap-smear based on segmentation and the analysis of cell features like shape, texture, and size of the nucleus and cytoplasm. The performance achieved accuracy, sensitivity, and specificity of 98.88%, 99.28%, and 97.47%. The main contribution of this technique is the time reduction by discarding the evident normal cells. This method relays in Fuzzy C-means; However, the author clarifies that it is worth a deep learning implementation to improve the results [22].

3   Methodology

The used pap images were retrieved from the Mendeley data repository and correspond to the liquid-based cytology of 460 patients. The original data-set image size is 2048 × 1536 pixels, but they were standardized to a width of 1080 pixels conserving the authentic width-height relationship, by using the "Open cv-python" library. This reduction was performed to facilitate visualization since the used computer had a resolution of 1920 × 1080 pixels, and original dimensions exceeded this limit. This modification was made to make observations but it is not essential in the proposed model.

A typical cervical pap test image contains an average of 20 cells, increasing up to approximately 50. It is not efficient to train a convolutional neural network with images containing this amount of elements because they represent too many objects to be simultaneously evaluated and with too many intricate details. A better approach, followed by human specialists, is to concentrate the attention and "zoom" into attractive individual cells, taking a closer look at them and assessing their characteristics for classification in pertinent categories. Following this line of action this projects develops a fast scanning process that takes a "quick look" with low resolution at the whole pap test sample and determine the coordinates of possible target cells. After that just the target cells are later zoomed in and fed to a high-resolution TensorFlow lassifier model.

3.1   Software

The language used for the implementation was Python 3.8. TensorFlow 2.2.0 library was used for the neural network implementation and the Opencv-contrib-python-4.4.0.46 library was used to display the analyzed images and track the process by making graphic representations.

3.2   Hardware

- Intel(R) Core(TM) i7-6500U CPU @ 2.50 GHz, 2601 MHz, 2 principal processors, 4 logic processors
- 12 GB RAM
- NVIDIA GeForce 940M.

3.3   Region of Interest

The region of interest (ROI) refers to the smaller current analyzed section of a bigger image. Since the proposed method requires a fast cell scanning system, the ROI size was set according to the cell average size. For the practical working software, the average cell size and the ROI size are 150 × 150 pixels. This value fits the 1080 width size pap test standardized measure, but the ROI size should be recalibrated for another dimensions.

3.4   Batch Size

The batch size defines how frequently weights and bias values in the convolutional neural network are updated. Both CNN models were implemented using a 32 mini-batch size since previous studies found that this and lower values yield better results [12]. Due to computing limitation the batch size was limited to 32, otherwise the used laptop collapsed. In principle this can be overcame using more powerful hardware involving CUDA and GPU.

3.5   Epoch

Epoch is a hyperparameter that always depends on the whole neural network architecture. Therefore, there is no rule to choose the best value but try several ones until good results are obtained, avoiding overfitting and underfitting. In the case of the cell recognition model, with 100 epochs training, good predictions were obtained. While in the classifier model, 200 epochs were necessary to get valuable predictions. It should be mentioned that, when training, the user classifier model showed overfitting above 373 epochs.

3.6   Activation Function

Activation functions depend on the task the neural network is performing. Based on a study made in 2017, the chosen function for all hidden layers in both models is the Relu activation function because it gives better results in most cases and is suitable for many hidden layers [16]. The chosen activation function for the output layers was softmax because its good performance in binary and multiple classifications, which fall in the category classification requirements of the two models.

3.7   Dropout

Dropout is a regularization technique essential for complex convolutional neural networks because it reduces or avoids overfitting probability. The dropout value determines the percentage of neurons that will be ignored; thus, values over 0.5 are avoided because they turn out sabotaging the model training [14]. Considering the mentioned information the classification model's dropout value was 0.3. On the other hand, the recognition model architecture does not include dropout layers to keep it as simple as possible to reduce its running time.

3.8   Maxpooling

Maxpooling is a technique used to lower overfitting by conserving just the neurons' group's most significant value. The value in the maxpooling filter determines the size of the evaluated group. Both models were set with maxpooling layers of 2×2 in both cases. Implementing the Cell Classification CNN without maxpooling layers produced the laptop to crash due to hardware limitation.

3.9   Filters

The dimensions of the images evaluated by the filters correspond to the standard size used to train each model. These models are explained in Sects. 3.11 and 3.12. Filters are a matter of try and error selection. However, using smaller filters usually detects small characteristics. Therefore the point of reference was to use small filters for the classifier model because cell features are essential to differentiate categories, choosing 3 × 3 filters for the 250 × 250 pixels images. On the contrary, the cell recognition model was set with more extensive filters because it does not need to identify all cell details to determine its presence, choosing 10 × 10 filters for the 20 × 20 pixels images. The number of filters was selected by trial and error, resulting in layers with 10, 32, 40, and 64 filters. The architectures' exact distributions are specified in 3.11 and 3.12.

3.10   Strides and Padding

Strides determine the steps filters move across the analyzed data, and padding completes the empty spaces with zeros when the filter stands in the image borders. For both cases, strides are set to 1 for vertical and horizontal displacement, which is the TensorFlow ambient's default value. Padding was deactivated since it's been shown that it affects the data variance and affects the CNN training [13].

3.11   Cell Recognition Model Implementation

Data Preparation. For this work it was necessary to select several images from the liquid-based pap smear dataset so that all the desired categories are covered. The photos are analyzed to recognize the average cell size and use this value for the ROI size in forthcoming processes. By experimenting, the average cell size selected was 150 by 150 pixels. Later, by using an available photo editor program, sections of the images containing cells were manually cut out and saved. The used photo editor program was Adobe Photoshop 2020, and the criteria used to select the mentioned sections were:

- Sections that meet the ROI size.
- Areas containing a centered cervical cell, regardless of its condition.
- Areas containing cervical cell cluster.

Besides these images, sections containing centered but larger cells that exceed the ROI size limit are also selected. As compliment, a group of pictures was edited to have samples of completed isolated cells. All the extracted images are stored with the "cell" category label.

A similar process is applied to extract images with the "no cell" category label. The difference radicates in the used criteria, and that the ROI size restriction is maintained in all cases. Also, non-images from this category were edited. The criteria used were:

- Sections that meet the ROI size limit.
- Empty sections.
- Areas containing one or more not centered cervical cells.

For the CNN to obtain good generalizations of the categories, it is necessary to choose enough images to represent as many cell shapes as possible. Then, data augmentation technique was used to generate more pictures and variability by zooming in, rotating, and flipping vertically and horizontally the images until they were enough to train the neural network. Data augmentation was performed until it generated two thousand images for each category. Finally, 25 % of each type was saved for validation and the remaining for training.

Fast Scanning Convolutional Neural Network Architecture. The convolutional neural network that recognizes cells shapes in the first fast scanning stage has to be as simple as possible to minimize the hardware resources required to make predictions [5]. Therefore, after some trial and error, the chosen architecture represented in Fig. 1 consisted in a four layers neural network. The first one is a convolutional layer with ten filters of 10×10. This layer is set to receive an input of 20×20 pixels. The second layer consists of a max-pooling layer of 2×2. The third layer is a flattened dense layer of 16 neurons. Finally, the output layer consists of 2 layers. The first and third layer uses a Relu activation function, while the output layer uses a softmax activation function.

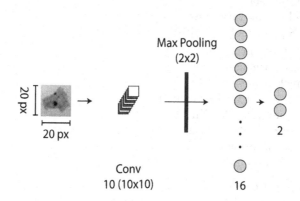

Fig. 1. Cell recognition model architecture (1st stage)

Training. For working purposes in the fast scanning stage the training and validation images are rescaled to fit an interval of $[0,1]$ and resized to 20×20 pixels. Then, images are transformed into tensors to fit the TensorFlow requirements and organized in batches of 32. Finally, training is performed during 100 generations, and the resultant model is saved. The CNN accuracy can be corroborated by testing it with the validation data by comparing predictions with the actual labels.

3.12   High Resolution Cell Classification Model Implementation

For the second, high resolution cell classification stage, a convolutional neural network capable of categorizing cells in the following categories was implemented:

- Negative for Intraepithelial Lesion (NIL).
- Low-grade Squamous Intraepithelial Lesion (LSIL).
- High-grade Squamous Intraepithelial Lesion (HSIL).
- Squamous cell carcinoma (SCC).

Training data and validation data were first prepared, in a similar fashion to the cell recognition model.

Data Preparation. From the liquid-based pap smear dataset, random images were selected. It is crucial to choose pictures from the four categories, ensuring that enough cells' variability is included. Using the same ROI size as the cell recognition model. Cells are extracted, saved, and labeled in the correspondent category using the following criteria.

- Low-grade Squamous Intraepithelial Lesion (LSIL):
  - Slight nuclear enlargement
  - Irregular nuclear contour
  - Hyperchromasia
  - Slight cell shape variations
- High-grade Squamous Intraepithelial Lesion (HSIL).
  - Marked Hyperchromasia
  - Hyperchromatic crowded group
  - Thick nuclear membrane
  - Marked irregular nuclear contour
  - Indented and irregular Nucleus
  - Usually parabasal-sized cell
  - Cell shape variations
- Squamous cell carcinoma.

- HSIL characteristics plus:
  * Macronucleus
  * Vacuolated cytoplasm
- Tadpole cell
- Fiber cell
- Cell cluster with enlarged nuclei
- Marked cell shape variations

- Negative for Intraepithelial Lesion (NIL):
  - Absence of the previously mentioned abnormal cell features

In the creation of the database for the second phase (High resolution), the images of extracted cells do not necessarily have to be centered, as all possible information and cases are considered for classification. Furthermore, certain relevant cells that exceed the standard cell size dimension were still included in the database. Later, all images were then standardized to a dimension of 250 × 250 pixels. Also some images of cells taken into account have vestiges of near by cells and other debris, in these cases the images were edited, erasing these extra elements to obtain the image of an isolated cell. In every case both the original end edited images were used for training and testing.

The data augmentation technique was used to increase the number of samples, obtaining more variations of the chosen images. The mentioned technique applies zooming, rotation, and flipping to the dataset elements vertically and horizontally. In this case, data augmentation was performed until each category had 1200 images, except for the NIL, which had 2200 images. Finally, 200 images of each type were saved for validation and the remaining for training.

High Resolution Convolutional Neural Network Architecture. The convolutional neural network required in the second stage to classify cells in high resolution needs to be robust, as seen in Fig. 2, to recognize cell features and make good predictions. Therefore, the chosen architecture consists of more layers and filters than the first stage. This convolutional neural network consists of 21 layers. The first one, a convolutional layer with 40 filters of 3 × 3. The first layer is set to receive an input of 250 × 250 pixels and three channels. The fourth and seventh are convolutional layers with 32 filters of 3 × 3 each one. The tenth, thirteenth and sixteenth are convolutional layers with 64 filters of 3 × 3 each one. The third, sixth, ninth, twelfth, fifteenth, and eighteenth are dropout layers set to eliminate 30% of the input. The second, fifth, eighth, eleventh, fourteenth, and seventeenth are max-pooling layers of 2 × 2. The nineteenth, twentieth, and twenty-first are a flattened layer of 128, 64, and 4 neurons. All the layers that require an activation function use a Relu activation function, while the output layer uses a softmax activation function.

Training. The training and validation images are rescaled to fit an interval of [0,1] and resize to 250 × 250 pixels. Like the recognition model, the images are transformed into tensors to fit TensorFlow requirements and organized in batches of 32. Finally, training is performed during 200 generations, and the resultant model is saved. The CNN accuracy can be corroborated by testing it with the validation data by comparing predictions with the actual labels.

3.13   Scanning Process

The prediction process needs of 7 steps, explained in this section and represented in Fig. 3

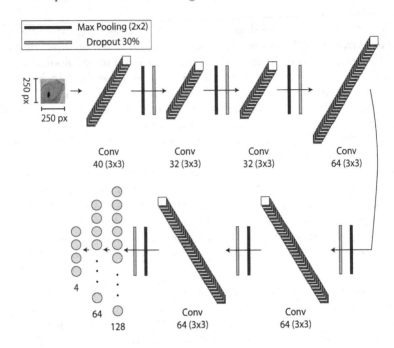

Fig. 2. Cell classification model architecture (2nd stage)Cell classification model architecture (2nd stage)

1. During the scanning process, several predictions are necessary; consequently, both previously trained CNN models are charged at the beginning of the process.
2. The Pap smear test file is loaded and resized to 1080 pixels to standardize all images but conserving the width-height relation allowing a correct visualization of the process on the monitor.
3. The whole matrix that makes up the picture is looped with steps of 70 pixels vertically and horizontally, extracting and storing matrix sections of ROI size. Also, the quadruple coordinates indicating where each of the pulled areas begins and ends are stored in a list B. Extracted images are stored in a list A to display them when desired. Nonetheless, displaying images is not essential for the procedure but helps track the process visually.
4. Two versions of each extracted section are stored as tensors to fit the CNN previously loaded TensorFlow requirements. Each version is stored in a different list to track them by their indexes; one version is resized to 250×250 pixels and stored in list C, and the other is resized to 20×20 pixels and stored in list D. Both are divided by 255.0 to rescale the tensor values to a [0-1] interval.
5. By looping every element of the list D, tensors are fed to the cell recognition CNN to start predictions. Whenever a forecast for "Cell" is thrown with an accuracy higher than 80%, list D's current index is used to track their

corresponding image, coordinates, and their tensor versions in lists A, B, and C; and store them in new lists to keep the index reference. Each time a cell is identified, coordinates in list B can be employed to draw a line in the Pap test sample image and have a visual representation of the process. The new lists for pictures, coordinates, and 250 × 250 pixels tensors are referred to as lists E, F, and G. This step should not consume much time since the predictions are made using a low-resolution CNN with few layers.

6. Then list G is looped similarly to the previous step using the classification cell CNN. Whenever a prediction corresponds to the following categories and accuracies, the coordinates on list F are used to draw their location with an indicative color.
   - Negative for Intraepithelial Lesion (NIL). accuracy > 70
   - Low-grade Squamous Intraepithelial Lesion (LSIL). accuracy > 50
   - High-grade Squamous Intraepithelial Lesion (HSIL). accuracy > 50
   - Squamous cell carcinoma. accuracy > 80

7. Finally, cells categorized as Negative for Intraepithelial Lesion (NIL) are labeled Normal Cells while the remaining categories are grouped in the Abnormal Cell Category.

4   Results

This chapter presents the results of the proposed two-stage cell classification system. Each time a pap smear sample is processed, the system saves an image with the respective classification, as seen in Fig. 4. Therefore, the program was executed through the whole set of photos available in the Mendeley pap smear data-set, and all the output images were stored for analysis.

The implemented system, composed of a low-resolution high-speed convolutional neural network for fast cell recognition and a high-resolution convolutional neural network for classification, demonstrates these two stage method could be used to improve the overall pap smear processing speed.

The detailed analysis was carried out by using correct individual cell recognition and classification as guiding indicators; instead of basing the examination on a generalized classification for the whole sample, as the original dataset does. Twenty random result images from each category were evaluated, and the obtained values were later fixed to fit the actual dataset proportion, getting the results shown in Table 1.

Table 1. Cell recognition and classification models results

	True Positive	True Negative	False Positive	False Negative
Cell Recognition	7004	111848	716	2930
Cell Classification	479	5525	152	1218

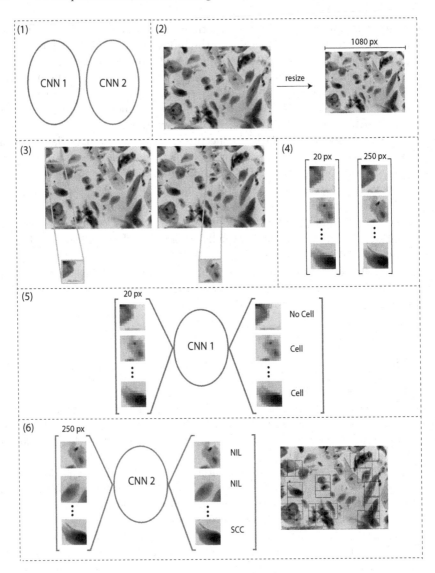

Fig. 3. General process

Table 1 shows how the cell recognition CNN obtained mostly true results and low negatives indicating that it can recognize actual centered cells. The cell classification CNN has the biggest value for true negatives, but it is followed by false negatives, showing that it misclassified 1218 abnormal cells as normal. Values in Table 1 were used to calculate performance metrics like sensitivity and specificity; these are the most common reference points to evaluate health technology assessments [10].

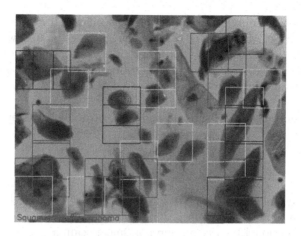

Fig. 4. Output

Table 2. Performance metrics

	Accuracy	Precision	Specificity	Sensitivity	Time
Cell Recognition (1st Stage)	0.970	0.907	0.993	0.705	5.76 s
Cell Classification (2nd Stage)	0.814	0.759	0.973	0.382	9.01 s

The following performance metrics are all shown in Table 2. Accuracy is an intuitive way of determining how well inputs were classified because it specifies how many images are correctly labeled from the whole group. The fast network reaches a value of 0.97, outperforming in this speciality at the HR network that got 0.81; this indicates that the fast network correctly differentiated cells from empty spaces and debris while the HR classifier hits only 20 percent of correct results.

Precision value tells how many of the images categorized as cells by fast network and abnormal by the HR network actually belong to those categories. The fast network performs better than the HR classifier when predicting affirmative results. That value also means that 10% of the images admitted by the fast network were later unnecessary analyzed by the HR network, even though they were not real cell images.

Specificity is an excellent indicator of how well our models work because its value reflects how many of the "no cell" images were categorized as such. In the same way, it indicates how many of the normal cells were classified correctly. The fast network reached a specificity of 0.99, with almost no empty region or debris classified as a cell. Also, the HR network specificity was 0.97, showing that normal cells are rarely misclassified as abnormal.

Sensitivity is the complement indicator of specificity. In this case, sensitivity shows how many of the existing cells were recognized and how many of the abnormal cells were efficiently found. There is a drastic difference between the two networks. The low-resolution, fast network correctly found 70% of all the available cells while the HR network correctly labeled just 38% of the abnormal cells.

Talking about speed, the time needed for both models to perform 140 predictions is lower for the fast network.

5   Conclusion

The main concern of this paper is to contribute with efficient methods to automatize pap smear analysis and improve medical services, especially in developing countries. Conventional high resolution pap smear scanning consumes computer resources and computing time, which difficult quick diagnoses. This project presents a two stage solution running in TensorFlow where in the first stage a fast, low resolution deep network scans the sample image at high speed, making fast predictions and extracting sample sections that contain cells or regions worth of taking a closer look. This information is passed to a more robust classifier model, where HR cells images are categorized as normal or abnormal. The resultant cell classifier achieves positive results where the fast network reaches 97% accuracy, 99% specificity, and 70% sensitivity and contributes with rapidly acquired information to the next stage. The second robust HR network contributes with a 38% of sensitivity for never seen pap smear and no training help from pap smear specialists. The obtained results prove that special multi stage networks architectures, assembled with Tensorflow libraries can produce improvements in the automatic analysis of pap smear and contribute with quality and quantity in medical services.

References

1. Agurto, I., Bishop, A., Sánchez, G., Betancourt, Z., Robles, S.: Perceived barriers and benefits to cervical cancer screening in Latin America. Prev. Med. **39**(1), 91–98 (2004). https://doi.org/10.1016/j.ypmed.2004.03.040
2. Canfell, K.: Towards the global elimination of cervical cancer. Papillomavirus Res. **8**, 100170 (2019). https://doi.org/10.1016/j.pvr.2019.100170
3. Gakidou, E., Nordhagen, S., Obermeyer, Z.: Coverage of cervical cancer screening in 57 countries: low average levels and large inequalities. PLoS Med. **5** (2008). https://doi.org/10.1371/journal.pmed.0050132
4. Global Cancer Observatory: Estimated age-standardized incidence and mortality rates (world) in 2020 (2020). https://gco.iarc.fr/today/online-analysis-multi-bars
5. He, K., Sun, J.: Convolutional neural networks at constrained time cost. In: Proceedings of the IEEE Conference on Computer Vision and Pattern Recognition, pp. 5353–5360 (2015)
6. Hussain, E., Mahanta, L.B., Borah, H., Das, C.R.: Liquid based-cytology pap smear dataset for automated multi-class diagnosis of pre-cancerous and cervical cancer lesions. Data Brief **30**, 105589 (2020). https://doi.org/10.1016/j.dib.2020.105589

7. Hussain, E., Mahanta, L.B., Das, C.R., Choudhury, M., Chowdhury, M.: A shape context fully convolutional neural network for segmentation and classification of cervical nuclei in pap smear images. Artif. Intell. Med. **107**, 101897 (2020). https://doi.org/10.1016/j.artmed.2020.101897

8. Jantzen, J., Norup, J., Dounias, G., Bjerregaard, B.: Pap-smear benchmark data for pattern classification (January 2005)

9. Kumar, R., Srivastava, R., Srivastava, S.: Detection and classification of cancer from microscopic biopsy images using clinically significant and biologically interpretable features. J. Med. Eng. **2015**, 1–14 (2015). https://doi.org/10.1155/2015/457906, /pmc/articles/PMC4782618/?report=abstract https://www.ncbi.nlm.nih.gov/pmc/articles/PMC4782618/

10. Lahue, B.J., Baginska, E., Li, S.S., Parisi, M.: Health technology assessment on cervical cancer screening, 2000–2014. Int. J. Technol. Assess. Health Care **31**(3), 171–180 (2015). https://doi.org/10.1017/S0266462315000197

11. Mangal, J., et al.: Unsupervised organization of cervical cells using bright-field and single-shot digital holographic microscopy. J. Biophotonics **12** (2019). https://doi.org/10.1002/jbio.201800409

12. Masters, D., Luschi, C.: Revisiting small batch training for deep neural networks. CoRR abs/1804.07612 (2018). http://arxiv.org/abs/1804.07612

13. Nguyen, A., Choi, S., Kim, W., Ahn, S., Kim, J., Lee, S.: Distribution padding in convolutional neural networks. In: 2019 IEEE International Conference on Image Processing (ICIP), pp. 4275–4279 (2019). https://doi.org/10.1109/ICIP.2019.8803537

14. Park, S., Kwak, N.: Analysis on the dropout effect in convolutional neural networks. In: Lai, S.-H., Lepetit, V., Nishino, K., Sato, Y. (eds.) ACCV 2016. LNCS, vol. 10112, pp. 189–204. Springer, Cham (2017). https://doi.org/10.1007/978-3-319-54184-6_12

15. Shanthi, P.B., Faruqi, F., Hareesha, K.S., Kudva, R.: Deep convolution neural network for malignancy detection and classification in microscopic uterine cervix cell images. Asian Pacific J. Cancer Prev. **20**, 3447–3456 (2019). https://doi.org/10.31557/APJCP.2019.20.11.3447

16. Sharma, S.: Activation functions in neural networks (2017). https://towardsdatascience.com/activation-functions-neural-networks-1cbd9f8d91d6

17. Simms, K., et al.: Impact of scaled up human papillomavirus vaccination and cervical screening and the potential for global elimination of cervical cancer in 181 countries, 2020–99: a modelling study. PLoS Med. **20** (2019). https://doi.org/10.1016/s1470-2045(18)30836-2

18. Sompawong, N., et al.: Automated pap smear cervical cancer screening using deep learning. In: 2019 41st Annual International Conference of the IEEE Engineering in Medicine and Biology Society (EMBC), pp. 7044–7048 (2019). https://doi.org/10.1109/EMBC.2019.8856369

19. Su, J., Xu, X., He, Y., Song, J.: Automatic detection of cervical cancer cells by a two-level cascade classification system. Anal. Cell. Pathol. **2016** (2016). https://doi.org/10.1155/2016/9535027, /pmc/articles/PMC4889791/?report=abstract https://www.ncbi.nlm.nih.gov/pmc/articles/PMC4889791/

20. The American College of Obstetricians and Gynecologists: Practice bulletin no. 168: cervical cancer screening and prevention, obstetrics & gynecology. Obstet. Gynecol. **128**, 111–130 (2016). https://doi.org/10.1097/aog.0000000000001708

21. United Nations Development Programme: Human development reports (2020). http://hdr.undp.org/en/countries/profiles/ECU

22. William, W., Ware, A., Basaza-Ejiri, A.H., Obungoloch, J.: A pap-smear analysis tool (pat) for detection of cervical cancer from pap-smear images. Biomed. Eng. Online **18**(1), 1–22 (2019). https://doi.org/10.1186/s12938-019-0634-5

23. World Health Organization: Screening as well as vaccination is essential in the fight against cervical cancer (2016). http://www.who.int/reproductivehealth/topics/cancers/fight-cervical-cancer/en/

Selecting and Acquiring IoT Devices Oriented to Older People: A Systematic Literature Review

Jorge Galán, Wilson Valdez⬤, Daniela Prado-Cabrera⬤, and Priscila Cedillo$^{(\boxtimes)}$⬤

Universidad de Cuenca, Azuay Av. 12 de abril s/n, Cuenca, Ecuador
{jorge.galang,wilson.valdezs,daniela.pradoc,
priscila.cedillo}@ucuenca.edu.ec

Abstract. The devices are crucial elements in the Internet of Things (IoT) applications. The correct selection of these elements influences the quality, cost, and adequate addressing of the application depending on the needs in each of the IoT verticals. In this sense, the need for methodologies for selecting IoT devices is an exciting field to explore in research. Therefore, this paper presents a Systematic Literature Review (SLR) based on the Kitchenham and Charters methodology, as the first step for designing a methodology for the selection and acquisition of IoT devices oriented to older people. The presented SLR describes the existing methods, technical criteria, context criteria (e.g., contracts, government restrictions), and other elements considered for selecting IoT devices from 2010 to 2021 year; this from the review in digital libraries, conferences, and journals. Sixteen articles were found following the methodology of systematics review. The obtained results are made up of studies for the selection of IoT devices, or criteria for the selection of technology related to IoT, such as IoT services, IoT platforms, sensors for IoT devices, among others. Most of the found studies are not directed to a specific domain, except for a few directed to people in general or companies. Overall, the study evidences a gap in the selection methodologies for IoT devices in applications-oriented to the elderly and the presence of some context-related selection methods.

Keywords: Systematic Literature Review (SLR) · Internet of Things (IoT) selection · Internet of Things (IoT) acquisition · Methodology

1 Introduction

Healthy aging in people is nowadays one of the most important challenges for governments and healthcare institutions [1]. The improvement of health services oriented to ensure physical and mental welfare in older patients directly influences their life quality, and reduction in health services costs [1, 2]. In this sense, technology is an essential ally to reach this goal. Besides, concerning older adults, new emerging technological paradigms such as the Internet of Things (IoT), Ambient Intelligence (AmI) and Ambient Assisted Living (AAL) are focused on improving their wellbeing [3–5].

The ideal field of application in for elderly-oriented solutions is AAL which is defined by [6, 7] as technical systems developed to support elderly or people with diseases in

© Springer Nature Switzerland AG 2021
J. P. Salgado Guerrero et al. (Eds.): TICEC 2021, CCIS 1456, pp. 345–361, 2021.
https://doi.org/10.1007/978-3-030-89941-7_24

346 J. Galán et al.

their daily activities giving them independent life as long as possible and improving their quality of life. Here exist a wide range of IoT applications (e.g., elderly care monitoring, chronic patient health monitoring, recognition of human activity, clinical applications), and all of them depending of the quality of the used devices to improve their impact [8]. In this sense, the IoT device selection is overriding to achieve an adequate technological solution for elderly-oriented or context needs. Therefore, having a structured method that considers steps such as mapping of requirements, classification, and weighting for choosing IoT devices is needed.

In this context, to know advances within this field of study and to establish a starting point to develop the bases to support the development of these kinds of methodologies, a Systematic Literature Review (SLR) is an ideal means to identify, evaluate, and interpret all the advances in this domain [9]. Although some research presents literature reviews about the acquisition of devices, there is no register about the presented in this paper which is n SLR to look for methodologies for selecting and acquiring IoT devices oriented to older people. The SLR follows three stages: i) Planification, ii) Execution of the review process iii) Report of the results, as suggested by Kitchenham [9].

This paper's remainder is organized as follows: Sect. 2 discusses the background, including existing SLRs or methodologies in this domain. Section 3 and Sect. 4 discusses an explanation of the research method and the systematic review results. Finally, a discussion of the results, methodology validation, and future work.

2 Background

This section gives initially an overview of the IoT application fields to create solutions for older people. Then, are discussed some important criteria and methodologies in selecting IoT devices that can be applied in solutions oriented to elderly.

In the last years, the needs in elderly care field have been addressed by technology. In this context, the IoT and AAL paradigms have applications or solutions-oriented to improve the quality of life in the elderly such as:

- *Elderly care monitoring.* These applications include devices that primarily intended to improve quality of life and promote safe and independent living. Examples include devices in AAL environments, active aging, therapy and entertainment, communication and social activities, health monitoring and diet [8].
- *Chronic patient health monitoring.* These applications include IoT devices specialized in monitoring and supporting older people with chronic diseases or disabilities, such as diabetes, Alzheimer's, among others [8, 10].
- *Recognition of human activity:* These applications include devices for constantly monitoring the elderly activities to detect abnormal conditions and reduce the effects of unpredictable events such as sudden falls [11]. This category also includes devices for the elderly location, navigation assistance and object locators.
- *Clinical applications.* These applications include IoT devices for the detection, diagnosis, prediction, and treatment of diseases (e.g., seizure detection) [8, 12].
- *Emergency conditions.* These applications include fall detection devices, fall risk management, emergency responses, and categorization of emergency patients according to their level of severity [8, 13, 14].

- *Mental health.* These applications include devices for the detection, prediction, and care of mental illnesses in elderly (e.g., dementia, depression) [8].
- *Movement disorders.* These applications include devices for continuous analysis or training of patient balance and gait based on portable sensors [8, 12].
- *Rehabilitation.* These applications include IoT devices to provide rehabilitation services and/or to generate feedback to patients and their caregivers about the progress of the rehabilitation process (e.g., exoskeletons) [8, 15].
- *Accessibility to health services.* These applications include devices that allow the generation of requests for health services, generation of information related to health areas, good habits promotion, and self-control in certain diseases [2, 8].
- *Accessibility for caregivers.* These applications include devices that allow remote monitoring and treatment of patients by healthcare providers [2, 8].

As presented, some of the applications are criticism due to its direct relationship with wellbeing and healthcare. Therefore, the quality of the devices directly influences the proper addressing of the solution. Hereof, an adequate selection of the devices depending of the context and the specific needs of the application is necessary.

The literature about IoT technology selection present some elements to consider when choosing adequately devices. On the one hand, the selection criteria, grouped into fifteen categories: *technical characteristic* [16–18], *device quality* [17, 19, 20], *safety* [17, 21], *sensors* [22, 23], *services* [22, 24], *software* [25], *communications* [17, 22, 26], *data type* [27–29], *IoT platforms* [28, 30], *patient needs* [31–33], *ethical considerations* [34], *marketplace* [19, 35], *contracts negotiation* [17, 21], *governmental regulations* [31, 36, 37], *and acquisition or fabrication* [38–40].

On the other hand, the IoT technology selection methodologies such as: *Analytical Hierarchical Process (AHP)* [41], *Analytical Network Process (ANP)* [42], *Additive Relationship Assessment (ARAS)* [43], *Decision Making Testing and Evaluation Laboratory (DEMATEL)* [44], *Elimination and Election Reality (ELECTRE)* [45, 46], *Convolutional methods* [47], *Primitive Cognitive Network Process (PCNP)* [48, 49].

Overall, there have been swiftly presented some specific elderly-oriented application areas, selection criteria for IoT technology and some selection methodologies. In the next section, these considerations are the starting point to the SLR.

3   Systematic Literature Review (SLR) Research Method

A Systematic Literature Review (SLR) lets obtaining, evaluating, and interpreting state of the art into primary studies about research questions related to a specific area of interest. These goals are reached by applying a scientific methodology that provides an objective assessment of the research topic in a reliable, repeatable, and replicable manner. Therefore, this paper applies the methodology proposed by Kitchenham et al. (Kitchenham & Charters, 2007a), to carry out the SLR.

The selected methodology consists of three stages, as shown and described in Fig. 1.

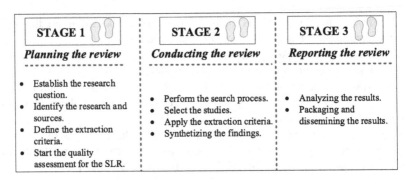

Fig. 1. Stages for the execution of a Systematic Literature Review according to Kitchenham.

3.1 Planning the Review

This stage defines the SLR protocol and research question to perform the review. Before beginning the review, it is necessary to verify the non-existence of similar previous works to avoid duplicating work. In this sense, a first search was carried out for SLRs related to the selection and/or acquisition of IoT technology and specialized in elderly-related aspects. As a result, the search did not return similar studies; for this reason, planning for the revision continues. Also, the guidelines proposed by Kitchenham [9] suggest the information extraction by considering several aspects as shown in Table 1.

Table 1. Extraction aspects during the SLR.

Aspect	Description
Population	Studies related to methodologies for selecting/acquiring IoT devices oriented to older people. Also, there are considered methodologies for selecting IoT devices
Intervention	The study contains a group of aspects related to the selection of devices
Comparison	This study aims not to compare the different aspects to be addressed when designing a methodology for selecting IoT devices oriented to elderly
Outcomes	To identify the main aspects addressed during the design of methodologies and aspects considered for the selection of IoT devices
Context	This study is developed in a research context, where the experts in the domain present primary studies

Afterward, are defined the research protocol steps from identifying the research question to the release of the results in order to carry out an orderly and systematic review. In addition to the data extraction and synthesis of studies.

Research Question. The overall objective of this review is to identify:

RQ: What factors are considered for proposing methodologies for the selection and acquisition of IoT technology?

Moreover, Kitchenham suggests dividing the main question into sub-research questions. In this case, the following were defined:

- *RQ1: What aspects are considered for selecting / acquiring existing IoT technology?*
- *RQ2: What domains are the selection and acquisition methodologies for IoT technology-oriented?*
- *RQ3: What method is used to weigh IoT devices?*
- *RQ4: How is research on methodologies for acquiring IoT technologies carried out?*

Research Strategy. According to the technological and medical field of the research, the libraries considered for the search were ACM, IEEE Xplore, ScienceDirect, and PubMed. The search string to submit to these sites is defined in Table 2.

Table 2. Search string.

Concept	Sub-string	Connector	Alternative terms
Internet of things	Internet of things	OR	
IoT	IoT	AND	
Acquisition	Acquisition	OR	
	Selection	AND	
Methodology	Method*	AND	It includes methodology, method
Search string	*(Internet of Things OR IoT) AND (Acquisition OR Selection) AND Method**		

In order to select the studies, there are considered the publications in the period 2010-January 2021. The selection is based on the IoT emergence milestone by 2008–2009 as presented in [50]. Therefore, it is expected that by 2010 there may have already been the first formal studies in this domain. In addition, manual searches of conferences and journals related to IoT applied in health and/or care of the elderly are included in SCImago Journal & Country Rank, Core Conferences, and Google Scholar.

Data Extraction Criteria. In order to extract data from the primary studies, a set of criteria is established for each research sub-question as set out in Table 3. These criteria are reviewed in each study to facilitate their classification.

3.2 Conducting the Review

This second stage starts with selecting and assessing the primary studies, then the monitoring and extraction by following the alignments such as the research questions and protocol proposed in the planning stage.

Table 3. Criteria to be analyzed for each research sub-question.

RQ1: What aspects are considered for selecting and/or acquiring existing IoT technology?

EC1	Analysis criteria	Technical characteristic	Sensors
		Quality	Manufacturing
		Safety	Business
		Software	IoT platforms
		Final user	Data
		Device market	IoT services
		Contracts	Communications
		Government regulations	

RQ2: What domains are the selection/acquisition methodologies for IoT technology-oriented?

EC2	Domains	Elderly
		People (in general)
		Enterprises
		None in specific

RQ3: What method is used to weigh IoT devices?

EC3	Methods	AHP (Analytical Hierarchical Process)
		ANP (Analytical Network Process)
		ARAS (Additive Relationship Assessment)
		DEMATEL (Decision Making Testing and Evaluation Laboratory)
		ELECTRE (Elimination and Election Reality)
		IPM (Multiple Information Process)
		Convolutional methods
		PCNP (Primitive Cognitive Network Process)
		Others (algorithms, models, etc.)

RQ4: How is research on methodologies for acquiring IoT technologies being carried out?

EC4	Focus	General IoT device selection
		Selection of IoT devices for medical use
		Process automation with IoT
		Sensor selection for IoT devices
		Wireless technology selection for IoT networks
		Selection of IoT services
		Selection of IoT platforms
		Selection of IoT systems
		General technology selection

Primary Studies Selection. The search string was applied in the metadata of title, abstract and keywords of the selected digital libraries. Then, since the results, the titles and abstracts were evaluated to filter the articles that did not align with the research question. Studies that at least comply with the selection or acquisition of IoT technology or analysis of aspects of IoT were kept. Introductory documents, same works in different sources, Not English written articles, books, workshops, and posters were excluded.

Quality Assurance of Primary Studies. Since the number of obtained results and that most of these have no more than three years old since their publication, it was decided to filter the papers published in an indexed journal or library. As a result of the search and filters described above, were obtained the following presented in Table 4.

Table 4. Automatic search results in digital libraries.

Search engine	Results	Just conferences and journals	Since 2010
IEEE Xplore	495	469	468
ACM	104	97	97
Science Direct	70	60	60
PubMed	42	40	40
		Total	665
Removing repeated			641

As a next step, the titles and abstracts of the 641 results were analyzed to extract only the articles that contribute to the research questions; thus, obtaining only two papers (*S01* and *S02* of Appendix 1). Additionally, 15 more reports were obtained from the manual search, giving 17 articles useful for research as total (*S03–S16* of Appendix 1).

3.3   Reporting the Review

The final stage presents the core of the SLR since the extraction criteria, the selection mechanism, and thus the current state of the art in this domain. All the researches were tabulated following the criteria to obtain a data summary. The summary results are in Table 5; where most of these do not have a specific domain orientation even to the elderly. Concerning current studies, it highlights the IoT sensors and platform selection.

Table 5. Results obtained by criterion of each sub-question.

Extraction criteria		#	%	Papers
RQ1: What aspects are considered for selecting and/or acquiring existing IoT technology?				
Analysis criteria	Technical characteristic	5	31%	S01, S04, S07, S09, S16
	Quality	5	31%	S01, S03, S04, S08, S11
	Safety	7	44%	S03, S04, S08, S11, S13–S15
	Software	0	0%	
	Final user	5	31%	S02, S04, S08, S09, S11
	Device market	3	19%	S02, S04, S11
	Contracts	0	0%	
	Government regulations	3	19%	S02, S08, S11
	IoT services	1	6%	S01
	Communications	4	25%	S01, S03, S04, S11
	Sensors	1	6%	S07
	Manufacturing	2	13%	S01, S16
	Business	4	25%	S03, S04, S08, S11
	IoT platforms	3	19%	S02, S14, S09
	Data	3	19%	S11, S14, S09
RQ2: What domains are the methodologies for selecting/acquiring IoT technology-oriented?				
Domains	Elderly	0	0%	
	People (in general)	2	13%	S08, S11
	Enterprises	1	6%	S03
	None in specific	13	81%	S01, S02, S04–S07, S09, S10, S12–S16
RQ3: What method is used to weigh IoT devices?				
Methods	AHP	5	31%	S01, S03, S06, S09, S16
	ANP	2	13%	S11, S13
	ARAS	1	6%	S08
	DEMATEL	1	6%	S13
	ELECTRE	1	6%	S16
	Convolutional methods	3	19%	S12, S14, S15

(continued)

Table 5. (*continued*)

Extraction criteria		#	%	Papers
	PCNP	*1*	*6%*	*S05*
	Others (algorithms, models, etc.)	*6*	*38%*	*S01, S02, S04, S07, S10, S15*
RQ4: How is research on methodologies for acquiring IoT technologies being carried out?				
Focus	*General IoT device selection*	*3*	*19%*	*S06, S09, S12*
	IoT device selection for medical use	*2*	*13%*	*S08, S11*
	Process automation with IoT	*1*	*6%*	*S03*
	Sensor selection for IoT devices	*3*	*19%*	*S04, S07, S10*
	Selection of IoT services	*1*	*6%*	*S13*
	Selection of IoT platforms	*3*	*19%*	*S02, S14, S15*
	Selection of IoT systems	*2*	*13%*	*S01, S16*
	General technology selection	*1*	*6%*	*S05*

Afterwards, from the obtained results, the trends in each sub question are shown. Figure 2 presents the analyzed criteria dispersion regarding the IoT device selection. Here highlight as most common criteria the quality, security and communications.

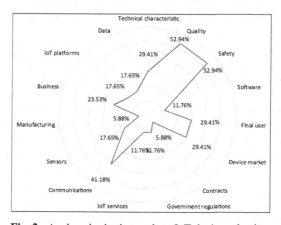

Fig. 2. Analyzed criteria trends to IoT device selection.

Figure 3 shows trends about used methodologies. It presents AHP as the most used. Then, are shown the Linear Convolution Method (LCM) and proportional method.

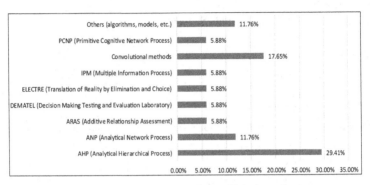

Fig. 3. Analyzed criteria trends to IoT device selection.

4   Results of the Systematic Review

This section presents a summary of the results from the searches about studies related to IoT devices selection both specialized in a single specific criterion, and multi-criteria selection methods. These results were complemented with research related to IoT technology such as the selection of IoT platforms or services, to obtain a broad set of criteria that will form part of a methodology for selecting IoT devices aimed at the elderly.

The range of the publications is 2013 to 2020 (Table 6). From 2013 to 2015, there is the least number of investigations (12%); where the selection of technology through selection methodologies (*S05*) or the search for sensors for middleware with IoT devices (*S07*) is already appreciated. Besides, in the period from 2016 to 2017, investigations reached 26%, where more specialized works in the selection of IoT devices can be observed, highlighting the *S04*, dedicated to the selection of IoT devices evaluated from the criteria of RFID and sensors; and *S06*, which proposes a multi-criteria decision model adaptable to different selection models in the search for the most convenient IoT devices. For the 2018 to 2020 period, the related jobs raise up to 63%, where 2019 has most publications (13). In this period, the research aimed at the selection of IoT platforms (*S02, S14, S15*) and the selection of IoT devices aimed at medical solutions (*S08, S11*) stand out. It is worth highlighting the importance of the S11 research that is oriented to the use of IoT for the implementation of Intensive Care Units (ICU) solutions.

EC1 Analysis Criteria. 75% of the studies include one or more technical criteria for the selection stage. The number of criteria is very dispersed and has different levels of abstraction. Within the range greater than 40% are the security criteria such as *S13* research, specialized in a security framework for evaluating IoT services; or *S03* research where a method for selecting IoT devices including security analysis criterion is proposed. In the range of 20 to 40% are the Quality, Technical Characteristics and Communications criteria, such as the research *S04* that analyzes the characteristics of radiofrequency sensors and identifiers (RFDI) in IoT devices from the quality view, technical characteristics, communications, among others. Another example is *S01* that includes these criteria for designing IoT ecosystems. In the 10 to 19% range are the Data, Manufacturing, and IoT Platforms categories such as the research *S16* that suggests some criteria for the IoT systems development; or the research *S14* that includes the criteria

Table 6. Research classification according to year of publication

Year	Papers	Year	Papers	Year	Papers
2013	1	2018	3	2019	2
2015	1	2018	2	2020	4
2016	2	2018	1	2020	2
2016	1	2019	4	2020	1
2017	2	2019	4		
2017	1	2019	3		

related to data management in IoT platforms. Finally, the range below 10% present the criteria for sensors and IoT services (*S07, S01*). None of the studies considers specific software criteria. Table 7 shows the papers' technical criteria classification.

Table 7. Research classification according to the technical criteria

Technical aspects	# Papers	% Papers	Rank	% Tech. aspects
Security	7	43.75%	>40%	75.00%
Technical characteristics	5	31.25%	20 to 40%	
Quality	5	31.25%		
Communications	4	25.00%		
Data	3	18.75%	10 to 19%	
IoT platforms	3	18.75%		
Manufacture	2	12.50%		
Sensors	1	6.25%	<10%	
IoT services	1	6.25%		
Software	0	0.00%		
None	4	25.00%	–	25.00%

EC2 Domain. In the results, 81% of the studies do not specialize in a specific domain. Only 13% are oriented to people in general, such as *S08* focused on patients requiring physical rehabilitation, or *S11* on people requiring hospitalization in an intensive care unit. 6% to a business vision (such as *S03* oriented to the automation of processes within a company). Besides, there is no study focused on the selection of IoT devices oriented to the elderly. Figure 4 shows the papers' classification according to the domain.

EC3 Methods. The studies found a wide variety of methods used for the selection of criteria. Of these, AHP stands out as the preferred one with 31%, made up of *S01, S03, S06, S09*, and *S16*. The next rank consists of the works that use convolution methods

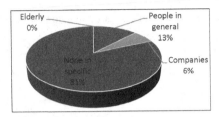

Fig. 4. Research classification according to the domain

with 19%. In this rank, the *S12*, which applies the Linear Convolution Method and the Ideal Point Method, stands out; and the researches *S14* and *S15* that apply the Linear Convolution Method. As the third most used methodology is ANP with 13% (*S11* and *S13*). We obtained 38% of studies that do not apply selection methodologies as such, but different options such as algorithms, metamodels, or simply do not specify a specific methodology. Within this range, the research *S01* stands out, which establishes a metamodel for the design of IoT ecosystems that allows the use of different selection methodologies such as AHP or ELECTRE. Table 8 shows the classification of the papers according to selection methods.

Table 8. Research classification according to selection methods

Methods	# Papers	% Papers	% Selection methods
AHP	5	31.25%	62.50%
Convolution methods	3	18.7n5%	
ANP	2	12.50%	
ARAS	1	6.25%	
DEMATEL	1	6.25%	
ELECTRE	1	6.25%	
PCNP	1	6.25%	
Others	6	37.50%	37.50%

EC4 Focus. There is no significant difference between the approaches of the studies, however, there are 3 trends: 19% of the studies have approaches to the selection of IoT devices in general, sensors for IoT devices or IoT platforms. Within this range, the research *S09* stands out, which presents a multi-criteria decision model for IoT device selection from different selection methodologies. 13% of the studies have approaches to the selection of IoT devices for medical use or selection of IoT systems such as those previously described: *S08*, *S11*, *S01* and *S16*. 6% of the studies focus on process automation with IoT, IoT services selection or technology selection in general such as the research *S03* that establish a selection method for IoT devices focused on process automation. Table 9 shows the classification of the papers according to selection methods.

Table 9. Research classification according to focus

Focus	# Papers	% Papers	Rank
General IoT device selection	3	18.75%	~19%
Sensor selection for IoT devices	3	18.75%	
Selection of IoT platforms	3	18.75%	
Selection of IoT devices for medical use	2	12.50%	~13%
Selection of IoT systems	2	12.50%	
Process automation with IoT	1	6.25%	~6%
Selection of IoT services	1	6.25%	
General technology selection	1	6.25%	

5 Conclusions and Further Work

The purpose of this work is to know the scientific advances regarding the offer of methodologies for the selection or acquisition of IoT devices to address contextual needs of older adults. After conducting the SLR, it is observed that, despite having achieved a significant number of valid initial studies (more than 600 papers), the number of valid papers for the purpose of the study was very low (16), which reflects that there is not much research about selection methods for IoT devices, even though IoT technology has been in existence for more than 10 years. In that way, there is no evolution of the studies that delve into any specific domain and focus. Hence, it is concluded that most of the reviewed articles focus on the selection of sensors or IoT platforms; Furthermore, a large percentage of studies have focused on AHP, a method that offers advantages such as considering all possible alternatives, encouraging reflection, and achieving an objective and reliable result. However, there is an absence of methods for the acquisition of IoT devices aimed at older adults; therefore, it is suggested to work in methodologies that consider aspects of this age group to set up high quality AAL.

Acknowledgements. This work is part of the research projects: "Design of architectures and interaction models for assisted living environments aimed at older adults. Case study: playful and social environments" and "Fog Computing applied to monitor devices used in assisted living environments; study case: a platform for the elderly", winners of the call for research projects DIUC XVIII and DIUC XVII. Therefore, the authors thank to the *Dirección de Investigación de la Universidad de Cuenca* (DIUC) of *Universidad de Cuenca* for its support.

Appendix 1

S01.   Silva EM, Jardim-Goncalves R (2020) IoT Ecosystems Design: A Multimethod, Multicriteria Assessment Methodology. IEEE Internet Things J 7:10150–10159. https://doi.org/10.1109/JIOT.2020.3011029

S02. Nikityuk L, Tsaryov R (2019) Optimization of the Process of Selecting of the IoT-Platform for the Specific Technical Solution IoT-Sphere. In: 2018 International Scientific-Practical Conference on Problems of Infocommunications Science and Technology, PIC S and T 2018 - Proceedings. Institute of Electrical and Electronics Engineers Inc., pp 401–405

S03. Durão LF, Carvalho M, Takey S, Cauchick-Miguel P (2018) Internet of Things process selection: AHP selection method. Int J Adv Manuf Technol

S04. Dalli, A., & Bri, S. (2016). Acquisition devices in Internet of Things: RFID and Sensors. Journal of Theoretical & Applied Information Technology, 90(1).

S05. Chen VQ, Yuen KKF (2015) Towards a hybrid approach of Primitive Cognitive Network Process and Self-organizing Map for computer product recommendation. In: Proceedings of 2015 International Conference on Intelligent Computing and Internet of Things, ICIT 2015. Institute of Electrical and Electronics Engineers Inc., pp 9–12

S06. Silva EM, Agostinho C, Jardim-Goncalves R (2018) A multi-criteria decision model for the selection of a more suitable Internet-of-Things device. In: 2017 International Conference on Engineering, Technology and Innovation: Engineering, Technology and Innovation Management Beyond 2020: New Challenges, New Approaches, ICE/ITMC 2017 - Proceedings. Institute of Electrical and Electronics Engineers Inc., pp 1268–1276

S07. Perera C (2013) Context-aware Sensor Search, Selection and Ranking Model for Internet of Things Middleware. CoRR abs/1303.2447

S08. Paramita RA, Dachyar M (2020) The Alternative Selection for Internet of Things (IoT) Implementation in Medical Rehabilitation. Int J Adv Sci Technol 29:3632–3640

S09. Silva EM, Jardim-Goncalves R (2017) Multi-criteria analysis and decision methodology for the selection of Internet-of-Things hardware platforms. In: IFIP Advances in Information and Communication Technology. Springer New York LLC, pp 111–121

S10. Zheng Z, Tao Y, Chen Y, et al. (2019) An efficient preference-based sensor selection method in internet of things. IEEE Access 7:168536–168547. https://doi.org/10.1109/ACCESS.2019.2953045

S11. Nadhira A, Dachyar M (2020) Selection Factor Analysis for Internet of Things (IoT) Implementation using DEMATEL based ANP and COPRAS Method at the Hospital Intensive Care Unit (ICU). Int J Adv Sci Technol 29:3614–3622

S12. Krapivina, H., Kondratenko, Y. P., & Kondratenko, G. V. (2019, June). Multi-criteria Decision-Making Approaches for Choice of Wireless Communication Technologies for IoT-Based Systems. In ICTERI PhD Symposium (pp. 73–82).

S13. Park KC, Shin DH (2017) Security assessment framework for IoT service. Telecommun Syst 64:193–209. https://doi.org/10.1007/s11235-016-0168-0

S14. Kondratenko Y, Kondratenko G, Sidenko I (2018) Multi-criteria decision making for selecting a rational IoT platform. In: Proceedings of 2018 IEEE 9th International Conference on Dependable Systems, Services and Technologies, DESSERT 2018. Institute of Electrical and Electronics Engineers Inc., pp 147–152

S15. Kondratenko Y, Kondratenko G, Sidenko I (2019) Multi-criteria decision making and soft computing for the selection of specialized IoT platform. In: Advances in Intelligent Systems and Computing. Springer Verlag, pp 71–80

S16. Silva EM, Jardim-Goncalves R (2021) Cyber-Physical Systems: a multi-criteria assessment for Internet-of-Things (IoT) systems. Enterp Inf Syst 15:332–351. https://doi.org/10.1080/17517575.2019.1698060.

References

1. Glisky, E.L.: Changes in cognitive function in human aging. In: Brain Aging, pp. 3–20. CRC Press (2019)
2. Garcon, L., et al.: Medical and assistive health technology: meeting the needs of aging populations. Gerontologist **56**, S293–S302 (2016)
3. Cedillo, P., Sanchez, C., Bermeo, A.: A systematic literature review on devices and systems for ambient assisted living : solutions and trends from different user perspectives. In: ICEDEG (2018)
4. Rashidi, P., Mihailidis, A.: A survey on ambient-assisted living tools for older adults. IEEE J. Biomed. Health Inform. **17**(3), 579–590 (2013)
5. Dohr, A., Drobics, M., Hayn, D., Schreier, G.: The Internet of Things for ambient assisted living, pp. 804–809 (2010)
6. Garcia, N.M., Rodrigues, J.J.P.C.: Ambient Assisted Living. CRC Press, Boca Raton (2015)
7. Erazo-Garzon, L., Erraez, J., Illescas-Peña, L., Cedillo, P.: A data quality model for AAL systems. In: Fonseca C, E., Morales, G.R., Cordero, M.O., Botto-Tobar, M., Martínez, E.C., León, A.P. (eds.) TICEC 2019. AISC, vol. 1099, pp. 137–152. Springer, Cham (2020). https://doi.org/10.1007/978-3-030-35740-5_10
8. Tun, S.Y.Y., Madanian, S., Mirza, F.: Internet of Things (IoT) applications for elderly care: a reflective review. Aging Clin. Exp. Res. **33**(4), 855–867 (2021)
9. Kitchenham, B., Brereton, O.P., Budgen, D., Turner, M., Bailey, J., Linkman, S.: Systematic literature reviews in software engineering – a systematic literature review. Inf. Softw. Technol. **51**(1), 7–15 (2009)
10. Memon, M., Wagner, S.R., Pedersen, C.F., Hassan, F., Beevi, A., Hansen, F.O.: Ambient assisted living healthcare frameworks, platforms, standards, and quality attributes. Sensors **14**, 4312–4341 (2014)
11. Wang, Z., Yang, Z., Dong, T.: A review of wearable technologies for elderly care that can accurately track indoor position, recognize physical activities and monitor vital signs in real time. Sensors (Switz.) **17**(2), 341 (2017)
12. Mancioppi, G., Fiorini, L., Timpano Sportiello, M., Cavallo, F.: Novel technological solutions for assessment, treatment, and assistance in mild cognitive impairment. Front. Neuroinform. **13**, 58 (2019)
13. Cheng, A.L., Georgoulas, C., Bock, T.: Fall detection and intervention based on wireless sensor network technologies. Autom. Constr. **71**, 116–136 (2016)
14. de Vries, O.J., et al.: Multifactorial intervention to reduce falls in older people at high risk of recurrent falls: a randomized controlled trial. JAMA Intern. Med. **170**(13), 1110–1117 (2010)
15. Jaul, E., Menzel, J.: Pressure ulcers in the elderly, as a public health problem. J. Gen. Pract. (2014)
16. Boeckl, K., et al: NISTIR 8228 considerations for managing Internet of Things (IoT) cybersecurity and privacy risks (2019)
17. USTelecom Media: C2 Consensus on IoT Security Baseline Capabilities (2019)
18. Abdallah, M., Jaber, T., Alabwaini, N., Alnabi, A.A.: A proposed quality model for the Internet of Things systems. In: 2019 IEEE Jordan International Joint Conference on Electrical Engineering and Information Technology, JEEIT 2019 - Proceedings (2019)

19. Mohammadi, V., Rahmani, A.M., Darwesh, A.M., Sahafi, A.: Trust-based recommendation systems in Internet of Things: a systematic literature review. Hum. Centric Comput. Inf. Sci. **9**(1), 1–61 (2019)
20. Kim, M.: A quality model for evaluating IoT applications. Int. J. Comput. Electr. Eng. **8**(1), 66–76 (2016)
21. U.S. General Services Administration: The Internet of Things (IoT): an overview on how to acquire "things" securely (2017)
22. Baranwal, G., Singh, M., Prakash, D.: A framework for IoT service selection. J. Supercomput. **76**(4), 2777–2814 (2019)
23. Rayes, A., Salam, S.: The Things in IoT: Sensors and Actuators. In: Internet of Things from Hype to Reality, pp. 57–77. Springer, Cham (2017). https://doi.org/10.1007/978-3-319-448 60-2_3
24. Li, Y., Huang, Y., Zhang, M., Rajabion, L.: Service selection mechanisms in the Internet of Things (IoT): a systematic and comprehensive study. Cluster Comput. **23**(2), 1163–1183 (2019)
25. International Organization for Standardization: Software engineering - Software product Quality Requirements and Evaluation (SQuaRE) – System and software quality models. ISO/IEC 25010:2011, vol. 2, no. Resolution 937 (2011)
26. Patel, K., Patel, S.: Internet of Things-IOT: definition, characteristics, architecture, enabling technologies, application & future challenges. Int. J. Eng. Sci. Comput. **6**, 6122–6131 (2016)
27. Nadhira, M.D.A.: Selection factor analysis for Internet of Things (IoT) implementation using DEMATEL based ANP and COPRAS method at the hospital intensive care unit (ICU). Int. J. Adv. Sci. Technol. **29**(7), 3614–3622 (2020)
28. Kondratenko, Y., Kondratenko, G., Sidenko, I.: Multi-criteria decision making and soft computing for the selection of specialized IoT platform. In: Chertov, O., Mylovanov, T., Kondratenko, Y., Kacprzyk, J., Kreinovich, V., Stefanuk, V. (eds.) ICDSIAI 2018. AISC, vol. 836, pp. 71–80. Springer, Cham (2019). https://doi.org/10.1007/978-3-319-97885-7_8
29. Valdez, W., Cedillo, P., Trujillo, A., Orellana, M.: A data infrastructure for managing information obtained from ambient assisted living. In: Proceedings - 2019 International Conference on Information Systems and Computer Science, INCISCOS 2019 (2019)
30. Nikityuk, L., Tsaryov, R.: Optimization of the process of selecting of the IoT-platform for the specific technical solution IoT-sphere. In: 2018 International Scientific-Practical Conference Problems of Infocommunications. Science and Technology (PIC S T) (2018)
31. World Health Organization: Medical Device Regulations, Geneva (2003)
32. Moreno, H., Ramírez, M., Hurtado, C., Lobato, B.: IoT in medical context: applications, diagnostics, and health care. In: Chen, Y.-W., Zimmermann, A., Howlett, R.J., Jain, L.C. (eds.) Innovation in Medicine and Healthcare Systems, and Multimedia. SIST, vol. 145, pp. 253–259. Springer, Singapore (2019). https://doi.org/10.1007/978-981-13-8566-7_25
33. Knight, A., Blessner, P., Olson, B.: Transforming the purchasing strategy of high-tech medical equipment in healthcare systems. J. Enterp. Transform. **6**(3–4), 170–186 (2016)
34. Chung, J., Demiris, G., Thompson, H.J.: Ethical considerations regarding the use of smart home technologies for older adults: an integrative review. Annu. Rev. Nurs. Res. **34**, 155–181 (2016)
35. National Institute of Standards and Technology: Cybersecurity Considerations in IoT
36. Asamblea Nacional de la República del Ecuador: Código Orgánico de la Economía Social de los Conocimientos, Creatividad e Innovación. Ecuador, p. 113 (2016)
37. Servicio de Aduana del Ecuador SENAE: Resolución Nro. SENAE-DGN-2013-0472-RE. Ecuador (2013)
38. Lee, H., Lee, S., Park, Y.: Selection of technology acquisition mode using the analytic network process. Math. Comput. Model. **49**(5–6), 1274–1282 (2009)

39. Kurokawa, S.: Make-or-buy decisions in R&D: small technology based firms in the United States and Japan. IEEE Trans. Eng. Manag. **44**(2), 124–134 (1997)
40. Steensma, H.K., Corley, K.G.: On the performance of technology-sourcing partnerships: the interaction between partner interdependence and technology attributes. Acad. Manag. J. **43**(6), 1045–1067 (2000)
41. Saaty, R.W.: The analytic hierarchy process-what it is and how it is used. Math. Model. **9**(3–5), 161–176 (1987)
42. Saaty, T.L.: Fundamentals of the analytic network process—dependence and feedback in decision-making with a single network. J. Syst. Sci. Syst. Eng. **13**(2), 129–157 (2004)
43. Alinezhad, A., Khalili, J.: ARAS Method. In: Alinezhad, A., Khalili, J. (eds.) New Methods and Applications in Multiple Attribute Decision Making (MADM), pp. 67–71. Springer, Cham (2019). https://doi.org/10.1007/978-3-030-15009-9_9
44. Li, C.-W., Tzeng, G.-H.: Identification of a threshold value for the DEMATEL method using the maximum mean de-entropy algorithm to find critical services provided by a semiconductor intellectual property mall. Expert Syst. Appl. **36**(6), 9891–9898 (2009)
45. Silva, E., Agostinho, C., Jardim-Goncalves, R.: A multi-criteria decision model for the selection of a more suitable Internet-of-Things device (2017)
46. Silva, E.M., Jardim-Goncalves, R.: Cyber-physical systems: a multi-criteria assessment for Internet-of-Things (IoT) systems. Enterp. Inf. Syst. **15**(3), 332–351 (2019)
47. Novikova, N.M., Pospelova, I.I., Zenyukov, A.I.: Method of convolution in multicriteria problems with uncertainty. J. Comput. Syst. Sci. Int. **56**(5), 774–795 (2017)
48. Qi, X., Yin, C., Cheng, K., Liao, X.: The interval cognitive network process for multi-attribute decision-making. Symmetry (Basel) **9**(10), 238 (2017)
49. Yuen, K.K.F.: The primitive cognitive network process: comparisons with the analytic hierarchy process. Int. J. Inf. Technol. Decis. Mak. **10**(4), 659–680 (2011)
50. Evans, D., et al.: Internet de las cosas: Cómo la próxima evolución de Internet lo cambia todo. J. Food Eng. **49**, 314–318 (2011)

Author Index

Printed in the United States
by Baker & Taylor Publisher Services